International
Economics

Salvatore Schiavo-Campo

University of Massachusetts at Boston

International Economics

An Introduction to
Theory and Policy

Winthrop Publishers, Inc.
Cambridge, Massachusetts

Library of Congress Cataloging in Publication Data
Schiavo-Campo, Salvatore.
    International economics.

    Bibliography: p. 376
    Includes index.
    1. International economic relations. 2. Inter-
national finance. 3. Commercial policy. I. Title.
HF1411.S2973   382.1   77-12591
ISBN 0-87626-386-4

Cover design by Designworks, Inc.

© *1978 by Winthrop Publishers, Inc.*
    17 Dunster Street, Cambridge, Massachusetts 02138

10 9 8 7 6 5 4 3 2 1

To
Hazel
And to
Ciuffo and Pia
(they also served who only
laughed and played)

Contents

PART III: INTERNATIONAL FINANCE   195

To the Instructor

International Economics is a relatively short, simple, and straightforward introduction to international trade, commercial policy, and international finance. It is explicitly intended as a one-semester text for students whose interests, general preparation, and background in economics vary widely. This is the audience to which I have become attuned in my years of teaching. The design and writing of a textbook inevitably reflect the author's own teaching experience and pedagogical aims. It is, of course, for others to decide whether the experience and aims are sufficiently general, and the book a good vehicle for its stated purposes. I am reasonably certain, however, that this book is at least faithful to its premise: that there is a need for an international economics text written exclusively as a teaching vehicle, specifically meant for a one-semester course and for a heterogeneous audience. This premise governs the coverage, level of presentation, and internal structure of the book. It also calls for a lengthier preface than is customary.

The *coverage* is fairly standard. Slightly greater emphasis than in other texts is given to the placing of policy and theoretical principles in historical perspective, and to the arguments for protection. The reader can be severely misled by a total absence of historical context into believing that economic theory is a static etching in rock, and that policy choices have no referent in prior experience. For example, it is hard to grasp the meaning of the 1975 Rambouillet summit if one knows nothing about the London Conference of 1933. The extensive discussion of the arguments for protection is motivated by a concern for giving students, as citizens, some intellectual defenses against the never-ending rhetoric for protection, as well, of course, as a sense of the conditions under which trade restriction may be justified.

Two subjects, touched on in most other texts, are deliberately omitted here: trade in centrally planned economies, and foreign problems of less developed countries. These are instances when a little bit of knowledge is indeed dangerous. These topics, and particularly trade and development, are much too complex and important to be dealt with in a short chapter somewhere outside the mainstream of the book. Nor does the scope of this book allow discussing them to the minimum extent necessary. Therefore, they have been left out altogether, although I have included repeated reminders of their existence and importance. Also, a separate chapter on international factor movements has been eschewed in favor of the alternative of incorporating its more salient points wherever appropriate in the analysis of trade and international finance.

With regard to the *level of presentation,* practically everything in this book should be accessible to students whose only economics background consists of an introductory course. Moreover, a heterogeneous audience and a homogeneous level of presentation do not match very well. A basic difficulty in the teaching of undergraduate courses, particularly in institutions in which the range of student preparation is great, is in the averaging out of the level of presentation. Inevitably, the better students then find the text too elementary while the less prepared ones are baffled by it. The alternative used here is: simple textual language, followed by a *recapitulation* of the argument in graphical language, with the mathematical formulation contained in footnotes and appendices. Students thus have the choice of studying the same material in whatever "language" they find comprehensible, with the better students given the opportunity to improve their understanding through following the argument in its diagrammatic and mathematical formulations as well as through the verbal explanation of it. The instructor, of course, also has the choice of which to stress, in light of students' preparation. This three-tiered approach cannot, of course, be used throughout the book. But many topics, such as the pure theory of trade, the effects of tariffs, the interaction of foreign trade and national income, and the analysis of devaluation, are suitable to this treatment.

The *organization* of the book places trade theory first, followed by commercial policy and by international finance. There is, however, enough flexibility to allow those who prefer dealing first with finance to do so easily. Also, chapters are ordered in such a way that material can be excised with a minimum of disruption. Thus, the least essential chapters are placed at the end of each part. And, within each chapter, there is an attempt to proceed from the very basic to the less fundamental. Though the book is tightly packed as it is, an instructor faced with a particularly severe time constraint can therefore cut it to the barest essentials (Chapters 1–6 and 9–13) without suffering the irritation of having to jump around the whole book cutting a few pages here and a few pages there.

Many international economics texts deal with foreign trade and national income within their chapter on balance-of-payments adjustment under fixed rates. Trade and income is, however, also an important topic in its own right, and is treated here in a separate chapter, although within the part on international finance. A second organizational problem familiar to anyone who has taught in this field is the efficient placement of the effects of tariffs and the arguments for protection. On the one hand, the only arguments that have possible validity are those grounded on some effect of tariffs. To explain those effects is at the same time to describe the possible arguments in favor of a tariff to produce them. On the other hand, this approach leaves out altogether discussion of the hardy fallacies with little or no economic content, or makes their placement awkward. In this book, a small amount of duplication has been accepted as the price of adequate treatment of protectionist arguments within a chapter of their own. Thus, in Chapter 6 the arguments founded on the existence of a real effect of tariffs briefly recapitulate what was said in the previous chapter concerning the effect itself.

A few assorted points deserve brief mention. Offer curves are not used here. In the author's experience, the improvement in analytical clarity they afford is not worth the time needed to explain them to an undergraduate audience. Second, the exchange rate is defined as the price of a currency in terms of foreign currencies, and not, as in some other texts, as the number of units of domestic currency one unit of a foreign currency can buy. No chapter summaries are included. For an introductory one-semester text, which is already a summary of sorts, chapter summaries can be either useless or positively dangerous if the student pays real attention to them. Instead, a short "What to Expect" section previews each chapter. Also, each chapter is capped by a review and discussion section, far more extensive than in other texts in this field. Instructors who have no need of these sections as openings for class discussion may still find them helpful as baskets of exam questions, ranging from short elementary problems to the broadest essay questions. A bibliography at the end of the book replaces the customary chapter bibliographies. Finally, all but the most elementary economic terms are briefly explained when they first appear in the text.

The author hopes to have successfully resisted the temptation to write for his colleagues rather than for their students. The book is liberally sprinkled with quotations, some pertinent to the subject at hand, some less so. One which is most pertinent to the intent of this book is a 140-year-old statement by Frédéric Bastiat in his *Fallacies of Protection:*

> ... *there are sciences whose influence upon the public is proportional only to the information of that public itself, and whose efficacy consists not in the accummulated knowledge of a few learned heads, but in that which has diffused itself into the reason of man in the aggregate. Such [is] political economy. Of these sciences Bentham might above all have said:* "It is better to circulate, than to advance them."

To the Student

You can hardly open a newspaper without noticing the attention paid to international economic issues. "Mr. Nixon Acts to Save Dollar in Move for World Currency Reforms," the *London Times* announces (August 16, 1971); "I.M.F. Publishes Gloomy Assessment of World Economy," headlines the *New York Times* (September 12, 1977). Imports, exports, common markets, devaluations, foreign exchange, Eurodollars, steel quotas—the number of newsworthy items that fall under the general heading of "international economics" are legion. Clearly, the subject must be of great importance to large numbers of people all over the world. Yet, it is cloaked in mysterious words and surrounded by an almost mystical aura.

The theoretical principles underlying international economic issues are, as most economic theory is, simple. *Not easy, simple.* This book tries to explain the essential principles of the theory of foreign trade, of tariffs and quotas, and of international monetary relations, by breaking them down into their component steps, each readily understandable provided that the previous logical step has not been skipped. The only prerequisite is some familiarity with the mode of thinking and the basic concepts of economics.

While the basic theory is simple, international economic policy issues can be extraordinarily complex, involving conflicting interests of different groups within a country and of different countries, as well as fundamental considerations of international politics. Readers are begged to keep in mind that they are shown here only the tip of the proverbial iceberg. To glean some of the ramifications of the subject, it is helpful to peruse the review and discussion questions at the end of each chapter, which can also serve as checklists to verify one's understanding of the material studied.

The subtitle refers to "theory and policy." Professor Carlo Greca, an Italian philosopher, used to warn his students that, whatever their future career, someone would always confront them with the false distinction between theory and practice. The "practitioner" claims superiority by quips such as: "He who cannot do, teaches"; the "theorist" retorts with sovereign disdain. But there is no conflict between sound theory and effective practice. On the contrary, they are complementary. Theory provides the map; practice provides the vehicle. The only valid distinctions are between good and bad policy and between good and bad theory. It is accordingly inadvisable, for an introductory text, to lay out the theory with complete exclusion of its policy implications, or to discuss international economic policy without reference to the underlying theoretical considerations.

This book is in three "languages." The verbal presentation is the main language used in the text. Where appropriate, the material is recapitulated in graphical "language" by the use of simple diagrams, and the mathematical formulation of it is shown in footnotes or appendices. After studying the verbal explanations, you are strongly urged to work your way at least through the diagrams. They are kept as simple as possible and can add considerably to the precision of your understanding. In any case, verbal explanations, diagrams, or math, this is a subject to be studied, not read. A careful, step-by-step study of the material will yield far better understanding (and, in the final analysis, take less time) than several cursory readings.

This book tries to serve as a solid foundation for those who will take their study of international economics further. For the majority of readers, whose exposure to the subject will stop with this book, the hope is to give them a lasting ability to understand and follow issues of international trade and finance at least at the level at which they are reported in the newspapers. The author would be genuinely grateful for readers' comments and criticisms. If the translation of a body of theoretical principles and their policy implications is not understood by the serious student, the fault can only be the translator's own.

Acknowledgments

Of all who helped in the development of this book, first mention must go to the hundreds of students of mine at the University of Massachusetts at Boston, who contributed over the past ten years to my sense of what did and did not "work" in the international economics classroom. Several persons offered valuable suggestions and criticism. Norman D. Aitken, Donald L. Friesen, Peter Kressler, Arthur MacEwan, Daniel Primont, Stephen E. Reynolds, William Roberts, Hazel McFerson Schiavo-Campo, and Mary Alice Shulman read various chapters. Peter B. Kenen and Leonard J. Kirsch read the entire first draft. Andrew Klein provided a student's viewpoint and gave competent research assistance. My thanks also go to Maureen Fallon, secretary and friend, who typed the entire thing along with Mary Durham.

It always feels a little peculiar to think of oneself as a colleague of his former teachers. Sometimes, this new status leaves intact the old respect and gratitude of the ex-student. For me, this is true, among others, of Peter Kenen. The subconscious is too resourceful a smuggler to allow one to record accurately his intellectual imports. If parts of this book should turn out to be especially effective teaching vehicles, I therefore cheerfully

Acknowledgments acknowledge the possibility that they may have been subliminally plagiarized from some of Peter's lectures of a short fifteen years ago.

Above all, I wish to single out the name of Leonard Kirsch, whose extensive comments on this book were among the last things he was able to accomplish before his premature death. To your memory, Lennie, dearest friend of all, this book is also dedicated.

*"If a little knowledge is dangerous, where is the man
who has so much as to be out of danger?"*

(Thomas Henry Huxley, 1877)

Introduction

What to Expect

This introductory chapter discusses the importance of foreign trade for all nations, outlines the main characteristics of international transactions, and provides a sense of the political and economic climate surrounding world economic relations. The section on characteristics of international transactions discusses the role of low mobility of resources, monetary differences between countries, and differences in national policies. The view is put forward that national policies in relation to the rest of the world can still best be explained by reference to the self-interest of the country establishing them. Thus, the true source of international cooperation is to be sought in the economic interdependence among sovereign nations. The chapter concludes by introducing the fundamental notion of the gains from trade and its implications for international economic interdependence. As an introduction, this chapter raises many more questions than it answers. Most of these, however, will be examined in some detail later in the book.

All nations of the world exchange some commodities or services with other countries. Although some people are less dependent than others, either owing to their fortunate economic circumstances or by deliberate choice, practically everyone has some economic contact with other persons. Similarly, international economic relations are significant for most countries and of extreme importance for many. International trade tends to be relatively more important for smaller countries. This is because a larger economic size allows a greater proportion of trading needs to be satisfied through internal exchange. But even for the largest countries, trade with other nations is too important to be disregarded. Moreover, trade is not distributed equally among the various economic sectors and groups in a country, so that its role for selected industries, groups of people, or regions, can be far greater than the average proportion indicates. For example, while exports account for about 6 percent of the U.S. national product, they constitute one-fifth of production of goods. Foreign trade can spell the difference between prosperity and economic disaster for many corporations and for large numbers of people.

The Characteristics of International Transactions

The principles underlying international economic transactions are essentially the same as those governing trade within a country. As will be seen again and again in this book, the fundamental concepts and tools of economic analysis (opportunity cost, production possibilities, supply and demand, and so forth) are applicable to economic activity regardless of whether it takes place within a country or across national frontiers. The scope and implications of these concepts, however, may be quite different in the international arena, and there exist important distinctions between international and national transactions. Why is this so? Are there in fact meaningful distinctions between the sale of Massachusetts shoes to a New Yorker and the sale of those same shoes to a Canadian? Why should these two apparently identical transactions be viewed as different merely because of the arbitrary interposition of a national frontier? Or, to phrase the question more generally, do national political boundaries have a significant influence on the sources and effects of economic activity?

The Classical Distinction: Differential Factor Mobility

The distinction made by classical economists between internal trade and international trade was grounded on the notion of geographic mobility of factors of production (economic resources). The assumption made was that, whereas the mobility of factors of production within a country is perfect, factors of production cannot be moved to a different nation. Perfect mobility implies zero costs of geographic transfer; complete immobility implies infinite costs. If internal mobility were perfect, then all factors of production, capital, labor, and even raw materials would respond quickly to changes in their prices and flow to the region where their price is higher. Even a minimal interregional difference in price would then be sufficient (under the idealized condition of perfect geographic mobility) to induce a flow of the economic resource away from the region where the price is relatively lower and toward the region where it is higher. In such a case, the price of any factor of production of a given type and quality must be the same throughout the entire country. For example, any regional differences in steelworkers' wages would be a purely temporary phenomenon, quickly eliminated by a move of steelworkers from the low-wage region.

Conversely, *between* nations factor mobility was assumed to be non-existent. Thus, any international difference in prices of factors of production, no matter how great, would not be sufficient to induce international movement of resources away from countries where their price is relatively low *to* countries where it is higher. In such a case, *ceteris paribus* ("other things being equal"), a difference in interest rates or in wages will persist indefinitely because there will be no flow of resources to eliminate it. (But, as explained later, trade can be a substitute for the movement of factors of production, and it also can serve to lessen factor price differentials between countries.)

Under these assumptions on factor mobility, if the wage rate of refinery workers in Louisiana rises above that in Texas, a move of some of these workers to the higher-wage state can be expected. With constant demand conditions, the wage rate will increase in Texas and fall in Louisiana, since the supply of refinery labor declines in Texas and increases in Louisiana. This mechanism will continue to operate until the wage rate is again the same in the two states. No such mechanism is at work between Louisiana and a foreign country. A higher wage in Louisiana than, say, in Venezuela will, other things being equal, persist indefinitely. (The implications of this point for international trade are explored in Chapter 3.)

Obviously, the classical assumption of perfect factor mobility within a country and zero mobility between countries is drastic and untrue. Movements of factors of production across national frontiers have occurred since the beginning of recorded human history. Also, there are internal obstacles to the movement of factors within a country, ranging from the simple matter of transportation costs to the more complex matters of discrimination and psychological resistance to geographic moves. But there is still significance in the distinction between the role of internal trade and that of international trade, provided that the degree of internal factor mobility is greater than the degree of international factor mobility (which is true for most countries).

International Monetary Differences

The distinction between internal and international trade is obvious in international monetary differences. Within a country, monetary differences are negligible. Monetary laws are the same, or very similar, for all regions. The financial institutions of a country operate on the basis of common procedures. Most importantly, a single currency is used throughout the nation. The price of any commodity or service is expressed in terms of the common national currency. This is not so between countries. The French seller of French perfume requires payment in French *francs*; but the U.S. buyer of the perfume is interested in the number of *dollars* he has to pay. In consequence, there are *two* prices relevant to an international transaction: the price of the commodity in terms of the currency of the producing country and the price of that currency in terms of the buyer's currency (the *rate of exchange*). Indeed, there are two transactions. The U.S. importer must first exchange dollars for French francs (which themselves are traded and have a price, like any other commodity). Only then can he exchange the French francs for the perfume he wishes to buy.

Clearly, monetary differences introduce a nuisance element in international transactions that is absent from domestic exchange. Imagine a Bostonian having to verify each dollar bill offered in payment for merchandise in order to see whether it is a Massachusetts dollar or not. If it is, say, a Texas dollar, it must first be exchanged into Massachusetts dollars (at whatever rate of exchange happens to prevail) before the transaction can take place. Imagine, when leaving for a camping trip, having to carry as many different currencies as the number of states you plan to go through or else resign yourself to visiting a bank to obtain local currency as soon as you cross a state line. Clearly, international economic transactions would be simpler if it were not for all these "funny moneys" floating around.

This situation is annoying, but it is not the really important consequence of monetary differences between nations. If the rate of exchange between currencies were fixed for all time, the nuisance element would be the entire story. (Countries would also have no monetary autonomy, as explained in Chapter 11.) The important point is that these differences introduce in international transactions an element of risk (and therefore of cost) that is absent from the domestic scene. The rate of exchange can, and often does, change. This influences the price paid for a foreign commodity in exactly the same way as would a change in the foreign price of that commodity. Suppose that 1 U.S. dollar is worth 5 French francs and that a bottle of French perfume sells for 100 francs; that bottle costs an American 20 dollars. If the price of the French franc changes to 4 francs for a dollar, that same bottle now costs 25 dollars, even though the French producer is still selling the perfume for the same 100 francs.

One can, of course, protect oneself from risks, including the risk that the rate of exchange may vary from the time of signing a contract to the time when payment needs to be made. Many institutions, such as insurance companies, absorb risks for individuals who are "risk-averters." There is an international institution that absorbs exchange risk. It is the so-called *forward foreign exchange market*, which will be discussed in Chapter 9. Of course, the service carries a cost, and an international transaction is subject to this additional cost.[1] (The possibility of changes in the exchange rate gives rise to even more serious difficulties for foreign investors who face a financial commitment of a long duration.)

But why should the exchange rate for a country's currency vary? What if there existed an international central bank, similar to the Federal Reserve System in the United States, with the power to carry out world monetary policy and with the authority to keep exchange rates between all currencies fixed at all times? All exchange risk would then disappear. Traders would simply face the relatively minor practical nuisances of having to deal with pieces of paper of different colors and of having to translate prices in one currency into prices in terms of other currencies. But an international monetary authority does not exist. Instead, there are many different countries,

---

[1] Of course, the exchange rate may vary up or down, and traders may end up with a windfall rather than an unexpected loss. The motivation of a trader is, however, to trade, not to speculate. Even if the losses from exchange rate variation are exactly matched by the windfalls, the trader will normally want to transfer the risk onto someone else and will thus have to carry the cost of doing so.

each with its economic sovereignty and with the authority to carry out its own *national* policy, including the authority to change the value of its currency by unilateral action. Thus, it is readily seen that the significance of international monetary differences is intimately linked to the fact of national economic sovereignty. These differences are only a symptom. The essential distinction between internal and international transactions is the influence of the different national policies of different countries.

National Sovereignty and International Economics

Different countries have different national goals and policies. Not only does a nation set and carry out its own policy with respect to the price of its currency and to its economic relations with other countries, a nation also has its own policies with respect to internal taxation, subsidies, money, employment, and so forth. Each national policy measure has some effect on external trade and investment as well as on the domestic economy. Its effects on the country's international economic position are not necessarily the same, nor of the same magnitude, as the domestic economic effects. It is necessary to make a distinction between a country's international transactions and its internal economic activity.

Although domestic policy measures usually do not have identical effects on all regions of a country, they are normally undertaken in response to a national, not a regional, need. For example, an increase in the sales tax on liquor will have more of an impact on towns where liquor consumption is greater than on areas where it is relatively low. The tax increase, however, is normally not motivated by a desire to worsen the economic position of areas of high liquor consumption but by some other general purpose, such as raising revenue or discouraging drinking. Increasing the "sales tax" (*tariff*) only on foreign liquor is usually not intended to discourage liquor consumption but to give domestic producers an advantage over foreign producers. Internationally, every act of national policy is expressly designed to advance the country's economic interests in a politically competitive world. The other effects of the policy are secondary. The reason the United States arrives at a tariff agreement with the European Common Market is not a desire to advance the interests of the world economy but is to be found in the U.S. national interests. If the world economy happens to benefit from national action, well and good. But from the viewpoint of the national policy-maker, that benefit is in a real sense incidental. A *national* government makes policy to pursue *national* goals.[2]

[2] An international government would make policy for international goals; but there is no international government. This is really a simple point and yet one that often is forgotten. By forgetting that every country acts in accordance with what it perceives to

Naturally, in an interdependent world, the distinction between the national and the international interests is often blurred. To an extent, a country's economic progress depends on the prosperity of its trade partners. Thus, the national interest partly coalesces with the international interest. It is, however, a very healthy distinction to keep in mind. Should a conflict arise between the interests of the international economy as a whole and the interests of a specific country, be assured that the country's economic self-interest will win out and that the country's economic policy will follow suit.

The distinction between the national and the international interests is important also because it highlights the true source of further international cooperation in the economic sphere, and thus, possibly, of a politically saner and safer world. That source is not the rhetoric of internationalism (helpful though it may be) with its moving but doomed appeals to national self-lessness. Further international cooperation can arise only from greater economic interdependence, with its attendant outcome of a tighter identification of the national interest with an international one. (This is increasingly recognized also in Communist countries. For example, the Hungarian economist Josef Bognar had occasion to state that "in the event of international tension common economic interests constitute a moderating force which cushions the political measures taken by the parties." [3])

Despite the frequent occurrence of clear instances of interference in the affairs of other countries (many examples can be found in the foreign policies of the United States and the Soviet Union), the concept of national sovereignty governs, at least formally, international relations, including international *economic* relations. Nations are political and social units: they view themselves as such and conduct themselves as such. The nation is the basic unit of analysis in international economics, just as the consumer or the firm are basic units of analysis in microeconomic theory.

The interaction of politics and economics is even stronger in the international arena than it is in the domestic arena. It may be possible, though not very wise, to identify the causes and the significance of a domestic economic event solely in economic terms. It is not possible to attempt to resolve any of the specific issues of international economic policy without an explicit consideration of the political dimension of those issues. Fundamental to an understanding of the interaction of politics and economics is the realization that, whereas income and wealth have meaning in absolute terms, political power is inherently relative to that possessed by other nations.[4]

---

be its national interest, unrealistic expectations are generated. These may turn out in the end to be more damaging than if a realistic point of view had been adopted to begin with.

[3] J. Bognar, "New Forces and Currents in the International Economy," *Studies on Developing Countries* (Hungarian Academy of Sciences, 1975) no. 83, p. 13.

[4] Of necessity, this book presents the main elements of the theory of international economics mainly from the perspective of their economic implications. Chapters 7, 8, 14,

It is the political, social, and cultural difference between countries that underlies the difference between international economic activity and domestic economic events and that gives international economics its claim to independent existence as a branch of economic theory. And it is the way in which differences between countries have been handled that leads to the identification of three broad stages in the modern history of international economic relations.

As we shall discuss in the next chapter, the guiding rule in the first stage (*mercantilism*) could be expressed as: "How do we best regulate internal economic activity or foreign trade in order to obtain a national advantage *and/or* to cause harm to other countries?" The mercantilist assumptions about the world led a government to consider an economic calamity suffered by another country almost as good a thing as an economic benefit accruing to its own country.

In the nineteenth century, the guiding government policy rule of international economic relations became: *laissez faire, laissez passer* ("let do, let pass"). National interests were no longer viewed as being in necessary conflict with international interests. On the contrary (provided that *within* the country economic activity is also free of governmental interference), unfettered pursuit of national self-interest was seen as the best route to maximization of worldwide efficiency and economic welfare in exactly the same way as pure competition on the domestic scene was supposed to result in maximum social gain. The "invisible hand" was seen as operating equally well internationally as within a country. In this view, therefore, national economic policy should concentrate merely on ensuring that competition prevails—internally as well as internationally.[5]

Finally, it has been argued that the international economy is currently in a third stage in which the guiding principle has become: "How de we best regulate economic activity for greater international cooperation and the mutual benefit of all countries?" But since international interests do not necessarily coincide with national interests, this correspondence between national and international benefit requires that national economic policies be coordinated and made complementary to one another. However, one could maintain that, on the contrary, this current "third stage" is nothing but a return to the first stage—a "neomercantilism" more sophisticated but

and 15, however, attempt to integrate political and economic considerations. The reader is fairly warned that to attempt analysis of a *specific* international issue solely in economic terms is liable to result in some very silly conclusions. For an interesting study of the interrelationships between politics and economics, see R. Gilpin, *U.S. Power and the Multinational Corporation* (New York: Basic Books, 1975).

[5] The one exception to this rule, accepted even by that most classical of economists, Adam Smith, was governmental interference for the purpose of national security: "Defence is more important than opulence." The national security argument for tariffs is discussed at some length in Chapter 6.

essentially as conflict-ridden as earlier mercantilist policies. (The trade and financial aspects of this question are examined in Chapters 8 and 15, respectively.) The issue is not yet resolved. The next few years should provide us with enough evidence to decide on either the optimistic or the pessimistic view of the prospects for international economic cooperation.

The Role of International Trade

The parallel between internal and international specialization is, in principle, a complete one. Internal economic progress is fostered by division of labor among individuals and groups; international economic progress is fostered by division of labor among countries. You are probably familiar with the demonstration that, under certain conditions, specialization among individuals is best for each individual—and for the country as a whole. Similarly, it will be shown here that, under certain assumptions, specialization among nations maximizes economic efficiency and welfare for each nation—and for the world as a whole.

The extent of specialization is, however, limited by the size of the market. Division of labor cannot occur unless the individual can dispose of his "surplus" production over and above his own wants and exchange it for the goods and services that other "specialists" produce. Similarly, international specialization can only occur to the extent that nations trade with one another. This clearly implies a degree of "dependence" on other countries. To the extent that a nation chooses to specialize in certain activities, it is at one and the same time choosing to specialize *away* from other activities. Its overall economic wants are still satisfied (indeed, they are better satisfied) since it can sell to other countries its goods and services in exchange for the wanted products that it no longer produces or produces in smaller quantities. But the country is "dependent" on foreigners for supplies of these products in exactly the same sense as you are dependent on the butcher for provision of meat, the hardware store for provision of paint, and so forth. To recapitulate: economic progress depends to a great extent on division of labor (specialization); division of labor depends on the possibility to trade; and trade implies dependence on "outside" sources of supply for the things you want but no longer produce yourself. Only if you grow your own food, sew your own clothes, build your own car—and generally take care of the satisfaction of *all* your material needs and wants *exclusively* by your own labor—only then are you truly independent in the absolute sense of the word. You are also materially much poorer. The same is true of countries and particularly true of small countries. It is the country's sovereign right (as it is the individual's right) to make such a choice of absolute self-sufficiency; there must, however, be an awareness that such "independence" carries considerable economic costs.

These remarks should not be interpreted as a criticism of any policy of self-sufficiency. Indeed, if such a policy is established for noneconomic reasons, it cannot be criticized on economic grounds. What can be criticized, however, is the pursuance of self-sufficiency without a recognition that such a policy can be economically costly, or, even worse, under the wishful fantasy that short-run economic conditions will actually improve if trade with other individuals or countries is curtailed.

Nor should these remarks be interpreted as denying that there are violations of national economic independence. Nor do they deny that the pattern of international division of labor currently existing is in part due to past or present policies designed to ensure a predominant role to the larger and richer countries. It is indeed quite possible that, under certain conditions, pursuing economic self-sufficiency in certain sectors may improve the long-run economic prospects of a country. "Imperialism" (or "neo-colonialism") is not a figment of the radical imagination. It was, is, and probably will continue to be a reality of international economic relations. Serious analysis, however, requires a distinction between different sorts of economic dependence. There is a kind of "dependence" on other countries that comes about merely as the inevitable consequence of economic progress and specialization. There is *also* deliberate international intervention that imposes on the target country considerable economic and political costs. It is essential to make a distinction between these two forms of dependence. In plain words, there is a basic distinction between the effects of importing foreign beer and the effects of having the bulk of the country's resources and economic decision-making controlled by foreign interests. The latter is harmful to national sovereignty; the former need not be.

Points for Review

1. Review the following basic concepts, by reference to the pertinent sections of any comprehensive introductory economics text.
a. Economic transaction
b. Opportunity cost
c. Production possibilities
d. Goods and services
e. Factors of production
f. Factor mobility
g. Supply and demand

h. Money (as medium of exchange, store of wealth, standard of value)
i. The "invisible hand" principle

2. Explain how an international transaction involves two different moneys and is thus influenced by two prices.

3. Why would it be almost the same thing to have completely and permanently fixed rates of exchange among national currencies as it would be to have a single international currency?

Questions for Discussion

1. Why should there be any tendency for smaller countries to be particularly dependent on foreign trade? Can you find instances of nations whose economic survival literally depends on their ability to trade with other countries? Can you think of a concrete example of a country for which foreign trade is entirely unimportant?

2. Consider the possibility of *complete* self-sufficiency, either for an individual or for a nation. Reflect on your own probable economic position and general well-being if you could not—or did not want to—rely on *anyone* for the provision of *anything*.

3. Is it realistic to state that, in general, the mobility of resources is greater within a country than between countries? Is it a more valid assumption for certain factors of production than it is for others? Can you think of a current instance where the obstacles to factor movement are greater between regions of the same country than they are between that country and other nations? What might be the implications of such a state of affairs for the efficiency of the country's economy? For its economic growth potential? For its political system?

4. Which side would you choose in an argument between a "realistic" view of international relations and an "idealistic" view? Is there a possibility of reconciling the two views?

5. What is the meaning of "national sovereignty" in the modern world? Is there an absolute dichotomy between "independence" and "dependence," or is there a continuum from one to the other? Is there indeed such a thing as full independence or complete dependence?

11

The Theory of
International Trade

"—. . . cloth is a useful article. Is the essential thing to make it, or to have it?

—A pretty question! To have it, we must make it.

—That is not necessary. It is certain that to have it someone must make it; but it is not necessary that the person or country using it should make it."

Frédéric Bastiat, *Fallacies of Protection*

The Effects of International Trade

What to Expect

This chapter attempts to answer the following important questions: Why do countries trade with one another? What are the effects of international trade on production and consumption? At what prices will imports tend to be exchanged for exports in the world market? First, the answers given to some of these questions in the historical past are summarized. Then the contemporary theoretical principles concerning the effects of international trade are outlined. These are explained first in a descriptive way and then through a simple diagrammatic analysis of trade under conditions of constant opportunity costs. The last section discusses the influence of foreign trade on the distribution of income within a country. The Appendix contains a more advanced diagrammatic analysis of the effects of foreign trade under conditions of increasing costs.

The Historical Antecedents of Contemporary Trade Theory

Current explanations of international economic phenomena are, of course, the result of continuing intellectual evolution and change grounded in large measure on earlier thinking about these phenomena. Some historical perspective is thus essential, both to a clearer understanding of theoretical principles and to an awareness of the fundamental fact that principles appropriate and useful in a particular historical context may become obsolete when economic conditions or policy goals change substantially. This was the fate of medieval economic notions, of the conventional wisdom of the mercantilist period, and of some among the more recent theoretical statements on international trade. One should keep in mind the possibility of gradual obsolescence of contemporary explanations of international trade as well and to have some sense of both their usefulness and their possible limitations. While we can only provide a capsule summary of the historical antecedents of contemporary international trade theory, even a "satellite view" can help to place current trade theory in some context.

Theoretical development is generally characterized by gradual building on, and occasional departures from, earlier thinking on the subject. Division of such development into "stages" is, therefore, to a great extent arbitrary. Still, from a historical distance it becomes possible to identify broad intellectual currents that differ from one another in fundamental respects. Thus, the body of contemporary theory outlined in this chapter traces the beginnings of its evolution to the late eighteenth century. It was preceded by a set of economic notions and policies (summarized under the general

The
Historical
Antecedents
of
Contemporary
Trade
Theory

label of mercantilism) that had held sway for the previous 300 years or so. Before the fifteenth century the prevailing attitudes and beliefs on economic activity were part and parcel of medieval ideology.

Throughout, one notices the close interrelationship between theoretical concepts, on the one hand, and economic conditions and policy goals, on the other. There is an ancient and knotty controversy between "idealism" (which stresses the supremacy of ideas over material things) and "material-ism" (which argues that ideology and theory are merely byproducts of the structure of economic activity). Whatever the merits of that controversy in the philosophical arena, it seems clear (at least in the international eco-nomics field) that theoretical ideas and economic conditions have been *both* the cause and the effect of one another. The manner in which inter-national trade theory evolved has indeed been organically connected to the historical conditions and specific policy interests of the times. After certain modes of thinking and general concepts became established, however, they acquired some independent influence on the very economic events that had helped shape them. To attempt to describe the complex interrelationship of ideas and economic realities appears of more interest than arguing whether the theoretical "chicken" came before or after the "egg" of material events.

Essential Medieval Views and Concepts of Economic Activity

Three major and interrelated perspectives underwrote virtually all thinking on economic and social activity in the Middle Ages. First, the world and everything in it has been created by God. Since God is infinite wisdom and perfect order, the existing order of all things embodies the will of God, and any imperfections observed must necessarily be defects of human interpre-tation. Second, the true purpose of life on earth is spiritual and religious salvation: the only "real" world is the hereafter. Third, human behavior is not divisible: economic activity must be subject to the same ethical and re-ligious norms that govern human behavior as a whole. These themes are summarized by Thomas Aquinas, the great medieval theologian, who wrote in 1273 (*Two Precepts of Charity*): "Three things are necessary for the salvation of man: to know what he ought to believe; to know what he ought to desire; and to know what he ought to do."

The metaphysical and theological nature of medieval thought consti-tuted an ideological disincentive to vigorous economic initiatives—either on the part of the individual or on the part of social groupings. Since the place of every person or social unit in the world order was seen as an expres-sion of the will of God, to try and change one's economic or social status was considered not only doomed to failure, but also sinful. To put it bluntly, "If God had not wanted a man to be a serf, he would not have caused him to be born in servitude." The economic status of individuals, regions, and the

17

world as a whole was thus viewed as being fixed (static) for all time. Clearly then, economic expansion—which by definition means *change,* if even only quantitative change—was considered to be out of the question for the world's economy as a whole and for every country, grouping, or individual in it.[1]

Two basic economic concepts emerged from this general perspective. First, since economic behavior must be moral behavior, it was expected that a seller would not charge his customer a price higher than the "just price" of the commodity, and that a buyer would not offer to pay less than that price. But the incentive to trade is, of course, the ability to sell something at a higher price than the price at which it was purchased. The notion of a just price was antithetical to trade, profit, and economic expansion. Second, medieval thought borrowed from Aristotelian writings the notion that "money does not beget money." If money is unproductive, the charging of interest (usury) for lending it is unethical.[2] The prohibition of usury acted generally to discourage whatever investment could take place. If you needed to borrow money in order to invest, but the prospective lender was prohibited from charging you interest, his incentive to finance your undertaking was not very strong.

The economic ideology dovetailed nicely with the political and economic realities of the time. The medieval economy was a constellation of basically self-sufficient, isolated, small, and static sociopolitical entities centered around the manor. It lacked both the incentive and the capability to specialize and trade. The fragmented and stagnant economy of those times was not such as to foster economic expansion and international commerce. The static view of economic activity thus was consistent with actual economic conditions and opportunities. That view, however, *also* impeded such change as could have occurred and, later on, somewhat slowed economic expansion after the seeds of economic growth had already been sown. Before effective changes can occur, there needs first to be a psychological recognition that changes are possible. Everything conspired against such recognition, from the ingrained experience of economic stagnation as far back as anyone could remember to the apparently unassailable theological

---

[1] In actuality, the medieval economy was not altogether stagnant. Particularly in the low Middle Ages (the twelfth through the fourteenth centuries), some significant economic expansion took place, as can be inferred from the growth in the European population during those years. Still, by comparison with the rate of economic growth during the mercantilist period and even more so by comparison with the pace of economic expansion in the nineteenth and twentieth centuries, the Middle Ages were indeed a time of relative stagnation.

[2] Remembering to place theoretical notions in the proper context, it should be noted that in times of economic fragmentation and stagnation much borrowing was likely to be for emergency consumption. It could indeed be considered unethical to charge interest on such borrowing and thus to take advantage of the misfortune of a fellow human being.

The
Historical
Antecedents
of
Contemporary
Trade
Theory

view that any attempt to change God's creation was doomed to failure from the start.

A number of events, occurring over many years, slowly forced the abandonment of medieval economic theories. On the political front, separate manorial entities were gradually consolidated into larger and larger political units. Concurrently, the power of the universal church diminished. Religious salvation slowly yielded the center of the stage to the power of the nation-state as the be-all-and-end-all of human efforts. No longer was it immoral to cause economic damage to others or economic gain to oneself, provided that the action resulted in a benefit for the state to which one belonged. On the cultural and scientific fronts, the Renaissance and the great geographic discoveries combined with the revolution in scientific method to produce a new curiosity about *this* world and new skills for discovering and measuring natural facts.[3] On the economic front, the growth of population, the breakdown of serfdom, migration to the cities, and other factors created a number of investment opportunities and consequent expansion of economic activity and international trade.

Under the combined effect of all these changes, medieval modes of thinking about economics eventually gave way. The apparently self-evident theological justification of the status quo was neatly turned around and used to legitimize modifications of it: "If God had not wanted the serf to run away and sell his labor services in the town, he would not have allowed it." Through continuing empirical proof that individuals and groups *could* succeed in changing their economic and social status, the view of an established role for everyone weakened. Eventually it was replaced by a recognition that everything *within* the world economy is potentially dynamic and changeable: the serf could acquire freedom; the free but impoverished urban dweller might become wealthy; the wealthy might obtain sufficient resources to expand operations with newly hired labor; the manor could expand into surrounding territories and become a sovereign state; the sovereign state had opportunities through diplomacy, war, *and trade*, to gain a dominant position in relation to rival nations.

Mercantilism

The general term *mercantilism* subsumes the diverse economic concepts and policies of several nation-states during a period in excess of three centuries. A unified view of the main elements of these policies necessarily masks important differences in thought and practice. Certain attitudes and general policy concerns, however, did underlie to a greater or lesser extent the

---

[3] It is noteworthy that the major scientific inventions of this period had to do with observation and measurement.

19

policies of most European states in the sixteenth through the eighteenth centuries.

In the mercantile period analytical efforts to explain economic phenomena began and economic policy came to be viewed as worth examining in its own right. As noted previously, during the Middle Ages economic concepts were but a corollary of the theological concerns and metaphysical theorems of the times. The purely deductive nature of medieval thought implied that any inconsistency between the theory and the apparent reality could only be attributed to an incorrect interpretation of the facts. As the medieval ideology slowly crumbled, there arose a new curiosity about the surrounding realities and a willingness to attribute inconsistencies between facts and theory to inadequacies of the *theory* itself. There followed the elaboration of new economic concepts and practices, within the new context provided by the purposes and requirements of the emerging nation-states. Regulation of individual action remained as a basic feature of economic activity, but its avowed purpose became the aggrandizement of the state rather than the greater glory of God.

From medieval thought mercantilist thinkers and practitioners retained *one* facet of its universal static perspective. While the political and economic status of the nation, and of individuals within it, was newly recognized as dynamic and capable of change, the conception of the world's resources as finite and of the world's economy as static persisted. The world came to be perceived as a cauldron full of boiling water, but with the lid on tight. Countries might, if wise and ruthless enough in their policies, increase their share of the world's economic pie, but only if other countries could be coerced into accepting a smaller share for themselves. There consequently arose the general notion that to cause economic damage to competing states was almost as good a thing as to procure direct economic gains to one's own country. The regulation of individual actions, as well as the modalities of mercantilist economic policies, was aimed at, and derived legitimacy from, the maintenance and strengthening of the power of the state—necessarily at the expense of other countries.

The mercantilist policy system, in its general aspects, had considerable coherence to it. The foremost instrument of state power was the country's military strength. But also, state power and prestige were in some measure a function of its economic wealth (which mercantilist writers by and large identified with the possession of precious metals). Gold and silver allowed one to hire mercenaries—whose only loyalty was to their employer—and to procure the material implements of war. If a nation had an abundance of gold and silver within its own borders, well and good. If it did not, some means had to be found to procure precious metals from elsewhere. One possible way, of course, was to take them by force from those who owned them. The Spaniards had gained a headstart in the conquest of South American Indian empires with fabulous treasures. Other countries had to devise less direct

The
Historical
Antecedents
of
Contemporary
Trade
Theory

means. The principal one was to ensure a surplus of exports over imports—a surplus in the balance of trade—which necessarily would result in an inflow of gold and silver greater than the outflow and thus enlarge the country's stock of precious metals. The attainment and maintenance of a balance-of-trade surplus became the main target of state regulation of economic activity.

Different countries followed different routes to that goal. While the entire array of policy means was utilized to some degree in most states during the mercantilist era, different countries did not assign the same weights to the different policies. For example, France generally tended to emphasize internal regulation of economic activity in the attempt to keep the prices of French products low and their quality high and thus make them especially attractive to foreign purchasers. England instead relied more on direct regulation of the foreign trade sector. *Internal regulation* (identified in France with Colbert, Louis XIV's minister) consisted primarily of the following measures: Stimulation of a prosperous agriculture, encouragement and regulation of industrial manufactures to assure their consistent high quality, and fostering of low prices of manufactures, particularly goods with export potential. In turn, low prices were thought to require low wages. Wages could be kept low by fostering population growth. High birth rates as well as immigration were encouraged. A large population had the added advantage of assuring a large pool of draftable males and thus contributed directly to the country's military strength.

External regulation through commercial policy was designed to minimize the expenditure of precious metals on imports and to maximize the inflow of gold and silver through exports. Thus, exports of highly processed commodities were strongly fostered and imports of such commodities restricted or prohibited outright. Correspondingly, importation of raw materials that could be worked up within the country and reexported elsewhere was viewed favorably, while sales of raw materials abroad were severely discouraged. In addition, it came to be realized that the selling or buying of transportation services was potentially as important as commodity trade. Most countries, and particularly England (through its Navigation Acts of the midseventeenth century), attempted to reserve the greatest possible share of trade for their own merchant marines. The protection given to the country's merchant fleet had the additional advantage (in England's case, a crucial asset) of strengthening the nation's naval position and thus directly contributing to its military power.

One policy feature that many states of the mercantilist period had in common was the acquisition of colonial outposts. Colonies were important for the country's strategic posture. They contributed to the effective military protection of the country's trade routes and afforded bases of potential usefulness to encroach on rival states' interests. Colonies could also be important suppliers of raw materials, thus lessening the undesirable de-

21

pendence on rival powers for the provision of needed resources. Quite independent of economic or military considerations, colonies were also, of course, the source of national prestige. Charles V of Spain could exclaim with pride that the sun never set on the Spanish empire.

The mercantilist policy system is summarized in Figure 2.1. Two qualifications must be stressed. First, it bears repeating that this summary covers the disparate policies of several different countries over a very long period of time and, as such, it masks significant differences between them. Second, the relationship among the various policy elements was far more complex than the few arrows shown in Figure 2.1. Nevertheless, in its essential features, this was the system of interrelated policies designed to serve the ultimate goal of state power that held sway until the advent of economic liberalism in the latter part of the eighteenth century.

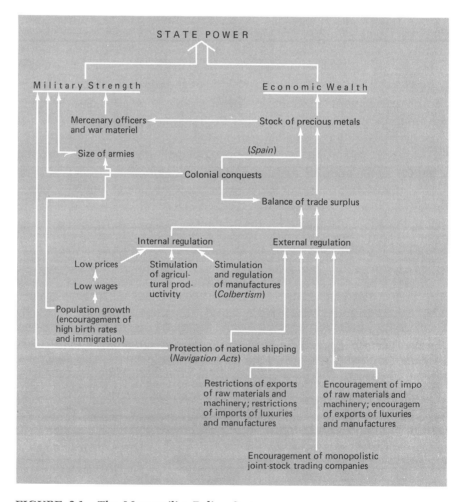

FIGURE 2.1   The Mercantilist Policy System

The
Historical
Antecedents
of
Contemporary
Trade
Theory

By the eighteenth century, the political and economic foundations of mercantilist practices came under major attack on several fronts. Eventually mercantilism was replaced by the laissez-faire ideology and practice that continues in modified form to this day. The intellectual movement known as the Enlightenment brought to the fore new ideas on individual rights, and on the proper limitations of the powers of the state, that robbed mercantilist practices of much of their political legitimacy. Also, after centuries of struggles for national preservation, the surviving nation-states had reached a certain balance of power. National policy could at best yield minor gains in status and acquisition of marginal territories—not absolute dominance. State regulation of economic activity accordingly came to be viewed as both increasingly less legitimate and less necessary for national survival.

Even more damaging was the demonstration that mercantilist policies were also self-defeating in terms of the very goals that they were intended to pursue. This demonstration arose from a new understanding of the relationship between the quantity of money circulating in the economy and the level of prices, and of the connection between the price level and the balance of trade. David Hume's *gold-specie flow doctrine* argued as follows: If policy succeeds in creating a balance-of-trade surplus, the country enjoys a net inflow of gold and silver. However, precious metals being an integral part of the money supply, the inflow of gold and silver constitutes an increase in the quantity of money in circulation. Next, an increase in money supply causes (other things being equal) an increase in domestic prices, making the country's exports more expensive and the country's imports relatively cheaper than before. You can then expect a decrease in the quantity of exports purchased by foreigners as well as a rise in the imports purchased by your own citizens. The result will be a lessening and eventually elimination of the balance-of-trade surplus.[4] Even when successful, therefore, mercantilist practices could do no more than procure to the country a strictly temporary economic advantage.

No policy can survive long when it comes to be considered devoid of political legitimacy, unnecessary, and self-defeating as well. The final blow to mercantilist ideology was the abandonment of the static view of the world's economy—that inheritance from medieval thinking—and the adoption of a universal dynamic perspective. If the world's economic pie is itself capable of expansion, it no longer follows that one country's economic gain must necessarily occur at the expense of the economic welfare of other nations. Instead, both parties to a transaction can gain through trade, and their separate national interests have a powerful common denominator. With the publication of Adam Smith's *Wealth of Nations* in 1776, it was only a matter

[4] Chapter 10 contains a detailed analysis of the relationship between foreign trade and national income. Also, monetary adjustment under a fixed-exchange rate monetary standard bears a general initial similarity to Hume's gold-specie flow argument (see Chapter 11).

of a few years before mercantilist policies were replaced by the economic liberalism and laissez-faire attitude that underlies the contemporary theory of international trade. (Note, however, that, from the viewpoint of international *political* power, which is inherently relative, the mercantilist rationale remained intact.)

This completes the satellite view of the principal conceptual antecedents of contemporary theoretical principles on international economics. Far-reaching developments have occurred in the theory of international trade from the classical views of Adam Smith and David Ricardo at the turn of the nineteenth century to the contemporary formulations of theoretical principles. However, trade theory is still in keeping with at least one of the basic premises of the liberal "revolution," that is, that the world economy is capable of expansion at the same time as individual nations increase their wealth. The fundamental implication is that a country's economic gains need not occur at the expense of its trading partners. The remainder of the chapter describes and explains contemporary trade theory without any further reference to its intellectual ancestry.

The Effects of Foreign Trade

Contemporary economic theory holds that free trade is advantageous to both sides. This section explains the basis for that conclusion. Possible circumstances under which a restriction of trade may be justified will be examined later, particularly in Chapter 6.

The General Effects of Trade

By far the most important effect of trading with another nation is the economic gains that accrue to both parties as a result of trade. The gains from trade arise from being able to purchase abroad wanted commodities or services cheaper than it would cost to produce them at home. In the example used by Adam Smith, in his critique of mercantilist policies, even the most hawkish English mercantilist would not have advocated suppressing all imports of wine, since it was so much cheaper to import it than to attempt to produce it domestically. But there is no conceptual distinction between the gains from trade when there are large price differences between the foreign and the domestic product and the gains to be obtained when the disparity in price is smaller. It is a distinction of degree, not of kind: As long as the wanted commodity can be obtained cheaper from abroad, there are gains from importing it rather than producing it at home (and, there are losses involved in preventing its importation).

Let us then start with the very simple proposition that a country (as well as an individual) will gain by importing goods, services and assets from abroad at a lower price than they carry domestically, and that it will pay for imports by selling to foreign countries those commodities whose domestic price is lower than the foreign price. *The immediate source of trade must be a difference in price.* Chapter 3 examines the possible reasons for a price difference to emerge. Here the effects of trade on the participating economies, given that a price difference exists in the first place, are examined.

The discussion should start by recalling the economic definition of *market:* A market is an organized mechanism of interaction between buyers and sellers, as a result of which *the same product sells for the same price.* It follows that intercountry differences in price for the same product necessarily imply the presence of separate markets.[5] In this context, however, *relative* prices, not absolute prices, matter. (For example, your economic position and behavior would be unlikely to change much if the dollars-and-cents price of everything you buy *and* of everything you sell were to double.)[6] The economically more relevant price of a quart of wine is not the $4.00 you pay for it, but the fact that a quart of wine sells for four times as much as a quart of beer. In a real sense, the price of a quart of wine is four quarts of beer, and the price of a quart of beer is one-fourth of a quart of wine.

This should bring to your mind the concept of *opportunity cost,* i.e., the benefit given up by not doing the next best thing. The principle governing gainful trade is indeed founded on the opportunity cost notion and is called *the principle of comparative advantage: A country tends to export products that carry at home an opportunity cost lower than they do in other nations and tends to import products that carry at home an opportunity cost higher than they do abroad.* Assuming for a moment that differences in relative prices emerge from differences in production efficiency, the principle of comparative advantage states that a country specializes in sectors where it is relatively more efficient and imports products where it is relatively less efficient. (Please note that to say "most efficient" is exactly the same thing as to say "least inefficient.") It follows that no country (and no individual) can have a *comparative* advantage in all sectors. A nation can be more efficient than other countries in the production of everything, but it can't be *most* efficient in everything. If you pardon the violence done to the English language, a country might be "better" in all economic activities than the rest of the world, but it still is to the advantage of that country to import prod-

[5] Attention is thus focused on the reasons for the separation of national markets from one another. Chapters 4 and 5 examine the economic separation caused by deliberate policies, such as tariffs.

[6] This chapter deals with "pure" theory in the sense that it abstracts from monetary considerations, which are analyzed starting with Chapter 9.

ucts where it is "less better" and specialize in sectors where it is "more better." For exactly the same reason, no country can suffer from a comparative disadvantage in all activities. The principle of comparative advantage is thus a hopeful one, for it implies that in principle any nation has an economic role to play in the international system (though the country may, of course, be less than pleased with the role that economic conditions and the influence of past policies have assigned to it).

The meaning of comparative advantage and the effects of trade can be explained by two hypothetical examples. First, suppose that a surgeon is faced with the decision to hire a nurse, who is less efficient *both* in surgery and in postoperative care. The nurse has therefore an absolute disadvantage in both sectors. The surgeon is, however, *most efficient* in surgery and least efficient at nursing tasks; correspondingly, the nurse is most inefficient at surgical tasks and *least inefficient* at nursing. It is clear that it is advantageous for the nurse to become employed.[7] Is it also advantageous for the surgeon to hire a nurse? Evidently yes; the doctor possesses an *absolute* advantage in both activities, but a *comparative* advantage in only one sector; and the nurse, who suffers from an absolute disadvantage in both sectors, possesses a comparative advantage in nursing. The essence of it is that the hiring of a nurse allows the surgeon to specialize in the activity of relatively greatest efficiency, and ultimately ensures the accomplishment of both more operations and more postoperative care.

The principle of comparative advantage is important enough to deserve a longer illustration. Let's pick this time an example closer to a student's experiences. Suppose that student A faces two tasks in connection with his course requirements: typing from rough draft a clean version of a termpaper, and editing other termpapers he has already typed up. Other things being equal, he can expect his grades to be higher if termpapers are both neatly typed and free of grammatical errors. Production in the two "sectors" is measured by number of pages typed and pages edited, respectively.

The student can accomplish a maximum amount of typing or editing if he employs his time fully and in the most efficient manner possible. That maximum depends both on the total time available and on his typing and editing skills. Suppose that he has one hour of labor time available (his "resource endowment"), and that his typing skills and grammatical knowledge are such that it takes him 10 minutes to type a page and 1 minute to edit one (the typing and editing "production functions"). Suppose further, for simplicity's sake, that he would choose to allocate his time equally between

---

[7] This is true only in static terms. In a long-run sense, it may be better policy for the nurse to sacrifice short-term gains, go to medical school, and possibly acquire a comparative advantage in surgery over the former employer. This is the "infant industry" argument for tariffs, which is described in Chapter 6.

the two tasks: in a half hour he could type a maximum of 3 pages, and in the remaining half hour edit a maximum of 30 pages. In these circumstances, how would one measure the *cost* of producing the 3 typed pages? It can be measured meaningfully only by reference to the opportunity lost, i.e., it is the 30 pages that could have been edited in the same half hour but weren't. Thus, the *unit* cost of typing is 10. Conversely, the relative opportunity cost of editing 1 page is 1/10 of a typed page.

Suppose now that his roommate, student B, is in similar academic circumstances. He has termpapers to type and papers to edit, and also has only one hour of time available. He is, however, less skillfull in typing *and* less knowledgeable of English grammar: it takes him 15 minutes to type a page, and 3 minutes to edit one. What is the relative production cost of typing for student B? It must equal the opportunity cost to *him*, i.e., 5 pages edited. Conversely, the relative cost of editing is 1/5 of a typed page. If we suppose that he chooses to allocate one-fourth of his time to typing, and the remainder to editing, his maximum output consists of 1 page typed and 15 pages edited.

Let's compare the very best each of these two people could accomplish *on their own* (given their choice of time allocation between the two activities):

Maximum Production

Student	Typing	Editing	Relative Cost of *Typing*
A	3	30	60/6 = 10
B	1	15	20/4 = 5

It is apparent that A would gain if he could get 1 page typed for *less than 10 pages* of editing it costs him to type it himself, and that B would gain if he can get *more than 5 pages* edited in exchange for typing 1 page. Assuming that such collaboration is permitted by their instructors, there is plenty of room for mutually beneficial "trade." [8]

Student A has an *absolute* cost advantage (is *more* efficient) in both typing and editing. However, he has a *comparative* cost advantage (is *most* efficient) only in editing and student B has a comparative advantage in

[8] If collaboration is *not* permitted, and A and/or B are honest, no division of labor and trade would occur and the difference in relative prices would persist. In such a case, academic honesty would be the barrier between the two "markets," which thus would remain separate. Even if A and B had no scruples, there is a probability that the cheating would be detected. The occurrence of trade would then depend on the degree of risk; if the price difference was not large enough to compensate for the risk involved, each would do his own work, the commerce would not take place and the price difference would persist. Risk is therefore also a barrier between different markets and can generally be expected to result in a lower volume of trade. This consideration is relevant to the discussion in Chapter 12 of flexible exchange rates.

typing. A can get the typing done cheaper if he "imports" it from B; he must, however, "export" in exchange the editing that B wants. As he was fully occupied to begin with, he can only take advantage of this opportunity for gainful trade by spending less time in typing, in order to free up time to produce additional editing. He thus becomes specialized in editing, while student B is reallocating his time out of editing and into typing. (In this case, specialization is complete, owing to the existence of only one scarce factor of production.)

If no obstacles exist between the two students, the two separate "markets" become integrated into a single one. One result of free trade is therefore the eventual merging of the two separate prices into a *single* price for 1 typed page and a *single* price for 1 edited page. The single "world" price cannot be higher than the higher of the two "pretrade" prices, nor can it be below the lower of the two—otherwise one of the two students would have no interest in trading. Normally, the single price after trade will be somewhere in between the two pretrade prices.

Suppose that the characteristics of "reciprocal demand" (to be discussed shortly) for typing and editing by the two students yield an agreement to exchange 1 page typed for 9 pages edited (10 and 5 were the pretrade prices). Suppose that student wants are such that B wishes to export 3 pages to student A and import 27 edited pages, and that A is willing to accept this exchange. The situation is as follows:

Production

Student	Typing	Editing
A	0	60
B	4	0

Consumption

Student	Typing	Editing
A	3	33
B	1	27

The most important result of trade is that both sides gain. A's skills (which have not been changed by trade) are such that if he produced the 3 pages of typing on his own, he would have half an hour left, during which he could edit at most 30 pages; by trading, he ends up with 33. B's skills are such that if he had been on his own, after typing one page he would have had 45 minutes left, during which he could have edited only 15 pages; by trading, he ends up with 27. It is important to note that the gains from trade, measured in terms of editing, are greater for student B (12 pages) than for student A (3 pages). Almost invariably, there are gains from trade to both parties (and never does either party actually lose). But the *distribution* of such gains is normally not equal. In our example, A gains less because the single price after trade is closer to his own pretrade price than it is to B's.

Exports are the difference between domestic production and desired domestic consumption, when production is larger; imports are the difference between desired domestic consumption and domestic production, when production is smaller. B's wishes to sell 3 typed pages in exchange for 27 edited pages are exactly matched by A's *reciprocal demand* to purchase them at that rate. They *can* exchange the two commodities at the desired rate because that rate is in fact the new agreed "international" price, and because at that price trade between the two students is balanced: A's desired exports equal B's desired imports and vice-versa. You notice from the table above that, for both students taken together, there is no excess demand or excess supply in either typing or editing. Four pages of typing are produced (supplied) and a *total* of 4 are consumed (demanded); 60 pages of editing are supplied, and a *total* of 60 are demanded. The quantity of editing demanded by B is indeed greater than the quantity supplied *domestically;* and the quantity of typing supplied is greater than the quantity demanded *domestically.* But the two separate markets have become unified through trade: equilibrium, or the lack of it, must now be assessed by reference to both markets taken together. It is clear that all typing and editing produced is demanded, either domestically, or in the form of exports.

The *terms of trade* are the rate at which products exchange in international trade. The most common definition of terms of trade is the relative price of exports, i.e., the unit price of exports divided by the unit price of imports. (This is technically known as the "net barter" terms of trade.) For A, who exports editing, the terms of trade are therefore 1/9; for B, who exports typing, the terms of trade are 9. The workings of reciprocal demand mean that the terms of trade (international relative prices) are at equilibrium when trade is balanced for both individuals. Since A's exports are obviously equal to B's imports (and vice-versa), if trade is balanced and exports are equal to imports for both individuals, there is no excess demand or supply in either sector. Relative prices are therefore stable. If, instead, trade were not balanced at the current international relative price, there would be excess demand for one commodity on the market as a whole, and excess supply of the other. The terms of trade would in such case change, and lead to eventual clearing of the market.

In general, what constitutes wise behavior for an individual is not necessarily also wise behavior for a whole country. In this case, however, the parallel between individual and national gains from trade holds. Trade is gainful for countries as it is for individuals, and for the same general reason. Foreign trade allows nations an avenue of escape from the limitations of their own productive potential, by enabling them to utilize each other's *relative* efficiency advantages so that they can *consume* (though not, of course, produce) beyond their production possibilities. In order for trade to be gainful, it is sufficient that relative prices after trade *differ* from relative prices in the isolated state. The gains from trade are greater the larger the price difference. If you were able to sell something for $1, and its price goes up to more than $1, you gain; if I had to pay $2 for that object, and can now obtain it for less than $2, I also gain. (But note the discussion of foreign trade and income distribution in the last section of this chapter.)

The Effects of Foreign Trade: A Simple Diagrammatic Analysis

Let us translate the numerical information of the termpaper example into graphic terms, from the viewpoint of student A. (Recall that the analysis is equally applicable to trade between countries as it is to trade between individuals.) In Figure 2.2, production of typing is measured along the vertical axis, and that of editing on the horizontal axis. The line P_1P_2 is student A's *production possibilities frontier*, which, as explained below, shows the maximum production made possible by the amount of labor time at his disposal (the factor endowment) in combination with the individual's knowledge in the two subjects (the state of technology). If student A dedicates the entire hour of available labor to typing, the typing production function (10 minutes needed to type 1 page) yields maximum production of 6. Since no time is left over, the corresponding production of editing is necessarily zero. It is *possible* for A to *produce* a combination of 6 pages typed and 0 pages edited; this "production possibility" corresponds to point P_1. It is obviously not the only possible combination. At the other extreme, if A dedicates his entire labor to editing, the editing production function (1 minute needed to edit 1 page) yields maximum production of 60. With no time left over, the corresponding production of typing is zero. A second production possibility is therefore point P_2, showing a combination of 60 pages edited and 0 typed. As there are any number of ways in which the student can divide up his time, there are any number of possible production combinations. As in the example in the text, if he chooses to allocate his time equally between the two activities, in one hour he can type 3 pages *and* edit 30 pages, a combination shown by point P_3 in Figure 2.2.

The production possibilities line P_1P_2 is thus made up of the points corresponding to all possible combinations of production if all scarce resources (in this case, labor) are fully employed with the maximum efficiency permitted by the state of technology. (It is a straight line in this special case

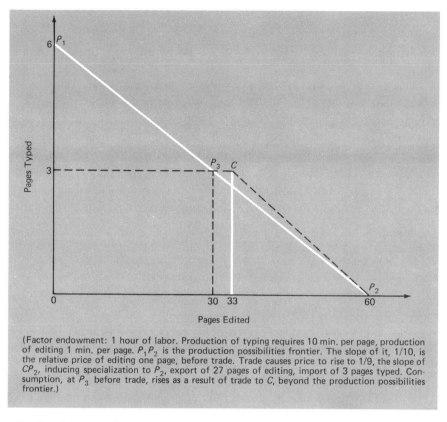

(Factor endowment: 1 hour of labor. Production of typing requires 10 min. per page, production of editing 1 min. per page. P_1P_2 is the production possibilities frontier. The slope of it, 1/10, is the relative price of editing one page, before trade. Trade causes price to rise to 1/9, the slope of CP_2, inducing specialization to P_2, export of 27 pages of editing, import of 3 pages typed. Consumption, at P_3 before trade, rises as a result of trade to C, beyond the production possibilities frontier.)

FIGURE 2.2   Graphic Representation of Student A's Gains from Trade

when only one factor of production exists. The diagrammatic analysis in the presence of more than one factor of production is presented in the Appendix.) It is quite possible for production to take place below the production possibilities frontier, which would result from unemployment, inefficiency, or both. But it is fundamental to realize that it is *impossible* for A to produce at a point to the right of P_1P_2. By definition, you cannot produce more than the very most you can produce with the available technology and resources. (Economic *growth* can thus be defined as a shift outwards—or rightwards—of the production possibilities frontier, owing to an increase in the availability of resources, to technical progress, or to both.)

The *slope* of P_1P_2 is significant. The slope of a line is equal to the vertical distance the line travels divided by the horizontal distance. As the vertical distance measures production of typing, and the horizontal measures production of editing, the slope of the production possibilities frontier is the ratio of typing production to editing production. Clearly, this is the number of pages typed which must be sacrificed if resources in the fully-employed economy are reallocated to edit one additional page. But that, of course, is the opportunity cost of editing, which (in a competitive market) represents the relative price of editing—the commodity on the horizontal axis. In this case, the relative price of editing is $6/60 = 1/10$, the slope of P_1P_2.

The example assumed that the relative price of editing after trading with student B went up to 1/9. The increase in price motivates student A to specialize in editing, with a view toward selling some of his editing production in exchange for the typing he wants done, but no longer does himself. In our example, he chooses a "consumption" combination of 3 pages typed and 33 pages edited (point C). This he attains by complete specialization in editing and by exporting 27 pages for 3 typed pages, which he can do at the posttrade editing price of 1/9. If A's consumption had been confined to his own production possibilities, it could not possibly have exceeded P_1P_2. By specializing and trading, A can evade his production limitations, and end up being able to consume more than he could do in isolation. On the simple assumption that "more is better than less," A gains from trade.

A's partner gains from trade as well. The diagrammatic demonstration is best handled through the use of a "box diagram," commonly known as an Edgeworth-Bowley diagram. In Figure 2.3, the production possibility frontier P_1P_2 at the left is exactly as drawn in Figure 2.2, and represents the economic situation before and after trade for student A. The production possibility line for student B can be derived in the same way as described earlier in the case of A, and is line $P'_1P'_2$, on the right-hand side of the box diagram. It is *upside down* so one can compare the two individuals' production possibilities in the same graph. Production of editing for B, while still measured along the horizontal axis, increases as you proceed to the *left*, and typing production increases as you go *down* on the vertical axis. Just turn the book upside down if you want to look at the situation from B's viewpoint.

The demonstration that both parties gain, even though one of them is absolutely more efficient in both sectors, is a simple extension of the demonstration of A's gains from trade shown in Figure 2.2. Since after trade, there must be a single set of relative prices, the slope of the dotted line P_2C represents the common relative price of editing for both individuals. With reference to B's editing price before trade, however, the new common price is *lower*, and the price of typing correspondingly higher, than before trade. Thus, B's situation is the mirror image of A's: the increase in the price of *typing* induces specialization in that sector, and an eventual shift of production from P'_3 to complete specialization at P'_1. B's desired exports are 3 pages of typing, and he can import in exchange 27 pages of editing. Thus, he also ends up consuming at point C, which lies beyond *his* production possibilities frontier and hence entails gains for him as well.

Finally, since the consumption point C is the same for both individuals (and B's diagram is upside down), the number of edited pages which A wishes to export at a relative price of 1/9 is exactly the same as the number

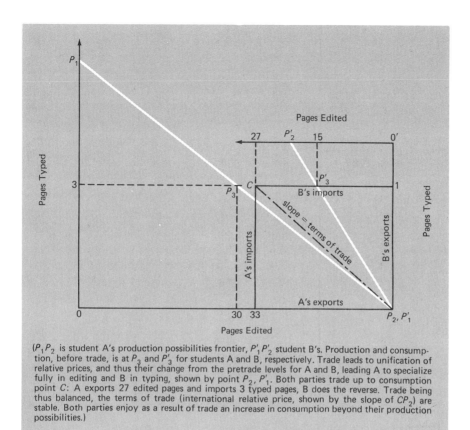

Pages Edited

Pages Typed

Pages Typed

27 P'_2 15 0'

P_3 C P'_3

B's imports

slope = terms of trade

3

P_3 1

A's imports

B's exports

A's exports

0 30 33 P_2, P'_1

Pages Edited

($P_1 P_2$ is student A's production possibilities frontier, $P'_1 P'_2$ student B's. Production and consumption, before trade, is at P_3 and P'_3 for students A and B, respectively. Trade leads to unification of relative prices, and thus their change from the pretrade levels for A and B, leading A to specialize fully in editing and B in typing, shown by point P_2, P'_1. Both parties trade up to consumption point C: A exports 27 edited pages and imports 3 typed pages, B does the reverse. Trade being thus balanced, the terms of trade (international relative price, shown by the slope of CP_2) are stable. Both parties enjoy as a result of trade an increase in consumption beyond their production possibilities.)

FIGURE 2.3   Graphic Representation of Gains from Trade for Both A and B

which B wishes to import at that price. And the number of pages typed which B is willing to export at a relative price of 9 is the same as the number which A wishes to import at that price. Thus, quantity supplied equals quantity demanded in both sectors, trade is balanced for both individuals, and the terms of trade are stable.

This simple analysis is sufficient for our limited purposes here. The Appendix contains a more complete diagrammatic analysis of trade under conditions of increasing opportunity cost. That analysis assumes, however, a certain familiarity with the graphic tools of economic theory. We may simply state here that trade is gainful to both sides also in the presence of more than one production factor and under conditions other than constant opportunity costs. The major difference is that under the more realistic situation of increasing cost, specialization in the activity of comparative advantage is only partial. Even after totally free trade a country continues to produce some of both commodities. This, of course, corresponds to what we know to be the case for most commodities in most countries.

Foreign Trade and Income Distribution

How does the simplified hypothetical situation involving the gains from trade of a single individual relate to the assessment of the role of foreign trade for an entire nation? The general conclusion of the simple analysis of the previous sections is valid also for a country as a whole. By specializing in the activities of comparative advantage, and trading with foreign countries, the economy benefits as compared to its standard of living when isolated from the rest of the world. The model becomes more complex, of course. Specialization and trade are not the result of a decision by a single person, but the aggregate result of myriads of economic decisions made by many individuals responding to changes in the market prices of the things they produce and consume. With many economic activities, a country has a comparative advantage in a number of them and a comparative disadvantage in others. Geographic distance needs to be reckoned with as an impediment to trade. The terms of trade, while still responding to the forces of reciprocal demand, must be expressed as a ratio between price indexes, as exports and imports include many different products. And so on.

The possible changes in the analysis, required by progressive elimination of the simplifying assumptions made earlier, are discussed and explained in the next chapter. One fundamental difference of the "real world" from simple models of the termpaper-commerce type, however, needs to be pointed out now. If foreign trade clearly benefits a nation as a whole, why do individuals and groups within a country so often advocate restricting it? The answer lies in the income distribution aspects, in the simple fact that actual international trade touches the lives of large numbers of different people. The valid conclusion that trade benefits the country *as a whole* should not be taken to mean that it necessarily benefits everyone in the country. The opening of foreign trade, or its expansion, tends to affect both the overall level of national income and its distribution among individuals, groups, and regions.

The opening of trade increases the demand for the country's commodities of comparative advantage. As, by definition, they were lower-priced than in the rest of the world, trade causes foreign demand to be added onto the existing domestic demand for those commodities. Therefore, their price goes up. Correspondingly, the price of the commodities of comparative disadvantage falls, compared to its pretrade level. If all individuals in the country had the same consumption pattern, what each individual loses as a result of the increased domestic prices of the exported commodities would be more than made up by gains from the lower prices of imported commodities. But this is never the case. If some persons are particularly heavy consumers of the commodities of comparative advantage, the opening or expansion of foreign trade causes them a net loss in favor of those individuals whose consumption basket is heavily weighted with imported commodities.

The distribution of national income among geographic regions can also be affected, when the "losers" and the "gainers" are concentrated in different localities.

Trade can also redistribute income among economic classes. This is a point that will not be fully covered until the next chapter, in which the "factor endowments" explanation of the source of comparative advantage is examined. In essence, the domestic owners of those resources that are used to a particularly great extent in the activities of comparative disadvantage lose from foreign trade, as lower-priced foreign supplies come in to take away some of the demand for their products. Correspondingly, the domestic owners of the resources especially useful in the comparative advantage sectors gain from the addition of foreign demand for their wares. Thus, for example, if labor is a particularly important factor in the production of "importables," and capital an important factor in the production of "exportables," foreign trade alters the distribution of income away from "labor-ers" and in favor of "capital-ists" as a group. (The rigorous formulation of this point is known as the Stolper-Samuelson theorem.)

To summarize, the opening or expansion of foreign trade, other things being equal, tends to harm the consumers of exportables (and the regions where they may be concentrated) and to benefit the owners of the resources needed to produce them (and the regions where they may be located). It tends to benefit the consumers of importables (and the regions where they may be concentrated) and to harm the owners of the resources needed to produce them (and the corresponding regions). The restriction or elimination of foreign trade tends to have exactly the opposite income redistribution effects. Application of this general principle is invaluable in assessing the probable impact of trade expansion or trade restriction on a group or locality within the nation.

If the undeniable static gains from trade for the nation as a whole are to be translated into actual benefits across the board, groups that stand to lose must in some fashion be compensated through national policy. Trade makes the nation better off in the sense that the overall economic pie is larger. Full compensation to those who would lose from trade can be made and *still* allow an improvement in the economic conditions of the other members of society. If, however, the compensation to the groups adversely affected does not take place, or is only partial, or it is believed that it will not take place, major political conflict is at hand. Foreign trade is viewed as beneficial or harmful depending on the specific economic circumstances of each interest group. Those who are likely to end up with a smaller slice of the national economic pie are not consoled by the fact that the pie itself will be bigger as a result of trade. Indeed, this may well add to their displeasure, as their *relative* income would decline even more than their absolute income.

These remarks are clearly not of mere academic interests. The income redistribution effects of foreign trade expansion or of trade restriction can cause civil wars. Chapter 8 points out how the tariff issue was an important contributing factor to the American Civil War. Part II of this book examines the types and effects of restrictions of foreign trade and the welter of arguments advanced in favor of such restrictions. At the very bottom of that controversy, aside from the specific arguments adduced, one usually finds income distribution considerations. The economy as a whole benefits from trade, but, in the absence of compensation, some people gain and others lose. The former tend to be protrade and the latter antitrade, a not unexpected reflection of their differing economic interests.

Appendix: A Diagrammatic Analysis
of Trade under Increasing Costs

The simple diagrammatic analysis in the text was subject to a number of assumptions, which will be listed and discussed briefly in the next chapter. Some of these assumptions bear little correspondence to economic reality. One was the assumption that marginal opportunity cost of production is constant; this is necessarily true (over a certain range, at least) when only one scarce factor of production exists (in the example used, the only scarce factor of production was the student's labor).[9] This is clearly not the case in reality where a number of scarce resources are needed in order for production to take place. This Appendix presents a diagrammatic analysis of effects of trade when more than one factor of production is present. The essential theoretical conclusions on the effects of trade are not impaired—merely modified—by the inclusion of more than one factor of production.

The presence of more than one production factor makes it unlikely that marginal cost is the same at all levels of production. Far more common is the case in which the opportunity cost of additional output increases as production expands. This is the case depicted by the familiar upward-sloping supply curve and, for the economy as a whole, by the equally familiar production possibilities curve that is concave from below. If the economy is at full employment, in order for production in one sector to increase, resources must be transferred into it from other sectors whose production therefore must decline. If more than one type of resource is involved, some resources will be relatively better suited to one economic activity than to others. It is reasonable to presume that at the initial stages of expanding production those resources are allocated to that sector which is relatively most productive for it. As output continues to expand, however, progressively less and less suitable resources must be transferred. Thus, for a given opportunity cost in terms of the decline in production of other commodities, the marginal returns (extra output of the sector in question) can be expected to decline as the scale of production increases. This situation may be termed one of "decreasing returns." But at the same time it is a situation of increasing costs. For it follows that in order to obtain equal production increments of one commodity more and more must be given up of other commodities. If this phenomenon is translated into graphic terms, you necessarily end up with a production possibilities curve that is concave from below, i.e., bulges outward.[10]

[9] This was the assumption used by classical economists in their analysis of trade. Classical economics—basically, the mainstream economic thinking of the nineteenth century—was founded in large measure on the labor theory of value, i.e., the notion that commodities derive their value in exchange from the quantity of labor needed to produce them. As will be shown at the beginning of Chapter 3, the labor theory of value becomes a handicap when one asks where comparative advantage comes from.

[10] Production possibilities under constant costs are instead depicted by a straight downward-sloping line, as in Figures 2.2 and 2.3. The slope of the production possibilities frontier reflects marginal opportunity cost. Since a straight line has the same

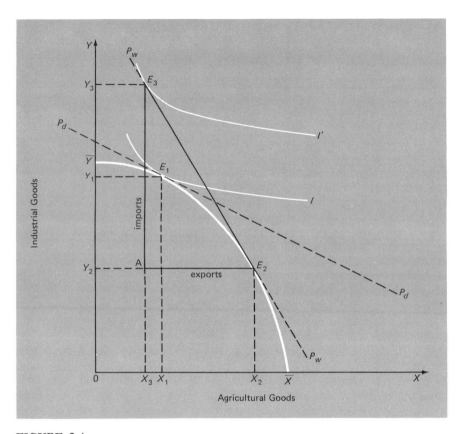

FIGURE 2.4

It is helpful to review the conditions for equilibrium in the national economy in the absence of trade. Figure 2.4 shows pretrade and posttrade national economic equilibrium under conditions of increasing cost for a simplified economy producing only two kinds of goods: industrial and agricultural.

In Figure 2.4, the curve YX shows the economy's production possibilities. These are determined by the availabilities of different resources and by the state of technology. Knowledge about the stock of different factors of production, and about the characteristics of the production functions for the two sectors, allows the determination of all combinations of production of agricultural and industrial goods that are possible if all resources available are fully employed and with the maximum efficiency permitted by the state of technology. The slope of YX at a point is the relative marginal quantity of industrial goods produced at that point: the ratio of the change in industrial production to the change in agricultural production. (The slope of a curve at a point is equal to the slope of a straight line tangent to the curve at that point; the slope of a straight line between any two points is given by the vertical distance divided by

slope at all points, relative marginal cost is in that case the same at all production levels. Finally, a situation of decreasing cost (scale economies) is reflected in a production possibility frontier that bulges *inward*, i.e., is concave from above.

Appendix:
A
Diagrammatic
Analysis
of
Trade
under
Increasing
Costs

the horizontal distance the line travels between those two points.) In a fully-employed two-sector economy, the opportunity cost of increasing production in one sector is the loss of production suffered in the other sector. Hence, the relative marginal quantity of industrial goods is the relative marginal (opportunity) cost of agricultural commodities. If the principle is understood, there is no harm in memorizing the fact that the slope of the production possibility curve is the relative marginal cost of the commodity on the *horizontal* axis. The steeper the curve (the greater the production level of the horizontal commodity), the greater the marginal cost of agricultural goods. (The slope of the production possibilities frontier thus represents the marginal rate at which one commodity can be "transformed" into the other through the production process.)

Producers are at equilibrium when they maximize profits. In a competitive market (one of the assumptions of this model), this occurs when marginal cost equals price. The required equality of relative marginal cost and relative price translates, in Figure 2.4, into the condition that producers must be producing at a point E_1, where the slope of YX (relative marginal cost of X), equals the slope of the price line P_dP_d (relative price of X), i.e., at the point of tangency between the price line and the production possibilities curve. (The slope of the price line represents the rate at which one commodity can be transformed into the other through market exchange. The significance of the price line lies exclusively in its slope, not in its position in space. The identical set of relative prices would be shown by any price line parallel to P_dP_d.) At such point E_1, therefore, the nation's producers are at equilibrium and production will consist of $0X_1$ of agricultural and $0Y_1$ of industrial goods.

What about consumers? In order for the entire system to be at equilibrium, they must be willing, given the relative prices indicated by P_dP_d, to consume exactly what is produced. Suppose that the preferences of all consumers in the country were added up and summarized by a *community indifference map*. (The conditions under which this procedure is permissible are extremely restrictive and quite unlikely to occur in reality. It should be clearly understood that the notion of community indifference curves is used here purely as a matter of analytical convenience.)[11] A given indifference curve shows all combinations of consumption that yield the *same* satisfaction to the nation's consumers as a group.

The slope of an indifference curve is the relative marginal quantity *consumed* of the commodity on the vertical axis (industrial goods). The opportunity cost notion applies here as well (though with a different meaning). The cost to the consumer of an increase in consumption of one commodity is measured by the loss in consumption of the other commodity. Thus, the slope of the indifference curve can be understood to indicate the relative marginal utility of *agricultural* goods. (More generally, that slope represents the rate at which one commodity can be transformed into the other in consumption.) If you assume that the satisfaction from consuming additional amounts of one commodity diminishes the more of it one is already consuming (decreasing marginal utility), each indifference curve will be concave from above, as represented in curves *I* and *I'* in Figure 2.4. Consumers will remain at the same total satisfaction level when giving up further and further units of one commodity only if they obtain greater and greater amounts of the other commodity to make up for the loss. Any

---

[11] Assuming a "classical" utilitarian welfare function, the indifference map can be used to predict market demand.

point on a given indifference curve thus indicates the very same level of economic satisfaction as any other point on the same curve. Instead, a higher indifference curve further away from the origin indicates a higher level of satisfaction throughout. A whole family of indifference curves exists (even though only two are shown in Figure 2.4), each reflecting a different level of economic welfare, with the entire family representing the structure of society's "tastes" for industrial and agricultural goods.

Consumers are at equilibrium when they maximize satisfaction. Satisfaction is at a maximum when relative marginal utility equals relative price. Geometrically, this condition translates into the equality of the slopes of the indifference curve I and of the price line P_dP_d. Consumers as well as producers are then at equilibrium at point E_1—the tangency of the indifference curve I and the price line P_dP_d—where they consume OX_1 of agricultural and OY_1 of industrial goods. (Consumers could also be at equilibrium on other indifference curves provided that the combination consumed yielded the same relative marginal utility of agricultural goods as at point E_1; but all consumption combinations to the right of E_1 are impossible since the economy does not have the capability to produce them, and all consumption combinations to the left of E_1 imply—under pure competition—that producers are not maximizing profits. Producers would also be at equilibrium if the price line were tangent to YX at some point other than E_1; but at any such point consumers would not be maximizing satisfaction.) Relative prices thus emerge from the interaction of supply (production possibilities) and demand (indifference curves) and settle at the point where both producers and consumers are doing as well as they can under the prevailing circumstances. (The rate at which commodities can be transformed into one another through market exchange equals the rate at which they can be transformed into one another in consumption as well as the rate of transformation in production.)

The country's situation *before trade* can be summarized as follows:

Production: OX_1 of agricultural goods, OY_1 of industrial goods
Consumption: OX_1 of agricultural goods, OY_1 of industrial goods
Relative price of agricultural goods: Slope of line P_dP_d
Economic welfare level: As indicated by indifference curve I

What happens if the country begins to trade with another nation where, for any reason, the relative price of agricultural goods is higher than P_dP_d? (It is immaterial whether the outside price is higher or lower than P_dP_d; it is the price difference that matters. Go through the following steps in the case where the outside price of agricultural goods is lower than it is in the country in question before trade.) It stands to reason that if foreign residents are free to do so, they will prefer purchasing agricultural goods from this country rather than from their own more expensive suppliers. This addition of foreign demand to the already existing demand for agricultural goods can be expected to push agricultural prices up. Correspondingly, industrial goods are relatively more expensive than in the rest of the world, and domestic consumers will turn to the less expensive imports, thus lowering industrial prices below their pretrade level. The increase in the relative price of agricultural goods is shown geometrically by a new line P_wP_w (for world price), which is steeper than the pretrade price line P_dP_d.

First, look at the production changes caused by the new price. Producers, remember, were maximizing profits at point E_1 because their marginal cost equalled the price at that point. They now face a higher price of agricultural goods and thus a discrepancy between price and marginal cost. They are no longer maximizing profits at E_1, for they can take advantage of the new higher price of agricultural goods by transferring resources out of the industrial sector and into expanding agricultural production. As they do so, however (increasing cost, remember?), marginal opportunity cost of agricultural production rises and progressively comes closer and closer to the new price. As they move to the right on YX, the slope of the curve becomes steeper and steeper until they eventually reach a new equilibrium (E_2 in Figure 2.4) where the equality of marginal cost and price is restored and further expansion of agricultural output is no longer profitable. At the new equilibrium E_2, the country's producers would like to produce a greater quantity of agricultural goods (OX_2) and a smaller volume of industrial goods (OY_2) than before trade.

Appendix:
A
Diagrammatic
Analysis
of
Trade
under
Increasing
Costs

The relative price change also calls for an adjustment on the consumption side. Consumers maximized satisfaction, hence were at equilibrium, at E_1 because of the equality of relative price with relative marginal utility. The new relative price of agricultural goods is now higher than before and thus also higher than their marginal utility at E_1. On this account, consumers would tend to substitute purchases of industrial goods for purchases of agricultural goods. At the same time, however, the newly-found ability to import industrial goods at a cheaper price from foreign sources is tantamount to an increase in real income—presumably leading to some increase in the consumption of both types of goods. Whether desired consumption of agricultural goods is now greater or smaller than before trade depends on whether the income effect is stronger or weaker than the substitution effect. (In Figure 2.4 the substitution effect is shown as stronger, and consumption of agricultural goods declines.) At any rate, what is important to note is that consumers would find a new equilibrium at point E_3 on the higher indifference curve I', where relative marginal utilities are again equal to relative prices. Given the new set of prices, consumers would like to consume OX_3 and OY_3.

There is now a clear discrepancy between the combination producers wish to produce and sell and the combination consumers wish to purchase. If the excess domestic supply of agricultural products can be fully absorbed by exports and the excess domestic demand for industrial products filled by foreign suppliers, the economy as a whole would again be in a general equilibrium state and at a higher level of overall economic welfare than before trade occurred. (Note that the gains from trade are measured by the overall increase in welfare. You can't measure them by the increased consumption of the two commodities, as the substitution effect may well decrease consumption of one.) After trade, the country's situation is as follows:

Production: OX_2 of agricultural goods, OY_2 of industrial goods
Consumption: OX_3 of agricultural goods, OY_3 of industrial goods
Exports: X_2X_3 of agricultural goods (equal to AE_2)
Imports: Y_2Y_3 of industrial goods (equal to AE_3)
Relative price of agricultural goods: Slope of line P_wP_w
Economic welfare level: As indicated by indifference curve I'

The country has a comparative advantage in agricultural production. By definition it therefore has a comparative disadvantage in the industrial sector. It follows that the country will specialize in, and export, agricultural products and import industrial goods. Specialization is, however, partial. As production of agricultural goods expands, their marginal cost rises, and, as industrial production contracts, its marginal cost falls until eventually the initial competitive disadvantage is wiped out. The country continues to produce some industrial goods at the same time as it imports them.[12] The economy has become integrated into a wider market and is enabled through trade to reap real economic gains (measured by the shift I to I'). The terms of trade (the relative price of exports) are given by the slope of P_wP_w. They will be at equilibrium if the country's trade is balanced, i.e., if the country can obtain from abroad exactly the quantity of industrial goods it wishes to import in exchange for the quantity of agricultural goods it wishes to export. Balanced trade means that the value of imports is equal to the value of exports. The value of imports is by definition equal to their price times the quantity imported, and the value of exports is the price of exports times the quantity exported. Thus, if Q_x stands for quantity exported, Q_m for quantity imported, and P is price, trade is balanced when: $P_xQ_x = P_mQ_m$. This expression may be rewritten as: $P_x/P_m = Q_m/Q_x$. But P_x/P_m is the relative price of exports, i.e., the terms of trade, and Q_m/Q_x is by definition the slope of P_wP_w. Thus, if trade is balanced, the country can do what it wishes to do under the circumstances—exactly because the rest of the world's intentions are the reciprocal of the country's own.

Points for Review

1. What was the general medieval perspective on human economic behavior? What were the two main economic principles arising from that perspective?

2. Describe the broad components of the change from the universal static medieval view to the universal dynamic *laissez-faire* view of the economic world, via the "intermediate" mercantilist perspective.

3. What was the mercantilist balance-of-trade doctrine? How was it related to the state's ultimate ends?

4. What was the main difference in emphasis between French and English mercantilism?

5. Was population growth encouraged in mercantilist times only because it allowed for a larger army?

6. What was the role of colonies in the mercantilist system?

7. What were the principal ingredients of the intellectual and political downfall of mercantilist concepts and policies?

8. What must be the immediate source of trade?

9. Review your understanding of the principle of comparative advantage.

[12] Partial specialization makes sense in light of what we know about the real world. Countries do not specialize entirely on one commodity and import everything else. Normally, a portion of their requirements is produced domestically even though some of it is imported. However, with only one factor of production (and thus a straight-line production possibilities frontier) specialization would eventually be complete.

10. Give examples, other than the ones in the text, of the workings of the principle of comparative advantage.

11. What is the general meaning of reciprocal demand? What is the meaning of terms of trade? What is the implication of the workings of reciprocal demand for the terms of trade?

12. In the presence of international trade, excess supply or excess demand in the domestic market can be perfectly consistent with the existence of overall equilibrium. Is this true? Why or why not?

13. Review your understanding of why, in a situation of increasing costs, the production possibilities curve is concave from below.

14. Review your understanding of the following statements:
a. The slope of the production possibilities curve is the "rate of transformation in production" and, hence, the relative marginal cost of the commodity on the horizontal axis (under full employment).
b. The equality of marginal cost and price is the condition for maximum profit and, hence, for producers' equilibrium (under pure competition).
c. The slope of the price line is the "rate of transformation in exchange" and, hence, the relative price of the commodity on the horizontal axis.
d. The significance of the price line lies only in its slope, not in its position in space.
e. As the consequence of the previous four points, for producers to be at equilibrium they must produce the combination indicated by the point of tangency between the price line and the production possibilities curve.

15. Review your understanding of the following statements:
a. The slope of an indifference curve is the "rate of transformation in consumption" and, hence, the relative marginal utility of the commodity on the horizontal axis.
b. The equality of relative marginal utility and relative price is the condition for maximum satisfaction and, hence, for consumers' equilibrium.
c. Thus, for consumers to be at equilibrium, they must consume the combination indicated by the point of tangency between the price line and the (highest) indifference curve.

16. Review your understanding of the following statement: As the consequence of the foregoing principles relating to production and consumption (points 14 and 15), the condition for general equilibrium is the equality of all three variables: marginal cost, marginal utility, and price.

17. Describe why the relative price of the commodity of comparative advantage rises as the result of the opening of trade.

18. Describe what happens to domestic production when the relative price of the commodity of comparative advantage increases (with constant tastes and the same production possibilities curve).

19. Describe what happens to domestic consumption as the result of the opening of trade.

20. Review your understanding of the notion of "gains from trade." Diagrammatically, review your understanding of the economy's move to a higher indifference curve as the result of the opening of trade.

43

Questions for Discussion

1. Can a theoretical statement be valid in a particular historical context, and not very useful in a different one? Can you think of some examples, not necessarily from economics?

2. The text argues that circumstances shape ideas, but also that human actions, which produce the surrounding economic circumstances, are themselves influenced by the prevailing conceptual climate. Do you agree? If not, can you find examples that appear to show otherwise?

3. Would you attribute the transition from medieval to mercantilist economics mainly to changed factual circumstances or to the emergence of new concepts? What about the transition from mercantilism to economic liberalism?

4. Were mercantilist attitudes in fact a recipe for continuous international conflict? If power is relative, does the mercantilist view of the world as a static entity still carry *political* relevance today?

5. Do you see significant differences between the motivations and modalities of colonialism in mercantilist times and the more recent colonial undertakings of the nineteenth and twentieth centuries?

6. The text does not mention a principle of "absolute advantage." What might be the meaning of such a principle? How would it differ from the meaning and workings of the principle of comparative advantage?

7. Does the gains from trade conclusion apply to commercial relations between a metropolitan power and its colonial territories?

8. List some possible reasons why the same commodity would sell for a different price, i.e., why different markets coexist for the same thing instead of a unified one.

9. On the *sole* basis of Figure 2.2, how would you identify which is the commodity of comparative advantage? (Hint: There are three ways, all of which are tantamount to saying the same thing.)

10. Are you persuaded that there are gains from trade? If not, why?

11. Trace the process of adjustment on the production and consumption side if the opening of trade causes the relative price of agricultural goods to *fall* instead of to rise as in Figure 2.4. Does it make any difference to the gains from trade conclusion?

12. Given that the opening of trade causes the country to move to a higher level of economic welfare (a higher indifference curve), what would be the general effect of restricting trade? How would such a restriction come about? Which segments of the country's population would be likely to favor restriction of trade?

"We only make progress through paradoxes."

Niels Bohr

"The artist may be well advised to keep his work to himself till it is completed . . . but the scientist is wiser not to withhold a single finding or a single conjecture from publicity."

Goethe, *Essays on Experimentation*

The Causes
of International Trade

What to Expect

This chapter deals with the remaining basic questions of trade theory: What is the source of comparative advantage? Are there systematic connections between the pattern of trade and the structure of the country's economy? What influence does international trade exert on the distribution of income within the country? The first section reviews the various possible causes of the pattern of trade and describes the major explanation, the factor endowments theorem. The second section examines the possible changes in the theoretical conclusions if some of the assumptions are modified, reviews several alternative explanations of the source of comparative advantage, and concludes with a capsule assessment of the validity and limitations of contemporary trade theory. The Appendix contains a mathematical proof of the factor endowments theorem.

The Source of Comparative Advantage

As great an improvement as the notion of comparative advantage and the gains from trade constituted over the earlier mercantilist ideas, it was not until this century that the source of comparative advantage was explained in a sufficiently concrete way. If, in David Ricardo's classical example, Portugal is relatively more efficient in the production of wine and England in cloth, both countries can gain through trade by utilizing each other's different relative cost advantages. But why is Portugal relatively more efficient in wine-making? Where does its comparative advantage in that sector come from? [1]

---

[1] The classical answer to this question was not very useful. Since the classical economists thought that value is determined by labor, and by labor alone, their answer boiled down to the following statement: "Portugal has a comparative advantage in wine production because Portuguese labor is more efficient in that activity." But is this due to some Portuguese tradition, or to an earlier start in that activity, or to the possibility that the Portuguese don't mind stomping grapes while the English do—owing to some "inherent," "natural" difference in labor efficiency? The classical answer thus turns out to be tautological: "Countries have a comparative advantage in those activities . . . where they have a comparative advantage." The recourse to the notion of "inherent" efficiency, by the way, bears the imprint of the moralistic basis of early classical economic thinking. Scratch a classical economist and you often find a moral philosopher or a physiocratic mystic. Thus, Adam Smith takes refuge in the notions of "parsimony" and "prodigality" in order to explain the source of saving, and Malthus offers his brand of obnoxious moralism when preaching on abstinence as a means to control the growth of population. Even Ricardo, in his lucid and dispassionate analysis of rent, occasionally slips into mystical language, as in his paean to "the original and indestructible powers of the earth."

In Search of a General Explanation

The immediate source of trade must be a difference in the price of the same commodity between different countries. This section examines the possible explanations of why such price differences can arise. Price is essentially determined by the interaction of supply and demand; thus, a price difference may arise owing to differences in demand conditions, in supply conditions, or both. The ingredients that are likely to be similar in the various countries and that are thus unlikely to be adequate explanations of intercountry price differences and of trade must be excluded first.

The Demand Side   The principal determinants of the quantity demanded of any product include the price of the product, the prices of related goods and services, income, and "tastes." Since comparative advantage emerges from differences in *relative* prices, the major demand factors in this context are income and tastes.

Income cannot be a major source of demand differences between countries whose income levels and distribution of income are similar. Thus, while income differences might perhaps be of major importance in explaining trade between developed and less developed countries (whose income levels are by definition widely divergent),[2] they must be excluded as a possible major explanation of trade among developed countries.

The *tastes* variable in the demand function is a difficult one to define, for it includes all residual influences on demand that cannot be specified separately. Still, in very general terms, tastes are related to the country's historical past and its prevalent social and cultural climate. Differences in tastes might therefore be quite relevant to the determination of patterns of trade between countries with different sociocultural orientations and/or of a diverse historical heritage (as, for example, between former colonies of different colonial powers). Even then, as trade occurs, tastes can be fundamentally altered and tend to become more uniform across the world (a phenomenon that Ragnar Nurkse termed the "demonstration effect"). Tastes, like jokes, do travel quite easily around the world: Just think of the spread of chewing gum in European countries after World War II, or the dissemination of the taste for Coca-Cola all over the world. In any case, differences in tastes are an unlikely candidate to account for significant demand differences—and thus for trade—between countries belonging to the

---

[2] Even then, it can be shown that income differences will not affect the structure of comparative advantage if demand functions are such that the income elasticity of demand is the same for all commodities and services. If income elasticities instead differ for different commodities, it is possible that commodities whose total demand (and therefore price) is greater than demand for other goods at one level of income, will rank lower in total demand (and in price) at a higher level of income. The technical term for this phenomenon is **demand reversal**. If demand reversals occur, a country may lose or gain a comparative advantage in a commodity owing to the impact of income changes on the pattern of demand.

47

same general sociocultural matrix. In particular, differences in tastes cannot be relied upon as a major explanation to trade among Western nations.

The upshot of these considerations on income and tastes is that *differences in the conditions of demand are unlikely to be an important aggregate explanation of international trade among developed Western countries.*[3]

The Supply Side In reasonably competitive markets, the marginal cost of production is by far the major determinant of the quantity of a product supplied. Marginal cost, as you know, depends both on the state of technology (the commodity's production function) and on the prices of factors of production. In turn, factor prices are related to the availability of those factors in the national economy (the country's factor endowment). Intercountry differences in supply conditions may therefore emerge from the intercountry differences in technology and/or from differences in national endowments of the various factors of production.

Technical innovations can generally move across national frontiers with far greater ease (albeit with some time lag) than can the factors of production themselves. Thus, intercountry differences in technology can be presumed to be less pronounced than intercountry differences in the availability of the various factors of production.[4]

This is the end of the line: If demand conditions are in all probability similar among developed Western countries, comparative advantage must be explained by reference to differences in *comparative cost.* Further, if technology is also fairly uniform, international variations in comparative cost—and thus in relative prices—should be attributed primarily to different national endowments of factors of production. *Differences in factor endowments thus remain as the likely major cause of international trade among developed Western countries* (which account for the bulk of world trade).

Trade and Factor Endowments

The analysis of the impact of different national endowments of production factors upon international trade is associated with the names of Eli Heck-

[3] They however remain possible explanations of trade between developed and less developed countries, or between "West" and "East," or between countries with widely different cultures. Also, demand differences may well be the cause of trade in specific commodities or services. The considerations presented here relate only to the general explanation of the overall pattern of trade.

[4] The classical model instead assumed similar factor endowments and attributed comparative cost differences to different production functions for the same commodity in different countries. As was emphasized in Chapter 2, theoretical development is in some measure organically connected to the historical conditions of the times. The assumption of technological differences between countries was an appropriate one in the late eighteenth and early nineteenth centuries, when the major technical innovations (mainly in iron manufacture, textiles, and steam machinery) had not yet spread from England to other countries.

scher and Bertil Ohlin, both Swedish economists, who independently set out its main points, and is summarized in the Heckscher-Ohlin theorem. This theoretical contribution does not invalidate the principal conclusions on the importance of comparative cost differences and on the gains from trade. It is more in the nature of an expansion of the earlier theory, in the direction of explaining in a sufficiently concrete fashion the source of differences in comparative costs.

The factor endowments explanation of international trade is grounded on the interaction between the nature of technology and the economic structure of a country. In a nutshell, the Heckscher-Ohlin (or factor-endowments) theorem states that a country is relatively more efficient in those activities that are better suited to its economic structure: A country does best with what it has most of. The analysis allows one not only to say that the principle of comparative advantage underlies trade and that there are gains from trade, but to predict which kind of an economy will tend to export or import which kind of product.[5]

The theorem states: *A country has a comparative advantage in those commodities the production of which is intensive in the country's relatively abundant factor; it will therefore tend to export those commodities and import commodities the production of which is intensive in the country's relatively scarce factor of production.* Differences in comparative costs are here attributed to the interaction of the characteristics of technology (which are assumed to be uniform throughout the world) and the structure of the economy (which is assumed to be specific to each country). If, for example, the United States has a greater total availability of capital relative to labor than other countries do, it will export those commodities the production of which requires a greater relative use of capital than other products do— and it will import the other products.

The theorem follows logically upon the assumption of the model. Let us see how. *First*, the labor theory of value is abandoned (see footnote 1) and more than one scarce factor is assumed to exist. This immediately allows for the possibility that greater labor efficiency might not be inherent at all, but may rather be due to the existence of a greater availability of other, complementary factors of production. In Ricardo's wine-making example, it stands to economic reason that Portugal's comparative efficiency in wine is probably due to its relatively greater abundance of grape-producing land. *Second*, once additional factors of production are introduced in the model, it becomes apparent that it is very likely for different countries to have different relative availabilities of the various factors of production. (Note that it is *relative* availabilities that matter, not absolute factor endowments. As Paul Samuelson stated it in a well-known article, "It is only proportions that

---

[5] This is so because, unlike the notion of inherent efficiency, a country's economic structure can be described meaningfully, measured, and quite possibly altered by deliberate policy.

49

matter, not scale.[6]) *Third*, while each commodity is assumed to have its own specific production function, a given commodity is assumed to have the same production function everywhere in the world. (We remain, however, in the static, purely competitive, full-employment world of the earlier analysis where transport costs, resource reallocation costs, international movement of production factors, and international differences in tastes, among other things, are assumed away.)

The uniformity of technology and of tastes in different countries implies that the conditions of demand for factors of production will also be the same, since the demand for factors of production is derived from the demand for the goods that they can produce. Simple supply-and-demand reasoning then tells you that, with identical demand conditions, differences in the relative supplies of a factor of production will lead to differences in the relative price of that factor between the two countries. A resource of a given type will have a lower relative price in the country in which it is relatively more plentiful. For example, if the United States has a relative abundance of capital and a relative scarcity of labor compared to the rest of the world (but the same conditions of *demand* for capital and labor) the relative interest rate (the price of capital) will be lower, and the relative wage higher, in the United States than in the rest of the world.

Next, it is assumed that production functions differ between commodities but are the same for the same commodity between countries. For example, the technology of automobile production is assumed to be the same in both countries, but different from the technology of clothing production. A difference in technique can be summarized by a difference in the relative use of factors of production: the ratio of capital to labor used in the production of automobiles differs from that used in the production of clothing. Each industry has a specific **factor intensity**.[7] Let's suppose that autos are the commodity with a higher capital/labor ratio (the *capital-intensive* com-

[6] P. Samuelson, "International Factor-price Equalization Once Again," *Economic Journal* (June 1949).

[7] The factor intensity taken as characteristic of a given industry is the one that applies when all of the economy's resources are fully used to their maximum efficiency. The condition for maximum efficiency of resource allocation may be familiar to you: the relative marginal physical product of a given factor of production must be equal in all its uses. The validity of the Heckscher-Ohlin theorem depends on the additional assumption that one commodity is more capital-intensive (or more labor-intensive) than the other at all factor price ratios. It is thus necessary to assume that production functions are such that, if a commodity is relatively more intensive in one factor at one production level, it is relatively more intensive in that same factor at all other production levels. This will be the case if production functions are such that the elasticity of substitution is the same in all sectors. If the elasticity of substitution differs in different activities, it is possible that commodities that are relatively capital-intensive at one level of production become relatively labor-intensive at other levels of production. The technical term for this phenomenon is **factor reversal**. You should easily see the parallel with the considerations made in footnote 2 concerning the effect of income differences on the pattern of demand If factor or demand reversals occur, a country may lose or gain a comparative advantage

modity) and clothing the commodity with a higher labor/capital ratio (the *labor-intensive* commodity). The cost of capital will clearly have an impact on the total production cost of automobiles greater than its impact on the cost of clothing production, since cars require for their production relatively more capital than clothing does. The opposite is true concerning the level of wages (the cost of labor).

Now join together the above considerations on production costs with the differences in factor prices between countries. It is easy to see that in the United States, where the relative wage is higher than elsewhere, the relative production cost of clothing (the labor-intensive commodity) must also be higher than elsewhere; conversely, the relative cheapness of capital causes the production cost of automobiles to be lower than in other countries. With identical conditions of demand throughout the world, and under pure competition, these cost differences will translate themselves into price differences. Thus, in the United States the relative price of automobiles will be lower and the price of clothing higher than in the rest of the world. Since those commodities are traded that it is advantageous to trade, the United States (capital-abundant, labor-scarce country) will export cars (the capital-intensive commodity) and import clothing (the labor-intensive commodity). This is, of course, what the theorem predicts as the result of different factor endowments. (A mathematical proof of the Heckscher-Ohlin theorem is presented in the Appendix.)

Trade and International Factor Prices

A difference in the relative prices of factors of production between countries, arising from a difference in the availability of these factors, is the most likely general explanation of differences in relative commodity prices and hence of international trade among developed Western countries. But the connection is not one-sided. If commodity prices differ because factor prices differ, can one not suspect that, once commodity prices have been rendered equal in all countries by trade, factor prices will have become equal also? It has been shown by Paul Samuelson that, under the strict assumptions of the Heckscher-Ohlin theorem, this is in fact the case.[8]

What is the significance of this conclusion? Under pure competition (one of the conditions for which is mobility of resources) the efficiency of resource allocation and utilization is at a maximum. (Competition in its pure form is a theoretical abstraction useful for analytical purposes, but it is not a reflection of economic reality.) If, therefore, the international mobility of factors is low, the efficient international utilization of resources is rendered

---

in a commodity without any change in relative factor endowments; hence, the Heckscher-Ohlin conclusion would not hold.

[8] Samuelson, op. cit.

even more difficult than it is within a country, where factors of production can be relied upon to move with greater ease.

There is, however, a possible substitute for factor movements: international trade. Although factors of production might not be free to move across national frontiers, something else can take the place of such movement. This "something else" is the movement of the *products* of the immobile resources, i.e., international trade. Through completely free trade, factor prices are progressively equalized in different countries, as would happen if the factors themselves were free to move. It is true that complete factor price equalization requires a set of conditions so restrictive that it is impossible for them to occur in reality. What remains fair to say, however, is that differences in the national prices of the same factor of production are very probably smaller as a result of trade than they would be otherwise. Free trade in the products is a partial substitute for free movement of the resources that produce them.

For example, a Japanese steelworker would find it quite difficult (for his own reasons as well as because of obstacles imposed by others) to migrate to Pittsburgh if steelworker wages were higher there. If he were free to do so, and the higher Pittsburgh wages corresponded to higher steelworker productivity, the efficiency of utilization of combined U.S.-Japanese resources would increase and the differences in steelworker wages between Osaka and Pittsburgh would lessen. But if Japanese steel were freely imported into the United States, the same result would obtain: the scarcity of U.S. steelworkers, relative to the demand for their products, would decrease owing to the fact that a portion of that demand was now satisfied by the products of foreign steelworkers. Combined U.S.-Japanese production would increase; U.S. and Japanese consumers would end up with more steel and more of everything else. There is a serious hitch in all this: steelworkers' wages in the United States would tend to fall. What is more, the decline in their wages would normally not be fully offset by a decline in the prices of goods and services that they buy. U.S. steelworkers' real purchasing power would decline, while that of U.S. steel consumers would increase. This is one of the important effects of trade on the distribution of income within a country (referred to as the Stolper-Samuelson theorem in Chapter 2), and the part of the continuing controversy over tariffs and quotas, which Part II examines in detail.

International Trade Theory: From Logical Certainty to Practical Likelihood

Modification of the Simple Theoretical Model

Here and there, in this and the previous chapter, certain assumptions were referred to as underpinnings of the analysis. It is time to assess how the essential theoretical conclusions are affected, if at all, by removing the explicit and implicit assumptions and thus bringing the model into closer correspondence with economic realities.

Multicountry, Multicommodity, Multifactor Trade   The discussion so far has been framed in terms of only one country, two commodities, and two factors of production.[9] This is clearly not a realistic reflection of the international trade situation. However, expansion of the model to encompass two or more countries, more than two commodities, and more than two factors of production does not cause the essential conclusions to change much.

With *more than two countries* the worst that can happen to one trading country is that it remains in the same situation as before trade, if it is so large as to cause international prices to coincide with its internal prices before trade. But it cannot lose from trading. Thus, the condition for trade to be advantageous for the world economy as a whole is an initial difference in relative prices in different countries. Since none of the trading countries can lose (incidentally, if they stood to lose from trade they would obviously not participate in it), and at least one country must gain, trade causes an overall benefit for the world economy as a whole.[10]

The existence of more than two countries complicates the situation somewhat, since it can no longer automatically be said that one country's comparative advantage in one commodity corresponds to the other country's comparative disadvantage. The various nations must now be ranked in order of their comparative efficiency in the sector being considered. The country on top of the list is unequivocally an exporter of the commodity, and the one at the bottom of the list is an importer of it. The countries in the middle either export or import the article depending on actual international prices (as determined by reciprocal demand).

A similar consideration applies to the extension of the trade model to encompass *more than two commodities*. The principle of comparative advantage still holds and so does the fundamental conclusion that trade produces gains for the individual participating countries and for the world economy as a whole. The specific commodity composition of countries' exports and imports, however, is no longer as clear-cut as in the two-commodity case. The various commodities produced by a particular country need now be ranked in order of the comparative efficiency of their production. It can unequivocally be said that the country has a comparative advantage in the

---

[9] Neither is there the space nor is it analytically appropriate in this text to pay more than cursory attention to the expansions of the model to encompass more than two countries, commodities, or factors of production. The interested reader is referred to the more advanced books in this area, for example, A. Takayama, *International Trade* (New York: Holt, Rinehart and Winston, 1972), chapter 6.

[10] It can be demonstrated that completely free international trade leads to *maximum* (not simply greater) efficiency and welfare in the world economy. This demonstration is left out for the sake of simplicity.

International
Trade
Theory:
From
Logical
Certainty
to
Practical
Likelihood

"top" commodity and a comparative disadvantage in the "bottom" commodity. But it cannot be said whether it will import or export the "middle" products unless actual world prices are known.

Finally, the assumption that no *more than two factors* of production exist (in the earlier discussion, capital and labor) is also at variance with economic reality but, as in the case of the limitations in the number of commodities traded and of countries, removing it does no great violence to the basic theory. The main conclusions still stand, provided only that the number of different factors of production is no greater than the number of different commodities traded. This is a perfectly acceptable restriction, once you consider that the different commodities traded internationally number in the thousands.

Making the theory more realistic by allowing for the existence of several countries, commodities, and factors of production, still leaves intact the conclusions that trade is gainful, that it takes place on the basis of comparative advantage, that international prices are greatly influenced by reciprocal demand, that the structure of foreign trade is a function of countries' factor endowments, that trade serves as a partial substitute for international movement of factors of production, and so forth.

Other Qualifications of the Static Trade Model In other respects, however, bringing trade theory into closer correspondence with the facts of international commerce does call for *possible* substantive modification of the essential conclusions. Some of these qualifications are briefly noted here; they will be discussed in detail in subsequent chapters.

No mention has been made so far of the obvious fact that products cannot be whisked instantaneously and at no cost from one country to another. *Transport costs* and their effects are examined in Chapter 4. *Tariffs* and other man-made obstacles to trade are discussed in considerable detail in Chapters 4–8.

A frequently stated assumption was that of *pure competition* in commodity and factor markets. The equality of relative marginal cost, relative price, and relative marginal utility is needed to demonstrate that the opening of trade produces gains for the economy as a whole. In turn, that equality requires pure competition or at least a reasonable facsimile thereof. The possibility that free trade may not be the best policy in the presence of significant market imperfections is examined in Chapter 6.

Also explicitly stated was the assumption of *full employment* of all resources, both before and after trade. Two broad possibilities may be distinguished here. First, it is possible that trade causes the economy to move to an underemployment position, as might be the case if the resources displaced by cheaper imports do not find their way in the sectors of comparative advantage and thus become unemployed. This possible adverse effect of trade on the level of employment is discussed in Chapter 6. Second, it is

International
Trade
Theory:
From
Logical
Certainty
to
Practical
Likelihood

possible that the economy was not at full employment to begin with, and that, in addition to the increase in efficiency due to specialization, trade also causes an increase in overall employment. This is examined later in this chapter under the "vent-for-surplus" explanation of trade.

Intercountry differences in the conditions of *demand* do not alter the gains-from-trade conclusion, but make it impossible to predict the pattern of imports and exports on the basis of production conditions only. Take the following example. A country has a comparative cost advantage in the production of cigarettes. However, the population's addiction to smoking is stronger than elsewhere in the world. The supply advantage may be more than offset by the greater intensity of domestic demand for cigarettes. Domestic price may thus be higher than in other countries, with the country importing that article even though it can produce it relatively more efficiently. Also, demand reversals (see footnote 2) may intervene to confuse the situation even when tastes are broadly similar. Thus, if the income elasticity of demand for cigarettes is lower than for other products, in poorer countries the effective demand for that product is relatively greater than in richer countries, and the pretrade price of cigarettes may be sufficiently higher to offset a relative advantage on the supply side. Finally, differences in the internal distribution of income between countries, with different groups exhibiting a different propensity to smoke, may also give rise to price differences in a direction opposite to that which would be predicted on the basis of the conditions of production.

The empirical evidence shows that, while tastes are generally similar in different countries, the income elasticities of demand for different commodities do vary widely. This supports the presumption of uniform conditions of demand among developed Western countries, which have similar income levels, tastes, and patterns of income distribution. But demand reversals must be reckoned with as an important possible determinant of trade between the industrialized and the underdeveloped countries. In a poor country, the demand for products of low income elasticity is by definition relatively greater than in a rich nation, and this may suffice to wipe out a possible comparative cost advantage. For example, if demand for foodstuffs in India is relatively much greater than demand for shoes—because of the country's poverty—the relative price of food may be higher, and that of shoes lower, than in the rest of the world. India might therefore end up importing food and exporting shoes even if it possesses a comparative *cost* advantage in the production of food.

As we have seen, the Heckscher-Ohlin explanation of trade on the sole basis of factor endowments differences rests, among other things, on the assumption that the same *technology* is used in all trading countries. If, instead, technology as well as economic structure differ, the Heckscher-Ohlin theorem no longer holds. For example, if good tobacco land is relatively abundant, but at the same time the techniques used in cigarette production are less advanced than elsewhere in the world, we can no longer predict whether or not the country has a comparative advantage in, hence exports, cigarettes. Also, factor reversals (see footnote 7) may invalidate the Heckscher-Ohlin conclusion even when technology is similar. If cigarette technology is the same, but production levels are very different in the various countries, the characteristics of the common production function may be such that cigarettes are a labor-intensive product in one country but capital-intensive in another. Relative availability of resources is thus no longer sufficient to predict whether a country will import or export the commodity.

Here the empirical evidence is highly ambiguous, with significant instances of apparent factor reversals having been found and frequent paradoxes emerging. For example, overall exports of capital-abundant Canada are capital intensive, as predicted by the Heckscher-Ohlin theorem; but Canada's exports to the even more capital-abundant United States are *also* capital intensive. This question will be brought up again later.

The model shown in the Appendix to Chapter 2 presumed increasing opportunity cost of production (a production possibilities curve concave from below), which is probably the more realistic assumption to make. If, instead, production is characterized by *constant costs*, two implications follow. First, as we have seen, trade leads to complete specialization. Second, constant costs mean that price is not affected by demand, but only by supply conditions. The equality of price and marginal cost in a competitive market obviously implies that, if marginal cost is constant, price will also be constant regardless of demand.[11]

If production is characterized by increasing returns to scale (also known as **economies of scale**), comparative advantage would be determined partly by the scale of production in different countries. A latecomer to an industry in which economies of scale are important might well suffer from a comparative disadvantage in that industry regardless of its advantageous economic structure or patterns of demand. This point will come up again later in this chapter.

The Dynamic Dimension of International Trade

The most important limitation of the trade theory discussed up to this point is undoubtedly its static nature, embodied in the assumptions of *given availability of resources, constant technology, and an unchanging structure of tastes*. The theory provides a solid framework for the analysis of the effects of trade on the current level of economic welfare and on the efficiency of utilization of available resources, and it tells much about how to use best what we have. However, it does not tell us how to increase what we have or

[11] A constant cost assumption would therefore obviate the difficulties caused by possible intercountry differences in demand conditions.

how to assess the effects of international trade on economic growth. Efficiency and growth, although in practice closely intertwined, are conceptually different problems. The effects of trade on growth are real and possibly more important than the static gains from trade. There are sophisticated works on trade and economic growth, and a very rich literature has evolved over the past thirty years on problems of trade and economic development. As emphasized in the preface, however, the issue is so complex and fluid that it would be quite misleading to give a summary of the theoretical contributions involved. They deserve separate and intensive study on their own merits. This book can do no more than note some possible major influences of trade on economic growth and development.[12] A nonexhaustive list follows.

First, not all of the goods traded internationally are for final consumption (as the simple theoretical model implicitly assumed), but also may be raw materials, intermediate goods, capital equipment. The introduction of such goods in the theoretical model does not cause any great change in the essential conclusions. It does, however, imply that imports are related both to economic growth and to the efficiency of allocation of current resources.[13] In particular, if there are no adequate domestic substitutes, the capacity to import certain types of capital equipment from abroad may be of far greater importance for the country's economic future than for its current well being. *Second*, the competitive stimulus from imports may be a catalyst for technical progress and industrial modernization. *Third*, exports can be an engine of economic growth through their linkages with productivity in the domestic sectors, and they can pull up the overall technical capabilities of the economy. *Fourth*, the increase in demand as producers break out into the world market may permit reaping substantial economies of large scale production. *Fifth*, the beneficial effect of foreign trade on current national income also creates the potential for more rapid economic growth. Growth is at least in part a function of investment, i.e., the increase in the capital stock of the country. But investment requires *saving:* some portion of the country's resources must be diverted from the production of consumer goods and services (thereby sacrificing current consumption) into the production of investment goods. And saving, in turn, is directly related to the level of income. Hence, since trade leads to specialization and greater efficiency of utilization of current resources, and thus to a higher national income, it also carries a potential for greater saving, investment, and economic growth. *Sixth*, "externalities" may be present. The term refers to those conse-

International
Trade
Theory:
From
Logical
Certainty
to
Practical
Likelihood

---

[12] Dynamic considerations will be brought up again in Chapter 6, under the infant industry argument for trade restriction. Also, the bibliography gives leads to those interested in a serious study of the relationships between trade and economic development.

[13] Other important implications of the introduction of intermediate goods are the theory of effective protection examined in Chapter 4, and the possibility of inflationary depreciation of the currency, discussed in Chapter 12.

quences of economic actions that affect, favorably or unfavorably, sectors other than the sector where the action is undertaken.[14] The importance of the phenomenon lies in the fact that those who are responsible for the creation of positive external effects do not benefit from them, while those responsible for unfavorable external diseconomies do not bear the corresponding costs. A discrepancy exists between actions and their eventual consequences. In the presence of externalities, therefore, current production and trade may be lower or greater than the volume that in the longer run would prove optimal for the economy as a whole.

Finally, on a more general plane, the opening up to foreign trade can cause a country to break out of a rigid socioeconomic structure dominated by custom and tradition. In particular, exposure to new products may create new wants and provide the incentive for greater economic efforts. On the other hand, if the structure of tastes changes, it becomes impossible to say whether or not trade leads to improved economic welfare. One would literally have to compare apples and oranges. Can you be sure that people are happier owning a TV set than they were before they even knew that TV existed, when they could not possibly have missed it? From the moment when the new wants come into being, it is quite true that one gains from being able to satisfy them more cheaply through specialization and trade. But there is an insurmountable qualitative gulf between the before and the after. The ancient Chinese equation of happiness states that

$$\text{Happiness} = \frac{\text{Results}}{\text{Expectations}}$$

The theory of trade, assuming constant expectations (tastes) and demonstrating greater results (income), shows convincingly that trade leads to greater happiness (welfare). But once you allow expectations (the denominator of the ratio) to increase as well, all bets are off. It becomes impossible to compare the level of subjective welfare before and after trade for a given individual since the new wants effectively mean that the individual *himself* has changed. (And it is even more hopeless to attempt such a comparison for an entire population.) The existence of benefits from trade is clearly demonstrable in the short and medium run, becomes conceptually ambiguous in the long run, and is wholly unprovable when the structure of tastes is radically altered by the very opening up of the economy to trade.

It is analytically necessary to command the economy to "stand still" while we leisurely go about our business of evaluating what happens to the

---

[14] An example of a positive external effect (external economies) is when investment in the training of steelworkers also has beneficial repercussions on the skill level of the labor force in other industries. An example of a negative external effect (external diseconomies) is when discharge of chemical waste into a river imposes water-purification costs on to other users of the river.

variables being examined. In fact, of course, everything that influences trade is changing all the time. The notion of comparative advantage must also be interpreted dynamically. Countries lose and acquire a comparative advantage in new industries as a result of any number of possible changes. Pioneering industries age into mature, and eventually into declining, industries. Exporters turn into importers, importers into exporters. Free traders become protectionists, isolationists become world-minded. And, probably fundamental from a decisional viewpoint, the analytical and policy questions are interrelated. Deliberate policies can have a significant effect on all variables that determine a country's comparative advantage: resource availability, technology, income, and even tastes. It is possible, although in practice a lengthy process fraught with dangers, for a country intentionally to set out to alter its structure of comparative advantage and its trade pattern, by policies expressly designed for that purpose. And this is where economic theory comes in, even when its direct applicability is severely limited by the assumptions it requires. It is not a universally valid map of every nook and cranny of economic reality, but a toolbox containing a variety of valuable principles and insights to be used as befits the policy purposes and the specifics of the situation. The next section adds to the "toolbox" by reviewing some alternatives to the factor endowments explanation of the source of comparative advantage.

International
Trade
Theory:
From
Logical
Certainty
to
Practical
Likelihood

Alternative Explanations of the Source of Comparative Advantages

The Leontief Paradox As you know by the factor endowments theorem, a relatively capital-abundant country tends to export commodities that are relatively capital-intensive and to import labor-intensive products. But the predictions from the theorem have not fared very well in empirical studies of the pattern of international trade. The theorem first appeared to flunk the empirical test in a 1953 study by Wassily Leontief. From input-output figures Leontief calculated that U.S. exports were less capital-intensive than U.S. import-competing production (and thus, on the assumption of uniform technology, U.S. imports themselves). But in the United States there is supposed to be a greater abundance of capital relative to labor than in the rest of the world. The finding thus seemed to contradict the Heckscher-Ohlin theorem.

The Leontief study motivated further empirical research. The empirical evidence accumulated since then shows many paradoxical results and contains serious, but not fatal, contradictions of the general applicability of the factor-endowments explanation. The **Leontief Paradox**, as it came to be called, sent economists scurrying after possible explanations and sparked valuable rethinking of an issue that had been considered satisfactorily closed.

Since the internal logic of the factor endowments theory is beyond dispute, explanations of Leontief-type findings can only be of two types: Those that attribute the paradox to a real-world violation of one or more of the Heckscher-Ohlin assumptions; and those that argue that the inconsistency between theory and facts is only apparent and results from faulty methodology.

The first class of explanations has already been indirectly discussed. The factor endowment conclusion does not follow unless production and demand functions (technology and tastes) are the same in the different countries and unless their characteristics are such that factor and/or demand reversals are ruled out. These are highly doubtful suppositions when the countries in question vary widely in production and income levels. Instead, as argued earlier, they are reasonably applicable to trade among developed Western countries. There is little evidence of significant *and* wide-ranging differences in technology and tastes among those countries; their similarity of income and production levels makes it unlikely that demand or factor reversals are a major influence on overall trade patterns.

Of the explanations alleging faulty methodology, the more important ones point out that a simple capital/labor ratio is inadequate as a measure of factor endowments when more than those two factors exist, especially when the very definition of capital and labor is open to question. Thus, as Jaroslav Vanek argues, if one considers the United States to have its greatest relative scarcity in natural resources, and not in labor, the factor endowments theory would predict imports of resource-intensive products; the theory is thus not disproved by a finding that imports are relatively labor-intensive. Peter B. Kenen took into consideration the "human capital" factor. If human capital (skilled labor) is relatively abundant, but is lumped in the category of "labor" in general, American exports will appear to be labor intensive whereas, in keeping with the factor endowments theory, they really are human capital-intensive.

These and other contributions have gone a long way toward explaining the discrepancies between the theoretical predictions and the apparent economic facts, but not all the way. It is probably fair to conclude that the evidence still supports the factor endowment theory, but only as *a* major explanation of the source of comparative advantage, and then primarily for trade among industrialized countries. Through the process of rethinking set in motion by Leontief, the factor endowments theory thus lost some of its generality. There is room for alternative explanations.

Comparative Labor Costs The less than satisfactory performance of the Heckscher-Ohlin theory in practice has rekindled some interest in a much older explanation of the source of comparative advantage, one that goes back to the early nineteenth century economics of David Ricardo. In the classical view, comparative advantage is determined solely by relative labor efficiency. Of course, labor is not the only scarce factor of production. Still, a

International
Trade
Theory:
From
Logical
Certainty
to
Practical
Likelihood

theory ultimately must be evaluated on the basis of its predictive value. Also, the Ricardian view has the great advantage of being much simpler than the factor endowments explanation. There need be no worry about the proper specification of several different factors of production nor, with the constant costs implied by the existence of only one factor, about possible international differences in demand, or about esoteric problems such as factor or demand reversals. By the theory of comparative labor costs,[15] all that is needed to predict comparative advantage is a relatively high coefficient of labor productivity. Higher labor productivity means lower labor costs; in the Ricardian world, lower labor cost is synonymous with lower production cost and, since demand conditions do not matter, the relative price of the product is lower than in other countries.

In a 1951 study of U.S.-British trade, G. D. A. MacDougall discovered a correlation between relative labor productivity and exports: the U.S. exported commodities where its labor productivity advantage over Britain was greater than the U.S. wage disadvantage, and it imported from Britain articles where the U.S. labor productivity was *relatively* lower.[16] This result, supportive of the comparative labor cost theory, was confirmed by other studies, but was severely shaken by still other research that found no significant evidence in support of the labor cost proposition.[17] Thus, while the simple comparative cost proposition should be welcomed back to our theoretical toolbox, it is highly dubious that it can replace the more complex factor endowment theory as the general explanation of trade patterns.

"Vent for Surplus" This explanation of the pattern of international trade also long predates the Heckscher-Ohlin theory, going all the way back to Adam Smith in the eighteenth century. Consider the following situation. A country has, before the opening of trade, some resources that are not used because of a surfeit of the commodities that they could produce. There may be, for example, a surplus of bananas in the country, and the population does not find it worthwhile to expend energies for increasing banana production up to its full potential. Foreign trade provides a "vent" for such surplus. As trade opens, the price that can be obtained for bananas rises, inducing an inflow of the unused resources into production of the export commodity *without* causing a decline in production elsewhere. The gains from trade are therefore greater than in the conventional situation of initial full employment. While the "vent for surplus" concept has little applicability

---

[15] The Ricardian proposition is sometimes referred to simply as the theory of comparative cost. This is seriously misleading, since the factor endowments explanation relies on comparative cost differences, too.

[16] G.D.A. MacDougall, "British and American Exports: A Study Suggested by the Theory of Comparative Costs," *Economic Journal* (December 1951).

[17] J. Bhagwati, "The Pure Theory of International Trade: A Survey," *Economic Journal* (March 1964).

to the pattern of *ongoing* trade, it is an interesting explanation of the gains from the initial opening up of the economy to foreign trade.[18]

The gains may be considerable for the rest of the world, which gets cheaper bananas. But are there true gains from trade for the country itself in a vent-for-surplus situation? Earlier the point was made that gains from trade are undemonstrable when tastes change through trade. What will the country purchase with the proceeds of the exports of bananas? It is not very likely that it will simply import commodities similar to the ones it had been producing before trade. The state of pretrade isolation implied by the vent-for-surplus theory would indicate that the opening of trade exposes the country's population to new products and thus causes a significant change in the structure of wants.

Indeed, in his version of the vent-for-surplus concept, the nineteenth century economist John Stuart Mill considered this change in tastes as an important gain in and of itself:

A people may be in a quiescent, indolent, uncultivated state, with all of their tastes either fully satisfied or entirely undeveloped, and they may fail to put forth the whole of their productive energies for want of any sufficient object of desire. The opening of foreign trade, by making them acquainted with new objects, or tempting them by the easier acquisition of things which they had not previously thought attainable, sometimes works a sort of industrial revolution in a country whose resources were previously undeveloped for want of energy and ambition in the people, inducing those who were satisfied with scanty comforts and little work, to work harder for the gratification of their new tastes, and even to save, and accumulate capital, for the still more complete satisfaction of their tastes at a future time.[19]

In this statement, however, the tail of effort wags the dog of satisfaction. It cannot really be said that individuals, or peoples, are worse off if their modest wants are "fully satisfied" than if their possessions are greater but their new wants greater still. And the long-term economic and political implications for the local population of the vent-for-surplus doctrine are no

[18] Of far greater interest than a possible vent for surplus *commodities* of a less developed country is the possible role of foreign investment as a "vent" for surplus *capital* of industrialized nations, a notion central to the classical theory of imperialism associated with Hobson and Lenin.

[19] J. S. Mill, *Principles of Political Economy*, W. J. Ashley, ed. (London: Longmans Green and Company, 1909), bk. 3, chapter 17, Sec. 5. In a famous controversy, Mill forcefully refuted the proslavery views of Thomas Carlyle. Carlyle defended slavery, in essence, because in his view the "indolent African" would spend all his time eating "pumpkins" (watermelons) unless he were forced to work. And, in Carlyle's puritanical (and flatly racist) perspective, hard work was the instrument of "civilization" and religious salvation. It is ironic that in the passage quoted, Mill exhibits the same puritanical attitude (though without the racist content) by implying that "putting forth the whole of productive energies" is an end in itself rather than simply a means to the satisfaction of human wants.

less dubious. Consider, for example, the long-term consequences for American Indians of their exposure to whiskey as a "new product" and the creation of a "new taste" for it. And, as someone has said: "Hawaii is beautiful, but where are the Hawaiians?!"

Availability How does one explain exports of petroleum by a country with large and easily accessible deposits of it? Why, simply because the oil is there. There is no need to resort to elaborate theoretical constructs. The sufficient basis for trade is here the availability of a scarce natural resource. Consider also the obvious fact that only Scotland can export genuine Scotch whiskey, only France can export Cognac and French perfume, only Switzerland can export Swiss watches, only Italy can export Italian shoes. The preference of world consumers for certain products because of their geographic origin is quite enough by itself to explain the pattern of trade in those cases. (Strictly speaking, all of these could be treated as special cases of the Heckscher-Ohlin theorem, by looking at the natural resource or "mark of origin" involved as factors of production that are *absolutely* scarce in the importing countries. But this would be unnecessary hairsplitting.) On the other hand, it is clear that the availability theory, while indispensible to explain the pattern of trade in certain commodities, cannot be a general explanation of the source of comparative advantage.

Economies of Scale and Technological Headstart Serious attention must now be given to the implications for international trade of the possibility of decreasing costs (economies of scale) and of the headstart some countries may have in the production of new commodities or in the application of new processes. The term *economies of scale* means that unit production costs decrease as production expands. Thus, a country may export a product simply because, perhaps owing to the larger size of its domestic market, it has a larger production volume than its international competitors, whether or not its factor endowments, technological level, or conditions of demand would otherwise lead to a comparative advantage in that industry.[20]

Static economies of scale apply within a given technical process, albeit

---

[20] Some economies of scale are a production phenomenon, arising from such things as the possibility to use specialized equipment when production is larger. Others are of a commercial and financial nature. Larger firms enjoy a number of advantages over smaller companies, ranging from discounts for bulk purchases of materials to easier access to financial markets. It is in recognition of these advantages that the Webb-Pomerene Act in the United States exempts from antitrust regulations associations of American firms on export markets, provided that such arrangements do not have unfavorable backlash effects on the extent of domestic competition. As another example, the government of South Korea was planning in 1976 to assign to only 10 existing Korean companies the responsibility and privilege of handling at least 30 percent of the country's total exports and to assist them through special financing and tax treatment to foster their amalgamation.

one characterized by a direct relationship between scale and efficiency. More important is the role of technical change, either in the form of introduction of new products or as technological innovations in the production of existing ones. A firm in a particular country introduces on the market a new product, nylon stockings, for example. It has a practical monopoly on it until firms in other nations learn how to produce it themselves. For the duration of the "imitation gap," the initiator is the only exporter on the world market. Similarly, when a firm discovers a different and more advanced technique of production, it may enjoy for a time a considerable cost advantage and come to dominate the world market, especially since in the usual case its innovation is legally protected from imitators by the international patent system.

To be sure, such an explanation of trade patterns is inherently temporary for specific products or processes. At the end of the imitation gap, the product is no longer "new," and countries' relative factor endowments may take over again as the principal determinant of comparative advantage. But *technological gap trade* (as Gary C. Hufbauer calls it) cannot be treated merely as a special case in our age of systematic and quickening technical change. By the time a formerly new product or process has become standard, other products and techniques have come to the fore. As long as technical progress is a continuing proposition, the technological gap explanation of trade patterns will continue to be of major importance.

Attention here is focused on how the technological advantage itself is obtained. One proposition has been well established by research: Inventions and innovations are no longer primarily due to individual geniuses working alone in basement labs, but to teams and to the amount of research and development expenditures (R&D). The cartoon image of a tiny lightbulb suddenly switched on inside the scientist's head, the "Eureka! explanation" of invention and innovation, has given way to a world where technological progress is itself *produced* through the fairly systematic use of the inputs required for it—scientists, engineers, libraries, laboratories, and so forth. This allows one to reconcile in principle the technological gap theory with the factor endowments explanation of trade, by looking at R&D as a separate factor of production whose relative abundance or scarcity in a country determines comparative advantage or disadvantage in technology-intensive products.

A major issue of relevance to this discussion is the possible relationship between the pace of technical advance and the structure of the industry. You might suppose that large firms spend proportionately more on R&D (because they have more money than small firms) and thus produce proportionately more new technology. Correspondingly, highly concentrated industries would be technologically more progressive. If this were the case, the standard economic argument against the undesirable effects of monopoly on static efficiency would carry much less weight, relative to the dynamic role of large corporations and monopolistic industries as carriers of technical progress.

But the proposition that corporate bigness is related to technological advance is far from obvious. True, large firms generally have greater profits and liquidity and are thus better *able* to finance R&D activities. But they also have a greater economic stake in the existing technology and more to lose from development of new techniques, and they may therefore be less *willing* to do so. Also, there is evidence that scientists, engineers, and technical personnel work less well in big outfits than they do in medium-sized ones, where their creative activity is freer from complicated rules and regulations and the individuals responsible for improvements or mistakes are more easily identified and thus rewarded or penalized accordingly. In economic terms, it appears that above a certain minimum threshold R&D suffers from *dis*economies of scale. If the facts justify associating a particular size of firm with the potential for technical progress, it is therefore the medium-size company, *not* the large company, that gets the nod.[21] This is welcome news for relatively small countries, whose capacity to participate advantageously in technological-gap trade is relatively unhampered by their economic size. It is also good news, at least in this limited context, for local firms in competition with giant multinational corporations.

The Basis of International Trade: A Capsule Assessment

This section has attempted to put the applicability of the theoretical explanations of the causes of international trade into realistic perspective. We hope that it has not generated and compounded doubts about the "relevance" of the theory to the realities of international commerce. In fact, the theory of trade by and large stands up rather well to the gradual removal of its unrealistic assumptions. Naturally, as one moves from a highly abstract model to a more complex representation of economic reality, one comes down from the realm of logical certainties to that of practical likelihoods. But the explanatory and predictive value of the theoretical contributions remains considerable.

With reference to the source of comparative advantage, we have seen that, while simple availability and a vent-for-surplus may explain special instances of international trade, differences in factor endowments do survive as the most general explanation of the pattern of "old" trade and that the technological gap emerges as a powerful explanation of trade in "new" products. Among industrialized Western countries, therefore, the overall structure of trade can be rather thoroughly explained either by differences in the domestic economic structure or by differences in technology. In the in-

---

[21] The major exception in the United States is the chemical industry.

dividual trade instance, we must still say "it depends," but we have a fairly specific idea of what "it" depends on.

With reference to the gains-from-trade conclusion, the theory is even more solid. The proposition that, on static grounds, trade benefits both parties remains valid even if the assumptions underlying it are removed, at least at the aggregate level and as a very strong presumption. The various possible exceptions to the free trade rule have not yet been examined. Part II does so in detail. But the gains-from-trade conclusion is the necessary backdrop against which any proposal for restricting trade must be viewed. The burden of proving that a restriction of trade carries specific benefits, which outweigh the general advantages from trading, rests squarely on those who advocate the restriction. The general case for free trade has been abundantly proved.

Appendix: Mathematical Proof of the Heckscher-Ohlin Theorem

If A and B are the only two commodities produced, and capital (K) and labor (L) are the two factors of production, knowledge of the production functions for A and B yields the following coefficients:

$$a_{11} = \text{capital per unit of output of } A$$
$$a_{12} = \text{capital per unit of output of } B$$
$$a_{21} = \text{labor per unit of output of } A$$
$$a_{22} = \text{labor per unit of output of } B$$

By the assumption of full employment,[22] we have:

$$a_{11}A + a_{12}B = K, \text{ where } K \text{ is total capital availability} \tag{1}$$
$$a_{21}A + a_{22}B = L, \text{ where } L \text{ is total labor availability} \tag{2}$$

Dividing through by L in both (1) and (2), we obtain:

$$a_{11}(A/L) + a_{12}(B/L) = K/L \tag{3}$$
$$a_{21}(A/L) + a_{22}(B/L) = 1 \tag{4}$$

In order to eventually solve for B/L, we must first isolate the term A/L. Subtracting the B/L term from both sides of equations (3) and (4), and then dividing both sides by the coefficient of A/L, we get:

$$A/L = \frac{K/L - a_{12}B/L}{a_{11}} \tag{3a}$$

$$A/L = \frac{1 - a_{22}B/L}{a_{21}} \tag{4a}$$

The left side of (3a) is equal to the left side of (4a); therefore:

$$\frac{K/L - a_{12}B/L}{a_{11}} = \frac{1 - a_{22}B/L}{a_{21}} \tag{5}$$

From: Ronald Findlay, *Trade and Specialization*, Penguin Modern Economics, Penguin Books, Harmondsworth, England, 1970; pp. 53–55 (with major adaptations, reproduced with permission).

[22] To have full employment *and* positive quantities of A and B, one must additionally assume:

$$(a_{11}/a_{21}) > (K/L) > (a_{12}/a_{22})$$

which is reasonable if the current stocks of factors of production were produced in response to past factor demands.

Multiplying both sides of (5) by the two denominators, a_{11} and a_{21}, the latter disappear. We may then bring to one side both B/L terms, factor out B/L, divide through by the resulting coefficient, and obtain:

$$B/L = \frac{a_{11} - a_{21}K/L}{(a_{11}a_{22} - a_{21}a_{12})} \tag{6}$$

Solving in the same manner for A/L (the intermediate steps are omitted), we obtain:

$$A/L = \frac{a_{22}K/L - a_{12}}{(a_{11}a_{22} - a_{12}a_{21})} \tag{7}$$

Note that the denominators are equal on both sides of equations (6) and (7). Dividing (7) by (6), therefore, we get:

$$A/B = \frac{a_{22}K/L - a_{12}}{a_{11} - a_{21}K/L} \tag{8}$$

Equation (8) is quite important, for it shows the exact quantitative relationship between factor endowments and commodity production. Specifically, (8) gives the ratio of outputs of the two commodities as a function of relative factor *availabilities* in the presence of certain technological parameters. The effect of changes in factor endowments on the ratio of outputs is obtained by differentiating (8) with respect to K/L, which after some cancelling out yields:

$$\frac{d(A/B)}{d(K/L)} = \frac{a_{11}a_{22} - a_{21}a_{12}}{(a_{11} - a_{21}K/L)^2} \tag{9}$$

You can easily see that $[d(A/B)/d(K/L)]$ is positive if (a_{11}/a_{21}) is greater than (a_{12}/a_{22}). Referring back to the definition of the a coefficients, this means that the capital/labor ratio in commodity A is greater than in commodity B, i.e., that A is the relatively capital-intensive commodity. An increase in the relative availability of capital will thus cause an increase in the relative quantity of A produced. Under pure competition, full employment [assumed in equations (1) and (2)], and international uniformity of demand conditions, the relative price of A will fall. It is therefore clear that the country with a higher relative availability of capital will have a comparative advantage in A, the capital-intensive commodity. (Strictly, this demonstration depends on fixed input coefficients.)

Points for Review

1. Explain how trade can take place because of a difference in tastes, even though conditions of production are identical in the two countries.

2. List each of the steps connecting differences in relative factor endowments to the Heckscher-Ohlin conclusion on the source of comparative advantage and disadvantage. List the assumptions mentioned or implied in the text as being necessary to that conclusion.

3. What is meant by factor intensity?

4. What is meant by demand reversals? How are demand reversals related to the notion of income elasticity of demand? Why do they invalidate the factor endowments theorem?

5. What is meant by factor reversals? How are factor reversals related to the characteristics of the production function? Why do they invalidate the factor endowments theorem?

6. What is the factor-price equalization theorem? What does it imply for the distribution of income among economic classes?

7. Are any of the basic theoretical conclusions of the simple model to be abandoned or modified when the model is made more realistic by allowing for the existence of many commodities, countries, and factors of production?

8. Review your understanding that specialization is total under a constant costs situation.

9. Review your understanding of the alternative explanations of the source of comparative advantage, including especially the existence of scale economies and/or of technological headstart.

10. Review the steps in the mathematical demonstration of the Heckscher-Ohlin theorem in the Appendix.

Questions for Discussion

1. Why does the discussion in the text limit the general a priori validity of the factor endowments explanation of comparative advantage to trade among Western developed countries?

2. Does the factor endowments theorem say, for example, that if a country has a much greater work force than another, it tends to possess a comparative advantage in labor-intensive products?

3. One of the several assumptions of the factor endowments explanation is international uniformity of technology. What can one say about the probable pattern of trade if *both* technology and relative factor availabilities differ between countries?

4. Conditions in the real world deviate significantly from the assumptions required by the factor-price equalization theorem. Besides, factor prices are not equal throughout the world. Is the factor-price equalization theorem then a mere academic exercise?

5. Why are the gains from trade not provable when tastes change as a result of trade? Is this statement equivalent to saying that differences in tastes between countries invalidate the factor endowments explanation (see review point 1)?

6. The text notes a need for dynamic interpretation of the notion of comparative advantage. Is this tantamount to a belated admission that static trade theory is useless as a predictive tool?

7. After reading through the discussion of the Leontief Paradox, do you see why the Danish physicist Niels Bohr stated, as quoted at the beginning of the chapter, that progress only comes from paradoxes? Indeed, doesn't the implicit definition of the word "paradox" mean that his statement is necessarily true? Can you think of examples in disciplines other than economics to which that statement would apply?

8. How convincing would you consider each of the various explanations of the source of comparative advantage? To which general type of country, or class of product, would each of those explanations be particularly applicable?

9. The text concludes that, the Leontief Paradox notwithstanding, the factor endowments explanation is still the most general explanation of the pattern of trade in "old" products. Do you concur?

10. [For the mathematically inclined] Why is it stated that the proof of the Heckscher-Ohlin theorem shown in the Appendix depends on fixed-input coefficients? How might one modify the proof to generalize it to variable-input coefficients? How would then the existence of factor reversals manifest itself to invalidate the conclusion?

The Theory
and Practice
of Commercial Policy

*"Ships are but boards, sailors but men: There be
land-rats and water-rats, water-thieves and
land-thieves; pirates, I mean; and then there is
the peril of waters, winds and rocks."*

Shakespeare, *The Merchant of Venice*

"A customs duty is a negative railway."

Frédéric Bastiat

The Nature
of Trade Restrictions

What to Expect

Much of the theory presented in earlier chapters assumed away the existence of any obstacle to the free movement of goods and services between countries. Such obstacles, however, do exist. This chapter examines the principal types of impediments to international trade. (Chapter 5 will analyze the effects of these impediments.) First, the natural barriers to trade—chiefly, the geographic distance between countries and the resulting costs of transport—are examined. The remainder of the chapter focuses on man-made restrictions, including the various types of policies that can be used to affect the flow of international trade. These are quotas, monetary restrictions, administrative and technical regulations, and, most importantly, tariffs. The discussion of the types of tariffs includes an examination of significant measurement problems and particularly the determination of the extent to which a given tariff reflects the effective degree of protection accorded to the domestic industry. The Appendix reproduces a short satirical piece by a nineteenth-century French economist. It is not essential reading, but I think you will enjoy it. Because of the intimate connection between the material of this and the subsequent chapter, Points for Review and Questions for Discussion are omitted here. Longer lists, covering the material of both chapters, are given at the end of Chapter 5.

The theoretical explanation of international trade presented in Chapter 3 required all sorts of assumptions. Many of those assumptions were obviously unrealistic. But any explanation of complex reality must of necessity first arrive at some general conclusions about "What would happen if. . . ." Only then is one in a position to examine how the general conclusions are likely to be changed if the assumptions on which they rest do not hold. (Many of the unrealistic assumptions were removed in the last section of Chapter 3. The net result of bringing the theoretical model into closer correspondence with economic reality is the demotion of the theoretical conclusions from a status of logical certainty to one of practical likelihood. By and large, however, those conclusions do survive.) Especially offensive to your common sense must have been the assumption that there are no obstacles of any sort to impede the free flow of goods and services between countries. It is perfectly obvious that you cannot instantaneously whisk a Toyota from Japan to San Francisco at no cost whatever. Barriers of all kinds do exist. It is the task of this and the following chapter to describe their types and analyze their principal effects. (It is the purpose of Chapter 6, in the light of the material presented here, to examine the validity of arguments for restricting international trade. Chapter 7 brings up the political dimension of the tariff issue, and Chapter 8 gives a summary of American tariff history.)

An easy distinction comes to mind between "natural" obstacles to international trade and those impediments that arise from human action. The first section of this chapter briefly examines the consequences for international trade of the existence of natural obstacles, mainly distance and geographic impediments between countries. The bulk of the chapter is dedicated to the man-made obstacles, the analysis of which is referred to as the **theory of commercial policy.** It is well to anticipate the conclusion that, broadly speaking, the influence of natural obstacles is similar to that of deliberate obstructions. For example, it makes little difference to a trader whether his route is obstructed by a natural pond or by an artificial reservoir of the same size and shape. It takes him exactly the same additional effort to detour around it.

Natural Obstacles: Transport Costs

Two general categories of natural obstacles to international trade can be identified. In addition to transport costs (discussed below), there is a complex of accidents and natural catastrophes that are bound to happen from time to time. Train wrecks, plane crashes, sinking of ships, truck collisions, storms, earthquakes, all give rise to certain risks connected with the movement of goods from one place to another. The list of possible sources of risk and uncertainty is virtually endless. The important point is that all risks entail the probability, however small, of economic damage to the buyer or the purchaser and to that extent tend to discourage trade. It is, of course, precisely to absorb risks that the insurance industry evolved. And, with the possible exception of life insurance, no other form of the industry is as widespread and well developed as insurance of international commerce. Still, the risk-absorption function of the insurance industry is not performed for free. Thus, to the extent that certain risks are specific to international transactions, international movement of goods and services carries an additional cost, namely, the cost of insurance. In international trade statistics, the practice is to record prices received and prices paid. Thus, exports are valued "free on board" (FOB), excluding all costs of transfer. The value of imports, instead, includes both transport and insurance costs and is recorded as "cost, insurance, freight" (CIF).

Transport Costs and International Trade

Additional costs are the principal manifestation of the second category of natural obstacles to international trade: distance and geographic impediments between countries. It takes real resources—ships, airplanes, people, equipment, fuel—to move something from one place to another. These resources are not a gift. Transport costs exert a significant influence on the prices and volume of goods and services traded.[1]

As you recall, in the absence of any barrier between two countries, the two national markets are one. In one market, there can only be one price for a unit of the same commodity. In the absence of any barrier, a commodity must therefore sell for the same price in both the exporting and the importing country. The price of an imported commodity must be identical to its world price. Any price difference between countries, not matter how slight, is sufficient to induce trade. If transport costs are present, it is no longer true that the slightest price difference is sufficient to reduce trade. The existence of an obstacle between the two countries separates the two national markets, and two different markets are, by definition, characterized by two different prices for the same thing. In order for trade to take place, the initial price difference between countries must be greater than the costs of transport. The price of imports is thus greater than the world price of the same commodity, with the difference due to the costs of transport.

The implications of transport costs for the volume of international trade are clearly related to the price increase. Other things being equal, tacking transport costs on to the international price of a commodity means an increase in the price paid by the purchaser (hence, a probable reduction in the quantity imported), a reduction in the price received by the seller (hence, a probable decline in the quantity exported), or, usually, some measure of both. The total volume of trade can thus be expected to be lower than it would be if transport costs were zero. In some cases, freight charges would be so high that no conceivable difference in production costs could suffice to induce trade.[2] The lower volume of trade reduces the real gains that nations could reap from utilizing each other's relative efficiency advantages. There are gains from trade accruing to both trading partners. These gains generally increase with the volume of trade. As a general rule, an increase in trade is beneficial in real economic terms. Correspondingly, a lower volume of international trade, as caused by the existence of transport costs, implies, in principle, a lower level of economic welfare for all countries concerned.

These considerations provide only the barest outline of the effects of transport costs. An extensive literature exists, exploring the implications of variable transport costs, of market interdependence, of balance-of-payments

[1] Other items incidental to the shipment such as handling and storage are included under transport costs.

[2] As an example, consider housing. The costs of shipping complete houses are so enormous that no country can succeed in exporting them, no matter how great a comparative advantage in housing construction it might have over the rest of the world. However, this does not preclude exports of construction materials, or equipment, or emigration of the plasterers and carpenters themselves to take advantage of the higher returns available in countries with a comparative disadvantage in construction.

mainder by importers, regardless of who is nominally charged with paying the freight. (This is because none of the curves drawn in Figure 4.1 are perfectly elastic.) Both the excess supply abroad and the excess demand at home are reduced, with a consequent decline in the volume of trade. At the new equilibrium, imports and exports are still equal, but they have now been cut to $A'B'$ and $C'D'$, respectively. The gains from trade are smaller.

This analysis is subject to the severe limitations of any partial-equilibrium approach, assuming, as it does, that everything else remains the same while the adjustment is proceeding, and thus that the position of all curves is not changed. More complex general-equilibrium models, both diagrammatic and mathematical, are available. While they do shed much additional light on the interaction of transport costs and trade, they do not alter the essential consequences of the introduction of transport costs: import price is different from world price; import price is higher than in the absence of transport costs; and the volume of imports is lower than it would be otherwise.

Man-made Obstacles to International Trade

There is an essential equivalence between natural and artificial obstacles to trade: They all constitute barriers between markets. To that extent, they cause prices for the same commodity to differ between countries. More specifically, if obstacles exist, import prices are higher and import volume is correspondingly lower. Frédéric Bastiat, the nineteenth-century French economist, in several satirical pieces, emphasized the basic similarity between natural obstacles and man-made barriers. One of these, "A Chinese Story," is reproduced in the Appendix. The quote at the beginning of this chapter is taken from Bastiat's devastating criticism of an argument of his time that the proposed railway from Paris to Madrid should offer a break of continuity at Bordeaux in order to increase employment and profits in the Bordeaux area. But then, Bastiat noted, if Bordeaux has a right to profit by a break in the railway line, and if this is consonant with the national interest, all intermediate places should also be entitled to gaps. For, the greater the number of gaps in the railroad line, the greater the positive employment effect on all areas affected. "In this way, we shall succeed in having a line of railway composed of successive gaps, and which may be denominated a Negative Railway." [5]

Suppose that an avalanche destroys a section of a major highway connecting Boston and Montreal. You would surely agree that the avalanche is a "bad" thing. Indeed, it would be important news, and the media would

[5] F. Bastiat, *Fallacies of Protection*, trans. from *Les Sophismes économiques* (London: Cassell, 1909), pp. 101–102.

dwell on the resulting inconveniences and probably attempt to estimate the loss. Existence of a functioning road between the two cities was advantageous to both New Englanders and Quebeçois. The road was beneficial because it lowered the cost of transporting people and things between Boston and Montreal. What then is the loss caused by the avalanche? One measure of the loss is the increase in transport costs caused by the accidental destruction of the road. Suppose that destruction of the road would increase the costs of transporting goods by 10 percent of their Boston price. Now suppose that there has been no avalanche, but that the Canadian government decides, for its own good or bad reasons, to increase tariffs on imports of U.S. goods by 10 percent of their U.S. price. Is the economic effect on Canadians not similar to that of accidental destruction of the highway? Would a TV set produced in Boston not cost more in Montreal after the tariff, just as it would after an avalanche? Is it not true that the Canadian and American markets will as a result be all that much farther away from each other? You can therefore expect a decline in U.S.-Canadian trade, and, if such trade is gainful to both sides, you may presume, at least as a first approximation, that the tariff also is a "bad" thing.

There are, of course, any number of important differences between natural and man-made barriers to international commerce. Their modalities vary, their frequency is not the same, and their specific effects on production, economic welfare, and the distribution of income can be different. One difference between natural obstacles and man-made restrictions is that the influence of natural obstacles has consistently declined in the past, and can be expected to decline further in the future, owing to human action itself. The technology of transportation has shared in the immense technical progress of the last few centuries, and unit transport costs have steadily decreased. Everyone is familiar with the commonplace that "the world has become smaller." This is as true of international transport as it is of communications. The *economic distance* between places has diminished. The ensuing decrease in delivered prices has resulted in an expansion of international trade, including in many instances international commerce of goods that had not been traded in the past because of very high freight charges. While human action will probably continue to operate in the direction of constantly lessening the influence of natural obstacles between countries, no such comfortable prediction can be made concerning man-made obstacles.

Among man-made obstacles, war is certainly a drastic barrier to commerce between nations. There is no more effective deterrent to trade than shooting at prospective buyers and sellers. Racial and social discrimination also constitute real walls between markets and can be particularly devastating in their political and economic impact when they coincide with national boundaries. Among the economic restrictions, some are expressly used to harm another country's economy; these go under the umbrella term of *economic warfare* and are outside the scope of this book (with the exception of the national security argument for trade restriction, discussed at length in the next chapter). Here the effects of instruments of commercial policy *on the nation that uses them* are discussed. They may be listed as follows: quotas, monetary restrictions, administrative and technical regulations, and tariffs.

Nontariff Barriers

Tariffs, the most common instruments of commercial policy, are described and analyzed in detail later. This section deals briefly with the various types of nontariff barriers, which mainly include direct restrictions of the volume of trade (the so-called quotas), monetary restrictions, and administrative and technical regulations.[6]

Quantitative Restrictions Quantitative restrictions, or quotas, are direct limitations imposed on the amount of trade. They can be imposed on exports or on imports, can set a limit in either absolute or relative terms, can be mandatory or voluntary. In all cases, trade is limited to an amount lower than would prevail under a free trade regime.

Quotas on exports, or outright prohibitions, were part and parcel of mercantilist policies. As we have seen in Chapter 2, the balance-of-trade doctrine called for discouraging exports of raw materials and equipment. Quantitative restrictions of exports have been used intermittently also as an instrument of economic warfare to deprive competing nations of goods or materials. In recent years, countries exporting raw materials have become more and more interested in establishing export quotas as a means of maximizing their revenue.

Much more widespread are import quotas. They never really left the international scene, but in the 1970s they have witnessed an increase in use. They can be set to limit imports either to a maximum absolute quantity or to a maximum percentage of total domestic consumption. In the former version, they naturally become relatively more and more restrictive as total domestic consumption grows. In the recent past, a more palatable alternative to imposing outright quotas has been for a nation to convince exporting countries to accept voluntary restraints on their exports. The United States has been a leader in this field. Voluntary restraints on foreign exports to the

---

[6] Other policies affecting foreign trade are multinational in scope. They fall under the general heading of *international commodity agreements*. These are arrangements to lessen fluctuations in international commodity prices, or to prevent prices from declining over the long term, or some measure of both. Also, virtually any domestic policy action has some connection with foreign trade. The connection will be examined at the aggregate level in Chapter 10. A more detailed analysis of the relationship between internal taxes and subsidies and international trade would take us too far afield. Such a relationship is examined here only in the limited context of the arguments for protection to correct market distortions (see Chapter 6).

United States were negotiated first in 1956 with respect to cotton textiles and, as of the end of 1976, they had been negotiated also with respect to meat, steel, and synthetic fabrics. This brief description of the types of quantitative restrictions will suffice for the time being. Their effects are discussed in Chapter 5.

Monetary Restrictions This is the first time in the book that money is explicitly introduced. While a fuller account of the role and consequences of international monetary phenomena must wait until the chapters on international finance, it is possible now to give a summary view of how monetary restrictions can be used as an instrument of commercial policy. Money is primarily a medium of exchange. Its value rests on people's willingness to accept it in payment for their goods, services, and capital assets. In turn, people will in fact be willing to accept your money if there are reasonable assurances that they will be able to use it to make purchases from others. If various forms of money are in circulation, they can be ranked in order of their greater or lesser acceptability as a medium of exchange. For example, your personal checks are very nearly as convertible into merchandise as U.S. currency itself when you are dealing with your friendly neighborhood store. This is usually not true if some checks have "bounced" before or if you are trying to use them in another city or state. Similarly, in the international market, some countries' currencies are fully convertible (*hard* currencies) and can be used for transactions anywhere in the world, because everyone who accepts them in payment is sure to be able in his turn to use them as a medium of exchange where and whenever he chooses. Other countries' currencies are fully inconvertible (*soft* currencies) and are accepted by foreigners only to the extent that they intend to use them for future transactions with the very country that issues the currency.

When a country's currency is not fully convertible, it is possible for a government to influence the volume and composition of imports by controlling the amounts of hard foreign currency made available to its citizens to pay for imports.[7] Thus, even though no tariffs and no direct restrictions on the volume of imports may be imposed, *foreign exchange control* accomplishes the same effect of limiting the quantity of imports.[8] Individuals are nominally allowed to import as much as they please, but they can only obtain enough hard foreign currency to purchase a fraction of their intended imports. It amounts to almost the same thing whether the government tells people that they cannot buy more than 1,000 pairs of foreign shoes (which cost the foreign currency equivalent of $10 each) or tells them that they can only

[7] Alternatively, imposing currency restrictions has the result of destroying, in part or entirely, convertibility of the country's currency.
[8] Currency restrictions are normally motivated by balance-of-payments difficulties. They had all but disappeared in industrial Western countries in the 1960s, but the mid-1970s witnessed renewed use of foreign exchange controls in some European countries.

spend the foreign currency equivalent of $10,000 on foreign shoes. (However, the pattern of purchasing may differ, with cheaper items being imported under foreign exchange control rather than under a physical quota regime.[9]) The outcome of foreign exchange control is thus in almost every respect the same as that of across-the-board quotas on imports, the effects of which will be discussed later.

Administrative and Technical Regulations   By their very nature, administrative and technical regulations encompass so many different hindrances to international trade as to defy cataloguing. They range from formal governmental guidelines and regulations concerning industrial, health, and safety standards to practical international differences in technical requirements, product specification, and even terminology. Almost all are alleged to exist for reasons other than limiting imports. For some regulations, the official reason is merely a cover for the desired protective effect. All in fact restrict trade, to a greater or lesser extent, whether or not they are intended to do so.

Anyone who has returned to the United States from abroad is familiar with the customs' restrictions on the bringing in of certain agricultural or food products. All these regulations have apparently persuasive reasons. Most do meet a genuine social purpose and prevent concrete risks to the population's health. A few never really did. And some no longer do, even though they may have been originally established on unimpeachable grounds. Contrast, for example, mandatory antipollution devices on automobiles, which of course "discriminate" against foreign automobiles not comparably equipped, and the now-discarded obligatory installation of seatbelt "buzzers," or the more recent regulations concerning safety caps on drug containers, the trade-restricting effects of which are much clearer than the social benefits they are alleged to produce.

Among the most objectionable of administrative regulations are labeling, packaging, and marking requirements, and practical customs' formalities. They are not important or objectionable in and of themselves, but can be a major source of uncertainty and a hindrance to commerce when they are arbitrarily and randomly enforced. A major importer has reported that European shipments of a certain commodity destined for the New York City market are imported through a distant Southern port owing to the greater simplicity of customs procedures in that city and the favorable attitudes of customs' inspectors concerning the interpretation of various regulations and the specific classification of the commodity. Consider the implications. Either the customs regulations in question serve a genuine national pur-

---

[9] Exchange control can also be used selectively to discourage the import of certain commodities. Also, different rates of exchange for different transactions (multiple exchange rates) can be used to influence the volume and composition of foreign trade. Exchange control and multiple exchange rates are discussed in Chapter 13.

pose or they constitute unwarranted red tape. In the former case, the national purpose is frustrated by the lack of clarity of customs' requirements, which allows officials in one port city to interpret them away. In the latter case, the regulations in question result merely in wasting valuable real resources and increasing prices to consumers by forcing a round-about route of delivery.

Differences in technical specifications and terminology have also constituted significant obstacles to international commerce. Fortunately, it appears that one of the major sources of semantic confusion and incompatibility of equipment is finally on the way out: in all probability the metric system will be almost universally adopted in only a few years.[10]

Given the heterogeneity of trade restrictions under this heading, only a few general observations can be made. First, as already pointed out, some regulations are established exactly for their trade-restrictive effect, although they may ostensibly meet some social purpose. Second, their overall impact on trade depends greatly on the degree of enforcement, and thus on the day-to-day practices of the country, and can hardly be reliably estimated. Third, however large or small that impact may be, it tends to grow relatively when tariffs are low and to become less significant in times of generally restrictive international commercial policies.[11]

The impact of one administrative measure can be assessed more readily. This is the practice, common to many nations, of giving preferences to domestic producers for government procurement. In the United States, such preference stems from the Buy American Act, passed in 1933 in the midst of the every-country-for-itself atmosphere of those years. Under the act, U.S. producers receive considerable preference over foreign suppliers in government purchasing, ranging from 12 percent to as high as 50 percent for defense materials and services.[12] Buy American provisions can also have a psychological dimension not too different from the attempts of monopolistic competitors to differentiate their product through advertising. A campaign of public interest TV and radio spots, urging citizens to give preference to their own national firms has, of course, some dampening effect on imports. The effect can be considerable or insignificant depending in large measure on the political climate and prevalent public attitudes.

[10] The benefits of uniform measures are great over the long term. The costs of conversion are considerable but have been consistently overstated. For example, in 1974 the steel industry estimated the cost of metric conversion at over $2 billion. In 1977 it was apparent that it would be far lower than that. The auto industry, and particularly General Motors, has been a leader in converting to the metric system.

[11] There has emerged in the 1970s a considerable interest in nontariff barriers, both in the professional literature and in actual intergovernmental negotiations. One major reason is unquestionably the greater influence of such barriers in our times of relatively low tariffs.

[12] Peter B. Kenen has noted that Buy American provisions have a far smaller restrictive effect than does similar administrative protection in other countries. This is compounded by the fact that public sector enterprises play a larger role in other industrial countries than they do in the United States.

Tariffs

The best-known and most frequently used instrument of commercial policy is the tariff (or customs duty). *A tariff is a sales tax applied only to transactions with foreigners.* This section describes the various types of tariffs and discusses important measurement problems. Chapter 5 analyzes the effects of tariffs.

Types of Tariffs   Tariffs may be expressed in absolute or in relative terms, may be discriminatory or nondiscriminatory, may be imposed on exports or on imports, and may be prompted by revenue or by protective considerations.

A tariff expressed in absolute dollars-and-cents terms is called a **specific tariff.** An **ad valorem tariff** is instead a percentage tax (*ad valorem* is Latin for "on the value"). There may also be a **compound tariff,** which combines a specific duty with a percentage tax.[13] Clearly, any specific tariff has an ad valorem equivalent and vice versa. On a $10 item, a tax of $1 is equivalent to 10 percent, and a 10 percent ad valorem tariff has a specific equivalent of $1. It does not therefore make any difference whether trade is restricted by a specific tariff or by an ad valorem tariff, except when base prices are changing. When prices rise, the incidence of an ad valorem tariff remains the same, while tariffs expressed in absolute terms lose more and more of their restrictive effects, for they constitute a smaller and smaller percentage of price.

A **discriminatory tariff** calls for a different rate of duty depending on the country of origin or destination of the product. A nondiscriminatory tariff imposes a uniform rate of duty regardless of geographic source or destination. Commercial policy discrimination is discussed in the last section of this chapter.

Export tariffs are motivated by considerations similar to those governing the imposition of export quotas. They might, first of all, be used for mercantilist purposes such as economic warfare or reserving the use of local raw materials and equipment for the country's own industry. They may also, by restricting exports of a commodity on which the country has a degree of monopoly power, drive up the world price of that commodity and improve the nation's economic position. Finally, they may be used for the purpose of affecting internal income distribution by reducing the domestic price of the exported commodity. Export duties are prohibited in the United States. Furthermore, it is **import tariffs** that have historically been far more

---

[13] There is occasionally also a "tariff-rate quota" under which a certain tariff rate applies to imports up to a specified amount and a higher tariff rate applies to imports above that amount. The U.S. shoe industry, for example, has been pressing for an arrangement of this sort.

frequent and have garnered most of the analytical and policy attention. The remainder of this chapter is thus focused on import duties.

Import duties produce revenue for the government. They normally also to some extent protect domestic industry from foreign competition. Before this century, sales taxes, including **revenue tariffs**, were the major means of financing government expenditures. Their importance has since declined in correspondence with the introduction and expansion of direct income taxes. In developed nations tariffs are today only a minor source of government revenue. **Protective tariffs** dominate in commercial policy. The effects of a tariff of a given height is of course the same regardless of whether the tariff is motivated by revenue or protective considerations. The overall structure of tariffs, however, differs. As will be shown in Chapter 5, the revenue and protective effects of a tariff tend to go in opposite directions: High revenue is obtained when the tariff causes only a modest decrease in the amount of imports; high protection is obtained when imports are very sensitive to price increases.

The Measurement of Tariffs Until recently, the measurement of a nation's average tariffs and of the degree of protection enjoyed by the domestic industry was thought to be a relatively simple matter. A country whose tariffs averaged 20 percent was seen as having a more liberal policy than a country with a 30 percent average. Also, a 10 percent tariff on a finished product was considered to be less protective than a 20 percent import duty on another finished product. In the 1960s, however, new theoretical and empirical evidence was developed showing that: (1) *average tariff* levels can vary significantly depending on how the averaging is done; and (2) the *effective protection* enjoyed by an industry can be quite different from that implied by the official tariff rate on the product. These are not issues of merely academic interest. They are of fundamental importance for international trade negotiations. Successful negotiations presuppose an acceptable measure of the degree of restrictiveness of the commercial policies of participating countries. Only then does it become meaningful to talk of concessions and of the extent to which mutual liberalization of trade policies is feasible and thus potentially acceptable to all negotiating parties. In general, the restrictive effect of a country's commercial policy is measured by the difference between its potential foreign trade, i.e., the volume of trade the country would engage in if it did not impose restrictions of any sort, and actual foreign trade. Potential trade can, however, only be guessed at, but not measured. Thus, one is forced to use as a proxy some measure of the restrictions themselves rather than of their overall effect.

(1) *Average tariffs:* A first difficulty is that trade in many products is subject to nontariff restrictions of various kinds, the precise impact of which is impossible to gauge. A country's policies may thus appear more liberal than another nation's only because the country relies to a greater extent on

nontariff restrictions. It is possible to exclude from intercountry comparisons of tariff levels those products (particularly agricultural commodities) that are subject to significant nontariff barriers. But a second problem is inherent in the tariff averaging itself. If individual duties are simply added together and divided by the number of products, a high tariff rate on an unimportant product has an unduly large influence on the overall average. A country that allows free trade in most fields may appear restrictive simply because of a few very high tariffs on products of minor significance for its total commerce. This seems to point to the necessity of using a weighted average of individual tariffs. But which weights does one use? If tariffs are weighted by the corresponding amount of imports, the difficulty arises that a very restrictive tariff carries a low weight in the overall average exactly because it allows in a small amount of imports, culminating in the paradox that a prohibitive tariff is not counted at all since it cuts imports down to nothing. Weighting by the amount of domestic production or of domestic consumption of the commodity is no solution either, since both production and consumption are distorted by the existence of the tariff itself.

A. Balassa's solution is to weigh the individual tariffs by the value of world trade in the product in question. The problem here is that countries whose average tariffs are being compared might not under free trade wish to have the same composition of imports. And finally, even if these thorny methodological difficulties were solved satisfactorily, one would still have to face the question of whether a higher but more uniform tariff structure is better or worse than a lower tariff average accompanied by great variability. By analogy, people may be less uncomfortable in an area with a uniform temperature of 85 degrees than in an area with an attractive average yearly temperature of 70 degrees but with summer temperatures of over 100 degrees.

(2) *The effective rate of protection:* One of the several assumptions of the trade theory discussed in the earlier chapters is that all goods traded are for final use. As we saw in Chapter 3, the taking into consideration of the fact that raw materials and intermediate goods are also traded internationally does not cause significant modifications of the theoretical conclusions. It does, however, introduce an important distinction between the nominal rate of protection afforded a domestic activity (as measured by the official tariff rate) and the degree to which the domestic activity is *effectively* protected.

Consider the following example. Suppose that in shoe manufacturing the cost of leather and other needed materials accounts for a total of 75 percent of the value of shoes, with value added in the industry thus accounting for 25 cents out of every dollar's worth of shoes produced. Imports of shoes are subject to a 20 percent tariff; the same rate of tariff applies to imports of materials. The shoe industry can be said to enjoy a 20 percent rate of protection.

87

If the tariff on materials is abolished, would not shoe manufacturing enjoy as a result an increase in its *effective* rate protection although the tariff on shoes themselves had not gone up? Everything else remaining the same, the ability to purchase needed inputs at a lower price than before improves the industry's competitive position and hence the degree to which it is shielded from the competition of foreign suppliers whose production costs have not diminished. This becomes apparent if you consider that the activity being protected is not the production of leather or of other inputs but the *manufacturing* of shoes, i.e., the value added by that activity. The effective rate of protection should thus be measured by reference to that value added. The 20 percent nominal tariff is equivalent to $2 on a $10 pair of shoes. But the $10 includes $7.50 worth of inputs, with only $2.50 as value added at the manufacturing stage. After abolition of the tariff on shoe materials, the effective rate of protection is the $2 tariff *relative to* the $2.50 in value added, i.e., 80 percent!

The nominal rate of protection (as reflected in the official ad valorem tariff) thus may or may not accurately measure the effective degree of protection enjoyed by the industry. It usually does not. Three elements combine to determine the effective rate of tariff protection. The first, of course, is the nominal tariff itself. Second, relative value added, i.e., the portion of the gross value of production that is not attributable to the cost of inputs, influences the effective rate of protection. Finally, the nominal tariffs on the inputs are also a relevant variable. The effective rate of protection is higher when, other things being equal, the nominal tariff is higher, or the relative value added is lower, or the tariffs on inputs are lower. The nominal tariff accurately measures the effective rate of protection only when the product does not incorporate any processing or when the nominal tariff equals the tariff on the inputs. If the nominal tariff is higher than the duty on the inputs, the effective rate at which the industry is protected is higher than the nominal tariff. If the nominal tariff is lower than the duty on inputs, the effective rate of protection is less than the nominal tariff rate.[14]

[14] The relationship between the nominal tariff, the tariff on inputs, the value added, and the effective rate of protection is expressed mathematically in the following way. If *ERP* denotes the effective rate of protection, T the ad valorem tariff on the product, t_i the ad valorem tariff on input i, and a_i the value of input i per dollar of output, we have:

$$ERP = \frac{T - \Sigma a_i t_i}{1 - \Sigma a_i}$$

The term $\Sigma a_i t_i$ is the weighted tariff on inputs. The expression $(1 - \Sigma a_i)$ is relative value added per dollar of output. It is apparent from the formula that *ERP*, the effective rate of protection, is directly related to the nominal tariff T and inversely related both to the rate of tariff on the inputs and to the relative value added. For example, if the nominal tariff is 0.10 (10 percent), the weighted average of tariffs on inputs 0.05 (5 percent), and relative value added 0.10 (10 percent), the effective rate of protection is $[(0.10 - 0.05)/0.10] = 0.50$, or 50 percent, five times as high as

The discrepancy between nominal and effective rates of protection is not merely a theoretical possibility. Research has discovered wide and sometimes enormous differences between nominal tariffs on various products and corresponding effective rates of protection. Also, average rates of effective protection in industrial countries turn out to be almost twice as high as the nominal tariff averages.[15]

Does this mean that generalizations on the basis of the official tariff cannot be made unless you possess a great deal of concrete information on the structure of production of the industry and of the economy as a whole? Fortunately, no. To begin with, it may be assumed that in most cases a *change* in nominal tariffs will correspond to an approximately proportionate *change* in the degree of effective protection *of the products directly affected.* Second, research findings indicate a rough concordance in the ranking of both industries and countries by nominal tariffs and by effective tariffs. That is, the nominal tariff on a particular industry and the nominal tariff average of a particular country differ widely from the effective rates of protection. *But*, an industry with a nominal tariff higher than that of other industries usually also enjoys higher effective protection, and if a country has average nominal tariffs higher than those of another nation, its average effective rate of protection is likely to be greater as well.

The theory of effective protection has substantive ramifications well beyond its contribution to the measurement of the restrictive effects of commercial policies. Three are worth mentioning here. The first, which was implied in the earlier example of shoe manufacturing, is that liberalization of customs' duties on raw materials and intermediates leads to *increasing* the degree of restrictiveness of existing tariffs on manufactured goods. Second, technical progress that saves on raw materials' use can result in an effective liberalization of trade in manufactures.

A third implication is one aspect of the *structural tariff discrimination* suffered by less developed countries.[16] Throughout the world, nominal tariffs

---

the nominal tariff. This is a first approximation, since the formula does not take into account, among other things, the fact that relative use of inputs is not independent of their price and hence of the tariff imposed on them. The expression shows clearly, however, that nominal and effective rates of protection are very unlikely to be similar. A further complication arises when an ad valorem tariff is computed on the basis of the domestic price rather than the foreign price. (In the United States, for example, tariffs on certain chemicals are calculated on the American selling price.) This practice usually results in a nominal tariff rate higher than the official one.

[15] On the other hand, research has also found instances of negative effective tariff rates, meaning that sometimes countries inadvertently injure industries they seek to protect.

[16] "Structural" discrimination because it is not necessarily the result of deliberate policies against less developed countries but the consequence of commercial policies designed by most developed countries to stimulate domestic processing. See S. Schiavo-Campo and H. W. Singer, *Perspectives of Economic Development* (Boston: Houghton-Mifflin, 1970).

are generally greater on products at a higher stage of processing. This feature of the world economy is in some degree a relic of mercantilist policies and attitudes.[17] In the main, however, it can be explained as follows. A domestic manufacturer using imported inputs suffers some cost disadvantage in relation to his foreign competitors if there are import tariffs on these inputs. There is therefore in most countries a tendency to keep tariffs on inputs low. By way of additional compensation to domestic manufacturers, tariffs on manufactured goods' imports are correspondingly increased. As a result, tariffs throughout the world generally increase as you go from raw materials to intermediate goods and capital equipment, with the highest tariffs imposed on consumer goods. This implies an even higher effective rate of protection of those goods. One can then expect that a prospective investor, other things being equal, would prefer locating his manufacturing facility in a developed country, near the major market, in order to benefit from the difference between the higher effective tariff on the finished product and the lower rate of effective protection of the needed inputs. Obviously, this creates a bias against the location of manufacturing facilities near the source of the raw materials, and hence against the development of manufacturing and of manufactured goods' exports by less developed countries.

[17] Frédéric Bastiat had something to say about the principle of preferring importation of materials in their unworked state: "On the same principle, why do you not ask that the trees of Russia should be brought to you with their branches, bark, and roots; the silver of Mexico in its mineral state; and the hides of Argentina sticking to the bones of the putrefying carcass from which they have been torn?"

Appendix: *A Chinese Story* by Frédéric Bastiat

Note: Through this allegory, Bastiat tries to show the similarity of the effects of artificial and natural obstacles to commerce and ridicules the employment argument for trade restrictions. The underscoring is my own. The *Moniteur Industriel* and the *Esprit Public* referred to in the story were French protectionist newspapers of the nineteenth century.

There were in China two great cities, Tchin and Tchan. A magnificent canal connected them. The Emperor thought fit to have immense masses of rock thrown into it, to make it useless.

Seeing this, Kouang, his first Mandarin, said to him: "Son of Heaven, you make a mistake." To which the Emperor replied: "Kouang, you are foolish."

You understand, of course, that I give but the substance of the dialogue.

At the end of three moons the Celestial Emperor had the Mandarin brought, and said to him: "Kouang, look."

And Kouang, opening his eyes, looked.

He saw at a certain distance from the canal a multitude of men *laboring*. Some excavated, some filled up, some levelled, and some laid pavement, and the Mandarin, who was very learned, thought to himself: They are making a road.

At the end of three more moons, the Emperor, having called Kouang, said to him: "Look."

And Kouang looked.

And he saw that the road was made; and he noticed that at various points inns were building. A medley of foot passengers, carriages, and palanquins went and came, and innumerable Chinese, oppressed by fatigue, carried back and forth heavy burdens from Tchin to Tchan, and from Tchan to Tchin, and Kouang said: It is the destruction of the canal which has given labor to these poor people. But it did not occur to him that this labor was *diverted* from other employments.

Then more moons passed, and the Emperor said to Kouang: "Look."

And Kouang looked.

He saw that the inns were always full of travellers, and that they being hungry, there had sprung up, near by, the shops of butchers, bakers, charcoal dealers, and bird's-nest sellers. Since these worthy men could not go naked, tailors, shoemakers, and umbrella and fan dealers had settled there, and as they do not sleep in the open air, even in the Celestial Empire, carpenters, masons, and thatchers congregated there. Then came police officers, judges, and fakirs; in a word, around each stopping place there grew up a city with its suburbs.

Said the Emperor to Kouang: "What do you think of this?"

And Kouang replied: "I could never have believed that the destruction of a canal could create so much labor for the people." For he did not think that it was not labor created, but *diverted;* that travellers ate when they went by the canal just as much as they did when they were forced to go by the road.

From *Sophisms of Protection,* second series (New York: Putnam, 1886), pp. 236–240.

However, to the great astonishment of the Chinese, the Emperor died, and this Son of Heaven was committed to earth.

His successors sent for Kouang, and said to him: "Clean out the canal."

And Kouang said to the new Emperor: "Son of Heaven, you are doing wrong."

And the Emperor replied: "Kouang, you are foolish."

But Kouang persisted and said: "My Lord, what is your object?"

"My object," said the Emperor, "is to facilitate the movement of men and things between Tchin and Tchan; to make transportation less expensive, so that the people may have tea and clothes more cheaply."

But Kouang was in readiness. He had received, the evening before, some numbers of the *Moniteur Industriel*, a Chinese paper. Knowing his lesson by heart, he asked permission to answer, and, having obtained it, after striking his forehead nine times against the floor, he said: "My Lord, you try, by facilitating transportation, to reduce the price of articles of consumption, in order to bring them within the reach of the people; and to do this you begin by making them lose all the labor which was created by the destruction of the canal. Sire, in political economy, absolute cheapness"—

The Emperor. "I believe that you are reciting something."

Kouang. "That is true, and it would be more convenient for me to read."

Having unfolded the *Esprit Public*, he read: "In political economy the absolute cheapness of articles of consumption is but a secondary question. The problem lies in the equilibrium of the price of labor and that of the articles necessary to existence. The abundance of labor is the wealth of nations, and the best economic system is that which furnishes them the greatest possible amount of labor. Do not ask whether it is better to pay four or eight cents cash for a cup of tea, or five or ten shillings for a shirt. These are puerilities unworthy of a serious mind. No one denies your proposition. The question is, whether it is better to pay more for an article, and to have, through the abundance and price of labor, more means of acquiring it, or whether it is better to impoverish the sources of labor, to diminish the mass of national production, and to transport articles of consumption by canals, more cheaply it is true, but, at the same time, to deprive a portion of our laborers of the power to buy them, even at these reduced prices."

The Emperor not being altogether convinced, Kouang said to him: "My Lord, be pleased to wait. I have the *Moniteur Industriel* to quote from."

But the Emperor said: "I do not need your Chinese newspapers to tell me that to create *obstacles* is to turn labor in that direction. Yet that is not my mission. Come, let us clear out the canal, and then we will reform the tariff."

Kouang went away plucking out his beard, and crying: Oh, Fo! Oh, Pe! Oh, Le! and all the monosyllabic and circumflex gods of Cathay, take pity on your people; for there has come to us an Emperor of the *English school,* and I see very plainly that, in a little while, we shall be in want of everything, since it will not be necessary for us to do anything.

*"Our present tariff laws, the vicious, inequitable,
and illogical source of unnecessary taxation, . . . as
their primary and plain effect, raise the price to consumers of all articles imported and subject to duty."*

Grover Cleveland, 1887

The Effects
of Trade Restrictions

What to Expect

The subject matter of this chapter is the core of the theory of commercial policy. The discussion centers on the effects of tariffs and quotas, although, as explained in Chapter 4, the effects of restrictions of trade are similar whether the obstacles to trade are natural or man-made. We first analyze the microeconomic effects of a tariff, both in words and through diagrams. These include effects on total consumption of the product affected, on its domestic production, on imports, on government revenue, on the distribution of income, on the extent of competition, and on the world price of the product. It will be shown that, after the redistributive effects of the trade restrictions are taken into account, there remains a net loss from the tariff for the economy's welfare and efficiency. The first section concludes with an explanation of the major effects of a tariff on the economy as a whole; on income and employment, on the balance of payments, on economic growth, and on international movements of factors of production. The second section explains the approximate equivalence of the effects of tariffs and quotas and argues that a quota is venerally worse than an equivalent tariff. Besides carrying the same costs as a tariff does, a quota usually carries some additional costs, too. The last section introduces the topic of economic integration.

Effects of Tariffs

The effects of the various man-made restrictions are generally similar. In some cases, however, they are very difficult to gauge with any accuracy. This is especially true of the influence of administrative and technical barriers to trade. Tariffs, by contrast, have a known height, and their consequences can be more readily estimated (but see the discussion on effective protection in the previous chapter). This section explains at length the principal effects of import restrictions by reference to the workings of tariffs.

The overall consequence of any barrier to trade is an increase in the economic distance between countries. The tariff is an instrument of economic separation of the national market from the world economy, as indicated by the resulting increase in the import price of the commodity over its world price. The domestic price is pushed upward by the full extent of the tariff or by a part of it (depending on the relationship between market conditions at home and abroad). Throughout the following discussion the assumption is made that imposition of a tariff causes some increase in the domestic price, which is true in almost all cases. *The increase in price is the chief consequence, from which follow all of the tariff effects on production, consumption, income distribution, and trade.*

A tariff (as any other trade restriction) has implications both for the specific industry affected and for the economy as a whole. It is convenient to examine those implications separately. Those effects of a tariff that pertain mainly to the market for the individual commodity on which the tariff is imposed will be called *microeconomic effects*. Implications for the economy as a whole will be called *macroeconomic effects*.[1]

The Microeconomic Effects of Tariffs

Imposition of a tariff on a product in which the country has a comparative disadvantage almost always leads to an increase in the price of imports of that product and in the domestic price overall. This price rise has an influence on total consumption of the product, on its domestic production, on imports, on the distribution of income within the country, on government revenue, on the overall level of economic welfare, and, probably, on competition and on the world price of the product.

The Consumption Effect   The law of demand posits an inverse relationship between the price of a product and the amount of it that people wish to buy. A price decline is accompanied by an increase in quantity demanded; a price increase, by a contraction of demand. One obvious and important result of the tariff is therefore the consumption effect: the *decline in total consumption of the product*. The size of the consumption effect is, of course, directly related to the height of the tariff. It is also related to the price elasticity of demand.[2] The tariff will have some depressing effect on consumption in all but the extreme case when the demand for the product is totally inelastic.

The Domestic Production Effect   The tariff does not result only in an increase in the price paid by consumers. While the tariff does separate the domestic market from the world market, domestic producers are still in

---

[1] These terms are used here for convenience. Everything has some effect on the economy as a whole. Still, in some cases it makes sense to presume that most of the impact from a tariff is concentrated on the market for the specific commodity affected. In these cases it is possible to analyze the tariff effects from a *partial equilibrium* perspective, as the description in the text does implicitly and as the diagrammatic analysis that follows does explicitly. It should be particularly noted that the tariff effects on government revenue and on the terms of trade, discussed in this section, are primarily macroeconomic in scope. They are dealt with here because they can be more easily explained on a partial equilibrium basis (unlike the other macroeconomic effects).

[2] As you know, the concept of price elasticity refers to the degree of "responsiveness" of the quantity demanded or supplied when the price changes. A highly elastic demand, for example, indicates that a change in price has a very considerable effect on the amount that people wish to buy. A relatively inelastic demand, instead, means that a price change will lead to only a small change in quantity demanded. If price elasticity is zero, the quantity will not change at all, regardless of the magnitude of the variation in the price of the product. More will be said about this later.

the same market as domestic consumers. The tariff also means an increase in the price received by domestic sellers of the product. (It does *not* mean an increase in the price received by foreign suppliers, for it is not they who receive the revenue from the tariff.) The increase in domestic price normally induces an *increase in the quantity produced domestically*. This increase may be termed the domestic production effect of the tariff, and, analogously to the consumption effect, it is directly related to the price elasticity of domestic supply. Domestic production goes up as a result of the tariff in all but the limiting case of completely inelastic domestic supply.

The Import Effect With a decline in total consumption and an increase in domestic production, it is evident that imports of the product are cut from both sides. Total sales are smaller, and a greater share of sales goes to domestic producers. The tariff will thus always reduce imports, except in the extreme situation when *both* the demand and the domestic supply are completely inelastic.

Consumers' and Producers' Surplus: A Required Digression We must ask at this point two basic interrelated questions: "Who loses from the tariff, and how much?" and: "Who gains from the tariff, and how much?" The preliminary answers to these questions are implicit in the description of the consumption and production effects. Consumers of the product lose from imposition of the tariff, and domestic producers gain. An adequate explanation of why, as well as the estimation of *how much* of a loss and gain is involved, requires a detour through two concepts of economic theory: Consumers' surplus and producers' surplus.

If you reflect upon your day-to-day transactions you will probably agree that very rarely do you have to pay for a product as much as it is worth to you *under the circumstances*. You may not be pleased with the high price of a particular commodity, but in most cases, *if you had to*, you would be willing to pay even more rather than not get it at all. It is certain that, if you have a choice, you do not pay more for something than it is worth to you. And it is very improbable that the situation is such that you are forced to pay just about as much as your "top" price. Thus, in most cases, the market price you have to pay is lower than the maximum you would be willing to pay rather than go without the thing. The difference, the satisfaction you get for free, is your "surplus" as a consumer. It follows that an increase in the market price, such as for example that caused by an import tariff, reduces this surplus and causes consumers to lose. Some lose by no longer being able to afford the product; the others by having to pay more for the same thing.

The notion of producers' surplus is quite similar. Producers differ in their efficiency of operations. Only the least efficient one (the marginal producer) receives barely enough in order to stay in business. All others receive a market price higher than their "bottom" price. Producers' surplus is this difference between the market price actually received and the minimum they would be willing to accept rather than not sell their product at all. When the market price goes up as a result of a tariff, therefore, producers' surplus increases. Some producers gain by being able to get into the business because of the higher price, the others by receiving more for the same thing.

This is of necessity an abbreviated explanation. (The next section includes a more rigorous diagrammatic treatment.) It should suffice, however, to show that an import tariff tends to cause a loss to consumers of the product and a gain to domestic producers of it.

The Redistribution and Revenue Effects Consumers pay for the tariff. Their loss is measured by the decline in aggregate consumers' surplus. This decline may be termed the *gross* welfare loss from the tariff. It is not all a loss to the economy as a whole, however. First it has to be determined if other groups or individuals in the country gain from the tariff. If others gained as much as consumers lost, the nation as a whole would not be worse off. The tariff would in such case cause a redistribution of income—a different way of slicing the economic pie—but would not affect the overall level of economic welfare. A portion of lost consumers' surplus does accrue to domestic producers of the product, and another part is taken by the government in the form of tariff revenue.

Producers' surplus increases as a result of the tariff. Some producers gain by being able to enter the market at the higher price, others by receiving more for the same product than they did before the tariff. The portion of the loss in consumers' surplus accruing to domestic producers in the form of an increase in producers' surplus may be termed the **redistribution effect.** The amount of redistribution from domestic consumers to domestic producers is directly related to the size of the domestic production effect, and thus to the elasticity of domestic supply.[3]

Any tariff, except one so high as to shut out all imports (called a prohibitive tariff), yields revenue to the government. This is the **revenue effect,** measured by the unit tariff multiplied by imports after the tariff. The revenue effect accounts for another portion of the gross loss to consumers, since it is they who pay the tariff. It is also a redistributive effect, since government expenditures financed by tariff revenues provide benefits for someone or some group in the economy. Unlike in the case of the redistribution effect, however, one cannot pinpoint the specific beneficiaries of the revenue effect. The size of the revenue effect from any given tariff is directly related

[3] When tariffs on needed imported inputs differ from the tariff on the product in question, the rate of effective protection differs from the nominal tariff. As observed in Chapter 4, this will affect both the extent of redistribution and the domestic production increase.

to the amount of imports. Since imports are cut by the tariff in direct relation to the elasticity of demand (which determines the decline in total consumption) and to the elasticity of domestic supply (which determines the domestic production effect), the amount of government revenue produced by a tariff of a given height is inversely related to the domestic elasticities of demand and of supply. The more elastic are demand and domestic supply, the lower is the government's revenue from the tariff.

Net Loss The redistribution and revenue effects make up for only a part of the gross loss from the tariff. There almost always remains a net loss to the country's economic welfare and efficiency.[4] By definition, the country has a comparative disadvantage in this product. Under conditions of full employment, the increase in domestic production presumably diverts resources from activities in which the country possesses a comparative advantage, and the tariff results in a less efficient allocation of the economy's total resources. Also, the rise in price has the effect of driving some consumers out of the market altogether: They no longer purchase imports nor do they buy the import-competing product either. Their loss is not offset either by a gain to the government in the form of tariff revenue or by a gain to domestic producers. There is a net loss from the tariff. The import restriction results in a shrinking of the economic pie in addition to causing a different distribution of it.

This conclusion should come as no surprise to the reader who remembers the general upshot of trade theory. Under most circumstances, expansion of foreign trade carries benefits for the economy; consequently, restrictions of trade can surely be expected to cause real economic losses. But, just as the general theoretical conclusion was qualified in a number of ways, so should the harmful effects of tariffs be viewed as the *probable* outcome. It is a high probability, to be sure, but there does exist some possible room for arguments to the contrary. One such conceivable exception to the rule is examined under the terms-of-trade effect.

The Competitive Effect Recalling that a tariff increases the economic distance between countries leads easily to the conclusion that it may have an *adverse effect on the degree of competition in the domestic industry*. Take a situation in which there is a pure monopoly in a given sector in each of 20 different countries. Under free trade, the 20 national markets become a single market, and the 20 monopolists find themselves competing with one another. If the market is enlarged, almost inevitably the number of sellers and buyers is increased. If such number is small enough on a national basis

---

[4] An exception is when both demand and supply are completely inelastic (or when demand is completely inelastic and there is no domestic production within the relevant price range).

to cause significant deviations from competitive behavior, enlargement of the market through foreign trade has a beneficial effect on the degree of competition.

The opposite, of course, is also true. If trade is restricted, through tariffs or otherwise, competition from abroad is by definition lessened. And, to the extent that the domestic market is not a competitive one, restricting competition from abroad is equivalent to restricting the overall degree of competition. The presence of significant monopoly power usually leads to a higher price and a smaller quantity produced and sometimes to a lower quality of the product. There is also a possibility that without the spur of competition the domestic industry will become stagnant and indolent. While the adverse effect of tariffs on competition cannot be measured precisely, it should be kept in mind as a possible additional cost to society. This is particularly true of tariffs in highly concentrated industries and of tariffs in very small countries, for in both cases the only significant competitive stimulus is likely to come from abroad.

The Terms-of-trade Effect Throughout the discussion in this section, the assumption was implicitly made that the supply of the imports being taxed is perfectly elastic, i.e., that the world price remains unchanged regardless of how much the country's imports may be cut by the tariff. This is a realistic assumption if the country imposing the tariff is too small, relative to the rest of the international economy, for its purchases to have a significant influence on the world market. For the United States, this is evidently incorrect: In the international market for most products the United States ranks as a major or dominant customer. It is thus probable that curtailment of U.S. imports of a commodity, ensuing from a higher tariff, constitutes a significant decline in the total world demand for that commodity. A decrease in total demand for a commodity leads, other things being equal, to a decline in equilibrium price. A tariff would then force down the world price of the commodity.

The most common meaning of **terms of trade** is the relative price of a country's exports (average price of exports divided by average price of imports). To the extent that prices of other imported goods and of exports do not change, the reduction in the world price of an imported commodity constitutes an improvement in the terms of trade. Through a tariff a country therefore can, with the same real expenditure in terms of exports, obtain a greater amount of imported goods and services, or, which is the same thing, purchase the same amount of imports at a lower real cost. In other words, the country is better off to the extent of the terms-of-trade improvement.[5]

---

[5] This will be sufficient for our immediate purposes. The reader is cautioned, however, that the welfare implications of an increase in the relative price of exports are not as unequivocal as all that.

This is the terms-of-trade effect of an import tariff, stemming from the country's influence as a significant buyer on the world market. The size of the terms-of-trade effect depends on the relationship between foreign and domestic supply and demand elasticities. For example, the lower the elasticity of the foreign supply of imports, the greater is the terms-of-trade effect. In turn, import supply is likely to be less elastic the larger the share of the world market accounted for by the country's purchases. Thus, the possibility of significant terms-of-trade effects of a tariff must be kept in mind whenever a country's imports are large relative to total world demand.

If there is a terms-of-trade effect, it is no longer true that domestic consumers must bear the entire burden of the tariff. Foreign sellers are made to pay a part of it, through the reduction in the world price caused by the tariff. It is extremely unlikely, however, that the world price falls by the entire extent of the tariff. It is still true, therefore, that domestic consumers suffer a loss, and, after redistributive effects are accounted for, that there will be on that score an adverse effect of the tariff. The terms-of-trade improvement must consequently be larger than the net loss in consumers' welfare, in order to conclude that on balance a particular trade restriction ends up improving the economic position of the country. Otherwise, we are back to the familiar conclusion that the restriction is economically harmful. (This issue falls under the heading of the *optimum tariff argument*, examined at some length in Chapter 6.)[6]

Market Conditions and the Size of Tariff Effects   It is useful at this point to pull together the various statements made earlier on the influence of the relevant elasticities on the size of the different effects of an import tariff. Some idea of how much of an effect a tariff of a given height might have on production, consumption, and trade is evidently useful in and of itself. In addition, this helps to evaluate whether a specific argument for tariffs is valid or bogus. For example, if market conditions are such that the domestic production effect of a tariff is likely to be quite small, the argument that a higher tariff would provide significant employment opportunities should be viewed with even more skepticism than it normally deserves.

Table 5.1 gives an idea of the probable magnitude of the various effects of a tariff in relation to the relevant elasticities. In that scheme, "+" indicates that the size of the effect is directly related to the corresponding elasticity, "−" that high elasticity leads to a smaller effect, and "0" that there is no correlation. For example, the scheme tells you that high elasticity of domestic supply has no influence on the extent of the decline in consumption, while it is negatively related to the amount of tariff revenue and exerts a positive influence on the extent of terms-of-trade improvement. It bears emphasizing

---

[6] Favorable terms-of-trade effects can also be achieved through restriction of *exports*, in cases when the country has a degree of monopoly power on the world market.

TABLE 5–1

Effects
of
Tariffs

Size of the Effect of a Tariff on: High Elasticity of:	Consumption Decline	Domestic Production Increase	Redistribution	Revenue	Net Loss	Terms of Trade
Domestic Supply	0	+	+	−	+	+
Domestic Demand	+	0	0	−	+	+
Import Supply	+	+	+	−	+	−

that this analysis gives only a partial and approximate idea of the influence of market conditions on the outcomes of a tariff. Nevertheless, it is a useful illustration of the interdependencies among the various effects and is well worth a few minutes of scrutiny.[7]

The Microeconomic Effects of Tariffs: A Diagrammatic Analysis

The several effects of a tariff (with the exception of the competitive effect) can be shown with more precision by means of simple supply-and-demand diagrams expanded to include the supply of imports in addition to domestic supply. Figure 5.1 shows the market situation for a homogeneous product in the importing country. The line D_d represents domestic demand. Domestic supply is shown by S_d. In the complete absence of foreign trade, the market would find its equilibrium at E_d, and the product would sell for price $0P_d$. The rest-of-the-world supply of imports is shown by S_{rw}. Assume here that S_{rw} is perfectly elastic. This means that the country can import as much or as little as it wants without having any effect on the world price. (We will shortly remove this assumption, which, as noted earlier, is very often unrealistic in the U.S. case.) In one market there is one price. The price is of

---

[7] In using this analysis to guess at the probable size of the various tariff effects on a particular product, keep in mind the main determinants of demand and supply elasticity. Demand is relatively price-elastic when there are many good substitutes for the product, when the product accounts for a significant share of the buyers' budget, and when buyers have time to adjust their purchases to changes in price. Supply is relatively elastic when unit production costs rise slowly as production expands and when producers have sufficient time to adjust their production levels according to price changes. In addition, the rest-of-the-world's supply *to a particular country* is relatively elastic if the country accounts for a small share of total world demand for the product or if such world demand is itself price-elastic. For example, you can easily predict that the quantity demanded of an inexpensive but essential commodity is likely to change very little in response to a price change, especially in the immediate aftermath of it. You would thus be entitled to doubt the validity of a claim that a tariff on this commodity would improve the country's terms of trade.

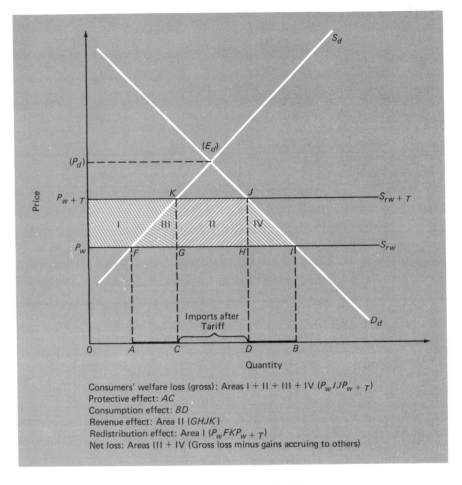

Consumers' welfare loss (gross): Areas I + II + III + IV ($P_w I J P_w + T$)
Protective effect: AC
Consumption effect: BD
Revenue effect: Area II ($GHJK$)
Redistribution effect: Area I ($P_w F K P_w + T$)
Net loss: Areas III + IV (Gross loss minus gains accruing to others)

FIGURE 5.1 Partial Equilibrium Effects of a Tariff

course the lower price, i.e., the world price $0P_w$. (The only situation in which the E_d and P_d are relevant is when no imports are allowed at all, either through an import quota of zero or through a prohibitive tariff.)

Domestic demand and supply conditions tell you that, at the ruling world price of $0P_w$, domestic production is $0A$ and total quantity demanded is $0B$. Owing to the existence of increasing costs (as reflected in the upward sloping domestic supply curve), as domestic production is replaced by imports, domestic costs eventually fall sufficiently to offset the initial disadvantage and allow for continuing domestic production (although, of course, at a lower level than before trade). Imports are AB, the difference between total desired consumption and domestic production.

Suppose that a 50 percent ad valorem import tariff is established. Graphically, this can be represented in Figure 5.1 by a shift of S_{rw} upward to S_{rw+t}, with the vertical distance between the two measuring the tariff. The tariff does not alter the perfect elasticity of import supply. Foreigners are still quite content to provide any amount at the ruling world price and none at all if the price is lower. Thus, with an unchanging world price, domestic consumers can purchase any given quantity only if they pay the world price plus the tariff ($0P_{w+t}$). The immediate consequence, from which everything else follows, is the increase in the price of imports and thus in the market price.

The increase in price causes both a decline in the quantity demanded and an increase in the quantity supplied domestically. Consumption falls to $0D$ and domestic production rises to $0C$. Imports are cut on both accounts to CD.

The **consumption effect** is consequently measured by the distance BD, the **domestic production effect** by the distance AC, and the **import effect** by $AC + BD$. As noted earlier, the size of the consumption and production effects is directly related to the elasticity of the demand and domestic supply curves, respectively. If the demand in Figure 5.1 were more elastic (flatter), the consumption effect would be more pronounced. Similarly, a more elastic S_d would imply a greater increase in domestic production. The consumption and/or production effects would be zero only if the demand and/or domestic supply were vertical (totally inelastic).

Recourse to diagrams illustrating consumers' surplus and producers' surplus is needed in order adequately to show the revenue, redistribution, and net welfare effects of the tariff. Figure 5.2 shows consumers' and producers' surplus before and after imposition of tariff. Before the tariff, consumers need only pay, and producers can only receive, a price of $0P_w$. The market demand curve D_d in Figure 5.2a tells you that, with the exception of the "last" buyer, all buyers would be willing to pay a higher price than $0P_w$, if they had to. Suppose that the commodity is cigarettes. The maximum amount the most inveterate smoker would be willing to pay rather than not smoke at all corresponds to the area under his (the highest) portion of the demand curve. The second most addicted person would be willing to pay, if he had to, up to an amount corresponding to the area under the second highest portion of the demand curve, and so forth. Since $0P_w$ is the maximum price that can be extracted from the *least* interested buyer, the *maximum* total consumers' expenditure (the sum of all individual expenditures) is the *whole* area under D_d and to the left of point B, i.e., the area of the quadrilateral $0BIL$. But no consumer need pay a penny more than the market price $0P_w$. Hence, they all get a free ride of sorts (with the single exception of the most casual smoker). *Actual* consumers' expenditure is then the total quantity bought ($0B$) multiplied by the unit price $0P_w$, hence, the area of the rectangle $0BIP_w$. The difference, area I, measures aggregate consumers' surplus in this market at a price of $0P_w$.

It is now easy to measure how much consumers as a group lose from a price increase to $0P_{w+t}$, resulting from imposition of a tariff. Some consumers

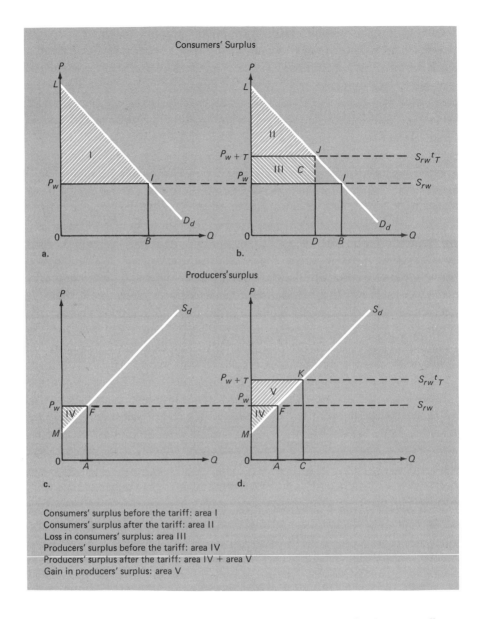

FIGURE 5.2 Consumers' and Producers' Surplus Before and After a Tariff

(those who were buying DB) lose by having to drop out of the market altogether; the others, by having to pay more for the same product. In Figure 5.2b, the loss to consumers as a group as a result of the tariff is measured by area III, i.e., the difference between total consumers' surplus before (area I) and total surplus after the tariff (area II).

The reasoning in the case of producers' surplus is similar. In Figure 5.2c, the supply curve S_d tells you that, with the exception of the marginal producer (the least efficient one), all sellers would be willing to accept a price lower than $0P_w$, if they had to. The most efficient producer (the one who is producing the commodity at least cost) could be forced to accept a price barely covering *his* cost, i.e., only the area under his (the lowest) portion of the market supply curve. The second most efficient producer could be made to receive an amount corresponding to the area under the second lowest portion of the supply curve, and so forth. If there were only one buyer, if each seller could be kept entirely separate from the others, and if $0P_w$ were the minimum price that the least efficient seller is willing to accept, total sellers' revenue (sum of the revenues of all individual sellers) would be measured by the area under the supply curve and to the left of A (the area of $0AFM$). If instead all sellers are in a single market, none need accept any less than the market price that the least efficient among them is willing to be paid, i.e., $0P_w$. All sellers but one, therefore, get some "gravy." Total revenue is given by the total quantity sold ($0A$) multiplied by the unit price $0P_w$ (the area $0AFP_w$). The difference, area IV, measures aggregate producers' surplus at a price of $0P_w$. If as a result of the tariff the market price rises to $0P_{w+t}$, sellers gain: some by being able to enter the market; the others, by receiving a higher price for the same product. Producers' surplus increases by an amount measured by area V in Figure 5.2d.

Let's now get back to Figure 5.1 and to the main point of this exercise. To begin with, you can now see more precisely why the burden of the tariff (in this case, the entire burden) is borne by the consumers. The sum of areas I, II, III, and IV in Figure 5.1 (corresponding to area III in Figure 5.2) is the decrease in consumers' surplus; it may be termed the **gross loss** from the tariff. Portions of that loss accrue as gains to other individuals or groups and are not losses to the economy as a whole. These are the redistribution and revenue effects.

The **redistribution effect** is that portion of the gross loss to consumers that is added to domestic producers' surplus. Only some of it can be attributed to entry of new domestic producers; the remainder of the redistribution effect is enjoyed by the more efficient among domestic sellers, in the probable form of higher profits. It is measured by area I in Figure 5.1 (corresponding to area IV in Figure 5.2).

The **revenue effect** is the other part of the gross loss to consumers that is distributed, via government expenditures, to someone else in the country. Government revenue is obtained by multiplying the tariff ($P_{w+t}P_w = KG$) times the quantity of imports after the tariff ($CD = GH$), area II in Figure 5.1. In the absence of information about the allocation of government funds at the margin, we cannot tell who ultimately benefits from the tariff revenue.

It is theoretically possible that the government will return the tariff revenue to the consumers who had to pay more for the imports. It is even conceivable that the redistribution of domestic producers could be taxed away and the proceeds given back to the consumers. Areas III and IV in

Figure 5.2, however, are lost to the consumer and not gained by anyone else. They are a preliminary estimate (remember the limitations of partial equilibrium analysis) of the net loss. That amount of economic welfare vanishes into thin air as the result of restricting imports.[8]

It remains for us to deal geometrically with the terms-of-trade effect. If the assumption of a perfectly elastic import supply is removed, the reduction of imports caused by a tariff induces a decline in the world price of the product, thus shifting a part of the tariff burden from domestic consumers to foreign sellers. This is really but a manifestation of the general phenomenon of tax incidence. The simple version of the tax-shifting problem is probably familiar to you from elementary economics. In Figure 5.3, before the tariff, equilibrium is at E and price is $0P_w$. World price, of course, is identical with import price ($0P_w = 0P_m$) in the absence of trade barriers. Suppose that a 100 percent ad valorem tariff is imposed. This will constitute for the domestic consumer a decrease in total world supply and will appear as a shift of S_{rw} leftward to S'_{rw}.[9] New equilibrium occurs at E', and import price rises to $0P'_m$. The quantity demanded of import falls. From the foreign sellers' standpoint, the tariff causes their total demand to shift to the left (not shown in Figure 5.3), with a consequent reduction of the world price from $0P_w$ to $0P'_w$. Thus, import price increases only by the distance $P_m P'_m$, less than the amount of the tariff. The remainder of the tariff is effectively paid by the foreign sellers in the form of a lower price ($0P'_w$) received for their product. In Figure 5.3, $E'E''$ is the tariff (equal to $P'_w P'_m$). Consumers pay for $E'F$; foreign sellers absorb the remainder.

We also notice that: (1) the gross consumers' loss and hence the redistribution effect and the net loss—areas I and (III + IV), respectively—are smaller than they would be if S_{rw} were perfectly elastic; and (2) the revenue effect is now split in two portions, with area IIa paid by consumers, but area IIb representing the country's revenue gain at the expense of the foreign sellers. The net loss from the tariff must now be weighed against the terms-of-trade effect. In Figure 5.3 the two are approximately equal, but it should be easy to see that there are a number of possible tariff rates under which IIb is greater than (III + IV), and which thus yield an overall net gain for the economy. Among these rates, the optimum tariff (discussed

[8] In general equilibrium terms (see Figure 2.4), imposition of the tariff modifies the slope of the price line by increasing the relative price of the imported good, thus proceeding backward in the direction of pretrade relative prices. A prohibitive tariff would bring the economy all the way back to the pretrade set of relative prices and, other things being equal, to the original level of economic welfare. A less than prohibitive tariff would cause the economy to move to a lower community indifference curve intermediate between the free-trade and the before-trade curves.

[9] With a constant percentage tax and a less than perfectly elastic supply, the two curves are of different slope, since the distance between S_{rw} and S'_{rw} must be in the same ratio to the distance between S_{rw} and the horizontal axis. They would instead be parallel if a specific tariff were imposed.

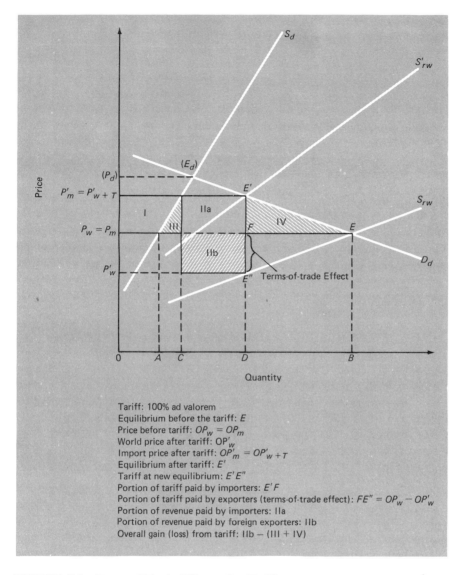

Tariff: 100% ad valorem
Equilibrium before the tariff: E
Price before tariff: $OP_w = OP_m$
World price after tariff: OP'_w
Import price after tariff: $OP'_m = OP'_w + T$
Equilibrium after tariff: E'
Tariff at new equilibrium: $E'E''$
Portion of tariff paid by importers: $E'F$
Portion of tariff paid by exporters (terms-of-trade effect): $FE'' = OP_w - OP'_w$
Portion of revenue paid by importers: IIa
Portion of revenue paid by foreign exporters: IIb
Overall gain (loss) from tariff: IIb − (III + IV)

FIGURE 5.3   Terms-of-Trade Effects of a Tariff

further in Chapter 6) is the one that produces the maximum possible such gain.

The Macroeconomic Effects of Tariffs

Tariffs may have significant effects on the economy as a whole, including a possible influence on national income and the level of employment, on the balance of payments, on the rate of economic growth, and on international movements of factors of production.[10] These effects are discussed here only briefly, since either they arise from theoretical considerations to be examined at length in later chapters or they form the substance of arguments for protection discussed in detail in Chapter 6.

The Effect on Income and Employment As Chapter 10 explains at length, in national income determination analysis imports carry a minus sign. A tariff may, therefore, via the decrease in imports and the resulting increase in aggregate demand, have a positive influence on the levels of national income and of total employment. This is only the initial effect, however, and is subject to a number of major qualifications. First, the increase in national income is in real terms only if the economy is not at full employment to begin with. If employment is high, the increase in aggregate demand for domestic production leads in all probability only to an increase in prices. Second, an import decline translates itself into an increase in aggregate demand only if some domestic component of aggregate demand increases by the same amount. The expression for national income may be written as:

$$\text{Income} = \text{Domestic Consumption} + \text{Domestic Investment} \\ + \text{Domestic Government Spending} + \text{Exports}$$

Imports in this case are deducted from each category of expenditures. (In the more familiar expression: $Y = (C + I + G + X - M)$, C, I, G, and probably X have some import components.) Thus the extent to which aggregate demand increases depends on the elasticity of domestic supplies. Also, if people view saving as an alternative to imports, i.e., if there are no good domestic substitutes for the imported goods, the decrease in imports engineered by the tariff may result in an increase in saving rather than in domestic spending. Finally, and most important, if other countries retaliate by raising tariffs, exports may be cut as much as imports, the level of national income and employment is not affected, and all that remains are the adverse effects of the tariff on economic welfare and on the efficiency of utilization of resources.

The Effect on the Balance of Payments Financial matters have not yet been discussed, but the basic point is simple. In the balance of payments, imports also carry a minus sign. A tariff that reduces them therefore has the initial effect of "improving" the country's financial position in relation to the rest of the world. The same qualifier applies here as to the income effect. Other categories in the balance of payments must not be affected. This is not the case if the imported item is an input needed for export pro-

---

[10] The revenue and terms-of-trade effects are also primarily macroeconomic in scope. As noted earlier they were dealt with in the preceding section because they can be more easily explained on a partial-equilibrium basis.

duction, for production costs in the export sector then rise and exports can be expected to fall. Also, an "improvement" in the balance of payments of one country is by definition a "worsening" in the balance of payments of some other nations. If the other nations retaliate against the country's exports, the net balance of payments may not be affected at all, and only the harmful effects of the tariff remain.

The Effect on Economic Growth   The various tariff effects discussed so far are all static in nature; they relate to the efficiency of utilization of the existing resources of a country and to its level of economic welfare, given a certain stock of factors of production and the level of technology. Trade, however, has important implications for the growth of the economy's productive capacity (some of which were noted in Chapter 3). On the one hand, the allocative inefficiency caused by tariffs may go hand in hand with a slower rate of economic growth. On the other hand, it is possible that a temporary loss in economic welfare and static efficiency may be the indispensable price of creating and expanding certain activities that can contribute to the longer term economic development of the country. This possible beneficial effect of tariffs is discussed at considerable length in Chapter 6 under the infant industry argument for tariff protection.

The Effect on International Factor Movements   The discussion of the factor-price equalization theorem in Chapter 3 showed that international trade is a partial substitute for international movement of resources. (Under the restrictive conditions of the theorem, trade is a complete substitute for factor movements and international factor prices are fully equalized.) A restriction of trade causes prices of products to differ between countries. The intercountry differential in the relative price of a factor of production can thus also be expected to increase if trade is restricted. Therefore, if the tariff-ridden product is intensive in the country's relatively scarce factor of production, and if resources are not fully immobile between countries, restricting imports may succeed in attracting an inflow of that factor of production.

Effects of Quotas

As noted earlier, a quota is a direct limitation on the quantity of imports permitted into the country in a given period of time. The effects of different kinds of barriers to trade are similar, but not identical. The effects of quotas, in particular, are similar to those of tariffs, but there are substantive differences worth examining.

The Approximate Equivalence of Tariffs and Quotas

Until the appearance of new contributions in the late 1960s and early 1970s (associated primarily with the names of J. Bhagwati and W. M. Corden), it was thought that the effects of quotas were exactly equivalent to those of tariffs, with the sole exceptions of the revenue and competitive effects. The more recent findings, however, have shown that in the presence of monopoly elements strict equivalence may not be the case. Nevertheless, a general similarity between quotas and tariffs still obtains.

This approximate equivalence has its roots in the functional relationship between price and quantity. A tariff acts directly on the price of the product and has an indirect effect on the quantity. A quota acts directly on the quantity of imports and has an indirect effect on the price. A tariff of a certain height reduces imports to a certain amount: it has a quota equivalent. A quota limiting imports to that same amount normally results in the same price increase as through the tariff: it has a tariff equivalent. This equivalence extends to all but two of the effects of tariffs described earlier. Since an import quota results in the same price increase and the same import reduction as an equivalent tariff, its effects on consumption, domestic production, redistribution, welfare, the terms of trade, national income, international factor movements, and economic growth are also the same as those of the equivalent tariff.

The Differences Between Tariffs and Quotas

The Revenue Effect Under a tariff, a portion of the gross loss to consumers goes to the government as tariff revenue. Under a quota that raises the price to the same extent, the same amount is lost by consumers, but the immediate recipient cannot be specified unless it is known how the import quota system is administered. The government could still collect the same amount in revenue if, for example, it charged a fee for import licenses equal to the difference between the world price and the higher price caused by the quota. Most often, instead, the quota system is administered in such a way that the "rent" or quota profit will be received by importers or exporters in relation to their respective influence over the market and to the specific procedures of quota administration.

In general, the large importers probably obtain the lion's share of the quota profit. Large domestic firms are more likely to be knowledgeable about the documentation required by import licensing and generally about the whole set of complex procedures and regulations necessitated by a quota system. They are also far more likely to have useful contacts in government. Since the quota profit can be quite considerable (verify the large area representing the revenue effect in Figure 5.1), there inheres in this difference between quotas and tariffs a huge potential for chicanery and corruption. There is at least a general presumption that the tariff revenue is spent by the government in accordance with some collective decision about national priorities. The distribution of the quota profit, instead, is in most cases haphazard and does not correspond to any accepted sense of social goals.

The Competitive Effect In the presence of significant monopoly power in the domestic market, an import quota might allow the domestic seller to behave as a monopolist when an equivalent tariff would not. Suppose that there is only one domestic seller, that a 50 percent tariff is imposed on a $10 world price, and that imports fall to 1 million units. The price rises to $15, and the domestic seller, of course, gains. But he still does not have the power to raise his price above $15, for his customers would switch to imports. Suppose that the seller manages to convince the government to convert the tariff into an "equivalent" quota that allows the same quantity of imports. Allowable imports now come in at the world price, but after the quota is exhausted the domestic seller is the only remaining source of supply. He can behave accordingly, equating marginal cost with marginal revenue, able now to reap monopoly profits without any further concern about the potential competition of foreign suppliers.[11]

Practical Differences Between Tariffs and Quotas There are several reasons why domestic producers, large importers, and even governments, may prefer quotas to tariffs despite (or, more accurately, because of) their added disadvantages. From a government's viewpoint, quotas may be administratively more flexible, easier to impose, change, or remove. Also, as R. M. Stern has noted, the international agreements on commercial policy are more permissive on quotas than they are on tariffs.

First, from the domestic producers' standpoint, the tariff required for a significant reduction of imports might have to be so high as to seriously damage the domestic industry's public image. An equivalent quota would achieve the same purpose without appearing to be quite so objectionable. Second, a quota expressed in absolute terms becomes more restrictive as total demand for the product grows. A tariff, instead, would not prevent foreign sellers from obtaining their share of a growing market. (On the other hand, a quota allows at least some imports into the country, while a tariff may become prohibitive.) Third, when the relevant elasticities are not known, the size of the effects of a tariff is in doubt. A quota establishes a definite limitation on imports and may be preferred owing to the greater

[11] Even a prohibitive tariff might not have the undesirable effect of transforming a latent domestic monopoly into an actual one. An "equivalent" quota of zero, of course, would do so.

certainty of its effects.[12] Fourth, highly concentrated domestic industries may push for a quota exactly because of its potential for allowing them a freer rein in the domestic market than an equivalent tariff would. Finally, from the viewpoint of large importers, the possibility of capturing a good share of the quota profit is a solid reason for preferring a quota to a tariff. It bears repeating, in conclusion, that from the viewpoint of national efficiency and economic welfare a quota is generally worse than an equivalent tariff. Besides carrying the same costs as a tariff does, it usually carries additional ones, too.

Economic Integration

Discriminatory Tariffs

We have implicitly assumed so far in this chapter that trade restrictions, whether high or low, are imposed uniformly on a specific product regardless of its geographic origin. What if the tariff or quota level differs depending on the country of origin of the product? What can one say about discrimination in commercial policy?

Let's start by noting that a tariff *preference* (a lower tariff) granted to one country is by definition tariff *discrimination* against the other countries to which the higher tariff applies, and vice versa. The theoretical issue is therefore the same (though not the political implications) whether we talk of preferences or of discrimination.

A theoretical presumption in favor of nondiscrimination exists in commercial policy, stemming from the general case for free trade. As you know, a tariff in general distorts the allocation of resources away from their most efficient allocation on the basis of the country's comparative advantages. A discriminatory tariff, in particular, *also* distorts the pattern of imports away from the most economical source. A 20 percent average tariff on TV sets, for example, causes domestic consumers to lose. If, in addition, the average tariff results from a 30 percent tariff on imports of *Japanese* TV sets, and a 15 percent tariff on imports from other countries, the consumer's loss is compounded by the additional obstacle placed in the way of importing from the most economical source.[13]

The issue of discrimination has even broader international political implications than the tariff question per se. There are serious political-

[12] As part of the new contributions referred to earlier, however, J. Bhagwati has shown that in the presence of monopoly elements the effects of quotas may be as uncertain as those of tariffs.

[13] James E. Meade offers a detailed explanation of the theoretical argument against tariff discrimination, in his *Theory of International Economic Policy*, vol. II (London: Trade and Welfare, 1955).

economic arguments on both sides of the issue.[14] The general theoretical case for nondiscriminatory treatment was accepted as the underpinning of the postwar international commercial rules. However, a major exception to the nondiscrimination principle was allowed when tariff preferences are part and parcel of an economic integration arrangement. (See the discussion of the General Agreement on Tariffs and Trade in Chapter 8.) The presumption here is that the benefits to the world economy from closer economic integration among some countries outweigh the distorting effects of the accompanying discrimination against nonmembers. Before analyzing this proposition, let us examine the semantics of economic integration.

The Meaning of Economic Integration

Economic integration is a continuum, going from total economic separation to fully integrated economies that have a central uniform policy and no barrier of any sort between them. As with all extremes—pure communism versus pure laissez-faire, full independence versus total dependence, and so on—neither total economic separation nor full economic integration have a counterpart in the real world. No country is totally isolated and no country can claim complete integration of even its internal economy. Thus, more important than countries' positions along the separation-integration continuum is their *movement* toward greater contacts and coordination, i.e., economic integration as a process rather than merely a state of affairs. Any division of a continuum into "stages" is arbitrary. Nevertheless, certain distinctions are widely used and practically convenient. It is important to note that of the following main stages of economic integration none is either an indispensable prerequisite for the more advanced one or necessarily a passage to it.

A *free trade area* implies the elimination of commercial barriers between the participating countries, but not the harmonization of countries' commercial policies for nonmembers. A *customs' union* calls for both the elimination of national restrictions on intra-union trade and the establishment of a common tariff and a uniform commercial policy of all member countries with respect to trade with outside countries.

As we saw when discussing the implications of the Heckscher-Ohlin theorem in Chapter 3, trade and international movements of factors of production are partial substitutes for one another. It follows that even the harmonization of countries' commercial policy does not ensure the effective liberalization of economic exchange in the absence of agreements not to impose additional restrictions on the movements of factors of production

[14] For a comprehensive discussion of the arguments pro and con, as well as an account of postwar tariff discrimination, see G. Patterson, *Discrimination in International Trade: The Policy Issues, 1945–65* (Princeton, N.J.: Princeton University Press, 1966).

between the member countries. A *common market* thus adds to elimination of trade restrictions and to harmonization of commercial policies, to abolition of national restrictions on the flows of labor, capital, and other resources to and from the other member countries.

The next stage in the economic integration process is an *economic union,* which goes far beyond a common market. It requires standardization of national economic policies, or even centralization of these policies into a "federal" economic authority. An economic union thus in effect means the abandonment of national economic sovereignty in favor of a supranational organism. The next, and last, stage is the political union of the member countries, into a United States of . . . .

One can find many historical examples of economic integration undertakings. For example, the Zollverein (customs' union) established in 1834 among the several small German states led to a unified German state in 1870. After World War II, Belgium, the Netherlands, and Luxembourg formed the Benelux union, and in 1951 sectoral integration was attempted in Europe in the field of coal and steel production (the European Coal and Steel Community), among the same six countries (Belgium, France, Germany, Italy, Luxembourg, the Netherlands) that agreed in 1957 to the formation of a European Common Market. The European Community membership was expanded in 1973, after years of difficult negotiations, to include Britain, Denmark, and Ireland. "Associated" status has been given to a large number of less developed countries that are economically dependent on one or another of the regular member nations. The European Community is today by far the most important economic integration undertaking among developed Western nations.[15]

In 1977, the European Community had gone a little beyond the common market stage but was a long way from economic union status. Internal tariffs were altogether abolished, uniform external tariffs established, re-

[15] In Eastern Europe, the Council for Mutual Economic Assistance (COMECON) is the principal organ for regional economic cooperation. Any number of attempts at economic integration have been made by less developed countries, most of them sadly unsuccessful. Economic union in East Africa has totally collapsed, owing to the political hostilities between Kenya, Uganda, and Tanzania. In Africa as a whole, prospects for badly needed regional cooperation are more remote than ever. The Latin American Free Trade Association (LAFTA) never really got off the ground, although the Andean countries' subgroup has exhibited some willingness to proceed to meaningful cooperation. An economically successful regional grouping, the Central American Common Market, was all but ruined in 1969 by war between two of the members (Honduras and El Salvador). In the Caribbean, however, a Free Trade Area (CARIFTA) rose from the ashes of the West Indian Federation, and recently evolved into a Caribbean Common Market. There are also moderately favorable prospects for selective economic cooperation among countries of the South Pacific. It may be a coincidence, but it is noteworthy that the only signs of hope for regional integration among less developed countries come from areas characterized by very small nations scattered across wide expanses of ocean.

strictions on labor and capital movements lifted. In addition, some fiscal policy harmonization was accomplished through the common adoption of a value added tax (VAT); a European policy was painfully hammered out in the field of agriculture; and some coordination in economic policy has been achieved. Also, European supranational political institutions have been established and are waiting in the wings for the moment when, if ever, member countries would be ready to proceed toward political integration. However, a common policy in the field of energy is conspicuous for its absence, and the international monetary turmoil of the 1970s (see Chapter 15) has caused severe setbacks to the progress toward European monetary unification.

The Theory of Second-best and the Static Effects of Economic Integration

It is time to return to the proposition mentioned earlier, that the benefits from economic integration outweigh the distortions caused by the accompanying tariff discrimination. To analyze this proposition, we need to make brief reference to a theoretical contribution known as the *theorem of second-best* (associated mainly with the names of R. G. Lipsey and K. Lancaster).

You undoubtedly recall the several assumptions needed for demonstrating the advantages of free international trade. The theorem of second-best states that if any one of those conditions does not obtain, then an optimum situation can be achieved only by departing in some measure from *all* the other conditions. Thus, an "improvement" with respect to only *some* other condition does not necessarily lead to an increase in economic welfare. To use a football analogy, if one wide receiver gets hurt, improving the accuracy of passing to the other receiver may or may not help the efficiency of the team; what is generally needed, instead, is a revision of the entire "game plan." (Departing from all the other conditions in order to "match" the initial violation is "second-best" to the optimal but unavailable policy, i.e., to remedy the initial violation itself.)

The link to the question of economic integration is as follows: if eliminating tariffs with respect to *all* countries is out of the question, eliminating tariffs only among *some* countries may or may not lead to an improvement in world economic welfare. It will have both positive effects (*trade creation*) arising from the reduction of tariffs within the customs' union, and negative effects (*trade diversion*) arising from the consequent *relative* increase in tariffs on trade with nonmember countries.

Let's spell this out a bit further. Countries A and B agree to eliminate tariffs on trade between them, but without a reduction in their tariffs on trade with other countries. You can expect trade between A and B to increase. Only a part of this increase, however, is trade creation, i.e., the replacement of comparatively inefficient domestic production with imports from the partner country owing to the elimination of tariffs. The remainder is trade diversion, i.e., the replacement of cheaper imports *from the rest of the world* with comparatively inefficient imports from the partner country. If trade creation is larger than trade diversion, the customs' union has a net beneficial effect on economic welfare; it has a negative effect if trade diversion is larger.

Much has been written on the probable size of trade creation and trade diversion, and thus on the conditions that make for a likely net beneficial effect. A fairly obvious point is that the chances for a net beneficial effect increase the greater the number of countries participating in the union. This point can readily be seen from the extreme case of a customs' union encompassing the entire world, which by definition precludes any diversion of trade. Empirical research has shown, however, that these static effects of economic integration, whether favorable or unfavorable, are quantitatively negligible.

Of far greater importance, but less amenable to precise quantification, are the dynamic effects of economic integration. Of the many such effects that can be claimed, three have received particular attention. First, the elimination of internal trade barriers creates a market larger than the individual national markets, and hence may allow for the reaping of substantial economies of scale (see Chapter 3). Second, and partly related to the first effect, there may be an increase in investment opportunities, and thus a spur to investment itself. Third, the restrictive effect of tariffs on competition is lessened, and the resulting stimulus to competition may accelerate technical and managerial modernization.

The Political Theory of "Second-best" and Economic Integration

As we have seen, the second-best argument implies, among other things, that a reduction of tariffs by some countries in relation to one another (economic integration of some, but not all, nations) is not necessarily in the best economic interests of the world as a whole.

A political internationalist would view national sovereignty as inimical to world peace, and rightly conclude that if *all* countries became politically integrated a major source of human conflict would disappear. But what if this "first-best" (from his point of view) were not an available policy option? Should he then be in favor of the political integration of *some* countries into a larger nation? Would this be a step forward in terms of the political interests of the world as a whole? The answer, as in the trade-creation/trade-diversion case, is that "it depends." Thus, one could make the conceivable case that the larger sovereign political unit resulting from the nineteenth-century unification of many small German states eventually became a much more serious destabilizer than if the various states had remained separate—

although the unification lessened political conflict *among* them. Similarly, one could argue that a United States of Europe will be a step toward world political integration, *or* that the "nationalism" of that larger political unit will be greater than the sum of its individual components.[16]

Political internationalization "from the top down" has been tried (League of Nations, United Nations) and has been notably unsuccessful. Political internationalization "from the bottom up" has had at best mixed results. What then? A possible intermediate route consists of cooperation involving most countries, but *selectively*, in respect to only certain issues. This is, in fact, the route that has been followed in the West since World War II, exemplified by *partial* international agreements such as the nuclear nonproliferation treaty, and the General Agreement on Tariff and Trade. Political interdependence is thereby increased, but at a slow enough rate to be practicable, though by no means assured. As we have seen, in the realm of economic integration it was just such a limited agreement on coal and steel that paved the way for the more comprehensive European Economic Community.

Points for Review

1. Review your understanding of the following effects of a tariff:
a. Consumption effect
b. Domestic production effect
c. Import effect
d. Redistribution effect
e. Revenue effect
f. Net welfare effect
g. Competitive effect
h. Terms-of-trade effect
i. Income effect
j. Balance-of-payments effect
k. International factor movements effect

2. Review your understanding of the effects of tariffs by working through the following exercise, either algebraically or graphically. You have the following information on an hypothetical market for men's shoes:

The demand function: Quantity demanded = 100,000 pairs — (2,000 × Price)
The domestic supply function: Quantity supplied = 10,00 + (3,000 × Price)
The world price: $10 a pair.

[16] S. Dell's analysis is generally founded on the latter point of view in his *Trade Blocs and Common Markets* (New York: Knopf, 1963).

Assume the world price to be constant (perfect elasticity of import supply), with no shifts in the domestic demand and supply curves, and initial equilibrium. Calculate the following effects of a 50 percent ad valorem tariff, after the market arrives at the new equilibrium:

a. Consumption effect
b. Domestic production effect
c. Import effect
d. Gross consumers' loss
e. Revenue effect
f. Redistribution effect
g. Net loss
h. The ad valorem tariff that would eliminate all imports (prohibitive tariff)
i. Terms-of-trade effect (This is really simple)

What would happen to the size of each of the above effects if demand elasticity were lower within the relevant range? If domestic supply elasticity were lower? If import supply were not perfectly elastic?

3. Refer back to Figure 4.1b and verify that if unit transport costs decline to less than 00′, import price falls and the volume of imports rises. Also, find how large unit transport costs would have to be to eliminate all trade.

4. What do the abbreviations CIF and FOB mean?

5. Check your understanding of the fact that the existence of transport costs (or of tariffs) usually means an export price *lower* than otherwise.

6. Identify and explain the following terms or principles:
a. The approximate equivalence of tariffs and quotas
b. Economic warfare
c. Major nontariff barriers
d. Voluntary quotas
e. Tariff rate quota
f. Specific and ad valorem tariffs
g. Revenue and protective tariffs

7. How is the elasticity of domestic supply related to the extent of the gain in producers' surplus resulting from a market price increase?

8. Should a protection maximizer prefer an ad valorem tariff to a specific tariff in times of declining prices?

9. Can you expect a change in the level of tariffs to have small immediate effects? If so, why?

10. Under what condition is it true that domestic consumers bear the entire burden of a tariff? When are they entirely unaffected by it?

11. Consider the following data on goods A, B, and C in an hypothetical country:

	A	B	C
Tariff Rate	10%	20%	200%
Domestic Consumption	250	500	5,050
Domestic Production	100	300	5,000
Imports	150	200	50
World Exports	1,000	1,000	2,000

Verify that a simple average of tariffs on *A, B,* and *C* differs from an average of tariffs weighted by domestic consumption, or domestic production, or imports, or world exports. Which would you choose as a reasonably good indicator of the degree of restrictiveness of the country's tariffs, and why?

12. If the import of silk ties is subject to a 20 percent tariff, the import of silk fabric to a 10 percent tariff, and silk fabric accounts for 66 percent of the production cost of ties, calculate the effective rate of protection of tie manufacturing. In the light of your result, can one say that elimination of the tariff on silk fabrics increases the restrictive effect of the tariff on ties?

13. What is the meaning of trade creation and trade diversion?

14. How does a customs union differ from a free-trade area?

15. What is the theorem of second-best?

Questions for Discussion

1. Think of examples (other than houses) of goods or services that are not traded internationally because of excessively high transport costs.

2. Reflect on the probable extent of the gains from trade for a geographically isolated country. Is there a geographic content to the category of Third World countries?

3. Is there a conceivable connection between the level of European import tariffs and the amount of U.S. investment in Europe?

4. Would you agree with John Maynard Keynes that there is nothing a tariff can do that an earthquake could not do better?

5. How would you personally assess, taking into account factors other than strictly economic ones, the merits and disadvantages of Buy American provisions?

6. As an example of the ways in which different technical specifications may affect international trade, consider the influence of the difference between the metric system and the U.S. measurement system on international trade in automobile parts and mechanics' tools.

7. The explanation of consumers' surplus given in the text is framed in terms of different individuals' desires for a unit of a given commodity. Can you think of illustrations relating to a *single* individual as his circumstances change? (Hint: Remember the "law" of diminishing marginal utility.)

8. The effective rate of protection formula given in the text is a first approximation, which assumes many other things to be equal. What factors should also be taken into account for a more accurate estimate of effective rates of protection?

9. Do less developed countries have a legitimate claim that the international

structure of tariffs generally discriminates against them? (This is an exceedingly broad question. Discuss it within the narrow limits of the points covered in the text.)

10. On which general category of product would a U.S. import tariff have a significant terms-of-trade effect? Would the same tariff imposed by Costa Rica on its imports of the same products accomplish the same result?

11. Is this statement correct: "Other things being equal, the revenue effect of a tariff is greater the larger the country's comparative disadvantage in the production of the taxed commodity?"

12. There are reasons to expect highly concentrated industries to prefer being protected by a quota rather than by an equivalent tariff. Can you find some examples in recent U.S. history? Would such a tendency be reinforced if the importing side of the market were also dominated by a few large firms?

13. In Bastiat's *Chinese Story* the labor created by destruction of the canal is said to be "diverted from other employments." What other employments? Why is it intimated that such diversion is "bad"?

14. Are you in favor of or opposed to European economic integration? Can you identify the reasons, economic or not, for your attitude?

15. How would you view the possibility of an economic union between the United States and Canada? Between the United States and Mexico?

"Protection concentrates on one point the good of which it produces, while the evils it inflicts are spread over the masses. The one is visible to the naked eye; the other only to the eye of the mind."

Frédéric Bastiat

Arguments for Trade Restrictions

What to Expect

Chapters 4 and 5 examined the various types of obstacles to foreign trade and their principal effects. This chapter uses that material as a backdrop for the analysis of the myriad arguments advanced in support of restricting international trade. First described are those arguments for tariffs or quotas that have no validity whatever, although they continue to surface in the debate on trade issues. Then arguments for trade restriction to achieve some noneconomic objective are examined. The focus then shifts to those arguments that under certain circumstances may constitute valid exceptions to free trade policy. They are classified under the following headings: Distributional arguments, which claim that protection is needed to induce a desired change in the internal distribution of income; mercantilist arguments, which view trade restrictions as a source of national advantage over other countries; arguments that trade restrictions are needed in order to correct economic distortions, either in the domestic or in the foreign market; and the infant industry argument, widely acknowledged as a possible justification for economic intervention on the basis of dynamic considerations. The review of the debate on the issue of trade restriction concludes with an overall assessment of the various arguments for protection. The Appendix is another satirical piece by Frédéric Bastiat.

As we have seen, there is a general presumption that trade restriction is economically harmful. It is a strong presumption and, at a minimum, it serves to shift the burden of proof on to those who would advocate such restriction. In the absence of convincing proof to the contrary in a specific case, it remains reasonable to view trade restrictions as inimical to the economic interests and welfare of the country imposing them and to the interests of its trading partners.

In assessing the possible merit of a specific argument for trade restriction, it helps to keep in mind that there are no internal logical faults in the theory of trade. The gains-from-trade conclusion is most definitely valid if the assumptions on which it is based hold. Any argument for interfering with the free flow of goods and services between countries must therefore rest, if it is to have any possible merit, on some evidence that one or more of the theoretical assumptions do not correspond to economic reality. This is, however, not sufficient to accept the validity of the argument. The deviation of the free trade model from the "real world" must also be shown to materially affect the conclusions drawn from that model.

There is a second possible line of valid reasoning for trade restriction. The economic losses from trade restriction are admitted, but it is claimed that they are more than offset by some noneconomic benefit resulting from it. In both instances, advocates of a trade restricting policy must also convincingly show that the desired purpose is best served by that policy rather than by some other available measure that does not interfere with the flow of trade. In a nutshell, any argument for tariffs or quotas should be subject to the following three tests: (1) Does the recommended trade restriction carry a benefit—economic or noneconomic—to the nation as a whole? (2) If so, is the expected benefit larger than the net loss a restriction of trade almost always carries? (3) If the benefit is real, and sufficiently great, is restriction of foreign trade the best policy to achieve it?

It generally helps in evaluating arguments for protecting specific industries to extrapolate them to the economy as a whole. Very often, an argument that appears sensible within its specific context is clearly seen as false when broadened to a more general context. The "fallacy of composition" consists of believing that what is true of a part is necessarily true of the whole. As an example, while it is true that students have a headstart in their search for summer jobs if their college shortens the spring semester, it does not follow that if all colleges ended the academic year earlier all students would have a greater chance of finding summer employment. The only result would be a shorter period of education. Similarly, one can correctly claim that a tariff yields a concrete benefit to the protected sector, but it does not necessarily follow that the tariff yields a similar benefit to the economy as a whole, and thus that the argument for protection is a valid one. Also, keep in mind the distinction between the possible validity of an argument and the application of it to a concrete case. An argument for protection may have merit in and of itself, but it may be used inappropriately to justify trade restrictions in situations to which it does not apply.

The possible arguments for protection are legion in number. The list discussed here does not pretend to be exhaustive, but it does try to be comprehensive by including both the most common as well as the soundest arguments (the two are not necessarily the same). Many of the false arguments are quite old and have stubbornly resisted repeated demonstrations of their lack of validity. They continue to surface in trade debates down to the present day because they have a strong superficial aura of common sense. They do not stand up to critical analysis, but they can sound quite persuasive to an uninformed audience exposed to them on a passing basis. One argument for tariffs that has virtually disappeared from the debate is the contention that tariffs are needed as a source of government revenue. Such argument, of course, would not hold much water in our times where tariffs account for an insignificant portion of government revenue (in the United States, less than 1 percent of federal revenues as against 95 percent in 1860).

Arguments in favor of restricting trade with foreign countries are discussed here in approximate ascending order of possible validity, beginning with those that make no sense, in economic terms or otherwise. The list is long, and it is a long trek from the nonsense arguments to the legitimate ones. But do try to reserve some of your attention for the latter part of the chapter, and particularly for the infant industry argument, the most powerful potential exception to the free trade presumption.

As you read through this chapter, you may wonder why some weak or nonsensical arguments persist in the public debate. Remember that trade expansion and restriction touch on very real economic interests of different individuals and groups. Those adversely affected by expanded trade want to marshal in support of their position as many arguments as they can to appeal to the public. These arguments are examined in this chapter. Chapter 7 discusses the political economy of trade restrictions. (You may find it useful to scan Chapter 7 before going into the material of this chapter, although a good grasp of the analytical aspects of the tariff debate is necessary before going in depth into the political economy of it.)

Nonsense Arguments

There are as many possible nonsense arguments for trade restriction as there are kinds of nonsense. The ones that have been most frequently used, and that still surface with some regularity, are the arguments that restricting imports is needed to expand the home market, to prevent loss of money to foreigners, to combat "unfair" low wages abroad, and to place international competition on a "scientific" basis. Each of these has a respectable variant to which serious consideration is given later in the appropriate section. These arguments are, however, most often advanced in a crude version lacking all validity.

Expansion of the Home Market

"Restricting imports reserves the national market for the national industry and, by fostering prosperity in the protected sector, it serves to expand the market for the other domestic economic activities, thus resulting in a general increase in prosperity."

Henry Clay was a major nineteenth century American proponent of this view. The answer is simple. Under conditions of full employment, the restriction of imports can only result in siphoning off resources from production of exportables, thus *replacing* the export market with domestic sales and causing the familiar loss in efficiency and welfare. With a lower real national income, the net result is therefore a *contraction* of the total market. (This nonsense argument should be distinguished from its less crude variant, discussed later under mercantilist arguments, which rests on the interaction of foreign trade and national income.)

"*When we buy the goods abroad, we get the goods and the foreigner gets the money. When we buy the goods at home, we get both the goods and the money.*" [1]

We discussed in Chapter 2 the mercantilist fallacy of identifying wealth with money, a fallacy that was exposed over two centuries ago by David Hume's gold-specie-flow doctrine and later by Adam Smith's demonstration of the true "wealth of nations." You cannot eat, wear, or drink money. Money is primarily a medium of exchange, an *intermediary* between our purchases of commodities and services from abroad and foreign purchases from us. As J. Nock stated, "Money does not pay for anything, never has, never will. It is an economic axiom as old as the hills that goods and services can be paid for only with goods and services." Exports are thus the real payment for a country's imports; foreigners accept the country's currency in payment for their refrigerators and automobiles because they can use it to buy other goods or assets. Again, under full employment conditions, an increase in import-competing domestic production requires reallocation of resources away from production of exportables and a decline in exports. (This crude argument has a more sophisticated variant, discussed later as the balance-of-payments case for restricting foreign trade.)

Counteract Cheap Foreign Wages

"*Foreign producers pay very low wages and often exploit the labor of women and children. Our industry instead provides its workers with a decent standard of living. How can we complete with imports produced by means of cheap foreign labor? Tariffs are needed in order to allow our industry to compete on a fair basis and to maintain the standard of living of our workers.*"

This is undoubtedly the granddaddy of the nonsense arguments and one of the most frequently used, appealing as it does to the citizens' sense of fairness for not supporting "labor exploitation" in foreign countries. (Would it be fairer perhaps to support import restrictions that would cause the "exploited" foreign workers to lose their low-paid jobs altogether?) Thus, for example, 70 years ago the U.S. glue industry claimed to be at an unfair disadvantage and to deserve tariff protection on the grounds that foreign producers used lowly paid women workers. [2]

 The argument is probably the hardiest weed in the field of trade debates. One may, however expect that it will be used in the United States

---

[1] This remark has been falsely imputed to Abraham Lincoln.
[2] Congressional Hearings on the Payne-Aldrich tariff bill, 1908.

to a lesser and lesser extent to justify protection against imports from other industrial countries, while it will continue as a frequent claim for protection against imports from less developed countries. This is because the wage differential between the United States and other major industrial countries has been decreasing, with labor costs rising far more slowly in this country than in its main trade partners. As Figure 6.1 shows, hourly compensation in the United States, far greater than in other countries in 1970, had become by 1975 comparable to the Canadian and West German levels, and lower than in Sweden.

There are several levels of reply to the cheap foreign labor argument. First, labor is only one factor of production. A cost disadvantage with respect to labor may well be offset by a cost advantage with respect to some other needed input. Second, higher labor costs usually go hand-in-hand with higher labor productivity.[3] An industry may appear at a cost disadvantage when only wages are looked at, whereas owing to higher labor productivity its labor cost *per unit of output* may be less than in low-wage countries. Third, and most important, differences in price of factors of production reflect to a large extent differences in the relative availability of those factors in various countries. Opportunities for gainful trade emerge exactly from such differences in comparative costs.

The main point, by far, is that to demand tariffs to offset labor cost differences is merely to claim that the country should be prevented to that

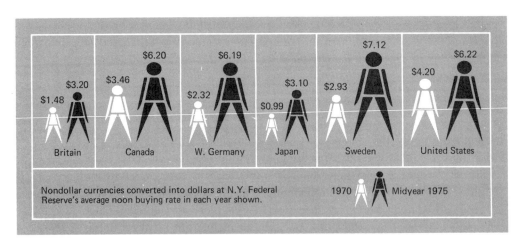

FIGURE 6.1 Hourly Compensation: 1970 and 1975

[3] A positive reaction to higher domestic wages was expressed in November 1975 by Thomas A. Murphy, Chairman of General Motors (Remarks before The Economic Club of New York): "We want our employees to continue to be paid more than their foreign counterparts and to enjoy the resulting higher standard of living. But to accomplish this and still maintain our competitive position we must be correspondingly more productive."

extent from taking advantage of the greater relative efficiency of foreign producers in certain areas.[4] You might as well argue, as *The Candlemakers Petition* in the Appendix does, that producers of lighting equipment should be protected from the unfair competition of sunlight, which is manufactured by nature at no cost at all. (The crude "cheap foreign labor" argument should not be confused with an economically meaningful interpretation of it, namely, the Stolper-Samuelson demonstration of the effect of trade on real wages; see the discussion of distributional arguments later in this chapter.)

The cheap foreign labor argument sometimes becomes the "cheap foreign *anything*" case for protection. In the U.S. Congressional hearings on the Hawley-Smoot Tariff Act of 1930,[5] witnesses for the brick industry argued for protection on grounds of "cheap foreign transport." Foreign plants located near ports enjoyed the advantage of lower ocean shipping rates, whereas U.S. manufacturers had to face the higher costs of railroad freight. (If this seems to you a valid justification for protection, perhaps you should read again the Appendix to Chapter 4.) The pumice manufacturers caught two birds with one stone, claiming an unfair disadvantage in their competition with Italian pumice, which was not only manufactured with "cheap labor," but was shipped at low cost as ballast in vessels carrying Sicilian citrus fruit exported to the United States. And the manufacturers of casein (a byproduct of milk used in the production of paints) argued for a 60 percent tariff on imports on the grounds of the unfair competition of "cheap foreign milk" from Argentina. It is only a short step from this kind of reasoning to advocacy of tariffs on a "scientific" basis.

"Scientific" Tariff

"Protection should simply represent the difference that exists between the cost of a commodity that we produce and the cost of the same commodity

---

[4] This, of course, is precisely the intent of the users of the argument, who have their jobs or their capital in relatively inefficient domestic industries. Protection of "fair labor standards" in domestic industries, as compared with "sweatshop" conditions in foreign countries, is the newer version of the cheap foreign labor argument. (Peter B. Kenen has remarked that fair labor standards are a public good, to be defended by general economic measures and not by restricting the flow of trade in specific industries.) A "covert" route to the same goal has also been followed. As reported by Philip Agee, an internal training course for CIA operatives in less developed countries emphasized that the agency's covert labor operations "must seek to develop trade unions in underdeveloped countries that will focus on economic issues and stay away from politics and the ideology of class struggle. This . . . when promoted in poor countries, should raise labour costs and thereby diminish the effect that imports from low-cost labour areas has on employment in the U.S." (P. Agee, *Inside the Company: CIA Diary* [New York: Stonehill, 1975], pp. 135–36.)

[5] U.S. Senate Finance Committee, and House Ways and Means Committee Hearings, June 1929.

produced by our neighbors. . . . Free competition exists only when there is
equality in the conditions and in the charges. In the case of a horse race,
we ascertain the weight that each horse has to carry and so equalize the
conditions." [6]

It is true, the argument goes, that labor is only one factor of production, and that productivity differences should be taken into account. Let us therefore place protection on a "scientific" basis and use trade restrictions to the extent needed to offset *any and all* differences in production costs, however small or large, and regardless of how they arise, thus "equalizing the conditions of competition."

The reply needs only a few words. Would you have handicapped the fastest horse if the purpose of the race was to tell people that "The British are coming"? Cost differences between countries being eliminated by the tariffs, the economic incentive to import would in most cases disappear, imports would be negligible, and exports could not very well be expected to continue unabated under those circumstances. A "scientific" tariff comes close to the definition of a prohibitive tariff. (This foolishness bears a very faint resemblance to a serious argument for trade restriction to correct economic distortions, examined later.) Let us move on to arguments of at least conceivable validity as justifications for restricting trade.

Noneconomic Arguments

It is possible to argue that the economic losses from trade restrictions are a necessary price to pay for the fulfillment of overriding noneconomic objectives. This is a legitimate line of reasoning; it cannot be dismissed out of hand as were the nonsensical arguments just discussed. Arguments for trade restriction on noneconomic grounds remain, however, subject to the tests mentioned at the beginning of this chapter: Restricting trade must yield a significant benefit, and, if the argument is to be accepted as valid, trade restriction must be shown to be the best means of obtaining that benefit. There are as many possible noneconomic arguments for protection as there are noneconomic goals. Among these, two have been most often used as justifications for tariffs or quotas: The political rationale, and the cultural-sociological argument. In turn, the political justification for protection can be advanced in three overlapping versions: safeguarding the country's military security, preserving the integrity of its foreign policy, and lessening its dependence on the outside world.

[6] Attributed to the Viscount de Romanet, *circa* 1830.

Adam Smith himself, that most ardent advocate of free exchange, had occasion to remark in a famous passage that national defense mattered more than national opulence. And nineteenth century British Prime Minister Benjamin Disraeli went as far as to say: "Free trade is not a principle, it is an expedient." The national defense justification for intervening in international commerce can be valid, depending on the circumstances of the specific case. In general, it is more applicable to intervention on *exports* than on imports. It would be hard to make a case for free exports of cruise missiles to the Soviet Union on the basis of the economic benefit accruing to the United States. The benefit would be real, but pales into insignificance by comparison to the national security cost of such exports. It is also possible to justify trade restrictions as part and parcel of economic warfare; *if* a boycott or blockade is sound from a political standpoint, the restriction of trade with the target country *may* accomplish the desired political objective.

It is, instead, harder to argue that *import* restrictions are needed for national security reasons. The reasoning in this case is that free imports of goods or services of military significance would lessen internal production capacity to the point where the domestic industry would not be capable of supplying the nation's military needs should a war cut the country off from its sources of imports. This was, for example, the rationale of England's Navigation Acts, which protected the merchant marine in order that England's navy, "the floating bulwark of the nation," would remain a strong military instrument.

Up to the emergence of nuclear weapons, there was merit to that argument. Today, for a major international power the national defense rationale of import restrictions must be seriously questioned. It hinges on the risk of a sudden cutoff of the nation from its sources of imports, which could only be caused by the outbreak of a war. A war that isolated a major power from *all* of its important foreign suppliers would almost by definition be a world war, considering how far flung is a major power's network of international commercial relations. And, as P. B. Kenen and others have pointed out, in the nuclear age the capability of the domestic industry to sustain conventional military production for an extended period of time is hardly relevant to the outcome of the war. Consider that even the war in Indochina, the largest military engagement in U.S. history except for World War II, did not significantly affect the U.S. capacity to import defense-related items. Besides, the very logic of the argument is in question: If the greatest possible availability of certain equipment or raw materials is the objective, restricting their import makes much less sense than importing as much as possible at the lower world prices and stockpiling the equipment or, in the case of minerals, conservation of domestic supplies by subsidizing exploration and development, but not production.

Another major problem of the national security argument is that it can be, and has been, advanced to justify protection in cases where the link between the industry and the nation's security is tenuous at best. In economics everything is related to everything else. "For want of a nail the shoe is lost, for want of a shoe the horse is lost, for want of a horse the rider is lost, for want of a rider the battle is lost." Anyone can trace a connection between military production and his own branch of economic activity, *because the connection exists.*[7] It can conceivably be argued that exclusion of foreign leather products is beneficial for the national defense: a healthy leather industry is needed to assure the country of adequate domestic supplies of belts and shoes, and soldiers could not very well fight barefoot and with their pants falling down. (There is as much merit in this preposterous argument as there is in some of the national defense claims actually made by various domestic industries.)

While every economic activity is in some way related to military needs, the connection is important and direct in a few cases, insignificant and remote in most. The crux of the matter is the availability of good substitutes for the product in question. The farther back you trace the connection, the greater is the total availability of substitutes. Also relevant is the geographic concentration of the country's imports. The more diversified its sources of supply, the less likely it is that the country will find itself isolated from all of them.[8]

In summary, the national security argument remains a conceivable justification for trade restriction, but it is subject to very heavy qualifications. The questions to ask when restriction of imports of a certain product is advocated for national security reasons are: (1) Is the specific security objective itself a valid one on its own terms? (2) If so, could the military make do reasonably well with some other product? (3) If the product is of direct relevance to military capabilities and has no close substitutes, could it not be imported from other sources should a country become separated from its traditional sources of supply? (4) Finally, could the national security objective not be accomplished through other means that do not carry the costs of trade restriction—such as a stockpiling of imported materials or a straight subsidy to the domestic manufacturers? By the time you have gone through all of these tests, the instances of trade restrictions genuinely justified on national defense grounds are certain to be reduced to a mere handful.

[7] Thus, if the national security rationale is pushed to its extreme conclusion, it becomes an argument for total economic isolation, since everyone can claim a connection of some sort to vital industries.

[8] The national defense argument is also sometimes applied in contradictory ways. C. E. Staley has noted, for example, that it is argued at one and the same time that imports of heavy electrical equipment should be restricted for national defense reasons *and* that such equipment should not be exported to China also for national defense reasons. (*International Economics, Analysis and Issues,* [Englewood Cliffs, N.J.: Prentice-Hall, 1970], p. 124.)

Integrity of Foreign Policy

C. E. Staley refers to the national security argument as the "strategy" justification for trade restrictions. It is a better term, for it encompasses national political considerations broader than strictly military ones. Indeed, preserving a country's autonomy to pursue its own foreign policy has probably become in the 1970s a more convincing rationale for protection than the national defense case narrowly interpreted. There may be a case for restrictive policies concerning imports of materials of great general importance for the economy as a whole in order to prevent foreign suppliers from acquiring an unduly large influence on the determination of the course of the country's foreign policy. The most dramatic example is given by the drastic post-1973 shift in many European and African countries' posture on the Middle Eastern question. There can hardly be any doubt that extreme dependence on imported oil from Arab countries contributed materially to such policy change. While the argument is therefore to be taken seriously, it is subject to qualifications similar to those that apply to the military rationale for trade restrictions. In particular, even when the commodity has no close substitutes and when stockpiling or subsidization are not practicable, preservation of the nation's independence in foreign policy is a much stronger rationale for *diversification* of the country's geographic sources of supply than for restricting total imports in the hopes of stimulating domestic production.

Excessive Political Dependence

There is sometimes the belief that consolidation of recent political independence may require a general lessening of dependence on outside sources of supply and/or on outside markets. (This belief is widespread in less developed countries, although it rarely is used to advocate trade restrictions in industrial nations.) To the extent that gains from trade and division of labor are paid for by a degree of international interdependence, it is true that curtailment of foreign trade will lessen, at a cost, a country's economic dependence on the rest of the world. As discussed in Chapter 1, it is a nation's sovereign right to pursue greater self-sufficiency as an end in itself. In the case of Central American countries, for example, the fostering of *regional* interdependence and the lessening of reliance on extraregional sources have been viewed as explicit policy objectives, separate from maximization of aggregate growth for the region as a whole and, indeed, avowedly in partial conflict with the latter goal.[9] The noneconomic nature of this objective brooks no criticism on economic grounds. In this case, the

[9] See S. Schiavo-Campo, *Import Structure and Import Substitution in the Central American Common Market*, Secretaría de Integración Economica CentroAmericana (SIECA), Monograph Series No. 1, Guatemala, 1972.

trade restriction is itself the objective and not an imperfect means to some other end. The only requirement on which economists must rightly insist is that the objective sought be made explicit and that the economic costs of pursuing it be assessed realistically. This is not always done. If it were, policy-makers might more often come to conclude that the game is not worth the candle.

The Cultural-Sociological Argument

The gains-from-trade proposition is a very dubious one when tastes change as a result of trade (see Chapter 3). In the presence of a significant potential demonstration effect, there is no way to show rigorously that opening up to foreign trade would improve the population's economic welfare. It is thus entirely defensible for an isolated national entity to continue to opt out of the international economy. Economic isolation is an even more defensible policy when the preservation of the country's "life style" and cultural pattern is considered desirable in and of itself and when it would be imperiled by exposure to new products and ways of doing things. The hitch is that the argument is valid only if economic isolation is virtually complete. If, instead, awareness of the new products and methods seeps in through the Great Wall and reaches significant numbers of people, their tastes do change anyway. Once this happens, we are back on the familiar grounds that abandonment of self-sufficiency and participation in the international division of labor carries net gains for the country's economy. There are involved here fundamental philosophical and political issues that cannot be resolved in this book.

There is also a cultural-sociological argument for restricting trade in *specific* products when a country is otherwise participating in the international system. Certain goods may be considered socially desirable (**merit-want goods**), and their exports may be curtailed in order to maintain the desired level of domestic consumption. Imports may also be restricted in order to preserve an economic activity or a "way of life" that are considered important components of the cultural and historical heritage of the nation. Or, certain goods may be deemed socially undesirable, and their imports restricted or prohibited in order to curtail consumption. Very few would argue, for example, that there should be free international commerce in narcotics or that the restriction on imports of hides of certain endangered animals is not justifiable. But now we can no longer assume that commercial policy is the best means to those ends: "Since the attainment of these objectives can be looked upon as introducing a policy-imposed distortion into the economy, it follows that the optimal policy is to create the distortion that directly affects the variable to be constrained." [10] In most cases, those

[10] R. M. Stern, "Tariffs and Other Measures of Trade Control: A Survey of Recent Developments," *Journal of Economic Literature*, September 1973, p. 864.

objectives are better accomplished through some combination of internal taxes and subsidies than through tariffs or quotas. Thus, for example, an import tariff to restrict consumption of socially undesirable commodities *also stimulates their domestic production.* If the consumption effect is the goal, and not simply a cover-up for protecting the domestic manufacturers, it is far better accomplished by an equivalent consumption tax, which reduces consumption just as much, but without the unwanted side effect of reallocating scarce domestic resources to production of the commodity that is deemed undesirable.

Distributional Arguments

We have discussed earlier how trade affects the distribution of income within a country. In general, expansion of foreign trade can be expected to benefit the producers of exportables, the owners of the relatively abundant factors of production, the population of regions with a high concentration of export industries, the consumers of the imported commodities. Correspondingly, a restriction of foreign trade can be expected to redistribute income in favor of the producers of import-competing goods, the owners of relatively scarce factors of production, the population of regions with a high concentration of import-competing industries, and the consumers of exportables.

Probably the best-known distributional argument for protection, and the most thoroughly worked out theoretically, emerges from the demonstration by W. F. Stolper and P. A. Samuelson of the relationship between trade and real wages. As was seen in Chapter 3, trade expansion stimulates an increase in the demand for those factors of production that are used intensively in the export sector and a decline in demand for resources used intensively in the import-competing sector. If the Heckscher-Ohlin theorem holds, it is the country's relatively scarce factor that is used intensively in import-competing production. A restriction of trade can thus increase the reward to that scarce factor, both in relative and in absolute terms. If labor is the relatively scarce factor of production, imposition of a tariff can increase both monetary and real wages.[11]

More generally, given the varied influence of trade on income distribution, a nondeceitful argument for trade restriction can simply make the case that one or the other of the distributional effects of such restriction is desirable from the nation's viewpoint. Thus, there is a plausible case for

[11] Stolper and Samuelson, "Protection and Real Wages," *Review of Economic Studies,* November 1941. The argument has since been refined and elaborated in a number of ways. For a review, see M. C. Kemp, *The Pure Theory of International Trade and Investment* (Englewood Cliffs, N.J.: Prentice-Hall, 1969).

trade restriction when the standard of living of the owners of the relatively scarce inputs is considered to be below some minimum acceptable norm, when regions where import-competing production is concentrated are economically depressed, when export commodities are a basic staple of mass consumption, and so forth. The argument is well within the proper bounds of the theoretical trade model and might well succeed in the specific case to show that the income redistribution sought is "worth" the net loss from the tariff.

The argument, however, fails the third test: The commercial policy recommended is not the most appropriate one for the desired end. As in the case of the cultural-sociological argument, the redistributive effect being sought can be accomplished through an appropriate mix of taxation (or devaluation) and direct subsidies that, by not causing an increase in import prices, avoids the net welfare loss resulting from trade restriction. (Subsidies do not, however, avoid the net efficiency loss. This and other considerations on subsidies as alternatives to trade restrictions are elaborated in Chapter 7.)

Is it acceptable merely to say that a relatively inefficient domestic industry should be allowed to wither away in the name of efficiency without any governmental action to alleviate the plight of those directly affected? Certainly not. But governmental action should be designed to minimize, if not entirely eliminate, the social and human costs of reallocating resources out of the declining industry, not to compound those costs by postponing indefinitely the needed transition. You may know of the tragic case of a young woman whose heart and lungs were for months kept functioning artificially despite the cessation of any significant brain activity. Whether to terminate the artificial life support systems involved extremely serious moral and legal questions in such a case, when she could not give or withhold her consent. But these questions are not at stake in the case of commercial protection. Manufacturing plants, buildings, machines, do not die: by allowing them to depreciate without replacement, these resources can gradually be transferred to healthier branches of economic activity.

What, then, is the rationale for keeping a declining industry in a state of economic coma through restriction of imports if it becomes clear that no long-term improvement is possible?[12] More specifically, why should society's resources be expended in such support for an indefinite period of time when a smaller expenditure, and on a once-and-for-all basis, could deal better with the human problems caused by the industry's demise? Which course of action would be considered more humane and socially responsible: A tariff, or quota, or production subsidy, leading the industry

---

[12] One should also consider the possibility that the industry's economic stagnation is *caused* by the import restrictions themselves and that the removal of commercial protection might force the industry to adapt and perhaps to become competitive on its own merits.

to hire young workers who will in all likelihood find themselves out of a job and without a marketable trade 20 years hence, when their occupational and geographic mobility is certain to be lower, or a probably smaller amount of temporary financial assistance designed to ease movement out of the industry for workers who can move, to preserve the standard of living of those who cannot, and generally to facilitate the transition of physical resources to more promising activities? [13]

Mercantilist Arguments

As we shall see in detail in Chapters 9 and 10, trade restrictions may have certain favorable effects on the economy as a whole. These include the possibility of a positive influence on the country's national income, its balance of payments, and its terms of trade, as well as on the inflow of scarce resources from abroad. To the extent that these favorable effects exist, however, they occur at the expense of other countries. An increase in employment through import restriction, an improvement in the balance of payments or in the terms of trade, successful attraction of scarce resources from abroad, all correspond to losses in employment, balance of payments, terms of trade, and resource availability in some other country. Arguments for protection on any of these grounds may therefore be grouped under the heading of mercantilist arguments. (During their heyday in the 1930s they also came to be known as "beggar-my-neighbor" arguments; see Chapter 8.) The "I'm all right, Jack . . ." thinking that underlies commercial policies under this heading is the source of their greatest practical weakness, for "Jack" will probably try to shift the problem onto someone else, too. Let's first look briefly at the income, balance-of-payments, and resource inflow arguments for tariffs or quotas, leaving for separate examination the optimum tariff case for trade restriction.

The Income, Balance-of-payments, and Resource Inflow Arguments

Both the income and the balance-of-payments arguments rest on violation of the full-employment assumption of the trade theory model. If in fact the economy is at less than full employment, tariffs or quotas may succeed in raising income and employment and in improving the country's international financial position. As noted in Chapter 5, however, this is true only as a first approximation. Since these positive effects take place at the expense of the

---

[13] As discussed in detail later, the 1974 Trade Act does recognize this difficult dilemma, although the specific provisions of the act have not really satisfied anyone, from the AFL-CIO to consumers' organizations.

level of foreign employment and the balance-of-payments position of other countries, the probable retaliation by those countries will at best cut down on the initial favorable effects and possibly offset them altogether. At any rate, the employment or balance-of-payments gain must be weighed against the loss suffered by consumers of the imported goods in the form of higher prices.

Similar considerations apply to the resource inflow argument. That argument rests on violation of the theoretical assumption of zero international mobility of factors of production. If factors of production can move across national frontiers, as of course they do, a trade restriction may succeed in raising the price of a relatively scarce resource sufficiently to induce an inflow of it into the economy (or to reduce its outflow when it is considered excessive), with a possible beneficial economic impact. That impact, of course, ought to be weighed against the losses of trade restriction. Also, two can play at the same game, and if foreign countries adopt countervailing measures to prevent the flight of the resource in question, the trade restriction loss is all that is left.

The use of the national income justification for tariffs has dropped off sharply since the 1930s rash of beggar-my-neighbor policies. The greater understanding and effectiveness of domestic fiscal and monetary policies have in most industrial countries lessened the temptation to export their unemployment problems abroad.[14] This development has been aided by the empirical finding that higher tariffs or quotas have a relatively small effect on the level of total employment. It should again be noted that import restrictions can have an *unfavorable* domestic effect if they are imposed in times of high economic prosperity, when they would contribute to inflation rather than to employment. On the other hand, it must be recognized that reduction of tariffs or quotas is not particularly advisable in times of high unemployment, when the resulting increase in imports would add to the recessionary forces at work in the economy. (This might not be true, however, if the recession is being transmitted to the economy via its export sector through higher restrictions abroad and if the tariff reduction is contemplated as part of a multilateral program to liberalize trade.) At any rate, it is unlikely that industrial countries will revert to using commercial policy as an instrument for creating employment.

Unfortunately, the same cannot be said of the balance-of-payments

[14] This enlightenment has progressed to the point that the turnaround in the U.S. balance of trade from a $12 billion surplus in 1975 to a small deficit in 1976 was labeled "good news" by U.S. Treasury officials, on grounds of the positive stimulus the deficit would have on *other* countries (as reported by Edwin L. Dale, Jr., *The New York Times,* May 23, 1976). It must not be inferred, however, that the income and employment argument for protection has entirely vanished from the commercial policy debate. The AFL-CIO in particular continues to emphasize heavily the "loss of American jobs" allegedly caused by foreign trade. (See, for example, its opposition to the 1974 Trade Act, and the platform proposals presented to the Democratic and Republican conventions in 1976).

rationale, which has continued to provide the basis for significant trade restrictions up to and including the 1970s. Recent examples include Canada in 1961, Britain in 1964, and the United States in 1971, when a 10 percent import surcharge was imposed partly on the grounds of the U.S. balance-of-payments deficit at that time (and partly as a bargaining tactic). And the 1974 Trade Act includes the granting to the President of considerable discretionary authority to impose temporary import surcharges or quotas as deemed necessary to deal with a balance-of-payments deficit.

The underlying reason for the continuing use of the balance-of-payments rationale for trade restrictions is the weakness of the international monetary system, which should perform the function of correcting balance-of-payments difficulties. This is, of course, an important topic that must be set aside until the later discussion of international finance. Suffice it to note here that, in principle, international *financial* problems are best dealt with by international *financial* policies, not by commercial policies. If, however, the international monetary mechanism is not working well, it is to be expected that countries will resort to second-best measures, such as restrictions of trade. This is one major reason why monetary questions can be of crucial importance to international economic activity.

The income, balance-of-payments, and resource inflow arguments for tariffs and quotas fail the last test: Restriction of foreign trade is not the single most appropriate policy to achieve the desired objectives. If an effect on the international movement of a factor of production is desired, it can be shown that the optimal policy does consist in part of a tariff or quota on goods and services traded, but it must also include the more direct means of taxing the reward to the factor of production itself.[15] If an increase in employment or an improvement in the balance of payments is desired, commercial policy is decidedly inferior to fiscal and monetary policies that can accomplish the same desired effect at a lesser real cost (see the discussion of subsidies in Chapter 7).

This is not true of tariffs or quotas that affect the country's terms of trade. The optimum tariff argument is the only one that is not "second best," and which, under certain conditions, justifies tariffs or quotas as the *optimal* policy. That argument thus constitutes a valid exception to the free trade rule.

The Optimum Tariff Argument

The optimum tariff argument rests on violation of the assumption that the country is too small for its purchases to have any effect on world prices. If instead import supply is less than perfectly elastic, the curtailment of

---

[15] For a mathematical demonstration of this point see M. C. Kemp, *The Pure Theory of International Trade and Investment* (Englewood Cliffs, N.J.: Prentice-Hall, 1969), pp. 195–200.

imports resulting from a tariff forces down the world price of the imported commodity[16] and, other things being equal, improves the country's terms of trade. As previewed in Chapter 5, the portion of tariff revenue paid by the foreigner in the form of a decrease in the *world* price is an economic gain to the country that may be greater than the net loss caused by the increase in the *domestic* price of imports. This difference provides a valid economic rationale for restricting imports. If the tariff is too high, the losses caused by it outweigh the terms-of-trade gain; if the tariff is not high enough, an increase of it may produce a net overall economic gain for the country. The optimum tariff rate is that which maximizes the difference between the terms-of-trade gain and the loss caused by the increase in domestic prices.[17]

The optimum tariff argument is the only one that successfully meets the requirement that the policy advocated be the best one for the purpose sought. Since the terms-of-trade gain arises from the reduction of imports, a tariff or quota is the most direct policy to achieve it. However, this is true only from the standpoint of the country imposing the tariff. From the *world's* economy point of view, instead, the partial shifting of the burden of the tariff onto foreign sellers is not a net gain, but a mere redistribution of income that cannot offset the net efficiency and welfare costs of the tariff. And if foreigners resist such redistribution by their own commercial policy actions, the country that attempts to improve its economic position by restricting foreign trade is not at all assured of ending up better off than it started. It should be noted, in conclusion, that the existing tariff may *already* be higher than its optimal level; in this case, the optimum tariff argument would be a reason for liberalizing trade rather than restricting it.[18]

[16] Except in the limiting case when domestic demand is completely inelastic.

[17] The optimum rate of tariff can be shown to be given by $[1/(e-1)]$, where e is the elasticity of the foreign offer curve. Offer curves (to be distinguished from supply curves) are not used in this book. The interested reader is referred to any of the more advanced treatments, such as R. E. Caves and R. W. Jones (see Bibliography). In any case, as M. C. Kemp, *The Pure Theory of International Trade and Investment*, pp. 171–72, has shown, there is an infinity of optimal tariff rates, one for each distribution of income, and the exact formula is much less useful than understanding of the general principle.

[18] In parallel with the optimum tariff argument, it is possible to make a case for an optimal rate of tax of foreign capital. In the absence of obstacles, the volume of foreign investment may be greater than the optimal level for a single country. That country may therefore improve its economic position by appropriate taxes on imports or exports of capital assets. (See A. Takayama, *International Trade* [New York: Holt, Rinehart and Winston, 1972], pp. 448–52.) There are possible reasons why the volume of foreign investment undertaken by citizens of a country may be greater than desirable from the country's viewpoint. J. M. Keynes noted that in case of default on foreign investment the country loses the physical capital assets, which of course is not true in case of default on the same amount of domestic investment. On the other side, it may be argued that imperfect knowledge of foreign investment opportunities (or the hindrances of foreign rules and regulations) causes the amount of foreign investment to be lower than optimal. This is a highly complex question the outcome of which is heavily dependent on the characteristics of the specific case.

A distant relative of the optimum tariff case is the often-heard argument that a tariff is needed for purposes of bargaining with foreign countries. Unlike the terms-of-trade rationale, however, the bargaining tariff is claimed to be a negotiating prerequisite for an eventual liberalization of foreign trade on a mutual basis, to set the stage for persuading foreign countries to lower *their* trade barriers in exchange for elimination of the initial tariff. There is a strong resemblance between this reasoning and the White House political argument of the early 1970s that the installation of new weapons systems by the United States was needed as a "bargaining chip" to induce the Soviet Union to make serious concessions in the Strategic Arms Limitation Talks.[19] The problem here is the familiar fallacy of composition: If *both* negotiating sides come to the table with commercial bargaining chips of all sorts, the imposition of bargaining tariffs will at best turn out to have been a useless exercise and, at worst, it may result in commercial escalation and in sabotaging otherwise good prospects for negotiated trade liberalization.

Correcting Distortions

A free trade policy rests on the presumed correspondence between the market prices of commodities and resources and their opportunity cost for society as a whole. Unfettered individual actions are then consistent with the general economic welfare. For this to be true, one needs to assume that markets are competitive, both at home and abroad; that external economies or diseconomies are absent; and that there exists no interference from government policies to accomplish objectives other than the most efficient utilization of available resources. A heavy list of assumptions, which are extremely unlikely to correspond to economic reality. Some markets do not function in a competitive manner, there often are external effects of individual economic actions, and governments do find it necessary to intervene into the economy for any number of reasons. Market prices may thus be imperfect measures of opportunity cost to society. The existence of distortions, whether from imperfect markets or from government policy, establishes a *prima facie* case for corrective measures, including appropriate restrictions of international trade.

The infant industry argument for tariffs to correct for the presence of externalities is discussed in the next section. Here we look at some of the justifications for tariffs to correct structural or government induced economic distortions. One of these justifications—the optimum tariff argument—has

---

[19] It is in our view not coincidental that one major recent example of a tariff for bargaining is the 1971 U.S. import surcharge (which was strongly hinted to be negotiable) imposed by the same Nixon administration that insisted on military bargaining chips for the SALT negotiations.

already been examined. It applies when the existence of monopoly or monopsony power on the world market permits the country to improve its terms of trade through the appropriate commercial policy measure. With that exception, tariffs or quotas are in general not the best antidistortion policy, for they do not deal directly with the source of the distortion. The most direct policy is instead an appropriate package of taxes and/or subsidies on consumption, production, or factor returns.[20]

Domestic Market Imperfections

Probably the best known under this heading is Everett Hagen's argument, which abandons the theoretical assumption of perfect internal mobility of factors of production between different occupations. If an economic disturbance (any change in basic market conditions) occurs, differences in marginal productivity of a factor of production between different sectors may emerge and give rise to differences in the return to the same factor of

---

[20] The various kinds of distortions and the policies to deal with them best have been analyzed by J. Bhagwati ("The Generalized Theory of Distortions and Welfare," in J. Bhagwati *et al.*, *Trade, Balance of Payments, and Growth*, Amsterdam: North Holland Publishing, 1971). Following Bhagwati, distortions can be classified as follows. Recall that the overall equilibrium condition for an open economy consists of the equality of relative marginal cost (domestic rate of transformation in production), relative marginal utility (rate of substitution in consumption), and relative world price (foreign rate of transformation in exchange). Equality of marginal cost and price assures producers' equilibrium under competitive conditions; equality of relative marginal utility and price is needed for consumers' equilibrium. In the absence of distortions, the price is one and the domestic rate of transformation in production equals the rate of substitution in consumption. Four kinds of distortions may thus exist. *First,* relative marginal cost may differ from relative world price, owing to the presence of an element of monopoly or monopsony in foreign trade. *Second,* relative marginal cost may differ from both relative world price and the rate of substitution in consumption, owing to the existence of production externalities. *Third,* relative marginal cost may differ from the rate of substitution in consumption but not from relative price, which is the case if sellers charge buyers the same premium on both imports and import-competing goods. *Fourth,* the economy may be operating below its production possibilities frontier, which can result, among other things, from market imperfections that do not allow the movement of resources to sectors where they are most productive (the Hagen argument). The optimal policy to correct the first distortion is imposition of a tariff at the appropriate (optimum) rate. (If that distortion arises from existence of a tariff when the country does *not* possess any influence over world market prices, the optimal response is of course *removal* of the tariff.) In the other three cases, however, trade restriction is inferior to other policies. To correct the second distortion, which relates only to production, a tax and/or subsidy on production in the sector affected by the externalities would do the job without the tariff-induced loss in consumers' welfare. To correct the third kind of distortion, which relates only to consumption, a tax and/or subsidy on consumption is best. And to correct the fourth type of distortion, which relates only to factor markets, taxes and/or subsidies on returns to the affected resource would, again, accomplish the desired purpose at a real cost lower than that implied by a restriction of trade.

production in various occupations. If mobility is complete, factors flow to the higher productivity, higher return sectors and the differences are quickly eliminated. If instead occupational mobility is imperfect, such differences can persist, leading to inefficient allocation of resources between occupations. National income is below its potential maximum, with production lower than economically desirable in the high return sectors and excessive elsewhere. If the high return sector produces import-competing goods, there is a preliminary justification for an import tariff or quota to induce the required inflow of resources into that sector and to raise production to the economically optimal level. (Correspondingly, if the higher returns are in the export sector, there is a case for a production subsidy to it.)

The argument is valid but fraught with serious practical problems, aside from the consideration made earlier concerning the superiority of subsidies to correct such distortion (the fourth kind of distortion in Bhagwati's scheme; see footnote 20). *First*, if the disturbance is reversible, the tariff should be removed once the initial situation is restored or else the tariff will from that point on cause an economic distortion instead of correcting for it. But it is in practice very difficult to gauge with any confidence when the disturbance has ceased and the need for the tariff has come to an end. *Second*, there is no reliable basis for estimating the rate of protection that will not over-correct for the insufficient factor mobility. Similarly, there is no assurance that protection will in fact increase occupational mobility, which may be limited almost absolutely by very rigid social and ethnic stratification. If the higher return to, say, labor, is due to barriers to the entry of certain groups into the privileged occupation or sector, protection of that sector compounds the initial inequity without doing anything to correct the economic distortion.

The Hagen argument has also a geographic dimension. If insufficient *geographic* mobility of factors of production is responsible for inefficient resource allocation, so that in regions where marginal productivity and factor returns are higher production is lower than economically desirable, there is a case for tariffs on imports of the main regional products (or subsidies if these are exported). Again, one must assume that geographic mobility will in fact increase as a result of the tariff or else the tariff will serve only to heighten the inequalities of regional income distribution. In any case, it is politically very difficult to argue for granting deliberate preference to those industries and regions that are better off economically, on the grounds that they are not *as much* better off as they should be for efficient allocation of resources.[21]

[21] There is a parallel here with the well-known economic development argument of W. Arthur Lewis, according to which redistribution of income in less developed countries in favor of the profit-receiving segment of the population, which has a higher propensity to save, would lead to faster capital formation and economic growth.

141

Foreign Market Imperfections: Dumping

Commercial policy might also be used to correct economic distortions existing abroad. One such possible argument stems from the technological gap explanation of trade in new products (see Chapter 3). If research and development expenditures are correlated both with monopoly power and with export strength, there may be a case for a tariff to protect would-be domestic manufacturers of new products from competition by foreign monopolists enjoying the advantages of an earlier start. But, first, if the advantage of an early start is as considerable as the technological gap explanation implies, the required tariff might have to be unacceptably high.[22] Second, if the new product is produced under patent protection, as in most cases it would be, in addition to restricting imports the country would have to opt out of the international patent system—a drastic step. Third, a domestic production subsidy would be better, although the last drawback mentioned applies to a subsidy as well.

Another case for tariffs on grounds of foreign market imperfections is the popular antidumping argument. This argument can be valid or not depending on how dumping is defined. **Dumping** is generally understood as selling in foreign markets below cost of production. *Persistent dumping is* quite different in its motivations and probable effects from *sporadic* (occasional) *dumping.* Sporadic dumping, in turn, can be *predatory dumping,* or *distress dumping.* There is a possible valid case for tariffs to combat sporadic dumping, although the argument differs depending on whether the predatory or the distress variety is alleged to exist.

Predatory dumping occurs when the foreign seller incurs deliberate losses in the attempt to drive his competitors out of business and eventually to acquire a monopoly with the ensuing higher prices and profits. Economic theory is firmly in support of preventing such an occurrence, and second-best tariffs or quotas may be justified on these grounds. The argument must, however, pass several tests before it is accepted in practice. First, the dumping must be verified as being truly of the predatory variety. Although there can be no absolute proof of motive, a finding that the commodity is being sold at less than *marginal* cost, i.e., at a loss, justifies the predatory inference. Second, there must be a concrete danger that the dumping practice will in fact succeed in its monopolizing purpose. If in the policy-makers' best judgment the danger of future monopoly is remote, it is far better to allow the foreign seller to lose his shirt in the attempt to acquire it. Considering the enormous size of the U.S. economy, it would be unusual (though not inconceivable) for a foreign firm to try to wipe out all its competition. In this

---

[22] For example, it took shocks of extraordinary magnitude to launch synthetic rubber and synthetic fabrics on a commercially feasible scale. The U.S. synthetic rubber industry, in particular, would not have come into being, and certainly not when it did, were it not for the urgent necessity during World War II to overcome the cutoff from supplies of natural rubber.

country a claim of predatory dumping ought to be greeted with some skepticism. Third, one must weigh the *certain* costs of the tariff against the *possible* costs of a future foreign monopoly.[23]

Distress dumping originates from honest mistakes or bad luck of foreign producers. Faulty production planning or unforeseen changes in market conditions may lead to overproduction and consequently to selling below original cost. While this is unquestionably a boon to importers—akin to distress sales or "going out of business" sales by a department store—it must be recognized that it may cause serious instability on the domestic market, with real costs from having to move resources in and out of the activity being "dumped on." A temporary tariff might protect the domestic industry against such instability (although it would also keep domestic consumers from taking advantage of an unusual bargain). It remains to be seen whether commercial policies could be used with the flexibility and timeliness implied by the argument.

There is instead no valid economic case for trade restriction to combat persistent dumping. Systematic selling abroad at a lower price than at home has a perfectly sound economic rationale. The elasticity of demand for a product in the world market is normally higher than it is in the domestic market, owing to the greater availability of substitutes from other sources of supply. There are cheaper substitutes for Toyotas in the U.S. market than in Japan. It is quite normal for an exporter who follows the profit-maximizing rules of the game to charge a higher price to home buyers than he can get away with in foreign markets. Since by doing so he is maximizing short-run profits, there is no inference of predatory intentions; and since he does so on a systematic (persistent) basis, there is no case for alleging market disruption either. Indeed, a claim for trade restriction to combat persistent dumping probably ought to be classified among the nonsense arguments for protection.

However, the unfortunate reality of antidumping tariffs, in all countries, is characterized by a lack of clarity on the meaning of dumping and by the indiscriminate use of the argument to justify restrictions in all sorts of quite different trading situations. In the United States, antidumping trade legislation dates back to 1921, and the 1974 Trade Act provides that, if it is found that the purchase price of imported goods is "less than the foreign market value" and that the domestic industry is being "injured," tariffs or other restrictions may be imposed on imports of those goods. It may be noted that the 1974 Trade Act also contains separate provisions to combat "unfair

[23] The 1974 Trade Act contains special provisions against predatory dumping, under the heading of "Unfair Import Practices." If it is determined that there exist "unfair methods of competition and unfair acts in the importation of articles into the U.S., . . . with the effect or tendency . . . to destroy or substantially injure an industry, efficiently and economically operated, in the U.S., or to prevent the establishment of such an industry, or to restrain or monopolize trade and commerce in the U.S. . . .," the articles concerned may be altogether excluded from entry into the country.

import practices," which clearly apply to instances of predatory dumping, as well as provisions to prevent "market disruption" from socialist countries' exports. Accordingly, one wonders if there is much of an economic case left for the antidumping provisions themselves.

Government-induced Distortions

If the fulfillment of some public purpose requires the introduction of certain distortions into the economy, there is a general case for corrective measures, subject to the general preference for offsetting the distortion in the same manner and in the same country in which it originates. Thus, if an *internal* sales tax on a product is established, for fiscal or other reasons, it is certainly sensible to provide domestic producers of it with an equivalent offsetting advantage. This practice, permitted under international rules, is termed an **import equalization tax.** However, the case rests on *differential* internal taxation, for only in such a case will a specific domestic industry be at a disadvantage relative to the other domestic activities. If, instead, the internal sales tax is uniform on all products, the allocation of resources among domestic economic activities is no different than it would be in the absence of the tax and, presuming the existence of a financial mechanism to assure equilibrium in the overall balance of payments, there is no valid case for protecting the import-competing industry. Furthermore, even when the import equalization tax is warranted, determination of the actual rate that exactly offsets the distortion is in practice quite difficult,[24] and the application of such a measure is correspondingly subject to contention. Still, with these qualifications, the argument is a valid one.

There is also a conceivable case for **countervailing duties** on imports when the foreign sellers' government subsidizes the commodity in question. This case parallels the antidumping justification. The duty is justified only if the foreign subsidy is predatory or if it causes market disruption. If the subsidy is instead persistent, the country simply obtains the product cheaper and gains, not loses, from this gift of foreign governments to domestic consumers. As L. B. Yeager and D. G. Tuerck emphasize,[25] the reason foreign goods are cheap is generally irrelevant to whether domestic consumers should be permitted to take advantage of a bargain, provided that this reason is not due to *domestic* distortions, whether built-in or government-induced.

The Infant Industry Argument

With the possible exception of the resource inflow argument, all of the principal tariff justifications discussed so far are framed in static terms and claim

---

[24] The difficulty is that a portion of the internal sales tax can normally be shifted to consumers, so that an import equalization tax equal to the sales tax will in fact overcompensate and effectively introduce a distortion of its own.

[25] *Trade Policy and the Price System* (Scranton, Pa.: International Textbook, 1966).

trade restriction to be beneficial within the context of *currently available* resources and technology. Also, the case for tariffs to correct economic distortions is the only exception up to now to the rule that trade restrictions are costly from the standpoint of the world economy as a whole. (The optimum tariff argument is not an exception; it is valid strictly from the viewpoint of the individual country.)

The infant industry justification for tariffs is a rationale characterized by both dynamic considerations and possible validity for the international economy as a whole. The argument has been traced by Jacob Viner back to the mid-seventeenth century and has been propounded in the eighteenth century by Alexander Hamilton in America; in the nineteenth century by John Stuart Mill in England, Jean-Baptiste Say in France, Friedrich List in Germany; and in contemporary times particularly by economists interested in the economic prospects and problems of less developed countries. Unlike in the case of the crude nonsense arguments, the historical persistence of the infant industry case is founded on a scholarly recognition of its considerable merit. The argument is also widely applicable and provides a theoretical underpinning to policies of **import substitution** (replacement of imports with domestic production), followed with varying degrees of success by many less developed countries.

As noted in Chapter 3, the principle of comparative advantage also has a dynamic dimension. Countries can acquire or lose a comparative advantage in an industry as a result of changes in demand, technology, and factor endowments. Some of these changes can be brought about as a result of conscious policy decisions. The analytical and policy questions are thus interrelated. For example, suppose that manufacturing of watches needs relatively large amounts of labor skilled in tasks requiring great manual accuracy and that such labor is *currently* relatively scarce in the country. If the conditions for the Heckscher-Ohlin explanation of trade hold, the country has a comparative disadvantage in that industry and imports watches. It is true that by specializing in other activities the country as a whole gains, and interference with the free importation of watches would normally cause the allocation of present-day resources to be less efficient. But suppose that the long-term prospects for watches on the international market are much more promising than for the country's current exports [26] and that a large segment of the labor force is *potentially* highly skilled in the required tasks. There may be a valid argument that specialization according to the current structure of comparative advantage, while maximizing static efficiency of resource allocation, is not the best policy for economic growth and efficiency in the long run. Accordingly, protection of the "infant" domestic industry

[26] This translates into the statement that the long-term income elasticity of demand is greater. The income elasticity of demand measures the degree of responsiveness of the quantity demanded to a change in income. A highly income-elastic product will thus face highly favorable market prospects as the world economy expands.

may be a means to foster the development of the required labor skills and to acquire a comparative advantage in watch manufacturing at some future time.[27]

The argument is really no different from one of the well-known reasons for attending college. The best *short-term* policy for a young person is certainly to specialize in the activity of current comparative advantage, perhaps gas-station attendant, typist, or check-out clerk. But, depending on the circumstances of the specific case, the best long-term policy *may* be to sacrifice a portion of current income in order to obtain advanced training in, for example, engineering and hopefully to acquire a comparative advantage in that field, leading to higher total income over one's lifetime.

Whether import restrictions are justified on infant industry grounds depends on several factors. *First,* the "infant" must have a reasonable chance to grow up strong. The prospective student must realistically assess the chances of getting a solid engineering degree. There must be some evidence, besides mere wishing, that the industry being protected will experience significant productivity increases, that it will in fact "learn by doing."

Second, there must be a reasonable expectation that the future economic advantages from getting an engineering degree are greater than the direct costs of attending school and the sacrifice in current income.[28] There are losses from import restriction, which obviously continue as long as the restriction is in place. Even if the protective policy accomplishes the stated purpose, it is not justified unless the cumulative gains after the acquisition of a new comparative advantage are greater than the cumulative losses from import restriction during the period of infancy.[29]

Third, there must be some reason why the industry in question needs society's assistance to grow and is not willing to invest its own resources in the learning process. If the industry can grow and become competitive, and if by

---

[27] There can also be a "macroeconomic" version of the argument when the infant industry rationale is applied not to a specific activity, but to the entire industrial sector of a less developed country. This version is intimately linked to the *balanced growth* view of economic development, according to which a poor country cannot break out of its poverty unless it engages in a large-scale program of simultaneous investments in a number of related activities. (See also the discussion of multiple exchange rates in Chapter 13.)

[28] The relevance of this framework for problems of higher education is apparent. The benefits of advanced training are related to the probability of finding a job in that field and to the salary advantage that occupation carries over present employment. The costs of training include both the direct cost of college and the income sacrificed by going to school. Other things being equal, any development that results in lower expected future benefits (such as a surfeit of people in the chosen activity) or in higher current costs (such as tuition increases) makes it less likely that an individual will choose to try and acquire training in the new field.

[29] Since the greater part of the costs and all of the benefits occur in the future, both costs and benefits should be discounted at some rate appropriate to the economy as a whole.

doing so the advantages to the investor are greater than the costs, the private interests that will reap the eventual benefits can certainly be expected to shoulder the costs as well. Granting of protection in such a case would simply be "gravy," an expensive toy for the pampered infant rather than the blanket needed to shelter him from the cold. Thus, there must be some evidence that some of the dynamic benefits made possible by protection would accrue to the economy as a whole and not be fully internal to the activity being protected. If this is true, then it may be that the share of the benefits going to the private sector is not sufficient to induce private investment in that activity, and a valid case exists for implicitly subsidizing the activity through restriction of competition from abroad.[30]

Fourth, the often-mentioned general superiority of direct subsidies over trade restrictions applies here as well. If the efficiency loss from diverting resources to a sector where they are currently less efficient is the unavoidable price to pay for future productivity increases, a direct subsidy can at least avoid the net welfare loss to consumers of the product.

Practical considerations are relevant, too. Since it is difficult to identify in advance which new industries are promising infants and which ones will remain forever retarded, protection granted on infant industry grounds often turns out after the fact to have been a mistake. It is because of the inherently speculative nature of the case that the infant industry argument is one of the most frequently used and abused in commercial policy pleading. For who can prove conclusively before the fact that any given activity does not have the potential to acquire a future comparative advantage? And if the protection given to the industry turns out not to lead to productivity gains, who can say with certainty that this was not due to the fact that the tariff was not *high enough?* Or that it was not maintained for *long enough?* This last hitch is the source of the second major practical problem with infant industry protection. The logic of the argument clearly calls for *temporary* protection. Yet, it is far easier to establish a tariff on a specific product than to remove it. Industries, like infants, become very attached to their

---

[30] As Harry G. Johnson stated it: "What is involved is an investment in a process of acquisition of knowledge which is socially profitable but privately unprofitable because the private investor cannot appropriate the whole of the social return from the investment" ("A New View of the Infant Industry Argument," in *Studies in International Economics*, 1970). Strictly speaking, the case for infant industry protection ought thus to be distinct from a justification for protection or subsidy when the private investors lack foresight or cannot borrow sufficiently to finance the undertaking. The latter two circumstances—uncertainty and imperfect capital markets—fall under the heading of economic distortions. Arguments for direct or indirect subsidization thus may be valid but do not rest on the "pure" infant industry rationale. The reader might consider this hairsplitting. To an extent, it is. But if there is a valid case for protection, it is of some help to be clear as to just what the problem is, for then attention is focused on the need for development of alternative policy measures aimed directly at its source. (See also Chapter 7.)

security blankets, and a commercial policy measure designed to subsidize growth and eventual competitiveness may in time turn into just some more heating fuel for an economic hothouse.

Arguments for Trade Restriction: A Purist Assessment

It may help after this lengthy catalog of the main ingredients of commercial policy debates to draw together the considerations made in evaluating each argument and to provide a summary assessment of the case for restricting foreign trade. As has been shown, some arguments do not succeed even in establishing a preliminary case for tariffs or quotas. These include expansion of the market, keeping money at home, cheap foreign labor, scientific tariff, and the argument for tariffs to combat persistent dumping. All of the other arguments at least merit some consideration. The noneconomic and distributional arguments are in principle acceptable, although in practice their applicability is quite narrow. Trade restrictions on mercantilist grounds, while possibly useful from the individual country's standpoint, are rightly saddled with the connotation of economic warfare and are very hard to justify and use with impunity in an interdependent world. The arguments for tariffs or quotas to correct economic distortions are, instead, valid and defensible as second-best policies, provided of course that the distortion really exists. This is especially true of import equalization taxes, although the determination of the *rate* of duty is questionable. Finally, infant industry protection extends the valid antidistortion rationale to a dynamic context and is thus also justifiable, although with heavy qualifications, as a contribution to worldwide, as well as national, economic efficiency.

But, (1) *only* the antidistortion and infant industry arguments are acceptable if a necessary criterion is that the restriction of trade must enhance current or future efficiency and welfare in the *world* economy; and, (2) *only* the optimum tariff argument is acceptable if the criterion is that the restriction of trade must be the *optimal* policy for the stated purpose. Therefore, from a purist viewpoint, *trade restriction is never the optimal policy from the world's economy standpoint*, whatever the real or alleged objective it is purported to achieve. The next chapter will come down from these lofty heights (high time, too) to expand on some of the considerations made here and use the material of this and the previous chapter to arrive at some generalizations on the political economy of trade restrictions.

Appendix: *The Candlemakers' Petition* by Frédéric Bastiat

PETITION OF THE MANUFACTURERS OF CANDLES, WAX-LIGHTS, LAMPS, CANDLESTICKS, STREET LAMPS, SNUFFERS, EXTINGUISHERS, AND OF THE PRODUCERS OF OIL, TALLOW, RESIN, ALCOHOL, AND, GENERALLY, OF EVERYTHING CONNECTED WITH LIGHTING

To Messieurs the Members of the Chamber of Deputies.

GENTLEMEN,—You are on the right road. You reject abstract theories, and have little consideration for cheapness and plenty. Your chief care is the interest of the producer. You desire to protect him from foreign competition, and reserve the *national market* for *national industry.*

We are about to offer you an admirable opportunity of applying your . . . practice—your practice without theory and without principle.

We are suffering from the intolerable competition of a foreign rival, placed, it would seem, in a condition so far superior to ours for the production of light that he absolutely *inundates* our *national market* with it at a price fabulously reduced. The moment he shows himself our trade leaves us—all consumers apply to him; and a branch of native industry, having countless ramifications, is all at once rendered completely stagnant. This rival, who is no other than the sun, wages war to the knife against us. . . .

What we pray for is, that it may please you to pass a law ordering the shutting up of all windows, skylights, dormer-windows, outside and inside shutters, curtains, blinds, bull's-eyes; in a word, of all openings, holes, chinks, clefts, and fissures, by or through which the light of the sun has been in use to enter houses, to the prejudice of the meritorious manufactures with which we flatter ourselves we have accommodated our country—a country which, in gratitude, ought not to abandon us now to a strife so unequal.

We trust, Gentlemen, that you will not regard this our request as a satire, or refuse it without at least previously hearing the reasons which we have to urge in its support.

And, first, if you shut up as much as possible all access to natural light, and create a demand for artificial light, which of our French manufactures will not be encouraged by it?

If more tallow is consumed, then there must be more oxen and sheep; and, consequently, we shall behold the multiplication of meadows, meat, wool, hides, and, above all, manure, which is the basis and foundation of all agricultural wealth.

If more oil is consumed, then we shall have an extended cultivation of the poppy, of the olive, and of rape. These rich and exhausting plants will come at the right time to enable us to avail ourselves of the increased fertility which the rearing of additional cattle will impart to our lands. . . .

The same remark applies to navigation. Thousands of vessels will proceed

From *Fallacies of Protection* (London: Cassell, 1909), pp. 60–65.

to the whale fishery; and, in a short time, we shall possess a navy capable of maintaining the honour of France, and gratifying the patriotic aspirations of your petitioners, the undersigned candlemakers and others.

But what shall we say of the manufacture of *articles de Paris?* Henceforth you will behold gildings, bronzes, crystals, in candlesticks, in lamps, in lustres, in candelabra, shining forth, in spacious warerooms, compared with which those of the present day can be regarded but as mere shops.

No poor *resinier* from his heights on the seacoast, no coalminer from the depth of his sable gallery, but will rejoice in higher wages and increased prosperity.

Only have the goodness to reflect, Gentlemen, and you will be convinced that there is, perhaps, no Frenchman, from the wealthy coalmaster to the humblest vendor of lucifer matches, whose lot will not be ameliorated by the success of this our petition.

We foresee your objections, Gentlemen, but we know that you can oppose to us none but such as you have picked up from the effete works of the partisans of Free Trade. We defy you to utter a single word against us which will not instantly rebound against yourselves and your entire policy.

You will tell us that, if we gain by the protection which we seek, the country will lose by it, because the consumer must bear the loss.

We answer:

You have ceased to have any right to invoke the interest of the consumer; for, whenever his interest is found opposed to that of the producer, you sacrifice the former. You have done so for the purpose of *encouraging labour and increasing employment.* For the same reason you should do so again.

You have yourselves obviated this objection. When you are told that the consumer is interested in the free importation of iron, coal, corn, textile fabrics— yes, you reply, but the producer is interested in their exclusion. Well, be it so; if consumers are interested in the free admission of natural light, the producers of artificial light are equally interested in its prohibition. . . .

But, again, you may say that the producer and consumer are identical. If the manufacturer gain by protection, he will make the agriculturist also a gainer; and if agriculture prosper, it will open a vent to manufactures. Very well; if you confer upon us the monopoly of furnishing light during the day, first of all we shall purchase quantities of tallow, coals, oils, resinous substances, wax, alcohol —besides silver, iron, bronze, crystal—to carry on our manufactures; and then we, and those who furnish us with such commodities, having become rich will consume a great deal, and impart prosperity to all the other branches of our national industry.

If you urge that the light of the sun is a gratuitous gift of nature, and that to reject such gifts is to reject wealth itself under pretence of encouraging the means of acquiring it, we would caution you against giving a death-blow to your own policy. Remember that hitherto you have always repelled foreign products, *because* they approximate more nearly than home products to the character of gratuitous gifts. To comply with the exactions of other monopolists, you have only *half a motive;* and to repulse us simply because we stand on a stronger vantage-ground than others would be to adopt the equation $+ \times + = -$; in other words, it would be to heap *absurdity* upon *absurdity.* . . .

Once more, when products such as coal, iron, corn, or textile fabrics are sent us from abroad, and we can acquire them with less labour than if we made them ourselves, the difference is a free gift conferred upon us. The gift is more or less considerable in proportion as the difference is more or less great. It amounts to a quarter, a half, or three-quarters of the value of the product, when the foreigner only asks us for three-fourths, a half, or a quarter of the price we should otherwise pay. It is as perfect and complete as it can be, when the donor (like the sun in furnishing us with light) asks us for nothing. The question, and we ask it formally, is this: Do you desire for our country the benefit of gratuitous consumption, or the pretended advantages of onerous production? Make your choice, but be logical; for as long as you exclude, as you do, coal, iron, corn, foreign fabrics, *in proportion* as their price approximates to *zero,* what inconsistency it would be to admit the light of the sun, the price of which is already at *zero* during the entire day!

Points for Review

1. Review your understanding of the logical certainty of the gains-from-trade principle when the theoretical assumptions hold.

2. Which three tests are to be applied to the evaluation of an argument for restricting trade?

3. The fallacy of composition appears in several arguments for protection. Which ones?

4. There is a sense in which each of the nonsense arguments for trade restriction has possible merit. Review the similarity and the main difference between each crude argument and its more respectable variant.

5. Is there anything scientific about the scientific tariff?

6. Think up some possible connection between the Hollywood movie industry and the nation's military needs. Is there a *conceivable* military security case for restricting imports of foreign films? Is there a *valid* case?

7. Is there a conceivable cultural-sociological argument for restricting imports of foreign films?

8. In which general way do import tariffs affect the distribution of national income among persons, socioeconomic classes, and geographic regions? Is it theoretically justified to use tariffs for income redistribution purposes?

9. Review your understanding of the effect of trade on real wages. Does the effect depend on the country's relative factor endowments?

10. Which justifications for trade restrictions fall under the heading of mercantilist arguments? Why "mercantilist"?

11. What is meant by the statement that the optimum tariff argument is the only one that is not "second best"?

12. By the logic of the optimum tariff argument, tariffs should be eliminated if the supply of imports is perfectly elastic. Verify your understanding of this statement.

13. What is a tariff for bargaining? Under what conditions is there a valid case for establishing bargaining tariffs?

14. In T. Lampedusa's novel *The Leopard,* one of the characters says: "Don't you understand that everything must change in order for everything to remain the same?" Is government intervention to correct economic distortions in keeping with free-trade principles? In particular, is a trade restriction for that purpose ever consistent with such principles?

15. Review the Hagen argument that a tariff is needed to correct for insufficient mobility of resources between occupations.

16. If you knew nothing about the subject, you would very probably be sympathetic to an industry's request for commercial policies to combat foreign dumping. Yet, dumping means different things. Which types of dumping are possible justifications for policy intervention?

17. Import equalization taxes are justified. However, if an internal sales tax of 10 percent exists, a 10 percent import equalization tax can introduce a distortion of its own rather than simply correct for the impact of the sales tax. Is this true? If so, under what conditions?

18. What is the essence of the infant industry argument for protection?

19. Which are the four major theoretical considerations relevant to evaluating a claim for protection on infant industry grounds?

20. What are the two major practical difficulties with infant industry protection?

Questions for Discussion

1. Do you see a general similarity between the thrust of this chapter and the presumption of innocence in criminal law?

2. Could a foreign producer threatened by competition from more efficient U.S. producers request protection from his government on grounds of "American exploitation of cheap machines"?

3. Find current examples of use of the cheap labor argument by an American industry.

4. "A nation does not live by bread alone. Economic well being is only one of several national goals, and occasionally it needs to be sacrificed for the sake of more important things." Discuss this statement, on any grounds you deem relevant, and see whether you are really in agreement with the considerations made in the text concerning the noneconomic arguments for trade restriction. If not, try to pinpoint the source of the disagreement.

5. Construct a hypothetical situation in which the United States would be entirely cut off from all major foreign suppliers of strategic materials in case of military conflict.

6. The national security argument most often calls for restricting imports of strategic materials. The Byrd Amendment (repealed in early 1977) used the national security as grounds for nonparticipation by the United States in the United Nations boycott of Rhodesian chrome. Do you see any inconsistency?

7. Suppose that the *small* farm is considered part and parcel of the nation's historical and cultural fabric and needs to be preserved. Does it follow that imports of farm commodities should be restricted for that purpose? Would such restriction also benefit large agribusiness? Similarly, are small farmers the principal beneficiaries of policies to promote *exports* of farm commodities?

8. It is humanly and politically difficult to allow a domestic activity to disappear because of competition from more efficient foreign producers without any governmental action to alleviate the plight of those affected. Yet, any such action carries costs for some other persons or groups in society. Discuss this dilemma, if possible with specific reference to a declining industry you may be familiar with.

9. Would it be possible to claim that an import tariff could *both* significantly bolster domestic production in a declining sector and cause a sizeable improvement of the country's terms of trade?

10. In South Africa, the policy of *apartheid* means, among other things, that high-wage, high-status occupations are exclusively reserved for whites. How would you assess the validity of the Hagen argument under these circumstances?

11. Following the order of presentation of the discussion of the infant industry argument, evaluate the merits of the case for governmental subsidies to your college education.

12. For which general types of industries would protection on infant industry grounds be especially questionable?

13. Other things being equal, is the case for infant industry protection stronger if the country's private credit market functions badly? Would protection under these circumstances be justified on *strict* infant industry grounds? Is there a point to this last question, or is it mere academic nit-picking?

14. The last section of the chapter gives an overall assessment of the case for trade restriction. What is your own personal assessment? If you disagree, try to pinpoint the source of the difference and analyze the situation further.

"You tell me whar a man gits his corn pone, en I'll tell you what his 'pinions is."

Mark Twain

The Political Economy
of Trade Restriction

What to Expect

This chapter draws together some of the generalizations on the practice of commercial policy that emerge from the theoretical material presented in the previous chapters. These so-called "laws" of commercial policy have characterized the political economy of trade restrictions and are useful guideposts in evaluating concrete foreign trade issues. The chapter also expands on some of the points touched on earlier, particularly retaliation and the superiority of alternative policies over tariffs and quotas, and concludes with a personal assessment of the issue of free trade versus protection. The Appendix provides a customary lighter touch with *The Three Aldermen*, the third and last Bastiat piece included in the book.

The "Laws" of Commercial Policy

The following are not laws in the sense of natural laws, nor are they legal provisions of international treaties. These laws are simply broad statements of the main recurrent themes of commercial policy theory and practice. They may or may not apply in the specific instance. They have to be taken with several grains of salt, but they have characterized the political economy of trade restrictions in the past and will probably continue to be useful guideposts for the informed citizen's evaluation of foreign trade issues.

All Trade Restrictions Can Be Presumed to Be Costly
(Or: "Make *him* prove it.")

This point has been made repeatedly in the previous pages. Just remember that it is not freedom of foreign trade that needs to be defended. The shoe is most definitely on the other foot. The burden of proof is on those who advocate trade restrictions.

One's Views on Foreign Trade Issues are Largely a
Function of One's Economic Interests
(Or: "Tell me what you do, and I'll tell you
where you stand.")

No assertion of inevitable correspondence between material interests and ideology is intended here.[1] It is, nevertheless, generally true that protection-

---

[1] The notion that the economic structure determines all aspects of ideology and culture originated with Karl Marx and is termed **historical materialism**.

ist views emerge from individuals or groups who stand to gain from restriction and free trade views from those who are associated with export industries. The theory surveyed earlier can yield useful preliminary guesses as to the probable attitude of different groups on foreign trade issues. For example, in a country characterized by relative scarcity of labor and relative abundance of capital, the return to labor tends to increase through protection and the return to capital to increase through trade expansion. Trade unions are likely to argue for trade restriction and manufacturers' associations likely to propound free trade views. In the United States one finds this to be the case. The AFL-CIO is generally protectionist and has become increasingly so in recent years, arguing not only for restriction of imports but also for discouraging certain types of exports. The AFL-CIO thus opposed passage of the 1974 Trade Act on the avowed grounds that it did not have a sufficient protectionist content. Conversely, the National Association of Manufacturers supported passage of the act, albeit guardedly, and with sympathetic nods in the direction of the interests of those of its members who were threatened by import competition.

Theory would lead to the expectation that products intensive in the relatively scarce factor would tend to be protected from imports to a relatively greater extent. Again, this is generally the case for this country. R. E. Caves and R. W. Jones have found that, with the exception of the most highly protected industries, there is a positive correlation between labor intensity and the height of the tariff; there is also a correlation between low wages and high protection, indicating that higher tariffs apply to products intensive in low-skill labor, precisely the factor that is in greatest *relative* scarcity in the United States.[2]

It would also be reasonable to presume protectionist sentiment to be stronger in depressed areas than in growing regions, since the depressed areas are likely to be characterized by a relatively high concentration of both declining industries and factors of production that are used intensively in those industries. Finally, a corollary of the proposition that a country's commercial policy is partly a function of its economic structure is the expectation that such policy will change as the structure of the economy changes. For example, free trade advocates were practically considered British agents in the protectionist climate of early nineteenth century France, the same country that was to become a major force for free international commerce a few decades later in correspondence with the growing export orientation of the economy.

---

[2] *World Trade and Payments: An Introduction* (Boston: Little, Brown, 1973), pp. 285–86.

Trade Expansion Benefits Large Numbers of People
by a Small Amount; Import Restriction Benefits a
Smaller Number of People by a Greater Amount
(Or: "There are more of 'us' than there are of 'them'.")

Tariffs harm the importers and benefit the import-competing domestic producers. In most cases, and certainly in the case of consumer goods, the number of buyers is much larger than the number of domestic sellers. Thus, while the overall losses from trade restriction outweigh the gains, the benefit accruing to the individual seller is likely to be substantial, and the loss suffered by the individual buyer is likely to be small. Accordingly, the tariff benefits are generally also more visible than its costs. This point is crucial to an understanding of why tariffs persist, at higher levels and on more articles than can possibly be explained on the basis of justifiable national interests and economic considerations. Consumers are unlikely to become upset enough about a tariff causing a 5 percent increase in the price of a Japanese color TV set to do something about it. But for a domestic producer of TV sets a 5 percent price increase might spell the difference between bankruptcy and prosperity, and it certainly means a substantial economic gain. This is a powerful reason for the domestic producer to invest time and money to lobby in favor of the tariff. At any one time, therefore, and for any given industry in which imports are significant, there is likely to exist a net political pressure in favor of protection. With the growth of organized consumer groups, this state of affairs has been somewhat altered, but there is a long way to go before the lobbying balance will come to reflect the overall gains and losses from tariffs.

Why then are tariffs not much *higher* than they are, if it is true that elected politicians face severe penalties when they incur the hostility of strong protectionist interests and reap little or no political advantage from resisting those interests?[3] The best single answer is that significant tariff reductions *can* be accomplished if they are across the board and negotiated with other nations, for in such a case the *overall* gains and losses of tariffs become apparent and the powerful pressures for restrictions can be offset by countervailing pressures for trade liberalization coming from manufacturers of articles for export. By the same token, it is unlikely for a country unilaterally to reduce its import restrictions. It is true that just because the "going" is difficult is no reason for not making the "coming" easier, but political realities indicate that serious efforts at liberalizing foreign trade must in general be made in the context of negotiations with the country's

[3] W. Krause has made the important point that Congressmen, who are elected on a local basis, are naturally more responsive to local interests than to national economic concerns. (*International Economics* [Boston: Houghton-Mifflin, 1965], p. 134.)

trade partners and be aimed at reciprocal reductions of foreign tariffs on the country's own exports.

The Weaker the Argument, the Stronger the Language (Or: "When they have no case, they yell like hell.")

The semantics of debates on international trade issues have often relied on fiery and emotional terms from international politics or war. Ralph Waldo Emerson said: "A good symbol is the best argument and is a missionary to persuade thousands." In general, the more objectionable the policy practice, the more flowery the language used to describe it; and the more successful the trade, the more obnoxious the words used to characterize it. This industry needs a tariff because it is being gravely "injured" by "unreasonable" or "unfair" foreign practices. That industry is at a disadvantage because of foreign "exploitation" of labor. Another industry is complaining of being "dumped on." The country's economy is "under attack," and is being "inundated" by an "invasion" of foreign products. In the 1930s, Mussolini, the Italian Fascist dictator, launched the "Battle of Wheat," a program of severe restrictions of wheat imports under the slogan "Italians must be freed from the slavery of foreign bread!" Can you just see a giant loaf of pumpernickel dragging 50 million suffering Italians in chains? (As historian Gaetano Salvemini later pointed out, Mussolini won the battle and the Italians lost the wheat.)

At the same time, very appealing terms have been invented to describe some highly questionable measures. The outstanding example is, of course, the "scientific" tariff. More recently, the very objectionable practice of blackmailing a foreign country into limiting its exports has graduated from "voluntary export restriction" (already a misleading term) to "orderly marketing arrangement"! It is wise to be leery of arguments that rely heavily on terms such as "fair," "just," "reasonable," particularly if they start with the phrase "I am entirely in favor of free trade, but . . . ," for it is very common to praise the virtues of free trade even as one is arguing in favor of effectively burying it.

A variant on the theme of the use of language to promote commercial vested interests is the frequent merger of different, and usually mutually contradictory, arguments for protection. Examples can be found in the record of virtually every congressional hearing on tariff bills. One notable argument is the 1908 statement by the magnesite industry during the hearings on the Payne-Aldrich tariff bill, which managed to hit *six* different birds with one stone. The industry requested tariff protection because expensive American labor was needed to mine the new deposits found in California and because land transport of the material was expensive, while the Greek producers enjoyed the advantages of *cheap labor* and *lower transport costs*. Also, protection was needed to allow the *infant industry* to develop. If no tariff were imposed, the United States would become *totally dependent* on foreign suppliers of magnesite. Not only that, but the consumers would eventually be charged *high prices*. Of course, the U.S. *balance of payments* would suffer, too.

Whatever You Do to Other Countries, They May Be Able to Do to You
(Or: "Don't throw stones at your neighbors' if your own windows are glass.")

The possibility of retaliation has been mentioned several times in the discussion of mercantilist arguments for protection. From a strictly economic viewpoint, one can assume that a country *would* pursue a mercantilist, beggar-my-neighbor, policy course if it thought that it could get away with it or considered that it would end up better off even if other countries did retaliate. Major instances of retaliation in postwar economic relations among industrialized countries are very few. One could infer from this that economic interdependence among industrial countries has become too close for any nation to presume complete or even partial immunity from retaliation. The potential for retaliation is a stronger disincentive to mercantilist policies than the actuality of retaliation, for once the process is set in motion all the participants have in a sense already lost.[4] It is also important, as R. M. Stern has noted, that such retaliatory actions as have occurred in recent years have been restrained by the existence of internationally agreed upon rules of policy behavior.

One should not forget that nations have international political objectives as well as economic ones. Nasty commercial behavior toward one's allies entails far more than the risk of an eventual reduction of one's exports. It can compromise or even destroy a very delicate edifice of military, political, and diplomatic cooperation, as well as economic cooperation in other areas. As a major example of the link between commercial policy and international political issues, consider the importance attached by the Soviet Union to receiving from the United States the same tariff treatment as other countries (the so-called "most-favored nation" treatment, discussed in Chapter 8), and the serious political repercussions when the "Jackson amendment" to the legislation made such treatment contingent on the Soviet Union liberalizing its emigration rules. (See the Appendix to Chapter 8.) It is probably no accident that the two major postwar instances of retaliation occurred in the same year, 1962, and involved the same protagonists, the United States and the European Common Market.[5] At that time, under

---

[4] The 1974 Trade Act gives the President substantial retaliatory powers "to assure a swift response to foreign import restrictions and price discrimination."

[5] The United States started the first, by increasing tariffs on carpets and glass on the grounds of injury to the domestic industry; the Common Market retaliated by raising their

the French leadership of General de Gaulle, relations between Europe and the United States were in a state of flux, and the tension inherent in any reassessment of political roles partly spilled over into the commercial policy arena.

Almost Anything a Restriction of Trade Can
Accomplish, Some Other Policy Can Accomplish at
Less Cost
(Or: "There must be a better way.")

With the exception of economic warfare, import equalization taxes, and the optimum tariff, the discussion of arguments for protection has included statements about the superiority of policies other than trade restrictions to accomplish the desired purpose. It is time to explain and expand on those statements.

Effective economic policy-making follows a few simple, but fundamental, principles. A *first* rule states that the number of different available *instruments* of policy must at least equal the number of different policy *objectives* being sought.[6] A *second* rule states that a given instrument of economic policy should be used in pursuit of the objective for which it is best suited. *Third*, when successful achievement of one objective is conditional upon prior achievement of some other goal, the various policies should be implemented in the appropriate sequence.

Perhaps a metaphor will help to explain. By the first rule, if you set two targets for your weekend renovating activities, scraping the living room ceiling and refinishing its floor, you need at least two instruments, in this case a scraper and a sander. If you have only one tool, you cannot accomplish both objectives effectively. If you have more than two, say the scraper and two kinds of sanding machines, there is more than one way in which to do the two jobs well. The second rule says something even more obvious: You should use the scraper to scrape the ceiling and the sander to sand the floor—each instrument to achieve the objective for which it is best suited.

---

tariffs on some U.S. exports. In the second instance, the Common Market started the "Chicken War" by applying higher tariffs to chickens, an article of major export interest to the United States; the United States retaliated by imposing equivalent restrictions on European products.

[6] This is known as the **Tinbergen Rule,** named after the Nobel prize-winning Dutch economist, Jan Tinbergen (see his *On the Theory of Economic Policy* [Amsterdam: North Holland Publishing, 1952]). Mathematically, there is one single solution when the number of independent equations is the same as the number of endogenous variables; there is more than one solution when the number of equations exceeds the number of variables; and none when there are more variables than independent equations. All of this assumes that the various objectives are not mutually inconsistent. If they are inconsistent, as for example when maximum labor productivity *and* maximum employment are sought at the same time, then no policies exist that can achieve them all.

Finally, by the third rule, it makes sense to scrape the ceiling first, in order not to have to sweep and vacuum the floor more than once.

The second rule is the one most closely applicable to an examination of the efficiency of trade restriction policies. In general, the best instrument for a given policy objective is the one that directly influences that objective. Of course any policy has indirect repercussions somewhere else in the economy, but it is preferable to take your chances with undesirable secondary effects than to use a roundabout policy that has unwanted *primary* effects. As has been seen, most of the arguments for trade restriction justify tariffs on grounds of their effect on *one* domestic variable, whether consumption, production, income distribution, or whatever. But trade policy has a direct effect only on trade and several indirect influences on the domestic economy. A restriction of trade affects indiscriminately production, consumption, income distribution, government revenue, and so forth, regardless of which one among these variables it is intended to influence.

Direct intervention on the target variable would, instead, have only secondary, indirect repercussions elsewhere. If, for example, the protective effect is the goal, it is more sensible to choose a policy aimed directly at increasing domestic production rather than a tariff bludgeon that indiscriminately affects all sorts of other things as well. If a drunk and disorderly person in an otherwise peaceful demonstration starts bashing in shop windows, the optimum policy response is to pick him out of the crowd and carry him off in a paddy wagon, not to arrest everybody in sight, including that person. In both cases the problem is solved. But the cost of the selective solution, aimed directly at the source of the disturbance, is usually lower than the cost of the indirect solution.[7]

As noted when examining the various arguments, in most cases the objective sought can be better accomplished by some appropriate combination of internal taxes and subsidies. Subsidies for infant industry or national security purposes, progressive taxation or regional development programs for income redistribution purposes, fiscal and monetary policies for income and balance-of-payments objectives, a mix of internal taxes and subsidies to correct economic distortions—all of these direct measures are in principle preferable to policies restricting foreign trade.

The superiority of subsidies over tariffs, in particular, needs a few special words. *First*, there is a question of simple equity at stake. The objective sought may be a gain for some specific group in society, but to deserve *national* policy attention it must somehow be accepted as a *national* goal. As you know, it is domestic consumers who pay for that portion of the

---

[7] The principle is important enough to deserve a second illustration. If before a race a horse is feloniously injected with a depressant drug by a competing trainer, there is a strong case for a measure to correct the "distortion." But if the horse in question is given an antidote, the distortion is corrected in the most direct way; if all other horses are injected with the same drug, the distortion is also corrected, *and* you get a dull race.

tariff that is not successfully shifted on to foreign sellers. It is contrary to simple fiscal justice to pursue a national goal at the expense of only a segment of the population. If the purpose is a national one, it should be financed on a national basis, i.e., through general taxation.

Second, subsidies are superior because they do not cause an increase in the price to consumers, and they thus avoid the net welfare loss caused by trade restriction. They do not, however, avoid the efficiency loss. The rise in domestic production does require channeling resources away from presumably more efficient economic activities, and it entails the same net loss in efficiency for the economy as a whole as an equivalent tariff.[8]

Third, direct subsidies are politically more wholesome. They are far more visible than the indirect subsidy implied by tariffs or quotas. They are subject to systematic periodic review, since they usually depend on annual appropriation of funds, whereas tariffs or quotas easily linger on long after any consensus on their use has disappeared. The beneficiaries of direct subsidies are more sharply defined, and the costs to the citizenry are far clearer and more measurable. On these grounds, direct subsidies are more likely than trade restrictions to correspond to a genuine social consensus. Unfortunately, these are also excellent reasons why vested interests and their political allies tend to prefer the indirect, but equally real, advantages of trade restriction. Contrast, for example, the justifiably heated controversy in 1972 over the mere federal *guarantee* of a $250 million private loan to the Lockheed corporation with the comparative lack of public understanding and concern over the far greater subsidies implied by the recently terminated oil import quotas.

In Chapter 5 we came down rather hard on quotas and their potential for corruption and abuse. A similar criticism can be made of direct subsidies. While there are problems inherent in the administration of tariffs, they are in all probability swamped by the bureaucratic maze created by the administration of direct subsidies on a vast scale and by the enormous possibilities for favoritism, corruption, and uncertainty. All in all, however, direct subsidies are economically and politically preferable to trade restriction for almost any purpose that restriction is alleged to have.

This is all well and good. But what if the theoretically optimal policy is in practice not available or does not work well? What if you do not have a sander or the one you have breaks down? If the job is important enough to you to justify the fatigue and inconvenience, you have no practical choice but to make do with scraping the floor by hand. You won't do a very good

---

[8] Referring back to Figure 5.1, the granting of a subsidy can be depicted by an increase in total domestic supply (a shift of S_d rightward) by a vertical distance equal to the amount of subsidy. It can readily be verified that for any given tariff or quota there is a subsidy that yields an equivalent effect on domestic production without causing a price increase.

Free
Trade
versus
Protection:
A
Personal
Assessment

job, and it will cost you considerably more effort, but if these drawbacks are realistically assessed, it is your privilege to go ahead and use a less-than-optimal instrument. Second-best tariffs and quotas are used. A major reason is that the optimal alternative policies are not available or are not practicable for any number of possible concrete reasons. Thus, subsidization of an infant industry may be entirely out of the question when a government budget deficit coexists with strong public opposition to the raising of general taxes. There may be no choice in practice, if the infant industry is to be protected, other than to do so through commercial policy. Or, suppose that the country's tax collection apparatus is ineffective. To be sure, the logical response should be to improve it sufficiently so that an increase in "paper taxes" corresponds to an increase in taxes collected. But in the meantime, if the objective is deemed worthwhile, tariffs or quotas may be the only instrument to achieve it.

You should not infer from this that the theoretical considerations on choice of policies are in any sense irrelevant when the optimal instruments are not available. A clear sense of the "ideal" course of action is a pre-requisite (not by itself sufficient, of course, but necessary) for future improvements in the range and functioning of economic policy instruments. Thus, as was seen earlier, commercial policies have almost entirely ceased to be used for national income and employment purposes. This clearly favorable development could not have occurred if the theoretical demonstration of the superiority of fiscal policies for those purposes had not provided the stimulus for improving their use and establishing appropriate institutional mechanisms to implement them. Similarly, the continuing use of tariffs and quotas for balance-of-payments reasons is related to the imperfect functioning of the international monetary system. But in turn, the realization that the optimal response to international *financial* disequilibria is international *financial* policy and not trade restriction is an effective spur to persist in efforts to improve the international monetary merchanism.

Free Trade versus Protection:
A Personal Assessment

In a well-known work of some years ago, L. B. Yeager and D. G. Tuerck assert that

. . . statements favoring free trade are extremely rare in textbooks of international economics. Practically all the texts canvassed avoid a clear-cut position. Quite a few authors straightforwardly analyze the gains from trade, show that each of the leading protectionist arguments is either wrong or of very limited applicability, clearly imply that the freer trade is

*the better, drop hints of personal preference for freer trade, but stop short
of flatly declaring for* free *trade.*[9]

Yeager and Tuerck criticize this timidity and make some telling points
in the process. Some of the conceivably valid justifications for tariffs are
indeed "theoretical curiosities." It is true that some of the exceptions to
free trade (such as the optimum tariff argument) have gotten too little
attention in the past but are probably getting to much now. The second-
best case for protection does suffer from the basic failing of being unable
to demonstrate just what level of protection does the job. And, yes, some
economists do compromise their views in an attempt to be politically
"realistic." These are thoughtful warnings of the real intellectual and political
dangers of "bending over backward," and, when they do apply, the Yeager
and Tuerck criticism is well taken.

But this author too will stop short of flatly declaring for free trade.
Awareness of the protectionist debating gimmick of pretending that free
trade propositions depend for their validity on a set of highly specific circumstances does not automatically demonstrate that the specific circumstances are never relevant. The exceptions may well be practically insignificant for certain countries and under certain historical conditions, while
so numerous elsewhere or at another time as to forbid a universal dogmatic
position.

We have been at pains to stress that the analysis in this book purposely
excludes afterthought commentary on problems of trade and economic development, to which it does not *necessarily* provide answers. The theoretical
conclusions depend to a great extent on the validity of the assumptions and,
mainly, a static context and reasonably well-functioning markets. If the
deviation from those conditions is minor, one is certainly justified in demand-
ing a fairly clear-cut stance in favor of free trade. If the deviation is extensive, the conclusion *must* be more ambiguous. The same "it depends"
attitude that can legitimately be criticized in the context of, for example,
North Atlantic trade, is the only possible intellectual course in the context
of foreign trade of less developed countries, where market imperfections
are pretty much the rule rather than the exception, where externalities are
an everyday economic reality instead of a theoretical curiosity, where efficient
allocation of current resources ranks much lower in priority than economic
development and *may* under certain circumstances be in conflict with it,
where disregard of income distribution considerations may result in blood-
shed and national disintegration.

Also the symbiosis between commercial policy and foreign policy in
general precludes a simple clear-cut recommendation with respect to either.
In a sense, a flat advice of unilateral declaration of complete free trade is as

[9] *Trade Policy and the Price System* (Scranton, Pa.: International Textbook, 1966),
p. 277.

Free
Trade
versus
Protection:
A
Personal
Assessment

romantic as early twentieth century political internationalism. While both have the merit of stubborn insistence on the right ultimate course of action, each has the mortal failing of focusing on only one facet of what is a "package" of interdependent policies. It would be very hard, for example, to view European trade liberalization as isolated from political integration objectives, or extension of nondiscriminatory commercial treatment to the Soviet Union as an issue separate from the general context of *détente*. The political coloration given to international economic issues may perhaps be decried (although, on the contrary, we believe that it has *helped* in recent years to liberalize international trade); or complete freedom in commercial policy may conceivably be viewed as a prerequisite for the lessening of international tensions. But unqualified advice about a single component of the international policy package is made impossible by the fact that each component is in fact qualified by the existence of the others.

If in practice first-best policies are not available (as they often are not), and the human and social costs of reallocating resources out of declining industries are to be alleviated, a flat out free trade policy is not invulnerable to criticism. It is quite true, and *almost* of determining weight, that "of the hundreds of variables in modern business success or failure, a tariff concession is only one"; [10] that equally or more severe human hardships are caused by a myriad of economic changes that have nothing to do with foreign trade; that governments do break explicit or implicit commitments to domestic firms at least as often as they lower protective levels on domestic production; that, in a word, the plight of the worker displaced by the closing of a military base is no less serious, and no less deserving of assistance, than the plight of a worker displaced by a tariff reduction. Valid political distinctions must rest on whether a prior government commitment has been broken, whether the human hardship is likely to be effectively alleviated by private means (such as the ease of finding alternative employment), whether the public assistance is in fact likely to go to the intended beneficiaries. There is no tenable distinction on the basis of whether the hardship is caused by removal of tariffs or by some other governmental action.

Having admitted all this, however, one is still faced with the bottom line question. Are restrictions of trade justified in those instances when the human costs are real and better policy instruments impracticable? Yeager and Tuerck phrase the question in an incisive, if a bit overstated, manner:

Perhaps assistance really should be generalized. But let us face the issue and not misconceive it as narrower than it is. Do we really want the government to go beyond assuming responsibility for monetary stability and other parts of an overall framework for general prosperity? Do we want it, in addition, to take on increasingly detailed responsibility for either protect-

---

[10] James Robertson, "Adjustment Assistance under the Trade Expansion Act of 1962: A Will-O'-the-Wisp," *George Washington Law Review,* June 1965, p. 1103.

ing people against all sorts of dislocations or else guiding and financing their readjustments? [11]

Fair enough. Our answer is "Yes." In all questions of income distribution, value judgments eventually must be faced up to. This author's personal view is that in some instances, although considerably fewer than claimed by protectionist interests, deviations from free trade policy are morally and socially necessary.

Requests for protection should be received with an open heart and a very keen nose. A keen nose is needed to smell out of the multitude of pleadings those that have genuine merit on either economic or social grounds and to assure that trade restrictions are used only as a last-resort measure when better policies are not available. An open heart must be maintained toward the plight of those affected, but *also* toward the equally real interests of the faceless mass of people who are not participating directly in the debate. In most cases, granted, the protectionist pleading should be rejected. But to reject it outright, on the basis of economic fundamentalism rather than of economic analysis and socially legitimate considerations, unnecessarily prevents society and its political representatives from helping out in those cases when such assistance *would* correspond to a wide social consensus. A recommendation of *relatively free* trade permits an appropriately flexible policy; a recommendation of *free* trade does not. We prefer to stick with the former, even in the case of developed economies, and most certainly as regards the less developed countries.

[11] Yeager and Tuerck, *op. cit.*, p. 261.

Appendix: *The Three Aldermen*
by Frédéric Bastiat

A DEMONSTRATION IN FOUR TABLEAUX.

First Tableau.

[The scene is in the hotel of Alderman Pierre. The window looks out on a fine park; three persons are seated near a good fire.]

Pierre. Upon my word, a fire is very comfortable when the stomach is satisfied. It must be agreed that it is a pleasant thing. But, alas! how many worthy people like the King of Yvetot,

"Blow on their fingers for want of wood."

Unhappy creatures, Heaven inspires me with a charitable thought. You see these fine trees. I will cut them down and distribute the wood among the poor.

Paul and Jean. What! gratis?

Pierre. Not exactly. There would soon be an end of my good works if I scattered my property thus. I think that my park is worth twenty thousand livres; by cutting it down I shall get much more for it.

Paul. A mistake. Your wood as it stands is worth more than that in the neighboring forests, for it renders services which that cannot give. When cut down it will, like that, be good for burning only, and will not be worth a sou more per cord.

Pierre. Oh! Mr. Theorist, you forget that I am a practical man. I supposed that my reputation as a speculator was well enough established to put me above any charge of stupidity. Do you think that I shall amuse myself by selling my wood at the price of other wood?

Paul. You must.

Pierre. Simpleton! Suppose I prevent the bringing of any wood to Paris?

Paul. That will alter the case. But how will you manage it?

Pierre. This is the whole secret. You know that wood pays an entrance duty of ten sous per cord. To-morrow I will induce the Aldermen to raise this duty to one hundred, two hundred, or three hundred livres, so high as to keep out every fagot. Well, do you see? If the good people do not want to die of cold, they must come to my wood-yard. They will fight for my wood; I shall sell it for its weight in gold, and this well-regulated deed of charity will enable me to do others of the same sort.

Paul. This is a fine idea, and it suggests an equally good one to me.

Jean. Well, what is it?

Paul. How do you find this Normandy butter?

Jean. Excellent.

Paul. Well, it seemed passable a moment ago. But do you not think it is a little strong? I want to make a better article at Paris. I will have four or five hundred cows, and I will distribute milk, butter, and cheese to the poor people.

From *Sophisms of Protection*, second series (New York: Putnam, 1886), pp. 273–78.

Pierre and Jean. What! as a charity?

Paul. Bah, let us always put charity in the foreground. It is such a fine thing that its counterfeit even is an excellent card. I will give my butter to the people, and they will give me their money. Is that called selling?

Jean. But call it what you please, you ruin yourself. Can Paris compete with Normandy in raising cows?

Paul. I shall save the cost of transportation.

Jean. Very well; but the Normans are able to *beat* the Parisians, even if they do have to pay for transportation.

Paul. Do you call it *beating* any one to furnish him things at a low price?

Jean. It is the time-honored word. . . .

Paul. To-morrow I will demand *protection,* and I will induce the Council to prohibit the butter of Normandy and Brittany. The people must do without butter, or buy mine, and that at my price, too.

Jean. Gentlemen, your philanthropy carries me along with it. "In time one learns to howl with the wolves." It shall not be said that I am an unworthy Alderman. Pierre, this sparkling fire has illumined your soul; Paul, this butter has given an impulse to your understanding, and I perceive that this piece of salt pork stimulates my intelligence. To-morrow I will vote myself, and make others vote, for the exclusion of hogs, dead or alive; this done, I will build superb stock-yards in the middle of Paris. . . . I will become swineherd and porkseller, and we shall see how the good people of Lutetia can help getting their food at my shop.

Pierre. Gently, my friends; if you thus run up the price of butter and salt meat, you diminish the profit which I expected from my wood.

Paul. Nor is my speculation so wonderful, if you ruin me with your fuel and your hams.

Jean. What shall I gain by making you pay an extra price for my sausages, if you overcharge me for pastry and fagots?

Pierre. Do you not see that we are getting into a quarrel? Let us rather unite. Let us make *reciprocal concessions.* Besides, it is not well to listen only to miserable self-interest. *Humanity* is concerned, and must not the warming of the people be secured?

Paul. That is true, and people must have butter to spread on their bread.

Jean. Certainly. And they must have a bit of pork for their soup.

All Together. Forward, charity! Long live philanthropy! . . .

Pierre. Ah, I forgot. One word more, which is important. My friends, in this selfish age people are suspicious, and the purest intentions are often misconstrued. Paul, you plead for *wood;* Jean, defend *butter;* and I will devote myself to domestic *swine.* It is best to head off invidious suspicions.

Paul and Jean (leaving). Upon my word, what a clever fellow!

Note: The other three tableaux describe respectively the City Council's approval of the import restrictions, the general impoverishment of Paris 20 years afterward, and, finally, the popular agitation that leads to the decision to abolish all restrictions on trade.

Points for Review

1. As a rough guess, what would be the probable position on the free-trade versus protection issue on the part of landlords in a land-rich country? On the part of the trade union movement in a low-wage country? On the part of manufacturers' associations in a high-interest rate economy?

2. Give an example of a *pair* of arguments for protection that would be mutually contradictory.

3. What are the three main "rules" of economic policy-making?

4. Review your understanding of the fact that a subsidy avoids the net welfare loss but not the net efficiency loss from a tariff.

5. Why can a tariff be preferable to a subsidy when the supply of imports is less than perfectly elastic?

Questions for Discussion

1. In light of the third "law" of commercial policy, examine the actual role played by consumer organizations in the Congressional hearings on any major piece of tariff legislation as compared to the intervention of manufacturing or labor interests.

2. Is there any systematic reason why the House of Representatives tends to be more responsive to protectionist demands that the U.S. Senate?

3. Tariff "wars" were common in late nineteenth century Europe. By contrast, commercial retaliation in Western trade since 1945 has been rare. What has changed?

4. Can you think of recent examples of economic policy (in the commercial field or elsewhere) when the second "rule" of economic policy-making was violated?

5. The word "subsidy" sounds vaguely paternalistic, the word "tariff" much less so. Is there any reason why the semantic difference in tone should correspond to a difference in substance?

6. What is your personal answer to the question posed by Yeager and Tuerck (quoted on p. 165)?

7. Totally free trade, relatively free trade, protection. Which would you advise, in the light of whatever economic and political considerations you deem most relevant, as general policy for the United States in the next 20 years?

"Our kind of tariff makes the competing foreign article carry the burden, draw the load, supply the revenue; and in performing this essential office it encourages at the same time our own industries and protects our own people in their chosen employment."
William McKinley, 1888

"We must reduce our own tariffs if we hope to reduce tariffs abroad. . . . There are many more American jobs dependent upon exports than could possibly be adversely affected by increased imports."
John F. Kennedy, 1962

From Independence to Interdependence: The History of Trade Restrictions in the United States

What to Expect

This chapter surveys the principal developments in the history of U.S. commercial policy. Until the Civil War, tariffs went up and down depending on the changing political fortunes of the Democratic party. From 1861 to 1934, protection became entrenched at a high level, with only a brief interlude about the time of World War I. Beginning with the Reciprocal Trade Agreements Act of 1934, a third phase can be identified, consisting of a sustained drive toward liberalization of foreign trade. The chapter continues with a more detailed account of U.S. trade policy after World War II, including a description of the General Agreement on Tariffs and Trade (GATT) and the other principal developments in commercial policy since 1945. These have consisted of the lowering of tariffs negotiated in the 1940s and 1950s under the aegis of the renewed Reciprocal Trade Agreements program, of the 1962 Trade Expansion Act that provided the authority for the significant trade liberalization accomplished by the Kennedy Round of tariff negotiations, and of the 1974 Trade Act. The last section attempts an overall assessment and explanation of the genesis of U.S. commercial policy through its history. The Appendix provides a detailed summary of the main provisions of the 1974 Trade Act.

The Years of the Seesaw: 1816–61

At the time of independence, the posture of the new republic was strongly protrade. As Tom Paine had written in his famous booklet *Common Sense*, for America "the plan is commerce." These views had their expression in the tariff of 1789, the first tariff legislation of the independent republic. The 1789 tariff was mainly a revenue measure calling for a uniform 5 percent duty on most products and slightly higher rates on a few articles. Protectionist arguments, beginning with the weighty infant industry case made by Alexander Hamilton in his 1791 *Report on Manufactures*, had no legislative impact for the following 25 years. Beginning in 1816, however, protectionist views and interests became increasingly influential.

The 1816 tariff act was the first piece of legislation with a clearly protectionist intent. Although the tariff continued to serve as the major source of revenue, the 1816 act gave special infant industry protection to textiles and iron, protection that was extended in 1818. In 1824, duties were increased further, to an average level of 30 percent, in great measure owing to the eloquence and political influence of Henry Clay, probably the foremost protectionist spokesman of the time. The 1824 bill commanded the support of the iron, textile fibers, lead, and glass industries and the Middle Atlantic states where these industries were concentrated, and was opposed by the South and the Northeast. Southern states' opposition to protection was one of the constants of nineteenth century commercial policy debates, and indeed the tariff issue was a contributing cause of the Civil War. The political stance of the Northeast, instead, changed from an earlier protrade position to protectionist advocacy from the 1830s onward, in parallel with the shift in the New England states from an economic structure dominated by commerce and shipping (including the slave trade) to one with important manufacturing interests.

The upward march of protection culminated in 1828 with the so-called "Tariff of Abominations." Some complicated buck-passing political maneuvers by supporters of Presidential candidate Andrew Jackson backfired; the 1828 tariff bill was approved by very narrow margins in both the House and the Senate. The bill raised duties to an average level of 45 percent, far higher than the sponsors of the measure and almost anyone else had intended.

This was clearly an aberration, even by the protectionist sentiment of the time, and a significant downward revision was carried out in 1832. The reduction of tariffs from their "abominations" peak split what had been monolithic Southern opposition; North Carolina and Virginia among Southern states supported the 1832 bill. South Carolina, instead, in an action foreshadowing the secession of 30 years later, declared the 1828 and 1832 tariff legislation "null and void" and not applicable to South Carolina. This drastic crack in the political fabric of the nation led the more farsighted protectionist advocates to "stop and think" of the political consequences of thoroughly disregarding the interests adversely affected by high tariffs. In a major attempt at conciliation, Henry Clay himself sponsored a bill, passed in 1833 and known as the "Compromise Tariff," providing for across-the-board cuts to take place gradually over a nine-year period to bring duties down to a final uniform level of 20 percent. In exchange, the Southern states tacitly accepted the principle of a permanent tariff. The provisions of the Compromise Tariff, however, had barely had time to be implemented when the victory of the Whig party (predecessor of the Republican party) in the 1840 Presidential election resulted in a temporary return to high protection with the 1842 tariff act, which raised duties to about pre-Compromise levels.

The seesaw continued as protection was again lowered as a consequence of the 1846 victory of Democratic candidate Polk. The 1846 tariff, associated with the name of Treasury Secretary Robert Walker, lowered average duties back to around the 20 percent level. It had three other significant features. First, import commodities were classed in five schedules. The tariff rate differed from schedule to schedule, but was the same on all products classified in the same schedule. This system instituted a sort of compromise between the across-the-board uniformity presumed desirable for revenue tariffs and the great variation of rates inherent in the principle of protection. Second, the Walker tariff replaced most specific duties with ad valorem tariffs, thus eliminating the problem of a changing incidence of protection as foreign prices fluctuated (see Chapter 4). Third, importers were permitted to postpone payment of customs duties, and re-exports of imported goods were exempted from duties, by placing the products in question in bonded government warehouses until their domestic sale or re-export. The Walker tariff also embodied the first major instance of reciprocity in American commercial policy. Passage of the bill was considered dependent on a reciprocal concession by England in the form of repeal of its agricultural protection measures (known as the Corn Laws). A vote on the bill was delayed until word arrived that removal of the Corn Laws was accomplished.[1] Duties were reduced further in the 1850s because of the existence of a large Federal budget surplus. Average tariffs reached a low of 16 percent in 1860.

The Age of Entrenched Protection: 1861–1934

The fall of the Democrats from power, and the Civil War, sparked the beginning of a gradual but steady increase in protection. U.S. commercial policies were to remain highly restrictive for the following 70 years, with the exception of a brief interlude at about the time of World War I.

The Morrill Tariff of 1861 first raised duties from their relatively low 16 percent average. Throughout the Civil War years, customs duties were raised again and again. By 1870 protection had climbed back to its 1842 level. This time, however, the high tariff would last. With the loss of Southern political influence, the freer-trade side of the seesaw had lost most of its weight. The 1885–90 Democratic interlude did not produce any trade liberalization, despite energetic efforts by President Cleveland. The structure of protection was instead extended and strengthened. The McKinley Tariff of 1890 imposed new duties and generally consolidated the protective system that had been built on a piecemeal basis over the previous 30 years. It resulted in a lower tariff average, but largely because of the substitution of a subsidy for the duty on imported sugar and the meaningless reduction of more-than-prohibitive tariffs. With the Dingley Tariff of 1897, imports were restricted even further and protection reached its highest level since the Tariff of Abominations of 70 years earlier, with tariffs on protected articles averaging over 50 percent.

By the end of the nineteenth century, exports of manufactures had become considerable and the South had regained much of its political clout. Also, 40 years of import restriction, combined with slow-rising wages and the growing resentment against industrial trusts and "Robber Barons," brought home forcefully the causal connection between import tariffs and the real income of consumers. A major effort to liberalize trade was made

[1] See S. Ratner, *The Tariff in American History* (New York: Van Nostrand, 1972), p. 23.

in 1908, but was successfully frustrated by the still tight Republican control of Congress. The 1909 Payne-Aldrich Act, as a result, called for very slight tariff reductions and did not affect in any major respect the structure of protection. It is possible that, had the heirs to Henry Clay's protectionist mantle shared in the farsightedness shown by their predecessor in the Compromise Tariff, and had they made some significant concessions in the Payne-Aldrich bill, the resentment against the tariff system could have been neutralized for many more years. Instead, the blatant disregard of the interests harmed by high tariffs and the animosity generated by the cosmetic reductions of the Payne-Aldrich bill contributed importantly to the election of Democratic candidate Woodrow Wilson in 1912 and led one year later to a much larger decrease in tariffs than would probably have been acceptable in 1909. This reduction was accomplished by the Underwood Tariff of 1913, which brought average import duties all the way back to the pre–Civil War level.

The 1913 tariff might well have constituted a turning point toward lasting liberalization of trade had it not been for the outbreak of World War I. After the war, the pleadings for protection by the new industries that had been built up during the war years combined with the return of the Republican party to the Presidency to produce in 1922 a resumption of restrictive commercial policies. The 1922 Fordney-McCumber Act restored tariffs to approximately their 1909 level. The act also gave some discretionary power to the President to change tariff rates. Lest you think that a nonsense argument for protection has no political impact merely because it is a silly argument, it is worth noting that the 1922 act embodied a version of the "scientific" tariff in its provision authorizing the President to change the existing rates of duty if it was found that they were not sufficient to "equalize production costs" between the United States and foreign countries.

The twentieth century equivalent of the Tariff of Abominations was the 1930 Hawley-Smoot bill, a veritable "orgy of logrolling" [2] that raised average tariffs to over 40 percent and average tariffs on dutiable products to 53 percent. The bill was opposed by most economists, who in vain petitioned President Hoover to veto it, and was vigorously protested by foreign countries, incensed that a major industrial power would carry out such restrictive actions in the face of a large surplus in its balance of trade. As Charles P. Kindleberger has noted, the Hawley-Smoot bill, as also much of the U.S. foreign economic policy action or inaction during the Great Depression of the 1930s, was a manifestation of a major power behaving in a manner more fitting its past adolescent economic status, a case of national self-image lagging behind economic reality. Commercial retaliation by other countries had, of course, taken place before, particularly in the frequent "tariff wars" between European countries, but the United States had generally been able

---

[2] P. B. Kenen, *Giant among Nations* (New York: Harcourt Brace Jovanovich, 1960), p. 41.

to pursue the tariff policy of a relatively minor power without any great need for concern about the foreign repercussions of such a policy. This was no longer the objective situation in the 1930s. The threats of foreign retaliation were in fact carried out. The enactment of the Hawley-Smoot tariff was followed by similar restrictive legislation in most other industrial countries and eventually by a drastic decline of U.S. exports (see Chapter 10).

Turning
Point:
The
Reciprocal
Trade
Agreements
Program
of
1934

Turning Point: The Reciprocal Trade Agreements Program of 1934

This was the background to President F. D. Roosevelt's request to Congress for authority to negotiate reciprocal tariff reductions with other countries. Largely at the urging and under the leadership of Secretary of State Cordell Hull, Congress approved in 1934 the Reciprocal Trade Agreement Program. The bill gave the President the unprecedented authority to negotiate agreements with foreign countries for a reciprocal reduction of tariffs on specific items, *without* the need for Congressional approval of the negotiated reductions. In its own unspectacular way, this step constituted one of the most important expansions of the powers of the Presidency.[3] The authority was to expire after three years, but the bill was renewed in 1937 and then again and again, for a total of eleven times, until replaced by the broader-ranging Trade Expansion Act of 1962. Significant tariff reductions were negotiated under the authority of the 1934 act and its renewals. By 1947 average tariffs on protected products had fallen to about 25 percent, or half of their 1934 average of 50 percent.

An essential feature of the reciprocal trade agreements program was that each agreement would contain an "unconditional most-favored nation" provision. The **most-favored nation clause** in a commercial treaty provides that if either of the parties should at some future time agree with a third country to lower tariffs still more, such reduction is automatically extended to the other party. For example, if the United States agrees in a treaty with Britain to lower its tariff on British cars to 20 percent (in exchange for a reduction of British tariffs on American products), and *later* the United States agrees with Japan to decrease its tariffs on Japanese cars to 10 percent, the most-favored nation clause of the U.S.-Britain treaty means that

[3] Historian Arthur Schlesinger, Jr., apparently agrees with this view, although he considers that this expansion of Presidential powers was in keeping with the intent of the Constitution, as "a century of American history had proved that [Congress] could not handle the tariff question in a rational way." (*The Imperial Presidency* [Boston: Houghton-Mifflin, 1973], pp. 402–03.) On the contrary, we have argued here that Congressional tariff actions were perfectly rational, from the viewpoint of those voting, although it is of course arguable whether or not they were in the national interest.

the lower 10 percent tariff automatically applies to imports of British cars as well. Most-favored nation treatment thus is simply nondiscriminatory treatment. As the number of commercial treaties multiplies, inclusion of the most-favored nation provision progressively renders tariffs on a specific product more and more uniform irrespective of the geographic source of the product. This point will be returned to in the discussion of the General Agreement on Tariffs and Trade.

The year 1934 was a major turning point, when U.S. tariffs began their slide downward eventually to reach a low level not attained in U.S. history since the War of 1812. America's policies and self-image began to match (and eventually to exceed) the reality of its new economic and political weight in the international system. The trend toward freer foreign trade begun with the Reciprocal Trade Agreements Program was to continue for 40 years, with only relatively minor deviations, the *only* sustained trade liberalization trend in the entire course of U.S. history.

Postwar Developments in U.S. Commercial Policy

Two interrelated phenomena mark the development of U.S. foreign trade policy since 1945: the support of, and participation in, international mechanisms for the orderly conduct of negotiations on commercial issues and, within that context, a remarkable comedown from the restrictive policies of the early 1930s.

The General Agreement on Tariffs and Trade (GATT)

Partly as the result of the unpleasantness of the 1930s, the United States and some of its allies were determined to place the conduct of commercial policy on an orderly basis after the war and to establish a set of agreed-upon rules of the game to avoid the chance of a return to disruptive national actions on an isolated basis. An International Trade Organization (ITO) was proposed to create a comprehensive code for commercial policy to parallel the establishment of the International Monetary Fund (IMF) to serve as a mechanism for financial stability. An International Bank for Reconstruction and Development (IBRD, also known as the World Bank) was proposed to provide investment funds to less developed countries. The IMF and the IBRD, which will be discussed later, did come into being and are in operation today. Congress, however, refused in 1950 to give approval to the ITO. Fortunately, a temporary agreement on ground rules had already been successfully negotiated in 1947 and had begun in 1948. This agreement, known as the General Agreement on Tariffs and Trade (GATT), did not require approval by Congress. Thus, as of 1977, the GATT was technically still operating as an executive agreement under the authority of the Reciprocal Trade Agreements Act and later trade legislation. The United States has generally abided by the general provisions of GATT as have the other contracting parties, which include practically all developed non-Communist nations.

The GATT is not a comprehensive commercial policy code, but it includes several important features. The fundamental feature is the prohibition of discriminatory tariffs or quotas. As explained in Chapter 5, a discriminatory tariff is one that subjects the same article to a different rate of duty depending on where it comes from. Not only is discrimination in international trade dangerous, as it invites retaliation in kind by the countries being discriminated against, but it also is generally inconsistent with the principle of comparative advantage. In a multicountry world, the gains from trade are maximized if products are purchased from wherever they are cheapest. A tariff in general distorts the relationship between foreign and domestic prices. A discriminatory tariff in particular also distorts the relationship between prices of imports from different countries, and it thus carries additional costs in terms of the economy's welfare and efficiency of resource allocation.

Discrimination in international trade is "outlawed" by the GATT through its provision for unconditional most-favored nation treatment. Article II of the agreement states that "any advantage, favour, privilege or immunity granted by any contracting party to any product originating or destined for any other country shall be accorded immediately and unconditionally to the like product originating in or destined for the territories of all other contracting parties. . . ." Although the agreement specifies several possible circumstances under which exceptions to the rule are allowed, the principle of nondiscrimination is the cornerstone of GATT and has in practice constituted an essential benchmark for commercial policy in contemporary times.[4]

[4] Discrimination is permissible, under the GATT, when it results from an already established system of preferences, as for example those between the member countries of the British Commonwealth. Also, discriminatory treatment is allowed when it occurs as part and parcel of an economic integration arrangement, such as a free-trade area or a customs union such as the European Community. Preferential treatment accorded to some countries is, of course, discriminatory treatment against products of the other countries. The presumption here is however that economic integration undertakings are a move toward freer trade among the member nations and, as such, justify discrimination against nonmembers. The GATT safeguard is the provision that the average tariffs of the integrating countries in relation to the outside world cannot be higher than they were before the economic integration agreement. The difficulties of meaningful measurement of "average" tariffs (see Chapter 4) explain why in practice the GATT safeguard has been the subject of much argument and contention in the negotiations following the formation of the European Common Market. Other important provisions of GATT include the outlawing of quotas except when imposed for balance-of-payments reasons or as counterparts of internal quotas on domestic production, and provisions to take into account the special trade needs of less developed countries.

Of equal importance to the legal rules has been the role of GATT as a forum, as an institutional mechanism to facilitate international negotiations on commercial policy issues. The necessity of an institution within which progress can be planned for mutual advantage, and disputes discussed and resolved in an orderly manner, would become most apparent if the institution did not exist. In the absence of an institutional framework to which all parties can turn, the best goodwill in the world may not be sufficient to make progress or to defuse dangerous conflicts in time. The constructive role of GATT in "containing" the instances of commercial retaliation that occurred in 1962 was mentioned earlier. The GATT has also provided the structure within which major liberalization of international trade could be, and has been, negotiated during the last 30 years.

It should be noted that the status and prospects of the GATT are in a flux. (This is also the case for the other two principal international economic institutions, the IMF and the World Bank, although to different degrees.) It may be, on the one hand, that the next few years will witness a strengthening of international cooperation on the rules of the commercial policy game, either through a broadening of GATT provisions and their implementation [5] or, just possibly, through an agreement on a new, more comprehensive instrument. It is also conceivable, on the other hand, that countries will increasingly make use of the exceptions with which the GATT is perforated and even progressively come to outright disregard of the agreement. This is a facet of the major question facing the international economy over the next few years.

Postwar U.S. Trade Policy

A major reduction of tariffs occurred in 1947 as an outcome of the same negotiations that gave birth to GATT. Average U.S. tariffs were reduced in that year by about 20 percent. In subsequent negotiations, again within the context of GATT, tariffs were further reduced by small amounts in 1949, 1951, 1956, and 1962. Trade liberalization of the magnitude of the 1947 reduction did not occur again until 1967.

The trend toward liberalization, started in 1934, was marred in the 1940s and 1950s by the introduction of devices to nullify significant tariff concessions. These were the escape clause, and the peril point provisions attached to renewals of the Reciprocal Trade Agreements Act. The **escape clause** allowed the government to "take back" a tariff concession negotiated with foreign countries if it was found that such concession was "injurious"

[5] The 1974 Trade Act charges the President to pursue steps toward GATT revision, mainly to deal with the growing problem of restrictions on raw materials exports and with the treatment of import equalization taxes and export subsidies (see this chapter's Appendix).

to domestic producers.[6] Since a significant tariff reduction must result in an increase in imports and thus in most cases in at least a relative decline of import-competing domestic production, the escape clause makes a mockery of the process of tariff negotiations, practically telling foreign countries that the tariff concession given to them will be allowed to stand only if it turns out not to be a meaningful one. **Peril point** provisions attempted to determine the minimum rate of duty below which the domestic producers would be "imperiled." They prevented the President from negotiating reduction of tariffs below that rate.

In part because of the increasingly restrictive provisions tagged on to renewals of the reciprocal trade agreements program, and also owing to the negotiating challenge posed by formation of the European Common Market in 1960, the Kennedy administration decided in 1962 not to seek a twelfth renewal of the program but rather to ask for Congressional approval of a broader instrument for further trade expansion. The Trade Expansion Act of 1962 was approved by huge majorities: better than two-to-one in the House and almost ten-to-one in the Senate. The Trade Expansion Act continued the basic authority given the President to negotiate tariff reductions and to have them implemented without Congressional approval, but in addition it contained two important new features. First, the President was given authority to negotiate on an across-the-board basis rather than item-by-item as in the Trade Agreements Program. The emergence of the European Common Market made this expansion of authority advisable. The President was authorized to reduce tariffs down to 50 percent of their 1962 level and by an even greater percentage with respect to industrial products. Second, the 1962 act embodied a recognition of the superiority of direct measures over trade restrictions as an instrument for alleviating the costs of import liberalization for the domestic producers. Accordingly, the 1962 act did not include peril point provisions. Instead, it provided for **adjustment assistance** to the industries and workers affected by tariff reductions. In light of the earlier discussion of the second-best nature of tariffs, the introduction of the principle of adjustment assistance must rank as a highly significant commercial policy innovation.

Under the authority of the 1962 Trade Expansion Act wide-ranging reciprocal tariff reductions were negotiated by the United States with other industrial countries in the so-called Kennedy Round of negotiations, completed successfully in 1967. Although the maximum 50 percent decrease authorized by Congress was not achieved, very extensive and sizable reductions were negotiated, averaging approximately 35 percent of the

---

[6] An escape clause provision is included in the General Agreement on Tariffs and Trade. Its impact is, however, moderated by the requirement of consultation with the other members of GATT before a country can invoke the escape clause to withdraw a tariff reduction previously negotiated and by the provision that the other members may retaliate in kind should the consultation prove fruitless.

1962 tariff level for the United States as well as for the European Economic Community, the United Kingdom, and Japan.

As the overall result of the 35 years of operation of the Reciprocal Trade Agreements Program and of the Trade Expansion Act, average U.S. tariffs had come down by the early 1970s to hover around the 10 percent mark. The decline in tariff levels of other industrial countries from the 1930s peak roughly paralleled that of the United States.

The last measures of trade liberalization under the negotiating authority of the 1962 Trade Expansion Act were taken in 1973. The following year the Trade Expansion Act was replaced by a new comprehensive program, actually signed by the President in January 1975 but known as the Trade Act of 1974. Major legislation of this nature occurs infrequently. In addition, the 1974 act has been deliberately designed as a flexible instrument, capable of serving both as a vehicle for further trade liberalization and as a justification of higher tariffs. It is very likely, therefore, that the basic provisions of the 1974 Trade Act will be with us into the 1980s (although the act is officially due to expire in 1980). The provisions are described in some detail in the Appendix.

The act has been seen by protrade advocates as a carrier of a dangerous potential for higher tariffs and by protectionist interests as an unacceptable continuation of the trade liberalization trend of the past 40 years. There is some truth to both of these views.[7] The act does continue in the tradition started by the Reciprocal Trade Agreements Program. Future Presidents may well use their authority under the act to negotiate further tariff and quota reductions. The 1974 legislation, however, also widens considerably the scope for exceptions, while fortunately stopping short of reinstituting the peril point provisions of the 1960s, instead reaffirming the superiority of adjustment assistance over trade restrictions. The 1974 Trade Act offers significant possibilities for higher tariffs or quotas, whether on grounds of import relief or of combating unfair import practices. The ambiguous direction of the act was in large measure deliberate. U.S. policy-makers, facing international uncertainties in the monetary as well as the trade arena, recoiled from mandating a definite course of action and chose to construct a piece of legislation that could in principle be suitable for use under diverse situations. Much will depend, therefore, on the views and priorities of future Presidents. The act is pliable enough to serve both as a vehicle for further trade liberalization in the hands of a protrade Administration in a cooperative international climate and as

---

[7] In the judgment of Edwin L. Dale, Jr., "The protectionist forces essentially lost the battle" ("U.S. Trade in Deficit and That's Good News," *The New York Times*, May 23, 1976). But W. D. Eberle, former Special Trade Representative, had earlier recognized the existence of widespread fears that the 1974 Trade Act can be used as a protectionist tool ("U.S. Trade Policy—Appearance and Reality," *The New York Times*, December 7, 1975). Eberle, however, considered these fears to be generally groundless.

an instrument for significant restrictions of trade in the hands of a protectionist Administration.

U.S. Tariff History: Some Conclusions

Table 8.1 and Figure 8.1, pieced together from various estimates by several
authors, condense the commercial policy developments discussed earlier.
The average tariffs mentioned in the previous survey and shown in Table
8.1 are extremely rough approximations. Recall also the considerations
made in Chapter 4 regarding the ambiguity of unweighted tariff averages,
as well as the discrepancies between nominal and effective rates of protection, and the existence of trade restrictions other than tariffs proper. The
average tariff levels shown do, however, indicate the general orders of
magnitude.

Current tariff rates of the United States are at a historical low, having

TABLE 8.1   Major Benchmarks in American Tariff History, 1789–1975

Years	Average Tariff Rate [a]	Enabling Legislation and Remarks
1789	8	First U.S. tariff. Almost solely for revenue.
1816	15 [b]	First tariff with protective elements. Textiles and iron protected on an infant industry rationale.
1824	30	Increase in protection, mainly due to influence of Henry Clay.
1828	45	Tariff of Abominations. Political maneuvers boomerang to yield tariffs higher than most people want.
1832	30	General retrenchment to 1824 level. Enactment of tariff is followed by South Carolina Tariff Nullification Act.
1833–42	20	Compromise Tariff of 1833 provides for progressive reduction of tariffs to an eventual average of 20 percent.
1842	29	Whig party wins Presidency. "Black Tariff" increases protection back to 1832 level.
1846–57	23	Democrats return to power in 1846. Walker Tariff establishes lowest level of protection since the early 1820s. Schedule principle introduced. Action helped by removal of British Corn Laws.
1856–61	16	Tariffs reduced further, owing to federal government budget surplus.
1861–70	30	Morrill Tariff of 1861 increases protection. Gradually, during the Civil War, tariffs crawl upward again to approximately the 1842 level.
1871–75	27	10 percent horizontal reduction in 1871, repealed in 1875.

TABLE 8.1 (*cont.*)

Years	Average Tariff Rate [a]	Enabling Legislation and Remarks
1875–84	30	Back to pre-1872 level. Tariff Commission established in 1882.
1885–90	30	Vain Democratic attempts to lower tariffs.
1890–97	22	McKinley Tariff of 1890 extends protection to several products. Average tariff reduction but mainly from removal of sugar duty. The system of protection is in fact strengthened.
1897–1909	30	Dingley Tariff. Highest in 70 years, with tariffs on protected articles averaging over 50 percent.
1909–13	26	Payne-Aldrich Tariff lowers protection slightly. Widespread freer-trade expectations disappointed.
1913	14	Democrats win. Extensive reduction of tariffs back to pre-Civil War level through Underwood Tariff.
1922	25	Republicans in power. Fordney-McCumber Act restores 1909 level of protection. Includes "scientific" tariff principle and gives discretionary power to President.
1930–34	41	Hawley-Smoot bill of 1930 brings tariffs to highest level since 1828, and highest ever on dutiable articles, with level of protection averaging 53 percent.
1934–62	25	Reciprocal Trade Agreements, first approved in 1934, and renewed 11 times, give President authority to negotiate reciprocal tariff reductions with other countries. Average tariff level progressively reduced throughout the period.
1962–73	10	Trade Expansion Act of 1962 strengthens President's negotiating authority. Under Kennedy Round and successive negotiations, average tariffs eventually come down to less than 10 percent in 1973.
January 1975		Trade Act of 1974 signed by President Ford.

Source: Pieced together from various sources, including S. Ratner, *The Tariff in American History* (New York: Van Nostrand, 1972); R. M. Robertson, *History of the American Economy* (New York: Harcourt, 1955); F. W. Taussig, *The Tariff History of the U.S.* (New York: Putnam, 1931); F. W. Tuttle and J. M. Perry, *An Economic History of the U.S.* (Cincinnati: South-Western, 1970).

[a] Percentage ad valorem equivalent. All figures are very rough approximations. See Chapter 4 for a discussion of the problems of averaging tariffs.
[b] Ballpark estimate. The only available figure is a 20 percent average on dutiable imports only.

descended all the way to their level prior to the War of 1812, when protective considerations were almost entirely absent from tariff policy. It should not be forgotten, however, that recent years have also witnessed a progressive resumption of the use of nontariff barriers to trade, particularly quotas. In the mid-1970s, about one-sixth of U.S. industrial imports and one-fifth of agricultural imports were subject to quantitative restric-

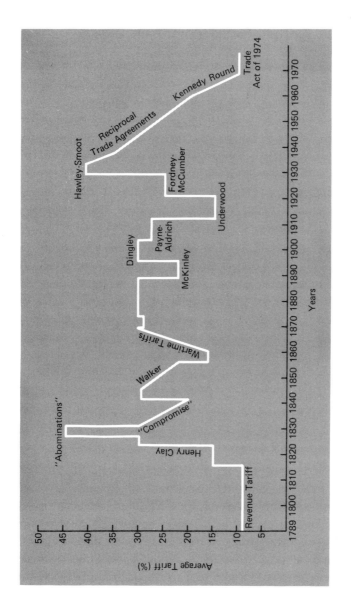

FIGURE 8.1   Major Benchmarks in American Tariff History, Average Tariff Rates

tions to some degree. Other industrial countries use quotas to a lesser degree than does the United States on industrial products but to a greater extent on agricultural imports. The European Community, in particular, has quantitative restrictions on about one-third of its agricultural imports. Also, there are constant quarrels over the use of other nontariff barriers to trade. Nevertheless, all in all, restrictions on international trade among Western industrial countries are currently at an historically low level. Is this a fortunate accident? Is it due to a broader acceptance of established theoretical principles? Is it grounded on permanent changes in international economic and political structure? Perhaps our satellite view of U.S. tariff history can provide some generalizations of possible relevance to these questions.

The Weight of Trade Theory

The discussion of the development of trade theory in Chapter 2 noted the close interrelationship between theoretical concepts on the one hand and economic conditions and policy goals on the other and concluded that theoretical contributions and economic events were both cause and effect of one another. The same mutual feedback of ideas and events has been present to some degree in the development of commercial policy. Thus, the powerful protectionist arguments of Alexander Hamilton's *Report on Manufactures* went ignored until real economic interests for protection emerged. Thereafter these arguments were used to legitimize and reinforce protective policies. And, in more recent times, significant liberalization of trade has depended to some extent on public understanding of the shallowness of protectionist arguments and on development of new theoretical contributions on the interaction of foreign trade and national income.[8]

The Weight of Economic Interests

Probably a more important explanation of the gyrations in tariff policy rests on the second and third "laws" of commercial policy presented in Chapter 7. By and large, tariffs were increased when those who stood to benefit were in control of the government's political machinery and were reduced when the balance of political power shifted in favor of those who stood to benefit from freer trade. In the United States, protectionist pressures came from the states with high concentration of import-competing industries and were resisted by exporting states (principally the South). Correspondingly, the Whigs and later the Republicans have maintained a

[8] Thus, contrasting the hearings on the 1974 Trade Act with hearings on earlier tariff legislation, one notices an increased skepticism of some of the conventional protectionist arguments and a correspondingly less favorable Congressional reception of protectionist pleadings.

protectionist stance and the Democrats have generally been protrade. In recent years, this political alignment has been in a state of flux, owing to the increasingly protectionist attitude of the AFL-CIO and to the substantial export interests of major manufacturers, but it was one of the constants in the political economy of U.S. tariffs until the 1960s.

The Haphazard Element in Commercial Policy

The theory of commercial policy may be reasonably precise. The politics of it is not. Tariff policies have often been promulgated in a haphazard way, without much thought given to the overall economic impact of a package of heterogeneous measures put together on a piecemeal basis. Passage of the Tariff of Abominations was the unintended result of political maneuvers to place the responsibility for disapproval of the tariff legislation onto political opponents. The upward creep of tariffs during the period 1861–90 did not correspond to any overall scheme; not until the McKinley Act was the ramshackle structure rationalized, although on a flatly protectionist basis. The extensive tariff cuts legislated by the Underwood Tariff in 1913 were to some extent due to the shortsightedness and stubbornness of a handful of Congress members only four years earlier in the context of the Payne-Aldrich bill. The catch-as-catch-can provisions of the Hawley-Smoot bill of 1930 mushroomed out of a proposal by President Hoover for a relatively modest increase in agricultural protection. And an extremely dangerous near-miss took place as recently as 1970, when only Senate adjournment prevented Congressional passage of the Trade Act of 1970, which would have imposed quotas on footwear, textiles, and oil, and opened a wide door for the establishment of quotas on a large number of other articles. Again, the origin of the 1970 act was an Administration request for an import quota on textiles only and for very minor tariff adjustments. Clearly, it is much easier to set in motion a process of trade restriction than to predict just where it will stop. This reality must give pause to any who would wish to predict commercial policy only on the basis of systemic elements of a broad economic or political character.

The Tariff "Cycle"

Even a quick look at Figure 8.1 shows an apparent cycle in the height of protection over the years. Historical tariff lows have occurred at approximately regular intervals: roughly 50 years went by between the low before the War of 1812 and the pre–Civil War trough and another 50 or so years before the next low of 1913–22. This book is being written at a time of a new historical tariff low which is *also* about 50 years after the previous one. Does this mean that we should expect an increase in protection in the foreseeable future? Is there a "method to this madness" that makes it inevitable for the pendulum to swing again toward high tariffs, and at approximately equal intervals? Certainly no one could assert that commercial policy fluctuations of a century ago or more dictate a similar pattern in the future. Indeed, considering that the last 40 or so years have been the only *sustained* trade liberalization period in American history (the previous instances of low tariffs lasted only a very few years) one could equally well predict that relatively free trade is here to stay and that the 1934 turning point represented the beginning of an entirely new trend rather than merely a downswing of the same old pendulum.

Has there in fact been a *systematic* cycle in U.S. tariff history? Surely not in the period 1816–60, when the political balance between protectionist and free-trade interests was so close that a substantial revision of tariffs was an almost automatic consequence of a change of the party in power. The sustained protection of 1860–1913 can be explained in terms of the loss of political weight by the free-trade interests. And the move back up to high protection after World War I can be attributed to the once-and-for-all inheritance of economic dislocations from that war combined with ten Republican years and with the onset of the Great Depression.

And yet, there is one consideration in favor of the systematic cycle view of tariff history. At any point in time and for a given product, the balance of lobbying efforts is tipped to the protectionist side since the *individual* losses from higher tariffs are too small to engender much aggregate political pressure. It is therefore especially hard to marshal internal resistance to demands for higher protection of specific products in times of low tariffs, when importers are unlikely to be terribly upset about a modest tariff increase. As the level of tariffs crawls upward, however, and protection is extended to more and more articles, the costs to importers mount. Eventually some threshold is reached at which the losses are visible and substantial enough to motivate importers to exercise some political pressure on their own. When combined with the efforts of those who find their *exporting* interests compromised by the import restrictions, sufficient pressure may be exercised to bring the whole structure of tariffs back down again. Thus, if you discount the very short-lived protectionist peaks of 1828 and 1930, in the almost one century and-a-half from 1816 to 1950, average tariffs fluctuated between only an approximate 30 percent ceiling and a 20 percent floor. When the average level of protection fell below 20 percent, renewed protectionist efforts brought it back up fairly quickly but never succeeded in keeping it above 30 percent for any appreciable length of time.

The swing of the pendulum away from high tariffs may in part be facilitated by the complacency of protectionist interests when the high tariffs have been in effect for a long time. The same, of course, is true of the other side. A prolonged regime of relatively free trade may lull its supporters into believing that this state of affairs has become permanent and into ignoring the roll of protectionist drums marshaling their forces to regain lost territory. Nothing is as effective in permitting a resumption of restrictive policies than the false conviction that the special interests who stand to benefit from the restrictions have somehow vanished or have been defeated for all time to come.[9]

Perhaps a determining factor for any prediction of the future course of commercial policy is the interaction of economic issues with international political relations. Given the continued existence of internal special interests for protection, it is fair to say that relatively free trade can be maintained only if international cooperation in the political arena continues and is strengthened.

---

[9] A recent case in point was the steel industry's push in 1976 for anti-dumping limitations of steel imports. In June 1976 the industry got President Ford to agree to impose a quota on specialty steels. In November they were at it again, this time asking for restrictions on imports of stainless steel pipe ("Steel Renews War on Imports," *The New York Times* headlined on November 28). Imports, however, accounted for less than *one-seventh* of American demand. It is interesting to note that a few days afterward several major companies announced an increase in steel prices. Could it be that the real goal of the industry was not maintenance of its share of the domestic market, but the profit increase which an import restriction can make possible for an oligopolistic industry such as steel?

Appendix: The Trade Act of 1974: A Summary of Important Provisions

Purposes of the Act

The statement of purposes of the 1974 Trade Act reads as follows:

The purposes of this Act are, through trade agreements affording mutual benefits—

(1.) to foster the economic growth of and full employment in the U.S. and to strengthen economic relations between the U.S. and foreign countries through open and non-discriminatory world trade;

(2.) to harmonize, reduce, and eliminate barriers to trade on a basis which assures substantially equivalent competitive opportunities for the commerce of the U.S.;

(3.) to establish fairness and equity in international trading relations, including reform of the GATT;

(4.) to provide adequate procedures to safeguard American industry and labor against unfair or injurious import competition, and to assist industries, firms, workers, and communities to adjust to changes in international trade flows;

(5.) to open up market opportunities for U.S. commerce in non-market economies [Communist countries]; and

(6.) to provide fair and reasonable access to products of less developed countries in the U.S. market.

Of these purposes, the first two represent a continuation of the tradition of negotiated reciprocal tariff concessions on a nondiscriminatory basis that was begun in 1934 and expanded in the 1962 act. Most of the public's attention centered on the objective of opening up commerce with nonmarket economies, seen as linked to the overall policy of détente and eventually enmeshed with the issue of Soviet policy toward emigration of its citizens.

Major Provisions of the Act

Negotiating Authority. The President, in the tradition started with the Reciprocal Trade Agreements Program, is given authority for 5 years to negotiate with foreign countries a lowering of U.S. tariffs down to 40 percent of their 1975 rates, as well as the authority to increase tariffs up to a maximum of 20 percent above the January 1, 1975, rate. The President can also completely eliminate nuisance tariffs, i.e., those below 5 percent. In keeping with the increased preoccupation with nontariff barriers, the President is also urged to arrive at agreements with foreign countries to reduce such barriers and to establish rules for their future use.

In particular, the Act is concerned with the use of import equalization taxes and calls for a revision of the rules of the GATT to "redress the disadvantage to countries relying primarily on direct rather than indirect taxes for revenue needs." The reference here is to the European use of import equalization taxes to offset their "value added tax." (The complexities of this issue were touched on in Chapter 6 under the discussion of government-induced distortions.) The Act urges that the GATT also be revised to recognize import surcharges as preferable to quotas to deal with temporary balance-of-payments difficulties and to introduce provisions to permit joint action by member countries to retaliate against restrictions of "access to supplies," a clear reference to the Arab oil boycott of 1973–74.

Finally, it is indicative of the uncertainties concerning the international monetary system that the President is given explicit authority to impose import surcharges of up to 15 percent, and/or quotas, for a period of not more than 5 months, when needed "to deal with large and serious U.S. balance-of-payments deficits," or to prevent depreciation of the dollar, or "to cooperate with other countries in correcting an international balance-of-payments disequilibrium."

Relief from Injury Caused by Import Competition. The stated purpose for regulations under this heading is "facilitating orderly adjustment" to import competition. Relief can be granted, upon the recommendation of the International Trade Commission (the new name of the Tariff Commission), in the form of restricting imports or as adjustment assistance to workers, firms, or communities adversely affected. It is clearly stated that restrictions of imports should be imposed only when direct help is not an effective remedy, thus reaffirming the superiority of direct assistance over trade restrictions (previously recognized in the 1962 Trade Expansion Act).

Upon petition for *import relief,* the International Trade Commission investigates whether the imports are "a substantial cause of serious injury, or the threat thereof, to the domestic industry." The Commission is given wide latitude in the conduct of the investigation. Of particular note is the provision by which the Commission may define as "domestic industry" only that portion which produces the article in question and only the segment of production located in a particular area. This allows the Commission, if it so wishes, to find "substantial injury" even in the case of a highly profitable domestic industry only a small segment of which is losing from import competition. However, the Commission must take into account whether or not the domestic industry has made significant efforts to compete more effectively, and it must hold public hearings. The President need not accept the recommendation of the Commission that higher duties or other forms of trade restriction be imposed if he does not consider it to be "in the national economic interest." Also, the President is mandated to take into account, among other things, the effect of the recommended action on consumers and on competition, a clear recognition of the theoretical consensus on the effects of restricting trade. If the President disagrees with the Commission, however, Congress can take its own favorable action on the Commission's report.

Adjustment assistance can be given, following certification by the Secretary of Labor or the Secretary of Commerce, respectively, to workers or to firms and communities affected by increased imports. Workers are eligible to receive adjustment assistance only if a significant number has been, or is about to be, laid off and the firm's production or sales have contracted absolutely with import increases contributing importantly to such a contraction. If eligible, workers can get a "trade readjustment allowance" of up to 70 percent of their wages (exclusive of unemployment compensation or other Federal assistance) for a maximum of one year. They are also entitled to placement services and/or to training for new jobs.

The criteria of eligibility for firms and communities are similar. If determined eligible for adjustment assistance, a firm can obtain loans of up to $3 million (obviously relevant only for small and medium-sized businesses) or technical assistance to ease the adjustment to import competition. For areas or regions adversely affected by import increases, adjustment assistance consists of public works and loan guarantees to be coordinated by special councils established for that purpose. Total loan guarantees for the whole country under this provision may not exceed $500 million, of which no more than $100 million can be allocated to a single state.

Relief from Unfair Trade Practices. Unfair trade practices are defined to include "unjustifiable," "unreasonable," or "discriminatory" restrictions of imports by foreign countries, foreign export subsidies, dumping, predatory or monopolistic practices by foreign sellers. The provisions under this heading are in principle applicable to all sorts of quite different trading situations, most of which provide no justification for actions to restrict imports.

Antidumping and countervailing duties may be applied when it is determined that the imports are being sold at "less than foreign market value" or that they are being subsidized by the foreign government. In cases of predatory practices, the products in question may be altogether excluded from entry. "If time permits," public hearings must be held before any trade restriction is imposed under these provisions, and the foreign sellers involved have an opportunity to participate in the hearings. However, the only real safeguard against excessive use of the "unfair trade practices" section of the law is the high probability of foreign retaliation in kind. Complaints of dumping were filed, after passage of the bill, by several industries, including principally autos, shoes, and specialty steels. Of the many requests for antidumping or countervailing duties, by early 1977 only a mere handful had been in fact accepted. This preliminary record may change depending on the make-up of the International Trade Commission, on the leanings of the Administration in power, on commercial policies of foreign countries, and on the general political climate on the world scene.

East-West Trade. The extension of most-favored-nation treatment to the USSR and to the Eastern European countries had been one of the principal themes of the Administration's request for new trade legislation. Nondiscriminatory treatment of nonmarket economy countries was considered an essential economic adjunct to the policy of détente. During the Congressional debate, however, the economic question became intermeshed with the issue of Soviet restrictions on the emigration of its citizens, particularly Jews. The Jackson Amendment succeeded in making most-favored-nation treatment conditional on liberalization of Soviet emigration policies: ". . . products from any nonmarket economy country shall not be eligible to receive non-discriminatory treatment . . . [if] such country: (1) denies its citizens the right or opportunity to emigrate; (2) imposes more than a nominal tax on emigration. . . ." The USSR viewed the amendment as an unacceptable attempt to interfere in its own internal affairs, the détente edifice was severely shaken, Soviet emigration policies did not change (if anything, they became more restrictive), and Title IV on East-West trade has remained so far a dead letter.

Generalized Preferences. The last substantive section of the Trade Act opens the

Generalized Preferences. The last substantive section of the Trade Act opens the possibility of exempting from customs duties articles imported from less developed countries. Special treatment given exports of less developed countries is referred to as "trade preferences." Preferential treatment was accorded by Britain to other members of the British Commonwealth, and the European Community agreed in the Lomé Convention of 1976 to give preferences to the products of its associated countries in Africa, the Caribbean, and the Pacific. By the 1974 Trade Act, duty-free treatment may be accorded to "beneficiary developing countries" with respect to "eligible" articles. The definition of "beneficiary country" and, even more so, of "eligible" articles is, however, quite restrictive.

Eligible beneficiaries must not be "dominated or controlled by international communism," or members of the Organization of Petroleum Exporting Countries, or of any other international arrangement to maximize foreign exchange revenues from the exportation of commodity resources. Nor is a less developed country eligible if it has nationalized without adequate compensation for properties of U.S. citizens.

These, and other, restrictions on the eligibility of countries to receive preferential treatment are at least defensible. But the definition of eligible *products* makes the system hollow. Duty-free treatment cannot be given on textiles and apparel, watches, shoes, certain kinds of electronic products, steel, and glass products, nor on "any other articles which the President determines to be import-sensitive." Since the manufactured products of export interest to the less developed countries are almost certainly in direct competition with the declining sectors of developed economies such as the United States, exclusion of articles that are "import-sensitive" takes the core out of the preferences scheme. If this were not enough, it is also provided in the act that preferential treatment ceases if in a given year an individual country manages to export to the United States in excess of $30 or so million (the ceiling rises according to the rate of growth of U.S. national income) or over 50 percent of total U.S. imports of a specific product. This is not to say that the Title V provisions are not of considerable significance to some less developed countries. To call them "generalized preferences," however, is more than a little ironic.

Points for Review

1. List the principal tariff laws of the period 1816–1934 and their main features.

2. Why does the text call the period 1816–61 "the years of the seesaw"?

3. It is true that the Democratic party has consistently been in favor of freer trade and the Republican party in favor of protection (at least until very recently)? To what is this stance to be attributed?

4. What is the "schedule principle" introduced in the Walker Tariff of 1846?

5. The McKinley Tariff Act of 1890 lowered the average level of tariffs. Yet, it is described as a protectionist measure. Why?

6. Why was the brief low-tariff interlude of 1913–22 interrupted?

7. Could one argue that passage of the Hawley-Smoot tariff was an expression of political immaturity on the part of the United States?

8. During what period was the Reciprocal Trade Agreements Program in operation? Was it successful in liberalizing international trade?

9. What is the "most-favored-nation" clause in commercial treaties? Give examples, other than the one in the text.

10. What is the GATT? What is its fundamental principle?

11. What is an "escape clause"?

12. What is a "peril point" provision?

13. The 1962 Trade Expansion Act replaced peril point provisions with adjustment assistance. In light of the money of commercial policy, would you consider this to be an improvement?

14. What is the main difference between the negotiating authority given the President by the 1962 Act and that of the 1934 Reciprocal Trade Agreements Act?

15. What are the main differences between the 1962 Act and the 1974 Trade Act?

Questions for Discussion

1. The text argues that, if protectionist advocates had been as farsighted in 1909 as Henry Clay was in 1833, the large tariff cuts of 1913 might not have been enacted. Do you think this thesis is valid? In light of your knowledge of U.S. politics just before World War I, would you consider that a similar move to liberalize trade would have taken place regardless of any concessions made earlier?

2. Is it conceivable that in the absence of the Compromise Tariff the Civil War might have been fought 30 years earlier than it was? If so, might the result possibly have been different?

3. A petition by over 1,000 economists opposed passage of the Hawley-Smoot Tariff Act in 1930. The act became law. Over 4,000 economists opposed passage of the protectionist Trade Act of 1970. That act did not become law. Was the different outcome due to 3,000 additional signatures on an economists' petition?

4. Which would you take to be the main lessons from passage of the Hawley-Smoot tariff and its aftermath?

5. The text argues that existence of an institutional mechanism is a neces-

sary, although not sufficient, condition for international cooperation in the conduct of commercial policy. Do you agree? Can you conceive of circumstances in which the existence of a *specific* kind of institution becomes a *hindrance* to international cooperation?

6. In which category of arguments for protection would you place a peril point argument for a minimum rate of duty?

7. In light of the considerations made in the text, of the summary of the 1974 Trade Act in the Appendix, and of your assessment of the political situation in the United States as you are reading this—what is your personal prediction of the trade policy of the United States over the next few years?

8. Do you see any similarity between Pandora's Box and the filing of tariff legislation?

International Finance

"Annual income twenty pounds, annual expenditure nineteen-nineteen-six, result happiness. Annual income twenty pounds, annual expenditure twenty pounds-ought-and-six, result misery."

Charles Dickens, *David Copperfield*

The Foreign Exchange Market and the Balance of Payments

The
Foreign
Exchange
Market
and
the
Balance
of
Payments

What to Expect

It is time to bring money into the picture and begin the analysis of international financial questions. This chapter explains the workings of the foreign exchange market and describes the balance of international payments. The other chapters in Part III analyze the workings and performance of various international monetary systems to correct imbalances in international payments.

The chapter begins by explaining how the foreign exchange market works to determine the exchange rate and how the forward foreign exchange market serves as a hedge against the risk of exchange rate changes. Next described is the balance of payments, i.e., the basic statistical record of a country's transactions with the rest of the world, and the principles on which the balance of payments is constructed. Various measures of balance-of-payments' equilibrium are briefly described: the liquidity criterion, the basic balance, the official settlements balance. Each is suitable for certain purposes but less convenient for others. Finally, the major trends in the international payments of the United States since World War II are briefly reviewed.

Appendix 1 contains an explanation of the relationship between "spot" and "forward" foreign exchange rates. Appendix 2 discusses the conceptual and methodological problems of measuring balance-of-payments' equilibrium. Also, the Points for Review contain a lengthy assignment that can be helpful in understanding the details of construction of a country's balance of payments.

This discussion of international finance begins with an explanation of some frequently used terms.

The **exchange rate** is the *price of a country's currency in terms of a foreign currency, i.e., the number of units of a foreign currency that can be purchased with one unit of the country's currency.* For example, if one U.S. dollar can buy four German marks, the dollar exchange rate is four marks. Conversely, the mark exchange rate is 25 cents. The latter is what daily U.S. newspapers list in their exchange-rate page. The quotations show the number of U.S. dollars (or, usually, U.S. cents) it takes to buy one unit of the designated foreign currencies. Strictly speaking, therefore, these are not the dollar exchange rates, but the exchange rates *of foreign currencies* in terms of dollars. Of course, the dollar exchange rate (the number of units of foreign currency a dollar can buy) is easily obtained as the reciprocal, i.e., by dividing into one the quotation listed. For example, if the French franc is listed at 20.16 U.S. cents, or 0.2016 dollars, the exchange rate of the *dollar* in terms of francs is: 1/0.2016, or 4.96 French francs. It is the *change* in the exchange rate, not the absolute level, that is economically more important. For example, the fact that the English pound is worth more than one U.S. dollar and the Japanese yen only a fraction of one cent means nothing about the strength of those foreign currencies, as shown by

The
Foreign
Exchange
Market
and
the
Balance
of
Payments

the marked decline in the value of the pound and the increase in the exchange rate of the yen in the mid-1970s.

As a price, albeit in many ways a unique sort of price, the exchange rate can go up and down. One speaks of **appreciation** of the currency when its exchange rate goes up and of **depreciation** of the currency when its exchange rate goes down. These terms are usually associated with a regime of flexible exchange rates. When the rise and fall of the exchange rate are instead due to a deliberate government policy decision in a regime of managed exchange rates, the corresponding terms are **revaluation** (or upvaluation) and **devaluation**. In these cases, the changes are usually "lumpy" and fairly large. When there is some government tinkering within a flexible rate regime, one speaks of "managed floating" or of "dirty floating."

The meaning and functions of the money used for international payments are the same as those of money in general. International money, whatever its specific form, serves as a medium of exchange, a store of value, and a measure of value. A thing is money to the extent, and only to the extent, that people accept it as a means of performing those functions. It is "good" money when it is readily accepted, "bad" money when it is not, regardless of whether it happens to be gold, silver, fishhooks, wampum, or a little piece of colored paper with a picture on it. One of the prerequisites for the efficient operation of any international financial system is that it be based on a monetary standard that is readily acceptable throughout the international economy as a means of payment, and a store of value.

A phenomenon called "arbitrage" is very important in international finance. *Arbitrage is a riskless operation of buying and selling of the same thing when the price of it is not the same within a single market.* It is the *arbitrageur* (from the Latin for "referee") who, by taking advantage of a price difference that is not warranted by the existence of real obstacles between markets, eliminates such difference and thus unifies separate markets when there is no systematic reason for their separation. For example, if the price of this book were higher in one bookstore than in an identical bookstore next door, you could realize a riskless arbitrage profit by buying the book where it is cheaper and immediately selling it outside the other store. As you did so, the mechanism of supply and demand would push the price up where it is lower and cause it to decline where it is higher, thus equalizing the price for the same book and in effect unifying the market for it. The existence of arbitrage of course means that an unwarranted price discrepancy rarely arises in the first place and is quickly eliminated if it does. Arbitrage operations can take place wherever an unwarranted price discrepancy emerges. There can be currency arbitrage, commodity arbitrage, and interest arbitrage, all of which will be discussed later at the appropriate time.

The
Foreign
Exchange
Market
and
the
Balance
of
Payments

Remember that arbitrage is a sure thing. It is thus quite different from **speculation**, which is *an inherently risky purchase or sale in the expectation that the future price will go up or down, respectively.* In the case of speculation you make money if your expectation turns out to be correct but lose if you were wrong, which you very well might be. Depending on the circumstances, speculation can be an element of market stability or instability, while arbitrage always has a stabilizing influence, preventing price fluctutations within a single market.

The Market for Foreign Exchange

General Characteristics of the Foreign Exchange Market

International transactions require payment or receipt in currencies other than the domestic currency of one of the two parties. The foreign currencies themselves must therefore be bought and sold. Their price is the exchange rate. *The international market on which currencies are exchanged for one another is the foreign exchange market.* In the foreign exchange market, as in any other market, there is an identifiable supply of and demand for a country's currency—supply and demand that are to a great extent derived from the underlying international conditions of supply and demand for the goods, services, and capital assets of the country. In a regime of completely flexible exchange rates, the price of a currency is determined entirely by the autonomous supply and demand for it. Excess supply of the currency causes its exchange rate to fall, excess demand drives the exchange rate up.

The foreign exchange market is not physically located anywhere. It consists of a worldwide network of telephones and cable lines. It is huge, with daily transactions in the principal currencies amounting to hundreds of millions of dollars every day. Thus, while conceptually similar, for example, to the market for ballpoint pens, in practice it is hardly in the same league. The very size of the foreign exchange market implies a larger cast of actors and calls for intermediaries between the individuals who ultimately want the currency and those who wish to sell it. Commercial banks are the principal **foreign exchange dealers**, acting as intermediaries for the parties to an international transaction. The banks themselves, however, do not want to hold either excessive amounts of a given currency or less· than they need for their daily operations. **Foreign exchange brokers** act as go-betweens for the banks in this respect. A bank temporarily short of one currency, for example, would use a foreign exchange broker to find and contact some other bank that happens to hold more of that currency than its business needs require.

Most international transactions are not "cash on delivery of merchandise," but what may be called "acceptance on delivery of documents." That is, the importer provides a written acceptance of his financial obligation to pay for the goods at some specified future time in some specific currency (usually the currency of the exporter) and gets delivery of the papers entitling him to take possession of the goods when the ship docks or the plane lands. When the bank, acting as intermediary, receives the importer's IOU (the **acceptance**) in exchange for the shipping papers, it sells the IOU on the financial market and pays the seller of the goods the money owed him. The exporter is now all squared away and so is the bank, which has of course received some compensation for its intermediary function. The importer gets the goods when they arrive; the transaction is rounded out when he pays off whoever purchased his acceptance at the time when the payment comes due.

Currency arbitrage is the mechanism that unifies the foreign exchange market. By taking advantage of unwarranted exchange rate differences, arbitrageurs make consistent the rates of exchange of the different currencies in various locations and with one another. *First,* arbitrage keeps the price of a given currency the same throughout much of the world (except for the small differences caused by the buying and selling costs). Suppose that £1 = $1.65 in London and £1 = $1.50 in New York. The pound is 10 percent less expensive in New York than in London. If there is no real reason for the difference (if London and New York are essentially in the same market), arbitrage emerges and works to unify the rate of exchange. The principle could not be more obvious. You buy a thing where it is cheaper and sell it where it is more expensive. In this case, you buy pounds in New York (in exchange for dollars) and sell them in London. For example, $1,000 will exchange for £667 in New York; the £667 can be sold in London for $1,100 for a 10 percent profit, equal to the discount on the pound in the New York market. The purchase of pounds in New York drives up their price there; the sale of pounds in London drives down the exchange rate, thus equalizing the exchange rate in the two locations.[1]

---

[1] Under gold arbitrage (see Chapter 11), gold must be actually shipped. The shipping costs delimit the range within which the exchange rate can fluctuate. For currency arbitrage, instead, one needs only to hold bank accounts in both London and New York; the operation takes place through changes in bank deposits. The "obstacle" is the fee received by the bank as the dealer in foreign exchange. The exchange rate of the same currency can therefore differ to some extent in different locations. However, the difference is usually quite small. The exchange rate of a given currency is nearly the same throughout the world. There is more. The shipping of gold takes time, so gold arbitrage is accordingly not *totally* risk free. With spot currency arbitrage, the buying and the selling are practically simultaneous and the risk accordingly nonexistent. Arbitrage involving the forward market, however, does carry the conceivable risk that foreign exchange controls might be imposed before the profit can be realized (see Appendix 1).

The
Foreign
Exchange
Market
and
the
Balance
of
Payments

Second, arbitrage keeps the exchange rates of various currencies in line with one another, and thus it allows one to refer to *the* foreign exchange market even though dozens of different currencies are traded there. Suppose that: £1 = $2.00; £1 = 9.00 DM; $1 = 5 DM. From the relationship between the pound, on the one hand, and the dollar and German mark, on the other, $1 should equal 4.5 marks instead of 5. The dollar is overpriced in terms of marks, and the DM is underpriced in terms of dollars.[2] The idea of arbitrage is just as obvious as in the previous case. You buy the underpriced thing and sell the overpriced one. In this example, selling $1,000 will get you 5000 DM. The 5,000 DM can be sold for £555, and at the current rate the £555 exchange for $1,110 or $110 more than you started with. The sale of dollars in exchange for marks, of course, lowers the exchange rate of the dollar in terms of marks to the level consistent with its exchange rate in terms of the other currency.

The principle of currency arbitrage is simple. With dozens of currencies actively traded every day, however, the practice of arbitrage operations is complex, although enormously simplified by the reference points provided by "vehicle currencies," such as the dollar. Thus, arbitrage is usually left to specialists in this field. Not so with speculation, which engages a lot of institutions and individuals, from the multibillion dollar international corporations to the doctors or hotel owners who dabble in foreign currencies partly because they love the notion of being "international financiers." Speculation arises from expecting the exchange rate to change in the future. Thus, while currency speculation is relatively unimportant in the pure gold standard with its permanently fixed exchange rates (see Chapter 11), it is part and parcel of a monetary system that allows exchange rates to be flexible (see Chapter 12). Chapter 13 examines the important issue of whether speculation is an element of stability or instability in the foreign exchange market under different international monetary systems.

The Forward Foreign Exchange Market

Recalling that the market for foreign exchange is the monetary reflection of millions of different international transactions, there are many reasons why, in the absence of government intervention, exchange rates can fluctuate. Changes in domestic prices affect a country's competitiveness and world

---

[2] You could equally well say, given the DM price of the dollar and the DM price of the pound, that the pound should exchange for $1.80 instead of $2.00, i.e., that it is overpriced with respect to the dollar. Or, given the DM price of the dollar and the pound price of the dollar, that £1 should really exchange for 10 DM instead of 9, i.e., that it is underpriced with respect to the mark. It quickly gets very complicated, and quite tiresome, but it all amounts to the same thing: The exchange rates are not consistent with one another, and there is a riskless arbitrage profit to be made therefrom.

demand for its goods and services. National monetary policies have an influence on interest rates, and the latter can have a considerable impact on capital flows. Expectations concerning the future price of a currency play an important role in the demand or supply of it. Even seasonal fluctuations, such as increases in imports of swimwear in summer, have an effect on the market for the country's currency. The possibility of exchange rate changes creates some problems for international traders.

So far, the "spot" exchange rate, i.e., the price of a currency when both the payment for it and the delivery of it take place immediately has been implicitly referred to. If, for example, you exchange dollars for lire at Rome's Fiumicino airport to pay for your tourist expenses in Italy, the spot rate is the one you are charged. But most international transactions take time, both for delivery of the goods and for payment. A contract is signed today, but the money is to be paid sometime in the future. Suppose that the contract, as in the usual case, calls for payment in the seller's currency. The price of the goods in terms of that currency is of course specified in the contract. But the price of the currency in which payment must be made is not specified. The price to the buyer is therefore also not specified, as it depends on both the price in terms of the foreign currency and the price of the foreign currency itself. If the latter goes up between the moment the contract is signed and the time when payment is called for, the buyer ends up paying more for the merchandise than he bargained for and his expected gain from the transaction can easily turn into an unexpected loss. Let's follow this through the example of an American purchase of a Mercedes automobile from Germany.

If a Mercedes sells for 28,000 German marks and the current rate of exchange is 2.5 DM per dollar (40 cents per 1 DM), the car would cost the American importer $11,200. Suppose that he figures to be able to resell the car for $13,000 and, after taking into account freight, insurance, and the costs of running his foreign cars dealership, that he can make $1,000 profit on the deal. There is no problem if the transaction takes place immediately. He buys the 28,000 DM for $11,200 at the current spot rate, turns the money over to the seller and gets the car. The importer might very well lose on the deal, if his business judgment of the U.S. market for Mercedes cars is incorrect, but for reasons quite unrelated to the international character of the transaction.

If, instead, the contractual commitment is signed today but the car is to be delivered and the payment is due 3 months from today, the importer can lose if the German mark goes up in price. If the spot price of one German mark 3 months from today goes up to 50 cents, the 28,000 marks the importer is obligated to pay cost him $14,000. Instead of a solid profit he suffers a considerable loss, entirely because of the exchange rate change and not because of bad business judgment. Of course, it is also possible for the mark to depreciate, in which case the importer enjoys an unexpected wind-

The
Foreign
Exchange
Market
and
the
Balance
of
Payments

fall gain. But his business is selling cars, not speculating on foreign currencies. He much prefers to avoid the exchange risk altogether.

What can the importer do to hedge on the risk of DM appreciation? Ideally, he wants to buy the 28,000 DM at a price agreed on today, but for delivery and payment 3 months from today. He signs *two* contracts: the first (with the Mercedes company) specifying the price of the car in terms of German marks, the second (with a foreign exchange dealer) specifying with equal certainty the price he will have to pay for the German marks when the time comes to deliver them. As a result, he no longer faces any uncertainty concerning the dollar price of the car. This is exactly the function performed by the forward market in foreign exchange, a market in currency "futures" whereby the price is agreed on today but the transaction is consummated at some future time.

Commercial banks are the main dealers in forward foreign exchange as they are in the spot market.[3] The importer thus buys 28,000 DM "3 months forward," at a price probably a bit higher than the spot rate of 40 cents per DM, say, 40.2 cents. When the payment is due he gives the bank $11,256, gets the German marks, turns them over to the Mercedes company, and gets the car. The hedge costs him $56, but he has rid himself of the exchange risk.[4] (Appendix 1 explains the relationship between spot and forward exchange rates.)

Does the bank absorb the exchange risk? No. The bank is no more of a speculator than is the importer. As a financial intermediary, the bank will want to obtain **cover** by at the same itself buying 28,000 DM three months forward from some *German* importer who wishes to hedge against *depreciation* of the mark. To the extent that expectations concerning the future price of the DM are "neutral," i.e., that there is no net worldwide expectation that it will differ significantly from the current rate, banks are able to obtain 100 percent cover, since the world exporters' desire to hedge is roughly matched by the importers' wish to hedge in the opposite direction.

The Balance of Payments: Definitions and Uses

Market equilibrium results from a correspondence between what people *can* do, and what they *would like* to do under the prevailing circumstances. But

[3] Recently, an organized "currency futures" market has emerged, functioning much like a commodity futures exchange, with a trading floor, open auctions, standardized contracts and delivery dates. Although, as in the forward market, the participants are mainly banks, brokers, and multinational corporations, the International Monetary Market of the Chicago Mercantile Exchange allows some participation by private individuals.

[4] The spread between spot and forward rates is usually about as small as in this example. Thus, the German mark was quoted in New York on September 29, 1976, at $0.4071 spot and $0.4093 six months forward, or a difference of only about one-half of 1 percent.

The
Balance
of
Payments:
Definitions
and
Uses

who knows what people would want to do? All there is to go on is the record of what they actually did. In international transactions, this record is the balance of payments.

It is essential not to think of receipts from abroad as necessarily good nor of outpayments to foreign countries as necessarily bad. Still, it is true that a nation's financial accounts with foreign countries must be looked at differently from the nation's own government budget. Internal taxes and government expenditures cause moneys to be transferred from some people to someone else in the economy. From the viewpoint of the country as a whole, these even out. The process is in a sense equivalent to shifting your wallet from the right to the left pocket. Expenditures and receipts from international trade and investment instead offset one another *only* in the context of the world economy as a whole, but *not* for the individual countries, which can experience net deficit or surpluses. This is why equilibrium in a country's international payments and receipts is an important question in its own right.

It is self-evident that a reasonably accurate record of a country's transactions with the rest of the world is indispensable as a basis for its economic policy, whatever the country's specific goals may be. *The balance of international payments of a nation is a summary statistical record of the transactions that have taken place between the nation's residents and residents of foreign countries over a period of time* (normally 1 year). Some important characteristics of the balance of payments (abbreviated as **BOP** from now on) emerge directly from this definition. Listing them quickly (they will be returned to later on), they are:

1. The *summary* nature of the record. It would be impossible to try to assess the country's general economic and financial position from the "raw" listing of the millions of individual transactions that take place every year.

2. The *ex post* ("after the fact") nature of the record. Only transactions that have already taken place are included. Their terms and volume may, or may not, have coincided exactly with the plans and desires of those entering into them. If they did not, you can expect some change in the future, but the state of the BOP is only an imperfect predictor of such change.

3. The BOP is a statement of *flows,* not of stocks.[5] Thus, it is not the counterpart of the balance sheets of corporations, but of their income statements, showing receipts and payments *over a period* of time rather than at one time.

[5] A *stock* is a quantity at one time, a *flow* over a period of time. For example, to say that a person has an income (flow) of $100 means nothing unless you know over what period the income accrues. $100 per week is vastly different from $100 per day. It is, instead, meaningful to say that his wealth (a stock concept) is $10,000 at one particular time.

The
Foreign
Exchange
Market
and
the
Balance
of
Payments

As an individual, or head of a family, you need a record of your economic transactions with other persons and families for two main reasons (aside from the need to substantiate your income tax returns!). *First*, you need the information to give you an idea of where you stand as a trader, i.e., as a buyer and seller of goods and services, for the extent to which you buy and sell goods and services affects your family's real income. And *second*, you must know about your debts, savings, and investments to evaluate your financial position and thus your future income prospects. Similarly, BOP statistics show the country's role as a trading unit in the international economy, and include a financial picture of the country's lending, borrowing, and investing operations.

Principles of BOP Construction

A straight account of the principles of BOP construction is hard to follow without a concrete reference point. Let us then start off with an example of bookkeeping by a hypothetical farm family, an example that will be used again when explaining further the concepts and principles underlying the BOP of a country.

The farm family engages during a given year in a variety of economic activities. Some are internal, as for example the cooking, washing of dishes, growing of food for the family's own use. The family also engages in external transactions with outsiders. It needs a reasonably good bookkeeping record of these various "foreign" transactions.

At one extreme, a minute record may be shown of all individual transactions, running into hundreds of pages. This is not very helpful, since the excessive amount of detail gives the family no idea of how it stands in relation to the outside world. At the other extreme, the family's financial record could consist merely of one single figure for total payments and one figure for total receipts. This is not useful either, as it eliminates all information on the types of activities or transactions responsible for the overall totals. The family would normally choose a middle course. It would "aggregate" the raw information on each detailed transaction into certain general *types* of transactions that may usefully be distinguished from one another. Suppose, then, that during the year in question the farm family:

1. Sold a total of $15,000 worth of produce and other tangible goods.

2. Bought a total of $20,000 worth of groceries and other tangible goods.

3. Earned $500 by occasionally renting rooms to visiting birdwatchers.

4. Paid $1,100 in trucking charges to transport its produce to market.

5. Gave $100 as a wedding gift to a neighbor's daughter.

6. Received $500 in dividends from shares of stock it owned.

7. Sold for $5,000 a parcel of land it owned.

8. Sold $500 worth of shares of telephone company stock it owned.

9. Lent $1,000 to a neighboring farmer, to be repaid in a few months.

10. Borrowed $500 on its credit card account.

How are these categories of transactions to be arranged in order to give the family some idea of how it stands in relation to the outside and hence of what it should or should not do in the future? The most obvious distinction is between transactions resulting in payments to outsiders and transactions resulting in receipts. If you add up the figures above, you will find total receipts of $22,000 and total payments of $22,200. How can this be? How can the family have paid out $200 more than it took in? Either something was left out or some errors were made in the recording of the various transactions. We do not know why the difference exists, but we do know that it just is not possible for the $200 to have materialized out of thin air. A "statistical discrepancy" item must be added whenever records are incomplete or inaccurate so that recorded payments do not equal recorded receipts as they should in principle. (Until 1976, this item was called "errors and omissions.")

Are there other convenient distinctions besides the obvious one between payments and receipts? The most general useful distinction is between transactions that affect the present income and well-being of the family and those that affect its wealth and indebtedness and hence its *future* income. The former may be termed *current* transactions, the latter *capital* transactions. The current transactions make up the **current account.** In the current account it is useful to distinguish gifts from trade, since the motivations underlying them are different. In turn, within the trade category, transactions involving merchandise (tangible goods) are shown separately from those involving services. The service category includes, it is important to note, the income from past investment (the stock dividends, in this example). In the **capital account,** it is useful to make a distinction between long-term transactions (such as the sale of the parcel of land) and short-term transactions (such as the credit card borrowing). A short-term debt, for instance, is obviously much more of an immediate concern. By the same token, however, you need not take it into account when making long-range economic plans, for by that time the debt will have been repaid already.

To show what the family's balance of payments looks like, let's agree on a simple rule. Refer to all transactions giving rise to receipts from the outside as *credit* items, carrying a "+" sign, and to all transactions giving rise to payments to outsiders as *debit* items, carrying a "–" sign. Table 9.1 shows the farm family's BOP, with the colloquial terminology on the right side and

The
Foreign
Exchange
Market
and
the
Balance
of
Payments

TABLE 9.1   Farm Family Balance of Payments
(U.S. Dollars)

Account	$	Account
Exports of Merchandise	+15,000	Sales of Produce and Tangible Goods
Imports of Merchandise	−20,000	Purchases of Groceries and Tangible Goods
Merchandise Trade Balance	− 5,000	
Exports of Services:	+ 1,000	Sales of Services:
Tourism	(+500)	Room Rentals
Investment Income	(+500)	Stock Dividends
Imports of Services (Transport)	− 1,100	Purchases of Services (Trucking Charges)
Total Trade Balance [a]	− 5,100	
Unilateral Transfers, Net	− 100	Wedding Gift
Current Account Balance	− 5,200	
Foreign Direct Investment	+ 5,000	Sale of Parcel of Land
Foreign Purchases of Securities	+ 500	Sale of Telephone Company Stock
Balance on Current Account and Long-term Capital [b]	+ 300	
Short-term Claims on Foreigners	− 1,000	Loan to Neighboring Farmer
Short-term Liabilities to Foreigners	+ 500	Credit-Card Borrowing
Statistical Discrepancy [c]	+ 200	?
Balance on All Accounts	0	

[a] Occasionally, you might find that the term "balance on goods and services" is used instead, with "trade balance" referring to merchandise trade only.
[b] This is known as the "basic balance," which excludes all capital flows of less than 1 year in duration. It is discussed further later on and in Appendix 2 of this chapter.
[c] Remember that this is not an independently-recorded item. Statistical discrepancy is simply the figure needed for the balance on all accounts to be zero, as it logically must be.

the corresponding technical terms on the left. Various subbalances are shown, each consisting of all transactions above the corresponding line. Total payments must equal total receipts. If an appropriate statistical discrepancy item is entered, *the overall balance on all transactions must be zero. It follows that the balance on transactions below any given line must equal the balance on transactions above that line, but with the opposite sign.*

Much more needs to be pointed out about the nature of the BOP and the interrelationships among the items listed above. The hypothetical farm family must now be abandoned, but with the hope that the concrete example will have served to lessen the inevitably abstract nature of what follows.

Major BOP Categories

Presentation of international economic and financial data is subject to the same difficulty that confronts the would-be user of great masses of information on a given subject. On the one hand, in a listing of millions and millions of separate transactions the mass of detail swamps any general characteristic of possible interest. On the other hand, too general a summary would eliminate too much detail and preclude analysis of the factors possibly responsible for the overall results. It is a practical problem, dealt with in a pragmatic fashion, with the fineness of the classification depending on the analytical and policy purposes of the users of the data. There is, however, close agreement in different countries as to the general classification of BOP data.

The first, very broad distinction is between *current* and *capital* transactions. Just as a family needs to make a distinction between weekly purchases of groceries and borrowing of money, so a country needs a record of its sales and purchases of goods and services separate from the record of its capital receipts and expenditures. The dividing line is in practice difficult to draw. The extremes, as always, are easy: buying a steak in cash at a restaurant for immediate consumption is a clear-cut current transaction; the purchase of a share of stock to hold until your children reach college age is clearly a capital transaction. But what would you call the purchase of a side of beef to hold in your freezer for months because you expect meat prices to go up? Or, conversely, the buying the stock shares on margin, to be resold next week? Many transactions affect both current and future income; their classification into the one or the other category is not unequivocal. The solution generally adopted by BOP statisticians is to include all purchases and sales of commodities and services into the current account. (The current account also includes gifts, although these are sometimes shown in a separate *unilateral transfers* account.)

The Current Account In the current account, the distinction between merchandise trade and trade in services is not due to a conceptual difference. It is usually true, however, that the trend and stability of trade in services (the so-called "invisible items") has historically differed from that of commodity trade. Within the services subdivision, the most important categories are *investment income* (from past investments abroad), *transportation, tourism,* and *insurance.*

Foreign trade in goods and services is linked to the country's national income. The relationship of trade and income is the subject of Chapter 10. The following fundamental proposition should be previewed here. In the absence of foreign trade, total national spending ("absorption") is limited by total national production: Nothing can be obtained that has not been produced at home. If the farm family were, and had always been, completely isolated, its total consumption could not exceed its own internal production. If instead the nation does trade with other countries, it becomes

The
Foreign
Exchange
Market
and
the
Balance
of
Payments

possible for it to overspend or underspend. If its imports are greater than its exports (a balance of trade deficit), the country's absorption is greater than its production. The country is in a sense "living beyond its means." (Remember that the income from past foreign investments is already included in exports of services.) How can it do this? In the same way as the farm family can consume more than it produces: It can borrow money (or run down savings), or it can sell off some of the economic assets it owns. Either way, the rest of the world is building up claims on the country running a trade deficit. If, instead, imports are smaller than exports (a trade surplus), the country's absorption is smaller than its production. The country is "living beneath its means." What is the result? The same as in the case of the family that consumes less than it produces: It can lend (or pay off past debts) or it can acquire economic assets elsewhere. Either way, the country builds up claims on the rest of the world.

This is why a surplus of exports over imports is termed **net foreign investment** in national accounting. If a country is not getting back goods and services equal in total value to those exported, it must be getting the difference in the form of claims to *future* goods and services, i.e., IOU's, money, shares of stock, factories, or such. The country is thus investing in foreign countries. (It can also make or receive gifts.)[6]

The Capital Account In the capital account, the distinction between *long-term* and *short-term* capital transactions is, in practice, fuzzy. A loan made today for repayment tomorrow is clearly short-term; a loan to be repaid 30 years hence is a long-term capital transaction. But since time is a continuum, the dividing line is necessarily arbitrary. By convention, sales and purchases of securities of an original maturity longer than 1 year are classed as long-term, the remainder as short-term capital transactions. The difficulty is that long-term securities are often bought with the intention of re-selling them in a short time and, conversely, that many short-term loans are continuously renewed.

A second important distinction is between government and private capital, since the motivations underlying each can be presumed to differ, and so do the policies affecting them. It is also useful to distinguish direct investment from portfolio investment. **Direct investment** (also called equity investment) is the acquisition (or increase) of controlling ownership of a foreign corporation. **Portfolio investment** consists of the purchase of shares of a corporation without acquiring control over it. Finally, of course, there is outright lending and borrowing.

It should be clear from the concept of net foreign investment that it is not possible for a net transfer of goods and services to occur in one direction

---

[6] There is also the possibility that foreigners will simply refuse to pay. But, aside from the obvious fact that this would not happen very frequently, you may still call such default a foreign "loan," albeit of course a forced one.

(unless they are gifts) [7] without an equivalent net transfer of financial claims in the opposite direction. Thus, strictly speaking, if there is a surplus in the balance of trade, there must be a corresponding deficit in the remainder of the BOP, and vice versa. It is therefore inconsistent for a country to be pleased about being able to import more than it exports, while bemoaning the existence of a deficit in the other accounts, just as it would be for the farm family to be happy that it is buying more than it is selling and to be at the same time surprised and upset about the resulting accumulation of debts. These are the proverbial two sides of the same coin. Whether a country is interested in living beyond or beneath its means, it cannot run a trade deficit without accumulating liabilities to foreigners, and it cannot maintain a trade surplus without accepting a capital account deficit (again, aside from gifts).

Also, the link between today's flows and tomorrow's stocks must be kept in mind. As a country, for example, accumulates foreign claims through running a trade surplus, its future income from foreign transactions increases. Nowhere is this more clearly illustrated than in the U.S. BOP in the last 20 or so years, which shows a current annual income from past foreign investment much greater than the annual flow of the new long-term investment.

The Varied Meanings of BOP Equilibrium

As repeatedly noted, if all BOP credit items are added, all debit items subtracted, and errors and omissions accounted for, the result must be zero. If all transactions are included, the BOP is always in equilibrium. To return to Table 2.1, the overall BOP of the farm family was zero. But such "balance" tells us nothing about the real financial situation of the family. In order to arrive at a useful conclusion about the state of equilibrium, deficit, or surplus in the BOP, those items that are relevant must be selected out of the total credits and debits and separated from the other transactions. The state of the family's BOP will depend on the balance of the relevant items, which, not encompassing all transactions, can indeed yield a disequilibrium in either direction.

To identify the relevant items, it is necessary to know much more about the nature of the transactions and about the purposes of the family's operations. Thus, if the family had wanted to sell the $5,000 parcel of land anyway, we could conclude that its current and long-term capital account showed

[7] In the matter of gifts, there is no apparent other side to the transaction. And yet, no present is ever given without *some* reason. The receipt of gratitude, the acquisition of influence, the satisfaction of helping, the expectation of future favors, the "strings" attached, any or all of these are among the possible counterparts of the gift itself.

The
Foreign
Exchange
Market
and
the
Balance
of
Payments

a $300 surplus. If, instead, the sale was forced by the excess of payments on the other accounts, we would conclude that a serious deficit occurred. Essentially, there is no cause for concern, nor any tendency for change, if the family was not forced to do anything it would not have wanted to do regardless of the state of its BOP. It should be clear, therefore, that the state of the BOP depends on the criterion of identification of the relevant items. If the various items are listed in order of their relevance, the question of BOP equilibrium depends on where the line is drawn between the relevant transactions and those that do not deserve independent concern. The state of the BOP is then determined by the balance of the credits and debits "above the line." (Since the total BOP must balance, it follows that the balance of the items "below the line" must be exactly the same but with the opposite sign.)

The farm family example illustrates the most important criterion for distinguishing those BOP items that should enter the calculation of equilibrium in a meaningful sense from those that do not. *Autonomous* transactions should be distinguished from *compensatory*, or *accommodating*, transactions. Equilibrium, or the lack of it, should be determined only on the basis of the autonomous transactions, i.e., those that did not take place in order to offset payments difficulties. The autonomous-compensatory distinction is a difficult one to translate into practice, for one cannot ever be sure of the motivations underlying any transaction, but it does serve as a general basis for defining BOP equilibrium. The rationale and implications of different BOP measures are examined in Appendix 2. It bears emphasizing, however, that the measure one uses normally has a significant influence on whether the BOP is considered to be in equilibrium, deficit, or surplus. The issue is relevant because inappropriate measurement often leads to inappropriate policies.

One final, easier point: Equilibrium, or the lack of it, must be assessed with reference to the nation's transactions with the rest of the world as a whole and not on a bilateral country-by-country basis. It would be as inefficient to attempt to equalize payments and receipts with each individual nation a country does business with as it would be to try to even them out on a day-to-day basis.[8]

The perceptive reader familiar with the *ex ante* ("before the fact") economic notion of equilibrium may have grown uneasy about the discus-

---

[8] If you go back to the theory of trade, you will quickly realize that an attempt to achieve balanced payments with each trading partner prevents the country from taking full advantage of its comparative efficiency. Think of how much less efficient your activities would be if you had to maintain payments equilibrium with each of the persons you do business with. This is in fact not the case: You specialize in your work, have a large surplus in relation to your employer (even if you eat in his cafeteria) and a deficit in relation to everyone else. You consider your accounts to be in balance if total receipts (wherever they come from) are equal to total desired expenditures (wherever they go to).

sion of equilibrium in the BOP, which by definition shows only what has already happened. Recall that, in the market for a particular commodity, equilibrium occurs when the quantity *demanded* (the quantity that buyers *want* to buy at the current price) equals the quantity *supplied* (the quantity that sellers *want* to sell at that price). This may or may not be the case. Instead, the quantity *bought* is always equal to the quantity *sold*. Similarly, the overall BOP always balances exactly because it is an ex post record. The picking and choosing of BOP items for a more meaningful definition of equilibrium can be seen as an attempt to use the accounting record of what people did as an indicator of what they wanted to do.

Fritz Machlup has identified three concepts of the BOP.[9] In addition to the accounting balance discussed above, a market balance and a program balance can be considered. **Market balance** corresponds exactly to the notion of equilibrium in supply-and-demand analysis: a *market balance is the difference between total receipts and payments of foreign currency on account of autonomous transactions* (those that are not intended to influence the price of the country's currency, the exchange rate). Under equilibrium in the foreign exchange market, by definition, there is no tendency for the exchange rate to change and thus no need for "compensatory" government intervention to prevent such change. If, therefore, the exchange rate is stable, and total autonomous receipts and payments are equal, it can be presumed that all private economic agents have in fact been able to do what they planned to do at the current rate of exchange and thus that the BOP is in equilibrium in a market sense. A deficit or surplus, instead, exists if and to the extent that the country's authorities have had to intervene in the market to keep the exchange rate stable, and/or to the extent that the exchange rate is changing.

This match of intentions and realities is also at the basis of the concept of **program balance.** Only here the benchmark is some overall economic plan of the public authorities and not only the aggregate intentions of private traders and investors. *The program balance is a statement of expected foreign receipts, and of planned uses for them, over some future period of time.* If international receipts over a number of years are estimated to equal the amounts needed to fulfill the country's planned economic targets, international payments over that number of years can be said to be balanced in the program sense. If estimated receipts fall short of the country's requirements, a **foreign exchange gap** can be said to exist.[10]

---

[9] F. Machlup, "Three Concepts of the Balance of Payments and the So-called Dollar Shortage," *Economic Journal,* March 1950.

[10] It is unusual for a surplus to exist in the program balance sense. If expected foreign receipts are greater than the amounts required by the economic plan targets, the usual response is to revise the targets upward and make use of the expected surplus, which therefore disappears. It should be clear, by the way, that a foreign exchange gap can exist only before the fact. After the fact, if the planned targets have been achieved, the needed foreign receipts must have come from some place. Alternatively, the foreign

The
Foreign
Exchange
Market
and
the
Balance
of
Payments

The concept of program balance is important when the economic plan cannot be fulfilled without a given amount of foreign currency, i.e., when it is not feasible to make do with substitute domestic resources should foreign receipts prove to be insufficient. This is far closer to the state of affairs in less developed countries than in industrial nations, and, as often stated, problems of trade and development are outside the scope of this book. Let us then from here on refer to BOP equilibrium in the market balance sense and its proxy measure, i.e., the accounting definition on the basis of autonomous transactions only.[11] Equilibrium in that sense is defined as a state of the BOP that will tend to continue without intervention by the public authorities. This is the general context of the discussion of alternative monetary systems in later chapters—those systems that by and large rely on private market forces for maintaining or restoring BOP equilibrium and those that call for government intervention under various terms and conditions.

Postwar Trends in the U.S. BOP

The U.S. BOP over the past 30 years has shown the following main features:

1. Exports and imports of merchandise have been the single most important source of receipts and payments (as they are in practically all countries), accounting for roughly three-fifths of total receipts and payments. Until recently, the United States had shown a positive balance of merchandise trade every single year. In the 1970s, however, the merchandise trade balance has often been in deficit, owing in some measure to the large increases in the price of imported oil.

2. By contrast, trade in services, while accounting for a smaller share of total payments and receipts (about one-fourth), has continued to show a significant surplus. The most important contributor to the surplus has been the income from U.S. investments abroad.

3. When taking into consideration the negative net unilateral transfers (private remittances abroad and U.S. government grants), however, the total balance on current account has turned from generally positive until 1967 to generally negative from 1968 on.

---

receipt requirements of the plan, or the foreign receipts expected, may have been incorrectly estimated. In this case, of course, there was no foreign exchange gap in the first place.

[11] Some autonomous transactions, such as direct food shipments under P.L.480 or other grants in kind or swaps of equipment for shares of foreign stocks and the like do not entail purchases or sales of foreign currencies. They therefore enter the autonomous transactions accounting balance but not the market balance, since any disequilibrium in those transactions does not affect the exchange rate. The correspondence between market balance and accounting balance is thus not a precise one.

4. The long-term capital account has consistently been in deficit, reflecting in large measure the continuing U.S. acquisition of assets abroad. As pointed out earlier, the net outflow of private long-term capital has been considerably smaller than the income from past foreign investments included in the current account. Still, the negative long-term capital balance, combined with a reduction of the current account surplus and eventually the appearance of a deficit in that account, has resulted in sizable overall basic BOP deficits from about 1965 on, reaching a 1976 peak of over $14 billion.

These trends are summarized in Table 9.2 and Figures 9.1 and 9.2. An elaboration of the implications of these data and of possible future prospects must await later chapters. The reader should be reminded, however, that, as noted at the outset, one must be careful not to assume that surpluses are necessarily good and deficits necessarily bad. Even a deficit clearly due to an excess of autonomous debits over autonomous credits may be desirable depending on what brought it about and on the country's economic perspec-

TABLE 9.2 Balances on Various Accounts, U.S. Balance of Payments, 1961–75 (Billions of Current Dollars)

Year	Merchandise Trade Balance	Services Trade [a] Balance	Total Trade Balance	Unilateral Transfers Balance	Current Account Balance	Long-term Capital Balance	"Basic" Balance [b]
1961	5.6	0.1	5.7	−2.6	3.1	−3.1	0.0
1962	4.6	0.6	5.2	−2.7	2.5	−3.5	−1.0
1963	5.2	0.8	6.0	−2.8	3.2	−4.5	−1.3
1964	6.8	1.8	8.6	−2.8	5.8	−5.8	0.0
1965	4.9	2.2	7.1	−2.8	4.3	−6.1	−1.8
1966	3.9	1.4	5.3	−2.9	2.4	−4.0	−1.6
1967	3.9	1.3	5.2	−3.1	2.1	−5.3	−3.2
1968	0.6	1.9	2.5	−2.9	−0.4	−0.9	−1.3
1969	0.7	1.3	2.0	−2.9	−0.9	−2.0	−2.9
1970	2.6	0.4	3.0	−3.2	−0.2	−3.5	−3.7
1971	−2.3	2.1	−0.2	−3.6	−3.8	−6.5	−10.3
1972	−6.4	0.4	−6.0	−3.8	−9.8	−1.4	−11.2
1973	1.0	3.2	4.2	−3.8	0.4	−0.6	−0.2
1974	−5.5	9.1	3.6	−7.2	−3.6	−7.3	−10.9
1975	9.0	7.5	16.5	−4.6	11.9	−10.5	1.4
1976[c]	−9.2	19.9	10.7	−5.3	5.4	−19.7	−14.3

Source: U.S. Department of Commerce.

[a] Including military transfers, purchases, and sales.
[b] Balance on current account and long-term capital. See Appendix 2 of this chapter for a discussion of this and other balance-of-payments measures.
[c] Preliminary figures.

The
Foreign
Exchange
Market
and
the
Balance
of
Payments

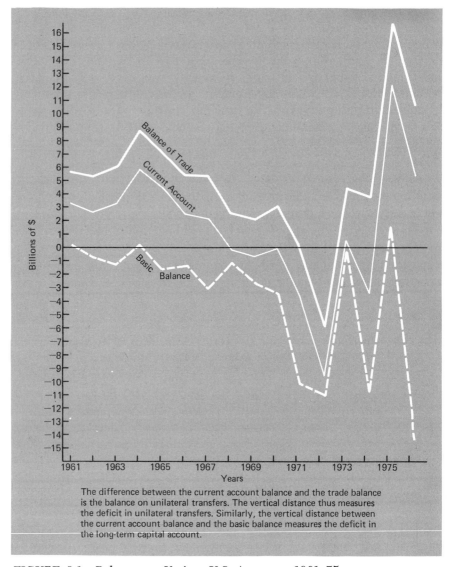

The difference between the current account balance and the trade balance
is the balance on unilateral transfers. The vertical distance thus measures
the deficit in unilateral transfers. Similarly, the vertical distance between
the current account balance and the basic balance measures the deficit in
the long-term capital account.

FIGURE 9.1   Balances on Various U.S. Accounts: 1961–75

tive. For instance, the resumption in 1976 of a deficit in the U.S. balance of
trade was not viewed with great concern. On the contrary, it was seen as
partly a symptom of a generally good development, namely, the recovery
from the severest economic downturn since the Great Depression of the
1930s. As will be examined in detail in the next chapter, imports can be
expected to rise when national income increases. Further, such an import
increase in the United States is good from the viewpoint of other countries
whose exports increase and contribute to their economic recovery, a desirable outcome also in terms of the U.S. interest in Western economic stability.

The Balance of International Indebtedness

Postwar
Trends
in
the
U.S.
BOP

The BOP, as a statement of flows, corresponds to the income statement of private corporations. The international accounting counterpart of corporations' balance sheets is instead the *balance of international indebtedness,* which is *the summary record of the stock of foreign assets and liabilities of the country's residents at one time.* The difference between a country's assets abroad and its liabilities is termed **net worth.** The country is classified as a *creditor* country if its net worth is positive, as a *debtor* country if negative. One must be careful not to assume that a positive net worth implies the absence of financial difficulties or vice versa. A country with heavy long-term indebtedness may nevertheless be in a favorable short-term position. Conversely, a country may be faced with liquidity problems (excess of short-term liabilities over short-term assets) despite its long-term creditor status. (This is in fact the current situation of the United States.)

There is an intimate connection between the balance of indebtedness and the BOP, as there is between any stock quantity and the corresponding flow. This year's flow of current receipts is partly a function of the stock of assets, which in turn stems from the flow of foreign investment in prior years. And past foreign investment was itself related to the state of the current account in past years. Projecting this relationship into the future, the by-now familiar concept of net foreign investment leads to a homely and puritanical, but inescapable, conclusion. To improve its debtor-creditor standing in the world economy, a country needs to increase its foreign assets or reduce its foreign liabilities. Neither is possible without net foreign investment. The country must therefore run a surplus in the balance of trade. National spending (absorption) must be restricted below national production. The essential problem of BOP policy for debtor country is how to plan for such eventual reduction of absorption, at the same time as efforts are made to increase national production itself, in order to avoid the painful effects of being forced at some future time to tighten the belt several notches all at one time. As will be discussed in later chapters: "International adjustment always takes place in some fashion, but this statement offers little more comfort than the observation that an airplane always gets back to the ground somehow." [12]

While the balance of indebtedness is a useful statistical record, the BOP receives the lion's share of public and policy attention. Economic policy has a greater chance of influencing what is in the process of happening than of effecting major changes in the cumulative result of what has already happened many years ago. Also, it is usually the case, although sometimes with disastrous long-term consequences, that today and tomorrow are considered far more important than the more distant future.

[12] R. Hinshaw (ed.), *The Economics of International Adjustment* (Baltimore: Johns Hopkins, 1971), p. 4.

Appendix 1: Relationship Between Spot and Forward Exchange Rates

It is obvious that there would be no difference between spot and forward rates if exchange rates were completely fixed. Indeed, there would be no forward foreign exchange market at all. If the exchange rate can vary, a forward market emerges, and the spot rate almost always differs from the forward rate. To explain the relationship between the two, start with the simple consideration that there is practically no difference between the spot rate now and the spot rate one minute from now, hence that the "1-minute forward" exchange rate would be identical to the spot rate. One might therefore suspect that the spot-forward differential widens the longer the duration of the forward contract. This is in fact the case if interest rates differ between countries. Under the assumption of neutral expectations regarding future exchange rates, it can be shown that the spread between spot and forward rates is mainly a function of interest rate differences between countries.

To explain this, let's go back to the U.S. importer of Mercedes cars. It probably occurred to you that he does not really have to buy DM forward to hedge against the risk of DM appreciation. He can instead buy the foreign currency now and simply hold it until payment is due. In fact, if he puts the marks in a German bank savings account, he draws interest. Suppose that the German rate of interest is 4 percent a year, or 1 percent for 3 months. If the importer buys the 28,000 DM spot and puts it in a German bank, 3 months from now he will be able to pay the Mercedes company and have 280 DM ($112) over and above that. Why does he bother with the foreign exchange market then? Does he gain anything at all?

Your economic common sense should at this point be whispering the words "opportunity cost." What else could the importer have done with the $11,200 it took to buy the DM spot and hold it for 3 months? Why, put it in a U.S. bank, of course, and draw whatever interest that bank is offering. Suppose that the U.S. rate of interest is 6 percent per year, or 1.5 percent for 3 months. By leaving the $11,200 in his U.S. savings account, the importer will 3 months from now gain $168 in interest. Obviously, if he buys the marks spot, he gains the interest paid by the German bank and loses the interest the U.S. bank would have paid him. If he buys the marks forward, he gains the interest the U.S. bank pays and loses the interest the German bank would have paid him. In this example, if he buys the marks spot, his net loss is $56, ($168 minus $112), but he has hedged against the exchange risk. The upshot is clear: If the cost of hedging through forward purchase is more than the cost of hedging through spot purchase (i.e., the $56 U.S.-German interest rate differential), the importer will not want to buy forward DM. If the forward premium on the DM is instead less than $56, *German* importers have no reason to *sell* forward DM. Thus, the difference between the spot and the forward rate is in principle equal to the interest rate differential between countries. This is known as the **interest-rate parity** principle. If the foreign interest rate is higher than the domestic one, the foreign currency sells at a forward discount as compared to the spot rate rather than at a premium.

The approximate mathematical formulation of interest-rate parity is as follows. If E_s is the spot exchange rate of a foreign currency, and E_f the 3-month forward rate, the forward premium FP is defined as

Appendix 1:
Relationship
Between
Spot
and
Forward
Exchange
Rates

$$FP = \frac{E_f - E_s}{E_s}$$

Hence

$$E_f = E_s + (E_s \times FP)$$

If I_1 is the domestic rate of interest on 3-month loans and I_2 is the corresponding rate of interest in the foreign country in question, the forward premium (or discount if negative), is given by:

$$FP = I_1 - I_2$$

In this example, I_1 is the U.S. interest rate of 1.5 percent for 3 months and I_2 the German interest rate of 1 percent for 3 months. The 3-month forward DM is thus sold at a premium: $FP = .015 - .010 = .005$ (or, one-half percent). If the spot rate is 40 cents, the interest-rate parity forward rate is therefore 40.2 cents.[13]

Should the forward rate diverge from the spot rate by more than the differential in interest rates, arbitrage comes in to take advantage of the discrepancy and brings exchange rates in line with the differential. This is interest arbitrage. It works in the same way as gold or currency arbitrage, but not quite as well, because of the element of time (see footnote 1).

One concluding point. So far, expectations have been assumed to be neutral. If they are not, the difference between spot and forward rates is only in part related to interest rate differentials. Thus, if there is a definite net expectation that the DM will appreciate significantly over the next 3 months, forward purchases of DM by *speculators* come into play, in addition to the traders' demand for forward marks. Since this additional speculative demand for forward DM is not matched by equivalent sales, banks cannot obtain 100 percent cover for their forward operations unless the forward premium on the German mark is higher than the interest rate differential. In times of financial stress and abnormal uncertainty, speculative flows may be so large as to altogether swamp the influence of interest rates on the forward foreign exchange rate.

---

[13] For a fuller explanation and elaboration, see L. B. Yeager, *International Monetary Relations* (New York: Harper & Row, 1976). Yeager also argues, contrary to the view expressed in this book, that "speculation *in itself* does not create forward premiums or discounts far out of line with interest parity" (p. 31).

Appendix 2: Various Measures of the Balance of Payments

As emphasized in the text, if all transactions are included, the BOP necessarily balances. Meaningful measurement of the BOP must therefore include fewer than the total credits and the total debits. Various measures are possible. Some differ from others because they are expressly intended to serve different policy purposes, to measure different things. Other measures are instead different because, while corresponding to the same general criterion of balance, they do not make the same assumptions concerning the best way to measure it. This undoubtedly sounds abstract, but should become clearer as the purposes, advantages, and disadvantages of the more common measures of BOP equilibrium or disequilibrium are examined.

The Balance of Trade   The balance of exports and imports of goods and services is useful as an indicator of the net foreign investment of the county, with a surplus resulting in an accumulation of claims on foreigners and a deficit resulting in an increase in liabilities to foreign residents. In addition, the balance of trade is intimately linked to the country's national income, as both cause and effect, in ways that will be discussed in Chapter 10. While a valuable measure in and of itself, the balance of trade has the obvious limitation of not taking into any consideration capital transactions, at least some of which are both autonomous and of a recurrent nature.

The Basic Balance   The basic balance is the net balance on the current account and the long-term capital account combined. It includes all imports and exports, unilateral transfers, and the balance on all capital transactions involving securities of an original maturity longer than 1 year. The assumption behind the basic balance concept is twofold. *First,* it is presumed that all short-term capital transactions (maturing in less than 1 year) are compensatory in nature, i.e., are undertaken as a way of offsetting surpluses or deficits in the other accounts. *Second,* and partly as a consequence of the first point, it is presumed that only long-term capital transactions are basic, whereas short-term transactions are soon reversed. It is thus natural to exclude short-term transactions from the measure of BOP, since they are assumed to be either compensatory, or volatile, or both.

The basic balance has the great merit of concentrating on the more fundamental changes. But many short-term capital movements are independent transactions in their own right. Not only do they pass the autonomous-compensatory test, but should be placed "above the line" also because they probably constitute a systematic source of payments or receipts. The basic balance concept thus tends to underestimate autonomous transactions. It will consequently tend to overestimate a BOP deficit (or underestimate a surplus) when there is a net inflow of *autonomous* short-term capital, and underestimate a BOP deficit when such short-term capital account is itself in deficit. Still, while hardly perfect in practice, the basic balance concept is a useful one, especially if applied to a number of years and as a means of comparing the BOP of different countries.[14]

Appendix 2:
Various
Measures
of
the
Balance
of
Payments

The Net Liquidity Balance In addition to current and long-term capital trans-actions, the net liquidity concept places above the line those short-term capital flows that are not liquid, i.e., not readily convertible into cash. The net liquidity concept (which includes the errors and omissions item) leaves below the line only movements of liquid private capital and of governmental reserves of foreign currency and gold. In other words, the concept places below the line all changes of international cash and near-cash items. A BOP deficit on this basis is a net decrease in the country's holdings of foreign cash and near-cash as compared to foreign holdings of its currency and liquid assets.[15]

The main practical difficulty with the liquidity concept rests in the distinction between "liquid" and "nonliquid" assets. The "cashability" of an asset depends on the willingness of people to accept it. And that ranges from zero, for an asset that nobody wishes to buy, to the perfect liquidity of an asset that is considered "as good as gold," and all gradations in between. Any dividing line between liquid and nonliquid is as arbitrary as a dividing line between short-term and long-term capital. Furthermore, the liquidity definition does not really satisfy the criterion of separating autonomous transactions from those that are "forced" upon the country by the need for offsetting imbalances in the autonomous accounts.[16]

The Official Settlements Balance The official settlements balance returns to the idea of distinguishing autonomous from compensatory items. The basic balance, as was seen, tries to make such distinction on the grounds of the *type*

---

[14] This is because the basic balance is a symmetrical measure of the BOP, in the sense that if the basic balances of all countries were added up, the total of deficits would about equal the total of surpluses. A country's exports would obviously equal the rest-of-the-world's imports from it, and a net outflow of longer-than-one-year capital would equal the net flow into the rest of the world from the country in question. The symmetry is present also in the trade balance, but is not characteristic of many other BOP measures.

[15] Many industrial countries use as a BOP measure the so-called balance of mon-etary movements, a similar measure to the net liquidity concept used in the United States.

[16] There is even less to be said for the particular variant of this concept that was the only one used by the U.S. government until 1965: This is the *gross liquidity balance*, which placed above the line only changes in liquid claims on foreigners while leaving below the line changes in liquid liabilities to foreigners. This is equivalent to saying that the country's overall liquidity is not improved by an increase in its own citizens' private holdings of foreign cash and near-cash, but is worsened by an increase in the foreigners' pri-vate holdings of dollars and liquid U.S. capital. The gross liquidity concept operated on the curious theory that foreign governments have total control over the currency and liquid assets held by their private citizens, whereas the U.S. government cannot draw at all on the holdings of foreign currency and liquid assets of U.S. citizens. The definition thus systematically tended to overestimate BOP deficits and underestimate surpluses. The gross liquidity concept had its defenders in the olden days of the "dollar shortage," when it was conceivable that the U.S. government would be able to single-handedly support the dollar exchange rate even against a wholesale cashing in of official and private hold-ings of dollars and liquid U.S. assets. But since that time, with the U.S. BOP deficits of the past 10 or so years, the total holdings of dollars and U.S. liquid assets held by foreigners (the so-called dollar "overhang") have increased so enormously that the con-cept has lost any relevance it might have had in the past. (See Chapter 15.)

The
Foreign
Exchange
Market
and
the
Balance
of
Payments

of transaction: The transaction is assumed to be autonomous if long-term, compensatory if short-term. The official settlements concept instead recognizes that one cannot be sure of the motivations underlying a particular kind of transaction. It replaces the short-term, long-term criterion with a private-official criterion, looking at all transactions by private individuals as autonomous and considering as compensatory only the changes in governmental reserves of international cash. The theory is that, since it is the function of the government, and only of the government, to undertake compensatory residual actions, compensatory transactions can be identified with the government's own acquisition or expenditure of monetary reserves. A BOP deficit, therefore, is said to exist if there occurs a net decrease in the monetary reserve assets relative to the liabilities of the *official* monetary authorities, a BOP surplus if there is a net increase. One of the difficulties with the official settlements concept is that monetary authorities sometimes do operate for their own autonomous reasons, as for example when the accumulation of official reserves is an independent official goal and not a passive response to offset a net surplus in the private transactions. Furthermore, with the much greater degree of exchange-rate flexibility in recent years (see Chapter 15) changes in government reserves are no longer an adequate measure of the disequilibrium on the foreign exchange market, as the disequilibrium can manifest itself through a change in the exchange rate. Still, the official settlements concept is widely used and is the measure employed by the International Monetary Fund.

In Summary All possible measures of the BOP, including those reviewed here, have their problems, some more than others. In general, there is no such thing as a universally valid concept of the BOP that can serve equally well the purposes of all countries and measure exactly what it is purported to measure. Furthermore, the differences between the various measures are not purely conceptual. The measure used has a significant effect on whether a deficit or a surplus is found to exist and of what size it is. This is exemplified in Table 9.3, which shows the calculation of various balances for the United States in the sample years 1973 and 1974. Thus, note that while the BOP showed a deficit on all three of the general measures, by the basic balance definition the deficit was smallest in 1973; by the official settlements definition, in 1974; and by the liquidity definition it was largest in both years. Also, while the deficit increased only slightly by the official settlements definition, it more than doubled on a liquidity basis and went up 11 times by the basic balance criterion.

In 1965, an advisory committee on U.S. balance-of-payments statistics (known as the Bernstein Committee from the name of its chairman, Edward Bernstein) recommended replacing the gross liquidity balance with the official settlements concept. At that time, when the dollar exchange rate was fixed, the relative merits of the notions of "capacity to defend the dollar" (underlying the liquidity definition) and of "degree of official intervention" (underlying the official settlements balance) could be discussed and assessed in a reasonably substantive fashion. The 1965 committee was thus able to arrive at a broad consensus on the official settlements definition as the single most desirable measure (although, by way of compromise, the U.S. Commerce Department continued to show the gross liquidity balance along with the official settlements balance).

In 1975, another prestigious advisory committee met to discuss the same BOP measurement issue. By that time, however, the world monetary scene had changed substantially. As Chapter 15 recounts in detail, the dollar had been

TABLE 9.3   U.S. Balance of Payments, 1973 and 1974
(Billions of Dollars) *a*

Appendix 2:
Various
Measures
of
the
Balance
of
Payments

Account	1973	1974
Exports of Merchandise	+71.4	+98.3
Exports of Services *b*	+30.7	+46.1
Imports of Merchandise	−70.4	−103.8
Imports of Services *b*	−27.4	−37.0
Trade Balance	+4.2	+3.6
Unilateral Private and Government Transfers, Net	−3.8	−7.2
Current Account Balance	+0.4	−3.6
Net U.S. Government Capital Flows (Excluding Reserve Transactions)	−1.5	+1.1
U.S. Direct Investment Abroad	−5.0	−7.3
Foreign Direct Investment in the United States	+2.7	+2.2
Net U.S. Purchases of Foreign Securities	−0.8	−2.0
Net Foreign Purchases of U.S. Securities (Excluding Treasury)	+4.1	+0.7
Net Change in U.S. Long-Term Loans to Foreigners	−1.4	−1.6
Net Change in Foreign Long-Term Loans to United States	+0.6	−0.5
Long-term Capital Balance	−1.3	−7.4
Basic Balance	−1.0	−10.9
Net Change in Nonliquid Short-term Claims on Foreigners	−5.1	−14.8
Net Change in Nonliquid Short-term Liabilities to Foreigners	+0.8	+1.8
Errors and Omissions	−2.4	+4.8
Net Liquidity Balance	−7.7	−19.0
Net Change in Private Liquid Claims on Foreigners	−2.0	−6.1
Net Change in Liquid Liabilities to Private Foreign Accounts	+4.3	+16.8
Official Settlements Balance	−5.3	−8.4
Net Change in U.S. Reserve Assets	+0.2	−1.4
Net Change in Liabilities to Official Foreign Accounts	+5.1	+9.8
Balance on All Accounts	0.0	0.0

Source: U.S. Department of Commerce.

a Figures may not add up to totals shown because of rounding.
b Includes military transfers, purchases, and sales.

formally devalued twice, in 1971 and in 1973, and had been practically allowed to "float" since mid-1973. Many other currencies were also on a floating basis. The measurement issue had become murky indeed. It was hardly possible to advocate one "best" indicator of the extent of intervention to prevent exchange rate changes when the exchange rate was in fact allowed to fluctuate. The 1975 committee did agree on some things. It agreed that there is no substantive economic difference between trade in merchandise and in services, and hence opposed using the merchandise trade balance as a measure of BOP equilibrium.

The
Foreign
Exchange
Market
and
the
Balance
of
Payments

It also agreed on the continuing usefulness of the balance on goods and services, owing to its link with domestic income and employment (discussed further in Chapter 10). Also, the committee saw clearly the irresistible temptation of both policy-makers and the media to latch on to a single figure, whether appropriate or not, as "the" measure of U.S. BOP deficit or surplus. Yet, it did not (and probably could not) recommend an overall measure of the BOP, and confined itself to urging that the entire BOP should be analyzed as an integral whole.

Points for Review

1. Review the following terms:
a. *The* foreign exchange market
b. Foreign exchange dealers
c. Foreign exchange brokers
d. Hedge
e. Cover
f. Acceptance
g. Spot and forward exchange rates

2. Define the exchange rate of a country's currency.

3. What is the difference between appreciation and depreciation, on the one hand, and revaluation and devaluation, on the other?

4. What are the three main functions of money?

5. Define "arbitrage." How does it differ from speculation?

6. How does operating in the forward foreign exchange market eliminate the risk of variations in the exchange rate?

7. On the basis of the following hypothetical data, calculate the interest-rate parity 6-month forward rate of the dollar in terms of the German mark.

Yearly interest rate in the United States: 8 percent
Yearly interest rate in West Germany: 12 percent
Spot exchange rate: $1 = 4.00 DM

8. This is a lengthy exercise, indirectly covering much of the material in the text. Construct the U.S. BOP on the basis of the information provided here, following the format and categories shown in Table 9.3 in Appendix 2. The transactions are in part hypothetical, but they do add up to the totals and subtotals in the U.S. BOP for 1974. Thus you should refer to Table 9.3 while doing the work, and use it as a check on the correctness of your results. Make sure you understand why the various items are credits or debits, why the balance on all accounts must be zero, and how the subbalances relate to one another. There is only one item missing from the following list, but you should not be surprised that it is "omitted." All figures are in billions of dollars.

U.S. firms and individuals sell to foreign residents 98.3 worth of goods.

U.S. corporations acquire control of a number of foreign corporations by purchasing a total of 2.0 in shares of stock.

U.S. portfolio holdings of foreign long-term securities increase by 2.0.

Foreign corporations import 0.7 worth of shares of stock of U.S. corporations that they do not control.

Foreign residents purchase from Americans a total of 15.1 in insurance, transportation, and various services other than tourist travel.

U.S. tourists spend a total of 7.1 on foreign travel, of which 1.0 goes for purchases of various services from U.S. firms.

U.S. residents send a total of 1.5 in remittances to their relatives abroad.

The U.S. government and its agencies make grants to less developed countries totaling 5.0.

Americans purchase from foreigners a total of 9.9 worth of insurance, transportation, and various services other than tourist travel.

U.S. corporations receive 26.1 in income from their invesements abroad.

CARE, The American Red Cross, and other private U.S. charities give a total of 1.2 in grants to foreign residents.

U.S. corporations purchase outright 2.1 worth of foreign manufacturing plants.

The U.S. government buys 0.6 worth of foreign long-term securities.

Foreign corporations receive 15.9 in income from their investments in the United States.

U.S. firms and individuals buy from abroad 103.8 worth of goods.

Foreign tourists in the United States spend a total of 2.0 net of their payments to non-U.S. firms and travel organizations.

The U.S. government adds a total of 0.1 to its reserves of monetary gold.

U.S. military sales abroad amount to 2.9.

Foreigners repay 0.4 of their long-term debts to U.S. banks.

Foreign corporations spend a total of 2.2 in direct investment in the United States.

The United States spends abroad 5.1 for direct defense purposes.

The U.S. government sells to foreigners 0.5 worth of its long-term securities.

Foreigners send a total of 0.5 in remittances to their relatives in the United States.

U.S. holdings of nonliquid, short-term, private foreign assets increase by 14.8 on a net basis.

U.S. corporations spend a total of 3.2 to purchase additional shares of stock of foreign corporations that they already control.

Foreign private holdings of short-term liquid U.S. assets increase by 16.8 on a net basis.

The U.S. government's liabilities to foreign monetary authorities increase by a net total of 9.8.

U.S. banks make a total of 2.0 in loans to foreigners repayable in a period longer than 1 year.

The
Foreign
Exchange
Market
and
the
Balance
of
Payments

U.S. exports to private foreigners nonliquid short-term assets worth a total of 1.8.

Americans repay 0.5 of their long-term debt to foreign private banks.

U.S. private holdings of liquid short-term foreign assets increase by 6.1 on a net basis.

The U.S. government's holdings of foreign currency reserves and other monetary reserve assets increase by a net of 1.3.

9. What are the three main uses of the BOP?

10. Review your understanding of the distinction between current and capital transactions and between short-term and long-term capital transactions.

11. Review your understanding of the concept of "net foreign investment."

12. Unilateral transfers abroad appear with a minus sign. Yet they are gifts. Why does the export of gifts not carry a plus sign like all exports should? Similarly, if a bank exports money by lending it abroad, shouldn't this transaction be a credit rather than a debit?

13. If the recorded total of credits and debits does not add up to zero, the only possible implication is that some items have been missed or that someone has made mistakes. Is this statement correct?

14. Review your understanding of the balance of international indebtedness and of its relationship to the flows shown in the BOP.

15. Review your understanding of the distinction between autonomous and compensatory transactions and of the rationale for that distinction as a basis for measuring BOP equilibrium.

16. No matter where you draw the line, the algebraic sum of BOP items above the line must be equal to the algebraic sum of the items below the line but with the opposite sign. Is this true?

Questions for Discussion

1. By the interest-rate parity principle, if there is no difference in interest rates in different countries, the cost of hedging against exchange rate fluctuations over a 1-month period is the same as the cost of hedging over a 6-month period. Is this correct?

2. What can in practice interfere with the neat operation of the interest-rat parity principle as the determinant of spot-forward rates differentials? Indeed, considering that in any economy there are many financial instruments, each carrying a different interest rate, degree of risk, and liquidity, just how does the interest-rate parity principle translate into actual practice?

3. It is stated in the text that BOP credits and debits should not be considered necessarily good or bad. Find an example of a deficit in the accounts of an individual family that the family would consider good and an example of a surplus that could be considered bad.

4. On the basis of your own receipts and expenses over some past period of time, try to distinguish those items that are of a current nature from your capital transactions.

5. On the basis of your own receipts and expenses, reflect on whether your finances are in equilibrium by the autonomous-transactions criterion.

6. On the basis of your estimated receipts and intended expenditures over some future period of time, reflect on whether your finances are in equilibrium in the "program balance" sense. If an imbalance shows up, what does this tell you about your future actions and possibilities?

7. Do chickens coming home to roost have anything in common with a continuing excess of absorption over national production?

8. Would you include unilateral transfers (particularly governmental foreign aid) in the trade account, or in the long-term capital account, or would you list them separately? (Think about it. The question is much less narrow than it seems.)

9. "The market balance and the program balance concepts both identify equilibrium with a situation where intentions (under the existing circumstances) match accomplishments. But the players whose intentions and accomplishments are relevant differ as between the two concepts." Discuss this statement, with particular attention to the ways in which the two concepts may in practice shade into one another.

"If you wish to avoid foreign collision, you had better abandon the ocean."

Henry Clay, 1812.

International Trade and National Income

The
Interaction
Between
Foreign
Trade
and
the
Domestic
Economy

What to Expect

This chapter introduces foreign trade into the analysis of the factors that determine the level of national income and employment. This topic is important in its own right and also is essential to understanding the mechanics of adjustment to balance-of-payments disequilibria under alternative monetary systems. The material of Chapters 11–14 will be difficult to follow without an understanding of both Chapter 9 and the material of this chapter. Particularly in this chapter, although this is generally true, do not proceed to a new point unless you are reasonably sure that you understand the previous ones. The chapter progresses from very simplified models of the economy on to a more realistic representation of the link between foreign trade and national income. The analysis starts with a review of the income determination model in the simple closed economy case with no foreign sector, followed by the parallel case of an open economy with no domestic saving or investment and by the case of a more realistic economy, with saving and investment as well as imports and exports. Next the effects of economic repercussions from foreign countries are analyzed. Finally, the chapter concludes with a discussion of some policy implications for an open economy. As elsewhere whenever appropriate in this book, the analysis is carried out in three "languages": words, diagrams, and algebra in the Appendix.

One important word of caution: Nowhere in this chapter is there any mention of the effects of monetary changes, much less an adequate discussion of those effects. Indeed, it is explicitly assumed throughout the chapter that the price level remains constant. This is not because monetary phenomena do not matter. They matter very much indeed. However, for the sake of a clearer exposition of international finance, the analysis of the effects of monetary changes is incorporated in Chapters 11, 12, and 13, which examine the complex process of economic adjustment to external disturbances under different international financial arrangements.

The Interaction Between Foreign Trade and the Domestic Economy

When calculating a businessman's total income, one needs to include not only the receipts from sales in his principal market but also those from sales to individuals in other regions of the country; also, one must subtract not only the cost of materials purchased from surrounding firms but also that of materials purchased from firms in other regions. Similarly, *national income* must include the value of exports to other countries; also, since national spending on consumption, on investment, and by the government partly goes to buy goods and services produced abroad, imports must be subtracted to obtain a satisfactory measurement of the value of national production.

Therefore, an intimate relationship exists between the foreign trade sector and the level of national income.

In introductory economics, the analysis of income determination usually begins with the instructor writing on the blackboard the familiar income equation:

$$Y = C + I + G + X - M$$

where Y is national income, C is consumption, I is investment, G is government spending, X is exports, and M is imports. Often, however, as soon as all the terms are explained, the instructor proceeds to erase X and M and continues the analysis under the assumption of a "closed economy," i.e., one that does not trade with other countries. The reason is that the picture is thereby made simpler, and the essential concepts of income determination analysis can be explained more easily and understood more readily.

This chapter reintroduces exports and imports into the analysis of the factors that determine the level of national income. It must be understood at the outset that the inclusion of the foreign sector is a straightforward expansion of the closed economy model and involves no conceptual change.

Model I: A Review of the Simple Closed Economy Case

Let's start with the simplest possible case: A hypothetical economy where national income can be spent only on domestically produced consumer goods and services; there is no government spending and no foreign trade. The essential operation of the economic system can be visualized as a **circular flow** of resources, goods and services, payments and incomes. The nation's business sector buys from the public a flow of resources that it needs in order to produce commodities and services that it hopes eventually to sell. Payments for the services of these factors of production (labor, capital, land, materials) constitute a reverse flow, from the business sector to the public. These payments are costs from the viewpoint of the businessman, but they are incomes to those who receive them. And **profit**, which is the difference between total revenue and total cost, is part of the businessman's own income. Therefore, the sum total of all incomes generated by the production process must necessarily equal the value of goods and services produced.[1]

---

[1] Suppose that in order to produce a typewriter that sells for $100 a businessman must pay out $50 in wages for the labor services required, $20 in rental of the needed space and machinery, and $20 to purchase materials and components as well as for all other costs of production. The sum of all costs is $90. These of course represent incomes totaling $90 for those who receive the payments. Does this mean that the value of production is $10 greater than the total incomes generated by production? Clearly not, for the remaining $10, which remains in the businessman's pocket, is his income. Thus, since profit is income and is always defined as whatever is left over after all production costs are paid, the sum of all incomes generated by production of the typewriter is necessarily equal to the value of it.

The
Interaction
Between
Foreign
Trade
and
the
Domestic
Economy

When incomes are spent, payments flow to the business sector in exchange for a reverse flow to the public of the goods and services that business has produced.

If all incomes are spent, the necessary equality of the value of national production and national income means that the entirety of national production is sold and that the national economy is at equilibrium. Other things being equal,[2] there is no net tendency for the level of national production and national income to change: The value of all the goods and services that the nation's business sector is willing to produce and sell (**aggregate supply**) is equal to that which the public is willing to buy (**aggregate demand**). The equality of quantity supplied and quantity demanded at the national level results in equilibrium of national income in the same way as the market for an individual commodity is at equilibrium when the quantity that people are willing to produce and sell is equal to the quantity that people are willing to buy.

But suppose that not all incomes are spent on consumer goods and services. The emergence of **saving** (which is by definition nonspending on domestic consumption) means that the national economy is no longer at equilibrium. If a portion of income is not spent, the corresponding portion of national production must go unsold. The level of national production (and hence of national income) must eventually fall as producers adjust their production downward to meet the smaller aggregate demand. National income can remain at equilibrium only if exactly that portion of it that is not spent by consumers is spent by other economic agents. In this first model, **investment** (spending on new capital goods) is the only possible injection of spending other than domestic consumption. The Model I condition for national economic equilibrium is thus that the portion of income that consumers desire to save be equal to desired investment spending by businessmen.[3]

As already noted, the general condition for national income equilibrium is always the equality of aggregate supply and aggregate demand. Thus, the total leakages out of the flow of spending on domestically produced consumer goods and services must be exactly matched by injections of spending from sources other than domestic consumers. It is only in this first model that saving must equal investment. This hypothetical economy may be lik-

---

[2] One of the assumptions of this analysis is that prices are constant. This means that any change in the national income and product is a "real" change, i.e., it is a change in the physical volume of production and not merely in the price level. In turn, this is equivalent to assuming that if income rises, unemployment will fall and that if income falls unemployment will increase.

[3] In simple algebraic terms, if NP is desired national production, Y is national income, C is the value of consumer goods and services produced as well as the expenditures on such goods and services, S is desired saving, and I is desired investment, we have: (1) $NP = C + I$ (2) $Y = C + S$ and, since $C = C$, in order for NP to equal Y, we need (3) $S = I$.

ened to a washing machine in operation. The agitator generates continuous internal movement of the water; but the water level remains constant as long as there is no leak. If a leak (saving) occurs, the water level (national income) can remain constant only if the same amount of additional water (investment) is poured in the machine. If the inflow of additional water (investment) is less than the leakage (saving), the water level (national income) will fall, and, if it is greater, the water level must rise.

What happens in this economy when there occurs an *autonomous* increase in investment?[4] In the absence of an increase in desired saving, aggregate demand is now greater than aggregate supply: with prices constant, aggregate supply, employment, and income will eventually rise. Ultimately, however, they will go up by more than the initial investment increase. This **multiplier** effect is not a magic trick, but a necessary result of the circularity of economic processes. The new investment spending generates an equal amount of new income for those who produce the goods newly purchased and of new employment of the resources needed to produce those goods. The individuals who receive the new income normally do not save the whole of it. What they do spend out of their additional income is itself new spending. It thus must go to buy goods and services that would not otherwise be produced, and it yields a second round of new income for the individuals who produce these goods and new employment of the resources needed. In turn, producers of these goods now see their income augmented, and they normally spend a portion of it. This chain of spending, income creation, and respending continues on, each link being weaker than the preceding one (since some income is saved at every round) but nevertheless calling forth additional production from the economy.

Suppose that a businessman decides to increase production capacity and spends an additional $100 per week to hire an extra worker. The $100 of additional spending immediately results in a $100 additional income for the worker hired (provided that he was unemployed to begin with). The worker will not usually save the entirety of his income increase; if he dedicates one half of it to new purchases and one-half of it to new savings, he will spend $50 a week on things that would not otherwise have been bought and hence would not have been produced, as, for example, a $50 radio. The producers of the radio now see *their* income augmented by $50. If they also spend half of the increase in income, yet another $25 will go to buy goods or services that would not otherwise be produced and will augment someone else's income by that amount. The ultimate increase in national income and production (which is given by the sum of the income increases at each round)

[4] **Autonomous investment** is defined as investment spending that is not related to the level of national income; "induced" investment occurs because of an increase in income. For simplicity's sake, here it is assumed that all investment is autonomous. Induced investment can, however, be introduced in the model without any conceptual difficulty (see Appendix).

The
Interaction
Between
Foreign
Trade
and
the
Domestic
Economy

is therefore obviously greater than the initial increase in spending and income. The increase in national income can be in real terms (i.e., correspond to an effective increase in production and not merely arise from price increases), however, only if there are unemployed resources in the economy. The increase in income will be permanent only if spending remains at the higher level. Otherwise income will drop back to its previous level. (It is left to the reader to trace the effects of a *reduction* in aggregate demand.)

Clearly, the greater the portion of new income destined to new spending at each round, the greater the strength of the multiplier effect. Thus, the **marginal propensity to consume** (or *MPC*)—the ratio of a change in consumer spending to a change in income—is directly related to the size of the multiplier. The greater the *MPC,* the greater the proportion of new income spent at every round and, consequently, the greater the ultimate increase in national production. And conversely, the greater the **marginal propensity to save** (or *MPS*)—the ratio of the change in saving to a change in income—the smaller the multiplier effect. At every round a greater portion of new income is siphoned off into new saving. In a closed economy, as the Appendix shows, the multiplier is equal to the reciprocal of the marginal propensity to save: $1/MPS$.

Model I is shown in Figure 10.1a. The only leakage out of the domestic spending stream is domestic saving (S), and the only source of spending aside from spending on domestically produced consumer goods and services is domestic investment (I). In Figure 10.1a, S and I are measured along the vertical axis and national income (Y) along the horizontal axis.

If it is assumed that planned investment is autonomous, i.e., that it does not change *as a result of a change in income,* the investment function I is a horizontal line. If some part of an income change is reflected in a change in saving and does not entirely spill over into a change in consumption (which is equivalent to assuming that the *MPS* is greater than zero), the saving function has a positive slope. The slope of that function is the *MPS.*[5] The condition for national income equilibrium is the equality of desired saving and desired investment; in Figure 10.1a, saving and investment are equal at an income of 250. Income is at equilibrium and, in the absence of a shift in the saving or the investment schedule, will remain constant at that level.

Suppose now that there occurs an increase in investment by 50 (from I to I'). Other things being equal, income will rise and eventually settle at

[5] The slope is the ratio between the vertical change and the horizontal change, in this case the ratio between the change in saving and the change in income. The intercept of the saving function is negative, for it is normally assumed that some consumption must go on even at zero income level; if so, at zero income saving must be negative. If you find this difficult to swallow, consider the situation of a newly unemployed person, who, with zero current income, must draw down accumulated savings in order to survive, i.e., has a negative current rate of saving.

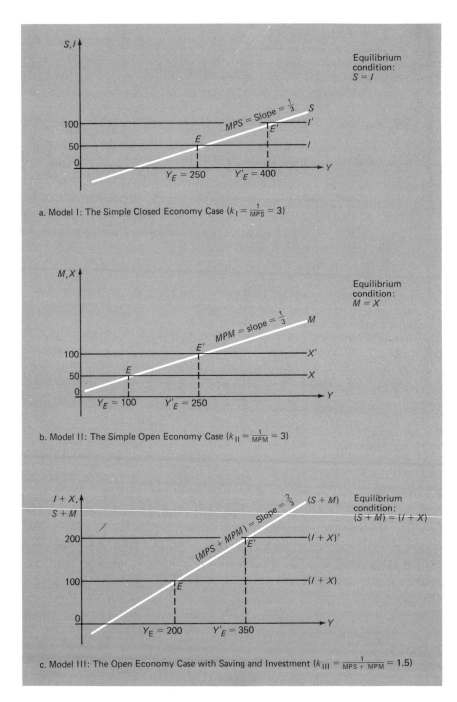

a. Model I: The Simple Closed Economy Case ($k_{\text{I}} = \frac{1}{\text{MPS}} = 3$)

b. Model II: The Simple Open Economy Case ($k_{\text{II}} = \frac{1}{\text{MPM}} = 3$)

c. Model III: The Open Economy Case with Saving and Investment ($k_{\text{III}} = \frac{1}{\text{MPS} + \text{MPM}} = 1.5$)

FIGURE 10.1

the new equilibrium level of 400. Only at that level is desired saving again equal to the (higher) desired investment. The ultimate increase in income (150) is clearly greater than the initial increase in spending (50). Specifically, in Figure 10.1a the income increase is three times as large as the investment increase. This is because in that diagram the MPS (the slope of the saving function) has been assumed to be 1/3; consequently the multiplier, $1/MPS$, is 3.[6]

What has been found then? In general, if the level of aggregate demand (desired national expenditure) increases, national production, income, and employment will eventually also increase and vice versa. Further, if the marginal propensity to consume is greater than zero, there is a multiplier effect such that the overall change in national production is greater than the initial change in spending. With specific reference to Model I, where saving is the only leakage out of the flow of domestic spending, it was found that *in the simple case of a closed economy the condition for national income equilibrium is the equality of desired saving and desired investment*, and the multiplier is $1/MPS$.

Model II: The Simple Open Economy Case

The relatively detailed review of the simple closed economy case allows proceeding speedily and simply to take into consideration the existence of the foreign trade sector. (The symmetry of these models is complete.) Consider a hypothetical simplified economy that does trade with other countries but where there is no saving and investment and no government spending. In this economy, national production can consist only of goods and services produced for domestic consumption and goods and services produced for export; and national income can be spent only on domestically produced consumption goods and services or on imports. Imports are by definition spending on goods and services produced abroad. Even though they may be expenditures by consumers, they are not expenditures on domestic production, and thus do not generate national income.

In this model, imports are the equivalent of saving in Model I. They also are a leakage out of the domestic spending stream. The emergence of imports means that national income can be at equilibrium only if "someone else" spends on national production that portion of income that consumers spend on imports. In this second model, where investment is ruled out, exports (spending by foreigners on domestically produced goods and services) are the only possible injection of spending other than domestic consumption expenditures. In the simple open economy case the condition for

[6] One can also see that the ΔS going from 250 to 400 Y is equal to the ΔI. Hence, since the economy was at equilibrium to begin with, it is also at equilibrium when income rises to 400, for S equals I in both cases.

nation income equilibrium is thus the equality between imports and exports.

What happens in this economy when, starting from equilibrium, there occurs an increase in exports? Aggregate demand is now greater than aggregate supply. At constant prices, national income, production, and employment will go up. Ultimately, they will go up by more than the initial export increase because of the operation of the multiplier. The multiplier effect operates in this economy as well and in exactly the same manner as it functions in a closed economy. It is still true that the multiplier is greater if the *MPC* is greater. Only now the concept of the *MPC* must be narrowed down to the marginal propensity to consume domestically produced goods and services. Since the possibility of saving has been ruled out in this model, imports are here the only leak out of the domestic spending flow. The **marginal propensity to import** (or MPM)—the ratio of the change in spending on imports to the change in income—is the exact parallel of the *MPS* in Model I. The greater the *MPM*, the smaller the multiplier effect, for at every round a greater portion of new income is siphoned off into new imports. As the Appendix shows, in Model II the multiplier is equal to the reciprocal of the marginal propensity to import: $1/MPM$.

Model II is shown geometrically in Figure 10.1b. The only leakage out of the domestic spending stream is imports, M, and the only injection of spending other than domestic consumption spending is exports, X. In Figure 10.1b, M and X are measured along the vertical axis, and national income, Y, along the horizontal axis. If fully autonomous exports are assumed, the export function X is a horizontal line. If a *MPM* greater than zero (in this example, $1/3$) is assumed, the import function M has a positive slope. The equilibrium level of income is 100, corresponding to the equality between desired imports and exports at a level of 50. Suppose that there occurs an autonomous increase of exports by 50, from X and X'; the new equilibrium income will be 250, where imports and exports are again equal, but at the higher level of 100. Income increases by 150, or three times the export increase, since the multiplier $1/MPM$, is in this case equal to 3.

It is still true in this model that changes in aggregate demand will cause national production to change in the same direction and that the ultimate change in national product will be a multiple of the initial change. But, since in this model there is no saving or investment, in the simple open economy case the *condition for national income equilibrium is the equality of imports and exports*, and the multiplier is $1/MPM$.

Model III: The Open Economy Case with Saving and Investment

Models I and II are obviously unrealistic representations of actual economic systems. Almost all countries do at least some trading with foreign countries

The
Interaction
Between
Foreign
Trade
and
the
Domestic
Economy

and have some domestic saving and investment. But now, after analyzing the simple cases, it should be quite straightforward to elaborate a model of income determination closer to actual economic reality. Let's keep for the moment the simplifying assumptions of no government spending, no induced investment, and no induced exports. But let's expand the definition of national product to include consumption goods, investment goods, and exports, and the definition of national expenditure to include domestic consumption spending, investment, and imports.

In this economy there are two possible leakages out of the domestic spending flow: a part of income may go into savings and some income may be spent on imports. But also, there are now two sources of spending other than domestic consumption spending: businessmen may spend on investment and foreigners may purchase some of the economy's production—exports. It should come as no surprise to the reader that in this economy the condition for national income equilibrium is that the sum of desired saving and desired imports, $(S + M)$, be equal to the sum of desired investment and desired exports, $(I + X)$.[7] The equality of domestic saving and investment is no longer required. An excess of saving over domestic investment will not cause national income to fall if it is exactly matched by *foreign* investment, i.e., a surplus of exports over imports. The equilibrium condition for an open economy may also be written, therefore, as: $S - I = X - M$. This clarifies the meaning of the proposition previewed in Chapter 9, to the effect that a trade surplus means an excess of production over domestic absorption, whereas a trade deficit implies that the country is "living beyond its means." If, starting from equilibrium, investment falls, in the absence of a corresponding decline in savings (increase in domestic consumption), the foreign trade balance will be in surplus. It is very instructive to spend a few minutes on the various implications of the $S - I = X - M$ equilibrium condition.

Starting from equilibrium, either a change in investment or a change in exports will cause national income to change in the same direction. And the multiplier is still related to the domestic MPC. But now, what is not spent on domestic consumption may be spent on imports or saved. Therefore, the greater the sum of the MPM and the MPS, the smaller the multiplier; it can be shown that in this case the multiplier is $1/(MPS + MPM)$. This is known as the **foreign trade multiplier** without foreign repercussions (which are discussed in the next section). The algebraic formulation of Model III is shown in the Appendix.

Model III is depicted in Figure 10.1c. Saving, S, and imports, M, are both leakages out of domestic spending. The saving function may therefore be added to the import function to form a combined $(S + M)$ function. The

[7] (1) $Y = C + M + S$; (2) $NP = C + I + X$; (3) $C = C$. Hence, in order for aggregate supply (NP) to equal aggregate demand Y, the condition here is
$$(S + M) = (I + X) \qquad (4)$$

slope of the combined function is the sum of the slopes of the separate ones, hence, the slope of the $(S + M)$ line is $(MPS + MPM)$: in this example, 2/3. Similarly, exports, X, and investment, I, are both components of total spending. The export function may be added vertically to the investment function to form a combined $(I + X)$ line. Equilibrium is here determined by the intersection of $(S + M)$ and $(I + X)$. An income level of 200 satisfies the equilibrium condition that the combined leakages be equal to the combined expenditures. Suppose that a doubling of investment plus exports occurs (whether from the investment or from the export side is in this model immaterial). The $(I + X)$ function will shift to $(I + X)'$, and national income will rise to its new equilibrium level of 350. The ratio between the income increase and the initial spending change is, of course, the multiplier, which can readily be seen to equal the reciprocal of the slope of the combined $(S + M)$ function: $1/(MPS + MPM) = 1.5$.

In general, therefore, the multiplier effect for an open economy is weaker than for a country that does not trade with the outside. But also, an open economy is subject to the possible additional "disturbances" coming from the export side. Whether an open economy experiences, on balance, greater or less economic instability than if it did not engage in foreign trade is an empirical question for which no general answer is possible. In any case, the foreign trade multiplier is smaller than the closed economy multiplier (in the assumption that the MPS is the same). Note, however, that so far it has been always implicitly concluded that a change in spending has exactly the same effect on aggregate income, whatever its source. In particular, nothing in the previous analysis calls for distinguishing between the income effect of an export change from that of an investment change. The next section, which takes into account the inevitable repercussions of domestic economic events on foreign countries will show that in reality this is not so.

Model IV: The Income Multiplier with Foreign Repercussions

The analysis so far has proceeded on the implicit assumption that economic policies have no effects except on a country's own economy. But a country cannot very well have a foreign trade sector unless the rest of the world trades with it. It is time to point out the obvious, but crucial, fact that *a nation's imports are the rest of the world's exports to it, and that its exports necessarily equal the total amount imported by other countries from that nation.* Thus, not only does a country's economic prosperity depend partly on events occurring elsewhere, but also, the country's economic activity exerts some influence on developments in other parts of the world. The country's influence on the international economy, in turn, is related to the nation's economic "weight," i.e., its importance as a major supplier or pur-

The
Interaction
Between
Foreign
Trade
and
the
Domestic
Economy

chaser of other countries' products. A large country must therefore take into account the effects of its economic policy on the rest of the world, for those effects will generate repercussions on the country's own economy that will modify the initial results of its economic policy. The foreign economic sector is the channel through which economic changes in large nations are transmitted to other countries, eventually flowing back to their source and modifying the impact of the initial changes. The fundamental implication of such economic interdependence in the world economy is examined in the last section of this chapter. This section describes how the income multiplier differs if foreign repercussions are taken into account.

In general, taking into account foreign repercussions results in a more complex multiplier formula because marginal propensities to import and to save elsewhere in the world must now be included in the analysis. In addition, while in the earlier simplified models the multiplier was the same regardless of the source of the spending change, in this more complete model the multiplier differs depending on whether the foreign repercussions lessen or reinforce the impact of the initial change in the country's economy. A change in a nation's foreign spending (an autonomous change in either imports or exports) is for other countries equivalent to a change in the *opposite* direction; in this case, the economic repercussions on the nation, originating from those other countries, will cut down the overall impact of the spending change. Instead, a change in domestic spending (an autonomous change in consumption, investment, or government expenditures) affects other economies in the *same* direction as it affects the country in question; the foreign repercussions will in this case reinforce the economic impact of the change.

Autonomous Change in Foreign Spending Suppose that the United States experiences an autonomous decrease in imports as the result of imposing higher tariffs. Other things being equal, the U.S. national income rises, with the eventual total increase being greater than the initial spending change owing to the multiplier effect. But a decline in U.S. imports necessarily means a fall in the exports of other countries to the United States, and this, of course, causes their national income to fall. With the decline in foreign income, foreign imports also decrease in proportion to the foreign *MPM*. A part of that decrease is at the expense of U.S. exports. In turn, the decline in U.S. exports, while almost certainly much smaller than the initial decline in the country's imports, does have a negative influence on U.S. national income and cuts down the U.S. multiplier effect. And so, in this case, the income multiplier is smaller than it would be in the absence of economic repercussions from abroad. This chain of events can be summarized in shorthand form as follows (where *RW* stands for the rest of the world)[8]:

---

[8] The income multiplier with repercussions, for an autonomous change in imports or in exports, can be shown to be given by:

$$M_{US} \downarrow \rightarrow Y_{US} \uparrow, X_{RW} \downarrow \rightarrow Y_{RW} \downarrow \rightarrow M_{RW} \downarrow, X_{US} \downarrow \rightarrow Y_{US} \downarrow$$

It is left to the reader to trace out the effects of an increase in imports or of autonomous changes in exports. Remember, in any case, that income changes can be in real or in money terms, depending on the assumptions one makes about the extent of employment in various countries. Therefore, a smaller multiplier can be bad or good depending on the direction of the change and on the initial circumstances. Thus, if in this example there happens to exist strong inflationary pressures in the U.S. economy to begin with, a decrease in imports would generally tend to worsen the situation; a weaker multiplier effect as the result of foreign repercussions would probably be considered advantageous.

Autonomous Change in Domestic Spending Suppose instead that the United States experiences an autonomous increase in domestic expenditure (whether in investment, consumption, or government). Other things being equal, the U.S. national income rises, with the eventual total increase being greater than the initial spending change owing to the multiplier effect. But now, as U.S. income rises, U.S. imports follow suit, and the rest of the world witnesses an increase in their exports to the United States. Foreign countries' national income goes up, and, with it, their imports from the United States, thus reinforcing the U.S. multiplier effect and ultimately leading to an increase in U.S. national income greater than it would have been in the absence of foreign repercussions. This chain of events can be summarized as follows [9]:

$$(C + I + G)_{US} \uparrow \rightarrow Y_{US} \uparrow \rightarrow M_{US} \uparrow, X_{RW} \uparrow \rightarrow Y_{RW} \uparrow \rightarrow M_{RW} \uparrow, X_{US} \uparrow \rightarrow Y_{US} \uparrow$$

For a country such as the United States, with enormous weight in the world economy, the foreign repercussions of domestic economic events are

$$k_{IVa} = \frac{1}{MPS_{US} + MPM_{US} + MPM_{RW}(MPS_{US}/MPS_{RW})}$$

The multiplier is smaller if the foreign marginal propensity to save is smaller and if the foreign marginal propensity to import is greater. The smaller the foreign MPS, the greater the foreign countries' income decline caused by the initial decrease in U.S. imports (their exports); the greater the foreign MPM, the greater is the fall in foreign imports as a whole (and in imports from the United States in particular) induced by the income decline. Thus, the greater is the extent to which the repercussions from abroad cut down on the U.S. multiplier effect. The mathematical derivation of the multiplier with repercussions is complex and need not be reproduced here. The interested reader can easily find it in more advanced treatises on international economics.

[9] The income multiplier with repercussions, for an autonomous change in domestic spending, is thus larger than for a change in foreign spending and can be shown to be given by the following formula

$$k_{IVb} = \frac{1 + (MPM_{RW}/MPS_{RW})}{MPS_{US} + MPM_{US} + MPM_{RW}(MPS_{US}/MPS_{RW})}$$

likely to be considerable. A small country, however, can afford to disregard foreign repercussions in its determination of national income changes. The repercussions do occur, but are too small to matter.[10] However, while the smaller economic entities in the world need not be concerned about the effects of *their* policies on the rest of the world, they had better be concerned about external economic developments, which are likely to affect their economy to a very considerable extent.

The International Transmission of Economic Disturbances

The previous section concluded with the observation that small countries need not be concerned with foreign economic repercussions, which are instead likely to be considerable for large nations. There is here a similarity to the argument made by contemporary political theorists, to the effect that in the modern world national power is to a large degree impotent,[11] owing to the unacceptable (nuclear) risks of any but the most careful and limited use of it: "... once it became clear that, being in a bottle, the two scorpions [the two superpowers] had lost some of their sting, other beasts decided they had their chance."[12] To be sure, there is merit in the notion that economically weak countries have somewhat greater policy freedom because of their very lack of economic weight (and hence the absence of concern about the effects of their actions on the international economy). What remains abundantly true, however, is that in far more important respects small countries are severely dependent on economic developments occurring outside their borders—and much more so than economically powerful states. As was pointed out in Chapter 1, there is an inverse correlation between the size of a country and the relative importance of foreign trade, since in a larger country a greater proportion of trading needs can be met through internal exchange. The greater relative importance of foreign trade for small countries thus implies that their economic prosperity, and their general capacity to set independent economic policy, depends in large measure on external economic developments. Compared to this constraint, the small

[10] Note that what is relevant here is the country's economic weight in relation to its trading partners and not in relation to the world economy as a whole. Thus, for example, even a very small nation should seriously consider possible foreign repercussions when its foreign trade is highly concentrated on the imports and exports of other small countries. In the extreme case of fully bilateral trade—when two countries trade with one another exclusively—foreign repercussions will be considerable even if the countries are quite small in relation to the rest of the world.

[11] The term "impotence of power" was coined by Raymond Aron (see "Macht, power, puissance," *Archives Européennes de Sociologie*, 1964, vol. 5, no. 1).

[12] Stanley Hoffman, *Gulliver's Troubles, or the Setting of American Foreign Policy* (New York: McGraw-Hill, 1968), p. 35.

nations' freedom from concern about the effects of their policies on the outside world is indeed puny.

At any rate, all countries depend on the international economy to the extent that they have economic relations with other states. The fundamental implication of the relationship between foreign trade and national income is the economic interdependence among different states. The main thrust of the discussion on the theory of international trade was that countries generally gain through trade and suffer real economic losses when they choose for any good or bad reason to restrict economic relations with other countries. That side of the coin is the economic gain reaped from specialization and division of labor. But there is (as always) another side to the coin: Specialization and division of labor require trading with—thus in a sense being dependent on—other nations. At least in the short run, you cannot both keep the cake of economic insulation and eat of the fruits of economic efficiency. (But keep in mind that for some nations, and particularly for less developed countries, certain short-term losses may be the inevitable price of developing a comparative advantage in fields of higher growth potential.) Of course it is perfectly legitimate for a country deliberately to choose to forsake some of the gains of international specialization to lessen its dependence on foreign sources of supply or on foreign markets. But if instead the decision falls on the side of maximizing short-term economic advantage, there must be a realization that this gain necessarily means greater economic interdependence with other countries. This is as true in the macroeconomic sense as it is of trade in specific commodities and services.

Foreign trade is the channel through which economic events in one country are transmitted to its trading partners. By and large, favorable economic developments in one nation have favorable effects on the rest of the world and vice versa. Take as an example the chain of events that was sparked, and fueled, by the U.S. economic downturn in the 1930s. It is a simplification, but a basically correct one, that the downturn was caused by a dramatic decline in domestic investment, accompanied by a reduction in the quantity of money. Even without the deliberate U.S. policies designed to improve the situation at the expense of foreign countries (policies discussed in Chapter 8), the U.S.-Europe economic interdependence would have worked, and did work, as follows: The decline in U.S. investment caused a fall in U.S. national income; the income decrease spilled over partly into a decrease in imports; the decrease in imports, which were of course the exports of other countries, spread the economic downturn to those countries. Nor was this the last of the ripples in the pond, for the onset of depression abroad meant, among other things, a decline in foreign imports, some of which constituted a decline in U.S. exports, thus aggravating the depression in the United States even further.[13] As a consequence of this

---

[13] Remember that for an autonomous change in domestic spending, as in this instance, the foreign repercussions reinforce the multiplier effect rather than cut it down.

process, in 1929 the United States sold $5,157 million worth of merchandise abroad and purchased from foreign countries $4,399 million worth of merchandise, for a balance of trade surplus equal to $758 million. In 1932, the worst depression year, U.S. merchandise exports had fallen to less than one-third the 1929 level, to $1,576 million, and its merchandise imports had dwindled to $1,323 million, for a trade surplus of only $253 million. U.S. (and international) trade did not recover until after the onset of World War II. In a very real sense, American unemployment was being exported abroad: The foreign trade sector constituted the vehicle by which the economic infection spread throughout most of the world.

The policies followed in those years by both the United States and Europe reinforced the transmission mechanism. The correct policy for both the United States and the European countries would clearly have been the *offsetting* of such transmission; the economic situation would have been alleviated for both sides. But in the absence of international cooperation (and of effective institutions to promote it) each side acted on the basis of what it saw as its own short-term self-interest, with the longer-term result just described.[14]

The great lesson of the 1930s was that unilateral action in an interdependent world invites disaster. To use a pedestrian, but essentially accurate, metaphor, your neighbor's housecleaning habits have a great deal to do with the cleanliness of your own house and of the entire block. You may be able to insulate yourself from vermin coming from next door (albeit at a cost), but by far the best approach is for everyone to keep his own house clean to begin with. That lesson was learned well by those responsible for creating the post–World War II commercial and financial international system, but might eventually be forgotten, as have been other lessons of long ago. In 1968, political theorist Stanley Hoffman expressed the view that: "Nations are economically interdependent enough not to indulge in the kinds of suicidal policies that marked the national responses to the great depression of the 1930s, yet they are not so interdependent as to be forced to break out of their national shells, or able to disrupt the world through isolated acts of autarchy."[15] Perhaps so. But international events in the 1970s make one wonder whether Hoffman's essentially optimistic diagnosis still applies and whether the lip service paid to the need for international cooperation will be translated into operational policies or whether we might be on the way to a repeat performance of the 1930s play, although on a different stage and with some new actors.

[14] Essentially the same mechanism can operate to spread inflationary pressures throughout the world. It is left to the reader to trace out the probable steps involved.

[15] *Gulliver's Troubles,* p. 42.

Appendix: Simple Algebraic Formulation of Income-Determination Models

Model I can be summarized in simple algebraic form as follows. For an economy at equilibrium, if Y is national income, C is consumption spending, and I is investment, we may write: (1) $Y = C + I$. If all invesement spending is autonomous, we have: (2) $I = I^*$, and, if we assume consumption to be a linear function of income, we have: (3) $C = c + MPC(Y)$, where MPC is the marginal propensity to consume and both MPC and c are constant. Substituting from (2) and (3) into (1), we obtain: (4) $Y = c + MPC(Y) + I^*$. Subtracting $MPC(Y)$ from both sides, factoring out Y, and dividing through by the resulting term, $(1 - MPC)$, we obtain: (5) $Y = (c + I^*)(1/1 - MPC)$, where $(1/1 - MPC)$ is, of course, the multiplier It follows from the definition of marginal propensities to save and to consume that, in a closed economy, their sum equals one. Hence, the multiplier, k, may also be written as: (6) $k_I = 1/MPS$.

Another way of arriving at the same result is the following. Call ΔSp the initial change in spending and ΔY the overall change in income. At each round, new spending will be given by new income (spending at the previous round) multiplied by the MPC. If the MPC is constant, we have

$$\begin{aligned} \Delta Y &= \Delta Sp + (MPC \cdot \Delta Sp) + MPC(MPC \cdot \Delta Sp) \\ &\quad + MPC[MPC \cdot \Delta Sp)] + \ldots \\ &= \Delta Sp + (MPC \cdot \Delta Sp) + (MPC^2 \cdot \Delta Sp) \\ &\quad + (MPC^3 \cdot \Delta Sp) + \ldots + (MPC^n \cdot \Delta Sp) \end{aligned}$$

Dividing through by ΔSp, we obtain a measure of the change in income per unit of change in spending, i.e., the multiplier

$$\Delta Y / \Delta Sp = 1 + MPC + MPC^2 + MPC^3 + \ldots + MPC^n = k_I$$

This is an infinite geometric progression; at the limit (if the MPC is constant), we have:

$$k_I = 1/(1 - MPC) = 1/MPS$$

The algebraic formulation of *Model II* is exactly parallel to that of Model I. The only required changes are the substitution of X for I and of M for S. It might be useful to go through the steps on your own. The multiplier is

$$k_{II} = 1/MPM$$

The algebraic formulation of *Model III* is perfectly symmetrical to that of Models I and II. It may be useful at this point to modify the model somewhat in order to add consideration of government spending and of induced exports and induced investment. Assuming that only government spending is autonomous and that all relationships between the induced variables and income are linear, we have

$$Y = C + I + G + X - M \tag{1}$$

$$C = c + MPC(Y) \tag{2}$$

$$I = i + MPI(Y) \tag{3}$$

where MPI is the marginal propensity to invest.

$$G = G^* \tag{4}$$

$$X = x + MPX(Y) \tag{5}$$

where MPX is the marginal propensity to export. The MPX has several possible economic meanings, ranging from an accelerator concept to a vent for surplus possibility.

$$M = m + MPM(Y) \tag{6}$$

Substituting from (2) through (6) into (1), subtracting all income terms from both sides, factoring out Y, and dividing through, we have

$$Y = (G^* + c + i + x - m) \; \frac{1}{[1 - (MPC + MPI + MPX)] + MPM} \tag{7}$$

But the term $[1 - (MPC + MPI + MPX)]$ is by definition equal to the marginal propensity *not* to spend on domestically produced consumer goods and services, i.e., the marginal propensity to save. Thus, the multiplier may be written as $k_{III} = (1/MPS + MPM)$ even when government spending, induced exports, and induced investment are taken into account. This expansion of the simple model looks, and is, easy on paper. However, incorporating induced investment and induced exports introduces serious practical difficulties, and the estimation of the model requires solving many weighty econometric problems. When, in addition, the assumption of constant prices is removed, monetary effects must also be considered and the policy solution to income determination becomes complex indeed. Nevertheless, the analysis here provides the basic theoretical foundations on which actual policy must rest, at least as a first approximation.

Points for Review

1. Review your understanding of the following basic concepts and principles:
a. Aggregate supply and aggregate demand
b. Circular flow of economic activity

c. Income-product identity
d. Income-product equality as condition of national equilibrium
e. Saving-investment equality as condition of national equilibrium in the closed economy
 f. Marginal propensities to save and to import
g. General meaning of the multiplier effect
h. Multiplier in the closed economy
 i. Multiplier in the simple open economy
 j. Foreign trade multiplier for an open economy with saving and investment. Why is it lower than for a closed economy?
k. Autonomous and induced changes in spending
 l. Foreign repercussions
m. Impact of foreign repercussions in the cases of domestic spending changes and foreign spending changes
n. Conceptual distinction between national economic equilibrium and full employment
o. General mechanism of international transmission of economic disturbances

---

Questions for Discussion

1. In the *ex post* sense, saving always equals investment: the condition for closed economy equilibrium is the equality of *intended* saving with *intended* investment. In the simple open economy case, the equilibrium condition is the equality of intended imports with intended exports. Is it also true in such a case that ex post imports must necessarily equal ex post exports?

2. Are not taxes a leakage out of the domestic spending stream? How can they be taken into account within the framework outlined in this chapter? What is the corresponding injection of spending? Is there any net effect on the level of economic activity if a tax increase is matched dollar-for-dollar by an autonomous decrease in imports?

3. If the quantities supplied and demanded are not equal in the market for a particular commodity, certain changes can be expected. What is it necessary to assume in order for the inequality of *aggregate* supply and *aggregate* demand to lead to changes in the physical volume of national production?

4. If it is generally true that aggregate supply follows aggregate demand, what can you expect if aggregate demand increases beyond the full employment level? Is it possible for such an outcome to result from changes in exports or imports?

5. "An autonomous change in exports causes a change in national income that in turn leads to an induced change in imports." Is this a correct statement?

6. The text uses a tariff increase as an example of a possible source of an autonomous fall in imports. Why is this decline termed autonomous? Isn't it in-

duced by the tariff increase? Can you think of other sources of autonomous changes in exports or in imports? (Hint: Refer to the basic determinants of supply and of demand.)

7. Is international economic instability good, bad, or indifferent? Why?

8. "A weak man is 'freer' than a strong man in the sense that he doesn't have to worry about the use of his strength." Does this statement bear relevance for the standing of small countries in the world economy? In your own mind, is power accompanied by responsibility preferable to powerlessness accompanied by freedom from concerns about the exercise of power?

9. Benjamin Franklin said in 1776 (in a different context): "We must all hang together, or assuredly we shall all hang separately." Do you see a parallel in the current international economic situation of the industrialized world?

10. Does your reading of recent international economic events lead you to conclude that we are headed toward fragmentation or toward renewed co-operation among industrial countries in the economic sphere?

*"... constant as the northern star, of whose true fixed
and resting quality there is no fellow in the firmament."*

Shakespeare, *Julius Caesar*

*"They would wonder much to hear that gold, which
in itself is so useless a thing, should be everywhere so
much esteemed, that even men for whom it was made,
and by whom it has its value, should yet be
thought of less value than it is."*

Thomas More, *Utopia*

Automatic Monetary Systems:
Fixed Exchange Rates

What to Expect

Disequilibrium in a country's international transactions engenders a tendency for several important changes. Whether this tendency is allowed to operate, and the manner in which the international payments' balance is restored, depends to a large extent on the characteristics of the prevailing international monetary system. Some international financial systems operate automatically without governmental policy intervention. Other monetary systems instead allow for the exercise of "discretion" by the authorities, and the process of adjustment to international payments' disequilibrium incorporates a degree of deliberate management through public policy. This and the following chapter examine the two automatic mechanisms of adjustment: permanently fixed exchange rates and completely flexible exchange rates. Chapter 13 discusses the discretionary international monetary systems intermediate between those two extremes, with special attention to the Bretton Woods system in existence from World War II until the early 1970s. Chapter 14 contains a sketch of twentieth-century international financial history and Chapter 15 outlines the political economy of international financial developments since 1971.

The consequences of BOP disequilibrium under a regime of permanently fixed exchange rates are examined in this chapter through a description of the workings of the gold standard, the best known among fixed-rate systems. The introductory section provides a general focus for the classification and analysis of alternative international monetary systems. The next section examines the workings of the gold standard mechanism, including an explanation of how exchange rates are fixed, the price and expenditure changes through which the system automatically restores BOP equilibrium, and the conditions under which the system operates effectively. The final section introduces the difficult problem of making policy for the achievement of domestic economic goals when the exchange rate is not allowed to vary.

International Disequilibrium and Adjustment

Chapters 9 and 10 have provided the basic concepts needed to analyze the workings of international finance. As usual, it is best first to set out the extreme forms of the international monetary system, in order to have a sense of the full range of possibilities, and leave examination of the intermediate forms until later.

To place the analysis of international monetary systems in perspective, recall very briefly the basics of supply and demand and the meaning of market equilibrium. The premise is quite simple. If you can do what you wish to do under the prevailing circumstances, you have no incentive to act and change those circumstances. If buyers can obtain all they want to buy at the prevailing price and sellers can sell all they want at that (same)

Automatic
Monetary
Systems:
Fixed
Exchange
Rates

price, no buyer has an incentive to offer a higher price and no seller is willing to accept a lower one. The market is in equilibrium because everyone can do what he wishes to do at that price. There is no tendency for the price, or the quantities bought and sold, to change. There is nothing good or bad about this situation—the meaning of equilibrium is quite simply that there is no net tendency for the situation to change.

Hence, disequilibrium necessarily implies the existence of a net tendency for change. If, for example, the quantity *demanded* equals the quantity *bought,* but the quantity *supplied* is greater than the quantity *sold,* buyers are effectively satisfied while some sellers are not able to sell as much as they would wish to sell at the prevailing price. This excess supply leads sellers to bid against one another, thus driving down the price. As the price falls, the quantity supplied declines at the same time as the quantity demanded rises, with the disequilibrium being corrected on both accounts.

This is very elementary and undoubtedly familiar to you. It is also one of the major ways in which an imbalance in a country's international transactions can be corrected. Take the case of a deficit in the balance of international trade (leaving aside capital transactions for the time being). The value of imports is greater than the value of exports *at the prevailing relative prices* of imports and exports. There is, in effect, excess demand for the foreign products or, which is the same thing, excess supply of U.S. products on the international market.[1] This disequilibrium can be expected to engender a tendency for relative prices to change, if they are allowed to, with the relative price of U.S. imports rising and the relative price of exports falling.

The crucial difference is that *two* prices are at work in international transactions. One, of course, is the price of the goods and services themselves, in terms of the currency of the selling country. The other is the price of the country's currency, i.e., the exchange rate. The price to the buyer is determined by both the foreign price and the exchange rate. Suppose, for example, that a Mercedes automobile sells for 27,000 German marks. The price of the car in terms of U.S. dollars depends also on the rate of exchange between the dollar and the mark. If the dollar exchange rate is 3 marks (the price of 1 mark is 33 cents), an American importer pays $9,000 for the car (abstracting from transportation and other transfer costs). The price to the importer can therefore change *either* through a change in the German price of the car *or* through a change in the exchange rate *or* through a combination of both. The dollar price of the car doubles to $18,000 either if the German price doubles to 54,000 marks (with the exchange rate fixed) or if the price of the German mark doubles to 66 cents instead of 33 cents (with the German price of the car remaining the same) or through any number of

---

[1] If you are unclear about this, go back to the notion of reciprocal demand explained in Chapter 2.

possible combinations of changes in both the internal price in Germany and the exchange rate of the German mark. The effect on the American demand for German cars is the same, since, obviously, that demand depends on the dollar price of the thing. Fewer German cars are imported, and the U.S. balance-of-trade deficit is lessened. The same kind of process is at work to increase U.S. exports through a decline in their foreign currency price.

In actuality, *the process of adjustment to a BOP disequilibrium always involves internal as well as external changes, whether or not the rate of exchange is fixed. Also, any mechanism of adjustment operates not only through price effects but, through changes in national income, expenditure, and quantity of money as well.* International capital flows also play a part. For a clear exposition, however, it is convenient to set out the two extreme cases of adjustment through price changes. At one pole, there is a system that keeps the exchange rate completely and permanently fixed and thus relies to a maximum extent on internal changes to correct BOP imbalances, implying, as will be seen, maximum international interdependence. At the opposite pole, there is a system that allows the exchange rate to change freely and thus relies to a minimum extent on internal changes, implying, as a first approximation, maximum independence in economic policy-making.

As a starting generalization (as will be seen, matters are far less simple), a flexible exchange rate system restores balance in the country's international transactions by allowing one important price to change, namely, the price of the country's currency itself; a fixed exchange rate monetary system restores balance by allowing a realignment of the country's internal price structure. Think of the operation of a flexible rate system as akin to unscrewing a burnt-out light bulb by standing in the same place and turning your hand. Think of the operation of a fixed rate standard as akin to grasping the bulb firmly and unscrewing it by walking around and around.[2]

Completely fixed and completely flexible exchange rates are at opposite extremes but, as extremes often do, they touch in one fundamental respect. They both operate automatically and need no government intervention to aid in restoring BOP equilibrium. Indeed, in their pure form, they permit no such intervention. This is not true of intermediate mechanisms, which rely on some combination of both exchange rate changes and internal readjustment, and thus incorporate a need for discretionary policies to limit both full exchange rate flexibility and full internal flexibility.[3]

---

[2] Lest you jump from this analogy to the premature conclusion that a flexible rate system is "obviously" more efficient, let it be emphasized that in practice some very complex issues are at stake. Pushing the same metaphor, ask yourself which system would be more "efficient" if your wrist were broken.

[3] Since there is an infinite number of such possible combinations, there are any number of conceivable international monetary systems. You could easily invent your own by simply picking on a particular combination of external and internal changes that has not already been incorporated into someone else's proposed system. One can still, however, make a general and meaningful distinction between intermediate sys-

Automatic
Monetary
Systems:
Fixed
Exchange
Rates

While it does sound appealing to have an adjustment mechanism that operates all by itself, one should not confuse automaticity with either efficiency or desirability. Remember, as so often repeated, that BOP credits and debits are not necessarily good or bad, that equilibrium may mean a stable but very unpleasant state of affairs, and that one person's "government meddling" is another person's "wise policy intervention," depending on whose ox is gored and on a host of other considerations, and not only economic considerations at that.

An important distinction exists, however, between government intervention that is a part and parcel of a mechanism to eventually restore external balance, and intervention that suppresses the disequilibrium by interfering with trade and capital flows. The latter policy has been called "quasi-adjustment." There is a presumption, as was seen in Part II, that this is harmful for the country and for the international system as a whole. For example, a balance-of-trade deficit can be "corrected" by raising import tariffs, but with the net losses such a step entails. To the extent that the international adjustment mechanism functions well, countries have less of a temptation to recur to quasi-adjustment policies and to increase restrictions on international trade and capital movements.

Adjustment Under Fixed Exchange Rates: The International Gold Standard

General Features of the Gold Standard

In a fixed-rate system the changes engendered by external disequilibrium are the same whether the international monetary standard is gold, silver, uranium, wheat, or, for that matter, the national currencies themselves. The crux of the matter is the existence of fixed rates of exchange among national currencies and a constant ratio between the stock of "international money" held by a country and the supply of money circulating in the domestic economy. The particular form of the asset that happens to be internationally accepted as a medium of exchange, store of value, and unit of account, is immaterial. Gold simply happens to be a metal that people have historically valued highly because it is especially scarce and pleasant to look at and is a convenient form of money because it is easily divisible, easily worked into ingots or coins, easily stored, hard to counterfeit, and so forth.

---

tems that are closer to the fixed rate extreme and those that rely primarily on exchange rate changes. The best example of the former type is the Bretton Woods system in operation until very recently; an example of the latter type is the operation of stabilization funds, which try only to smooth out exchange rate fluctuations rather than prevent them. Both are examined in Chapter 13.

Adjustment
Under
Fixed
Exchange
Rates:
The
International
Gold
Standard

A mechanism similar to that of the international gold standard operates to correct balance-of-payments disequilibrium of regions within a country, which, of course, all use the same currency. A system of permanently fixed rates of exchange among different currencies is almost equivalent to the existence of a single currency. What does it matter to have to pay in German money for purchases of German products, if you can freely obtain it and you know for certain that there exists an immutable relationship between the German money and the dollar? As previewed in Chapter 1, the importance of international currency differences rests on the possibility that exchange rates might vary and not on the relatively minor inconvenience of having to deal with differently colored pieces of paper.

The main general features of the gold standard are as follows:

1. The exchange rate of the national currency is fixed in terms of gold and therefore in terms of all foreign currencies that are also linked to gold.

2. The process of adjustment to BOP disequilibria operates automatically, without government intervention beyond its firm commitment to buy and sell gold at the price implied by the "gold content" of the national currency.

How Is the Exchange Rate Fixed?

The exchange rate between currencies emerges indirectly from the separate actions of national governments to link their currency to gold. Suppose, to take the simplest example, that the U.S. government decides that all the money circulating in the economy will consist of gold coins with George Washington's face stamped on them, each called a "dollar" and containing exactly one-tenth of an ounce of gold. The government commits itself not to change the gold content of the coin. Across the ocean, at the same time or later, it does not matter, the German government decides to mint a coin with Otto von Bismarck's face on it, containing exactly one-fiftieth of an ounce of gold, calls it a "Deutsche mark," and commits itself not to change the gold content of it. The exchange rate of the dollar in terms of gold, and of the Deutsche mark in terms of gold, is fixed. But equally fixed, though indirectly, is the exchange rate of the dollar in terms of the mark. If: $\$1 = 1/10$ oz gold, and $1 \text{ DM} = 1/50$ oz gold, then

$$\frac{\$1}{1 \text{ DM}} = \frac{1/10 \text{ oz gold}}{1/50 \text{ oz gold}} = 5, \text{ and } \frac{1 \text{ DM}}{\$1} = \frac{1/50 \text{ oz gold}}{1/10 \text{ oz gold}} = 0.2.$$

The dollar exchange rate in terms of marks is 5, and the Deutsche mark exchange rate in terms of dollars is 0.2. One dollar buys 5 marks, and one mark is worth 20 cents. (Remember that U.S. newspaper listings actually give the exchange rates *of foreign currencies* in terms of the dollar.)

Automatic
Monetary
Systems:
Fixed
Exchange
Rates

Actual circulation of gold coins is not necessary for the gold standard. The same result obtains if the United States and Germany print pieces of paper with Washington's and Bismarck's faces on them and keep their gold respectively in Fort Knox and in the Bundesbank basement, *provided* that the paper money is legally declared to correspond to a certain quantity of gold, that the two governments are committed to buy and sell gold at the price implied by the gold content of each national currency (in our example, $10 per ounce and 50 DM per ounce), and that no governmental restrictions exist on international shipping of gold. As long as these conditions obtain, the exchange rate between the dollar and the DM cannot deviate significantly from the "mint parity" of 5 DM for $1.

The reason it cannot is arbitrage (discussed in Chapter 9). Suppose that the dollar actually sells for only 4 DM instead of 5 DM, i.e., at a 25 percent discount from the mint parity. You could make a riskless 25 percent profit by:

1. Selling 1,000 DM on the foreign exchange market and obtaining in return, at the current rate of exchange, $250.

2. Exchanging the $250 for 25 ounces of gold, which the U.S. government is legally obligated to buy and sell at $10 per ounce.

3. Shipping the 25 ounces of gold to Germany.

4. Buying 1,250 DM in exchange for the 25 ounces of gold, which the German government is committed to buy and sell at 50 DM per ounce.

Through such a process of sales of marks and purchases of dollars on the foreign exchange market, the price of the mark would be driven down and the price of the dollar would go up. The opportunity for quick, riskless profit would be present and hence arbitrage would continue until the exchange rate went back to the level implied by the gold content of the two currencies, i.e., 5 DM = $1.

In practice, of course, one cannot ship gold across the Atlantic at no cost. Thus, arbitrage is profitable only if the deviation of the exchange rate from the mint parity is greater than the cost of transporting gold. Even in a "pure" gold standard, therefore, the exchange rate can fluctuate by small amounts up and down, although within very rigid upper and lower limits. These limits are called the *gold export* and the *gold import* points. When the exchange rate of a country's currency (as defined earlier) rises to a level higher than the mint parity by an amount greater than the cost of transporting gold (i.e., is above the gold import point), it becomes profitable to sell that currency in exchange for foreign money, exchange the foreign money in return for gold from the appropriate foreign government, import the gold into the country, and exchange it for a greater sum than one started with. As this happens, the exchange rate is driven back down into the gold points range. Similarly, the exchange rate cannot fall below the gold export point for any but the briefest period of time.[4]

Adjustment
Under
Fixed
Exchange
Rates:
The
International
Gold
Standard

The Adjustment Process under the International Gold Standard

Chapter 2 outlined one partial explanation of the process of adjustment to BOP equilibrium in a regime of fixed exchange rates. This was Hume's gold-specie-flow doctrine, which, based on a rudimentary formulation of the relationship between the quantity of money and the price level, concluded that trade surpluses and deficits could only be temporary, and hence that mercantilist policies were self-defeating. The economic changes caused by external imbalance are far more complex than the operation of the simple gold-specie-flow mechanism. As is true of all international monetary systems, the fixed exchange rate regime of the gold standard relies on both price effects and real expenditure changes to bring about BOP equilibrium. Let us follow them through starting from the hypothetical case of a U.S. external deficit, whether originating in the current account or in the capital account. A clear understanding of the material presented in Chapters 9 and 10 is essential to follow the process detailed here.

Price Effects You will remember from Chapter 9 that a net inflow of imports of goods, services, and capital assets over the corresponding exports necessarily means an equal net outflow of international cash and near-cash to pay for the import surplus. In the gold standard, gold is ultimately the only international money. A deficit in the autonomous transactions thus necessarily causes a compensatory outflow of gold.

The country's holdings of gold, in turn, are in a fixed relationship with the total money supply circulating in the country. The gold outflow thus causes a decline in domestic money supply in proportion to the ratio between the total quantity of domestic money and the stock of gold. For example, if a total of $5 circulates for every dollar's worth of gold held in the United States, a gold outflow causes a contraction of the money supply five time as large. Actually, gold is incidental to the operation of the system. Provided that the exchange rate is not allowed to vary, and that a constant relationship is guaranteed by the government at all times between the stock of international money and the domestic money supply, a deficit causes a contraction in the domestic quantity of money regardless of the form of the money asset that is acceptable to settle international transactions. (This is why in Figure 11.1 the "Gold Stock" link is shown in parentheses.)

---

[4] The general knowledge that the exchange rate does not go higher or lower than the gold points motivates short-term capital flows as an additional mechanism of exchange rate stability *within* the gold points spread. As the dollar exchange rate gets close to its upper limit, everyone knows that it has no place to go but down. Americans will want

Automatic
Monetary
Systems:
Fixed
Exchange
Rates

The decline in the domestic supply of money causes a general tightening of credit throughout the economy. With money less readily available, but the same conditions of demand for funds, the general result is an increase in the price of money, i.e., a movement upward of the entire structure of interest rates in the economy, from the **prime rate** (the interest rate charged to the most credit-worthy borrowers) to mortgage rates, interest for home improvement loans, personal loans, and so forth. (As the various rates of interest are to a great extent linked to one another, so that they all tend to go up and down together, it is possible to speak more simply of an increase in "the" interest rate.)

This increase itself contributes to correcting the deficit, for the following reason. Portfolio investment responds to some degree to the international structure of interest rates. Individuals and institutions hold a certain mix of securities from different countries partly as a function of the interest yields carried by those securities. An increase in the U.S. interest rate makes U.S. securities relatively more attractive than before to international portfolio investors and thus leads to some increase in the net inflow of long-term portfolio investment. This effect may or may not be sufficient to "improve" the long-term capital account as a whole. This is because the inflow of foreign *direct* investment might be reduced owing to the reduction in profit opportunities accompanying the contraction in the U.S. economy (to be explained shortly). But it might itself increase because of the opportunity to acquire American productive assets at a bargain price.[5] On balance, it is likely that the long-term capital account, and on this score the BOP as a whole, improves. It is also very likely, however, that this effect would not suffice to wipe out the initial BOP deficit. Nor does it have to all by itself, since other important mechanisms are at work.

The increase in interest rates tends to discourage domestic expenditure as well. With money tight, certain higher-risk loans are no longer granted, and the corresponding investment may not take place. More generally, the rise in interest rates means an increase in the cost of borrowing and, other things being equal, investment becomes less profitable and its amount de-

---

to pay off their short-term debts to foreigners very quickly, while the high value of their dollars lasts, and it is convenient for foreigners to delay as long as possible payment of their short-term debts to residents of the United States, waiting for the value of their currency to go back up. The resulting net outflow of short-term funds contributes to bringing the price of the dollar down. Note the difference between this process, which has an element of speculation in it, although fairly safe speculation, and the riskless arbitrage gold flows that ensue when the exchange rate moves beyond the gold points.

[5] There is, first, the inverse relation between the prices of stock shares and the level of interest rates. An increase in the rate of interest pushes down, under normal conditions, stock prices. Foreign investors might then find it financially feasible to try and acquire control of a corporation by purchasing its outstanding shares of stock. In addition, the general decline in domestic prices discussed later may well encompass the market price of productive assets of various types, possibly leading to a greater inflow of foreign equity capital.

Adjustment
Under
Fixed
Exchange
Rates:
The
International
Gold
Standard

clines. The construction industry is particularly affected, since even a small increase in mortgage rates means (over the long life of the mortgage) the addition of many thousands of dollars to the financing costs. Potential home-buyers are discouraged, new construction projects are postponed, refinancing of existing mortgages is held off until easier money comes back. An interest rate increase also contributes to cutting down on purchases of durable goods, such as cars, which are usually bought partly on credit.

As you know from Chapter 10, investment and consumption are both components of aggregate demand, i.e., the total national expenditure on do-mestically produced goods and services. The initial decline in aggregate de-mand is eventually followed by a greater decline in national income and production, through the working of the spending multiplier. If prices are not completely rigid in a downward direction, the decrease in national income pushes the general level of domestic prices down, or at least prevents them from increasing as much as they otherwise would have.

We are now back in Hume's world. The decline in domestic prices, relative to foreign prices, tends to cause the prices of the country's exports to fall in relation to prices of imports. The exchange rate being fixed, U.S. exports become cheaper in terms of the foreign buyers' currency and im-ports become relatively more expensive in terms of dollars. This change leads to an increase in the quantity of exports and a decline in the quantity of imports, with the size of the quantitative change being a function of the elasticities of the foreign demand for American exports and of the American demand for imports. This is a straightforward improvement in the balance of trade and thus a major corrective of the initial BOP deficit. (But see the discussion of the stability condition in the next chapter.)

Expenditure Effects The process has already been traced to the point where aggregate demand falls. If the economy is at, or below, full employ-ment, and if prices are not sufficiently flexible downward, the decline in aggregate demand is partly translated in a reduction of real income, employ-ment, and production. The direct connection between changes in income and in imports is measured by the marginal propensity to import (discussed in Chapter 10). With a reduction in real national income, all consumption is curtailed, including consumption of imported goods and services. The in-come-induced decline in imports contributes to the restoration of BOP equilibrium.

In addition, if the initial BOP deficit stemmed from the trade account, the autonomous import increase itself directly caused national income to de-cline. Even in the absence of the gold-money-interest-investment chain of effects, therefore, national income would decline and the import surplus would be partly corrected because of this.

A third source of expenditure changes correcting the external imbalance is the **real cash balances** effect associated with the name of the British econ-

Automatic
Monetary
Systems:
Fixed
Exchange
Rates

omist Arthur C. Pigou. The gold outflow and decline in domestic money supply in all probability would cause a decrease in the real cash balances held by individuals and firms. Since people want for any number of reasons to hold a certain amount of cash on hand, they are led by the decline in money supply to curtail their overall expenditures, partly at the expense of imports of consumption goods, services, and foreign capital assets.

The economic changes engendered by a BOP disequilibrium under the gold standard are summarized in Figure 11.1. Merely reverse all the up-and-down arrows to trace the process of adjustment to a BOP surplus. An evaluation of the conditions under which the gold-standard process of adjustment is effective is left to the next section. Keep in mind, however, the general point that if any one of the links of the chains—from the initial BOP deficit to the internal price and/or expenditure changes required to correct the deficit—is broken by government policy or by structural imperfections, the following links, of course, no longer operate. To that extent the adjustment process is prevented from taking place and the external disequilibrium persists.

Conditions of Gold-standard Effectiveness

A mechanism for monetary adjustment, in order to be considered effective, must pass at least the following two tests: The restoration of BOP equilibrium must be complete; the adjustment should be comparatively less "painful" than in alternative mechanisms.

"Completeness" of the Adjustment The first condition implies that the adjustment process must continue to operate as long as the disequilibrium persists, for only then will it eventually restore complete balance. Obviously, if the changes set in motion by a disturbance in the country's external payments do not suffice to adjust to the disturbance completely, some imbalance persists and something else would have to happen outside the confines of the adjustment system in use. Incomplete adjustment is by definition ineffective adjustment.

Of the several changes that are engendered by BOP disequilibrium under the gold standard, two are normally insufficient by themselves to restore balance. The change in interest rates does in all probability affect the capital account in the right direction, but this is by and large a one-time effect that cannot be relied upon to wipe out the BOP deficit. Similarly, the direct effect of a balance-of-trade deficit on national income is only a partial corrective. It is true that, other things being equal, an autonomous import

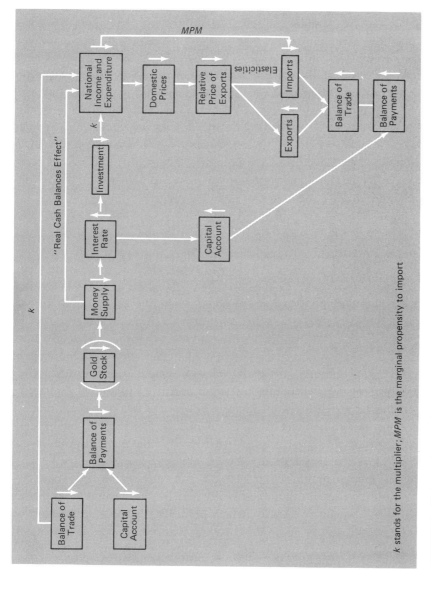

FIGURE 11.1 Balance-of-Payments Adjustment Under the Gold Standard

k stands for the multiplier; MPM is the marginal propensity to import

259

Automatic
Monetary
Systems:
Fixed
Exchange
Rates

increase lowers aggregate demand, but it is virtually certain that only part of that decline will be at the expense of imports themselves, with the remainder constituting a decline in demand for domestically produced goods and services.

Instead, the price effects and the indirect expenditure effects resulting from the reduction in the quantity of money in circulation do not cease until the BOP disequilibrium has been eliminated. Sooner or later, something has got to give. The continuing outflow of gold and consequent decline in domestic money supply—which under the gold standard necessarily go on as long as a deficit exists—will at some point cause enough of a decline in domestic prices and/or domestic income and employment to restore external balance. Similarly, the inflationary effects of a gold inflow and the increase in the quantity of money arising from a BOP surplus must eventually so reduce the competitiveness of the country's exports as to restore overall BOP equilibrium. When all facets of the process of adjustment under fixed rates are taken into consideration, therefore, the gold standard passes the test of "completeness."

Costs of the Adjustment   The gold standard fares much less well, however, on the "painfulness" criterion. All adjustments hurt, but some more than others. As was seen, under fixed rates a BOP disequilibrium sets in motion chains of effects on both prices and national expenditure. To the extent that one set of effects is weaker, the other must bear the brunt of the adjustment.

Let us expand a little on the earlier statement that the gold-specie-flow doctrine rested on a rudimentary notion of the connection between money and prices. This connection is usually referred to as the **quantity theory of money**. The theory arises from the following **quantity equation of exchange,** where M this time stands not for imports but for the total supply of money in circulation, V is the velocity of circulation of money (i.e., how many times it "turns over" during a given period), P is the general price level, and Y stands for national production in physical terms: $MV = PY$. The quantity of money multiplied by its rate of turnover in the economy equals physical national production multiplied by the general price level. Actually, this is merely an identity, which is necessarily true and hence tells us nothing about the workings of the economy. The left side of this expression is the total of all money expenditures on final goods and services; the right side is of course the money value of goods and services produced. It just is not possible for the sellers to receive a different amount of money than the buyers have paid them.

The equation, however, becomes a meaningful theoretical statement if certain assumptions are made. Thus, if it is assumed that V is constant and Y is always at full employment, and hence in the short run also constant,

Adjustment
Under
Fixed
Exchange
Rates:
The
International
Gold
Standard

you arrive at the simple but important prediction that the price level P goes up or down as the supply of money M increases or decreases. There is an on-going controversy as to whether V is in fact constant, but hardly any controversy that the assumption of constant national production and employment does not accord with the facts. Thus, a change in money supply can be expected to have an effect on both the price level and national production.

To put the question differently: With constant velocity of money, the change in the quantity of money caused by a BOP disequilibrium must affect both the price level and real national income and employment *unless* prices change up or down to the full extent implied by the money supply change. It is, on the contrary, a well-known feature of modern industrial economies that prices go up rather easily but come down with great difficulty. A number of structural characteristics, including the presence of monopoly elements in the manufacturing sector and of well-organized trade unions, make it unrealistic to expect a substantial lowering of prices and money wages, with the consequence that much of the realignment of the domestic economy must take place via changes in real national income and employment.

To take the case of total downward price rigidity, if the economy is at or near full employment before a BOP deficit, the entire gold-standard adjustment takes place through unemployment and recession. This is an extreme case. Prices in fact eventually do come down following a decline in demand,[6] but since their flexibility is certainly not complete, a real economic downturn is part and parcel of the gold-standard process of restoration of BOP equilibrium. To be sure, the downturn could be prevented by appropriate government policies to maintain full employment. In such a case, however, the gold standard would in effect be abandoned. As was stated earlier, to the extent that policy cuts any one of the links in the adjustment chains, the adjustment process is stopped in its tracks.

[6] A good example is the effect on automobile prices of the extensive decline in demand during 1974–75. Sticker prices did not come down, despite the accumulation of tens of thousands of unsold cars in dealers' lots, making more than one student wonder if the laws of supply and demand had stopped operating. What did emerge was price reduction in disguised forms, but price reduction nonetheless. First, trade-in values went up. But the trade-in value is determined largely by the new car dealers; for them to offer more money for the same used car is equivalent to lowering the price of the new car. A couple of months later the rebates policy began in earnest. You can surely see that there is hardly any difference between selling a car for $300 less and selling it for the same price but later giving back $300 to the customer. However, the failure of sticker prices to decline was unmistakable evidence of the extreme reluctance of corporations to lower prices. Also, it is true that effective automobile prices did not come down as much as needed to clear the market. When demand picked up again in the following years, instead, prices did go up to the full extent allowed by the more favorable market conditions.

Automatic
Monetary
Systems:
Fixed
Exchange
Rates

Most governments of industrial nations are committed, or at least claim to be, to policies to prevent unemployment. One can hardly expect that they would be willing to allow the full unpleasantness of adjustment through production and employment declines. Nor could a government get away with that kind of attitude in a democratic society. Imagine telling your constituent that you have deliberately allowed him to lose his job because it was necessary to restore BOP equilibrium!

The unpleasantness of the gold-standard mechanism of adjustment is seen by its advocates as an *advantage*. If the consequence of profligate domestic policies is very painful, the system would work to foster economic "discipline" within each country. In turn, as was discussed in Chapter 10, international economic stability does depend to a great extent on each country keeping its own economic house in order. Thus, the very harshness of the gold-standard penalties on those who would trespass against monetary self-discipline would prevent international monetary instability. This reasoning, however, fails entirely when a mechanism of international enforcement of the gold-standard rules is lacking. All nations may be perfectly well aware of the destabilizing effects of irresponsible actions. And yet, confronted with the lack of assurance that other countries will in fact behave according to the rules, the temptation to cheat on the part of each individual state would be irresistible. As will be seen in Chapter 14, the international gold standard held sway during a period when one power, Britain, had uncontested supremacy and could generally be relied upon to abide by the gold-standard rules. In addition, the considerable international mobility of Britain's capital by and large offset its large trade surpluses and financed other countries' trade deficits, thus preventing large BOP disturbances in the international economy from arising in the first place.

These are really the two necessary (but not sufficient) background prerequisites for a functioning international gold standard or, indeed, fixed exchange rate systems in general: *one* state whose dominance and role in the system is so unquestioned that all countries tend to follow its lead, and sufficient international mobility of capital to prevent the worst instances of imbalance in the *overall* external economic relations of the participating countries. In fact, these are similar to the conditions that prevail within a country and are among the reasons why balance-of-payments disequilibria of regions within a country are adjusted to with a minimum of fuss: the unchallenged predominance of the national government and the considerable mobility of capital (and labor) from one region to another. Of course, a region within a country does not have any monetary sovereignty and its economic policy autonomy is severely limited. But so is the economic sovereignty of nations participating in a fixed exchange rate international regime.

Full Employment, Fixed Exchange Rates, and BOP Equilibrium? The Policy Problem

Consider the following policy dilemma that may arise in a fixed exchange rate system. Suppose that the country is in a recession while its BOP is in deficit. The appropriate policy to cure the recession is expansion of the economy: cutting taxes, increasing government spending, easing credit, or whatever. To the extent that the expansionary policy is successful, of course, employment and national income rise. But some of the increase inevitably spills over, through the marginal propensity of import, into additional imports. The external deficit becomes greater. Take the mirror image of that situation: The country is experiencing severe inflation, and its BOP is in surplus. Contractionary policies reduce the rate of internal price increases, but at the same time make the BOP surplus even greater. There is, however, no dilemma when a recession is accompanied by a BOP surplus or when a BOP deficit coexists with inflation. In both cases the same general policy, expansion in the former case and contraction in the latter, can accomplish both objectives. Table 11.1 summarizes the various possibilities.

The term "internal balance" refers to a situation of reasonably full employment with price stability, and "external balance" to a situation of BOP equilibrium. The underlying reason for the existence of policy conflicts is implicit in the terminology used so far: *two* separate goals, internal and external balance, and *one* single policy, either general expansion or general contraction of the economy. Do you remember the Tinbergen rule, discussed in Chapter 7? Here it is again. Policy dilemmas arise when there are more objectives being sought than there are policy instruments actually available. The general solution is plain: either lower your sights and give up on some of the objectives or work at evolving new instruments of policy. The logic of the pure gold standard essentially reduces to allowing the domestic economy

TABLE 11.1   The General Policy Problem under Fixed Exchange Rates

Internal Situation		External Situation	
		BOP Deficit	*BOP Surplus*
Unemployment	I	**Conflict:** Unemployment calls for expansionary policies, BOP deficit for contraction.	II **No Conflict:** Expansionary policy improves both the external and the internal balance.
Inflation	III	**No Conflict:** Contractionary policy improves both the external and the internal balance.	IV **Conflict:** Inflation calls for contractionary policy, BOP surplus for expansion.

263

Automatic
Monetary
Systems:
Fixed
Exchange
Rates

to undergo whatever unemployment or inflation may be needed to restore BOP equilibrium.

As the gold-standard policy of deliberately harnessing the domestic economy to the vagaries of the foreign sector became less and less tolerable, countries began to resort to the quasi-adjustment policies of restricting trade and foreign investment. As discussed in Chapter 10, this tendency became most apparent in the beggar-my-neighbor policies of the 1930s. We can now see that, in addition to their primary "nasty" purposes, these policies contained a defensive element. For, trade restrictions can also be seen as the additional policy instrument needed to reconcile internal economic objectives with the need for some sort of external balance. A costly policy instrument, to be sure, as Part II has abundantly demonstrated. Yet, faced with a choice between the continuation or worsening of domestic depression, and the costs of suppressing external disequilibrium, it should not be surprising that the various countries acting in isolation saw competitive currency devaluations and tariff restrictions of foreign trade as the lesser of two evils.

Fortunately, since the 1930s the general term "economic policy" has been better understood as really subsuming two separate policy tools with different impact on external and internal balance: **fiscal policy,** encompassing mainly changes in taxation and government spending, and **monetary policy,** which influences the supply of money and the level of interest rates. It is now considered that, while both affect domestic as well as external economic variables, fiscal policy is generally more effective for internal purposes and monetary policy for influencing the BOP.

On the internal front, monetary policy is deemed less effective than fiscal measures as a cure for recession: The easing of credit permits greater investment, but cannot guarantee it if profitable investment opportunities are scarce. Fiscal policy, by changing the level of aggregate demand directly through changes in government spending and indirectly by changes in taxes, is instead thought to be effective in recessions as well as in inflationary situations. There is some controversy about that, too. But there is virtually no argument about the *relative* superiority of monetary measures as a means of BOP policy.

Monetary policy not only influences the BOP in the same manner as fiscal policy, through its indirect effects on domestic prices and expenditures, *but directly as well*, through the influence of interest rate changes on the capital account. It then becomes possible, through an appropriate mix of fiscal and monetary policies, to reconcile the objectives of internal and external balance when a conflict exists. Take for example a situation of inflation and BOP surplus (case IV in Table 11.1). A package consisting of fiscal contraction and monetary expansion would operate as follows. Taxes are increased or government spending is cut more than would be sufficient to restore price stability. By itself, this step would plunge the economy into a recession. At the same time, however, the money supply is increased and

Full
Employment,
Fixed
Exchange
Rates,
and
BOP
Equilibrium?
The
Policy
Problem

interest rates are lowered just enough to offset the fiscal policy "overcorrection." But interest rates have also their own independent corrective effect on the external sector. The fall in interest rates increases the net capital outflow (or reduces the net capital inflow) and goes some way toward correcting the BOP surplus. It is clear that in principle there exists an appropriate fiscal-monetary package that restores internal price stability without generating unemployment, while also bringing the BOP back into equilibrium.[7]

The dynamic nature of economic phenomena does not tolerate pat answers to complex questions for very long. Just when people become a little relaxed with the current state of policy-making knowledge something happens to toss the whole issue up for grabs again. In the matter at hand, two new developments have recently emerged to muddy the waters. First, the huge increases in the price of petroleum have swamped, for countries heavily dependent on imports of oil, whatever influence interest rate changes do have on the capital account (see Chapter 15). Second, in recent years domestic inflation *and* unemployment ("stagflation") have been present at one and the same time, adding new complexity to what used to be comfortably called "internal balance." We have been forcefully reminded that a country's economy is like a very intricate and sensitive mobile. To try to move one piece of it results in oscillations throughout the system, with repercussions on the original piece as well. Moreover, since the outside world does not stand still, the mobile is in constant motion even if there is no deliberate policy interference with it.

To this complex challenge different economists have responded in very different ways. Some argue that flexibility in the exchange rate is the additional policy instrument required to eliminate, or at least lessen, policy-making difficulties. Others instead see in the situation a prescription for greater international coordination of economic policies. The overall issue is summarized in the fundamental generalization that, of the three objectives of: (1) economic policy sovereignty, (2) fixed exchange rates, and (3) BOP equilibrium, you can have only two. Sacrificing any one of the three objectives entails some probable costs. If you pursue "sovereign" economic goals, and have the certainty of fixed exchange rates, sooner or later the BOP is sure to get out of whack and stay that way until some sort of adjustment is eventually forced on you by circumstances. You can have both fixed exchange rates and BOP equilibrium (as in the gold standard), provided you give up your independence of economic action. Finally, you could have national policy autonomy and BOP equilibrium, but fixed exchange rates

---

[7] The difference between monetary and fiscal policy is therefore a function of the importance of the capital account. If trade dominates the country's BOP, the independent corrective influence of interest rate changes is minimal; it is zero when capital transactions are altogether nonexistent. Fiscal policy and monetary policy would have in this case the same quantitative influence on the internal and the external sector. They would in fact no longer be different policy instruments in this respect.

Automatic
Monetary
Systems:
Fixed
Exchange
Rates

would have to be abandoned. The controversy over the choice of monetary systems basically hinges on which of the three objectives is to be forsaken. Preferences for one or another international monetary mechanism thus depend to a large extent on the individual economist's assessment of the relative costs of sacrificing any one of the three objectives. This chapter has shown that the gold standard, as any system of fixed exchange rates, in essence sacrifices to the altar of BOP equilibrium the first objective, i.e., the country's freedom to make policy for internal goals. The next chapter explores the functioning of a floating rate system and delineates some of the possible costs of abandoning the second objective, i.e., fixed exchange rates.

Points for Review

1. What is meant in the text by "extreme" monetary systems?

2. Review your understanding of why the pure gold standard requires a strict hands-off policy on the part of the government.

3. If: $1 = 1/10 oz gold; £1 = 1/5 oz gold; 1 DM = 1/50 oz gold, and Fr.Fr.1 = 1/1,000 oz gold, calculate the following mint parity rates.

$1 = ?DM $1 = Fr.Fr.? $1 = £?
£1 = ?DM   £1 = Fr.Fr.?   1 DM = Fr.Fr.?

4. Given the data in the previous question, calculate the dollar's gold points in terms of pounds if it costs 10 cents to ship one ounce of gold between London and New York.

5. In a fixed exchange rate regime, a BOP disequilibrium sets in motion chains of events that eventually cause domestic prices and national expenditure to change and restore BOP equilibrium. What are the five such chains of events explained in the text and summarized in Figure 11.1? Review your understanding of each link of those chains.

6. Which of the several changes set in motion by BOP disequilibrium are complete, in the sense that they continue as long as the disequilibrium persists?

7. What is the quantity equation of exchange? How does it change from a tautology to a meaningful theoretical statement?

8. Review your understanding of the reasons for the policy conflicts shown in Table 11.1.

Questions for Discussion

1. All monetary systems operate through the same basic mechanisms of adjustment, mainly price changes and domestic expenditure changes. What then is the point of talking of different monetary systems? Aren't they all merely variations on the same theme?

2. What policies might fall under the heading of quasi-adjustment? Why the implication that these policies do not produce "true" adjustment to BOP disturbances?

3. There may exist a gold-standard type of mechanism without using gold. Conversely, the international monetary system might have little in common with the operation of a gold standard even though gold may be a major international money asset. Comment.

4. The text states that fixed rates are almost equivalent to having a single currency. Elsewhere, it states that regional payments disequilibrium is corrected in a manner similar to the operation of the gold standard. Why almost and similar? Isn't the parallel between regional adjustment within a country and international adjustment under fixed exchange rates a complete one?

5. Can you imagine a set of circumstances under which the exchange rate in a gold-standard regime might lie outside the gold points for an extended period of time?

6. By reference to Figure 11.1, try to make an inventory of the various ways in which government policy can block, partially or entirely, the operation of the gold-standard mechanism of adjustment.

7. "If you want to learn to walk straight, put a stick covered with barbed wire down the back of your shirt." Is this an unfair metaphor for the discipline argument of some gold-standard advocates?

8. Would you consider that adjustment under fixed rates is in general more or less effective in countries where foreign trade is a high proportion of national income than it is in countries with a comparatively small external sector?

9. If the existence of fixed exchange rates is likely to engender greater recourse to quasi-adjustment policies, why did the extensive liberalization of tariffs since World War II (discussed in Chapter 8) take place in a context of generally fixed rates? (This question really belongs at the end of Chapter 14. It is important enough, however, to begin thinking about it now.)

10. A fixed-rate adjustment mechanism can be economically very painful. By the same token, would not a region of a country then be better off by becoming independent and acquiring control over its own currency?

"How sweetly do they float!"

Milton, *Comus*

"Money, which represents the prose of life . . . is, in its effects and laws, as beautiful as roses."

Ralph Waldo Emerson, *Essays*

Automatic Monetary Systems: Flexible Exchange Rates

What to Expect

General
Features
of
a
Flexible
Exchange
Rate
System

This chapter examines the other extreme form of automatic adjustment to BOP disturbances—a monetary system that allows the exchange rate to fluctuate freely. The structure of this chapter is similar to that of the previous one, proceeding from the general features of the system to a discussion of how the exchange rate is determined, of the exchange rate mechanism of adjustment to BOP disequilibrium, and of the conditions under which this form of adjustment is effective. It concludes with certain policy considerations. Thus, after a brief listing of the general features of a flexible exchange rate system, the principal mechanism of exchange rate adjustment is examined: the changes in exports and imports brought about by a change in the price of the country's currency and the process by which these changes restore BOP equilibrium. The first part of that section examines the adjustment mechanism in words; the second part goes over the same ground by the use of simple diagrams. The conditions under which exchange rate changes are an effective mechanism of adjustment to external disequilibrium are then discussed. In the process, we examine the elasticities, absorption, and monetary approaches to the analysis of the effects of exchange rate changes. The final section of the chapter returns to the general policy question that concluded Chapter 11 by indicating some of the possible costs of abandoning fixed rates of exchange, as well as touching on the important question of whether a flexible rate standard in fact insulates the domestic economy from the impact of foreign disturbances. Appendix 1 carries the diagrammatic analysis further. Appendix 2 discusses the possible influence of currency depreciation on the terms of trade.

General Features of a Flexible Exchange Rate System

First, a word about the title of this chapter. The international monetary system being discussed has variously been referred to as "floating" rates, "free" rates, "fluctuating" rates, and "flexible" rates. These are different names for the same mechanism, one in which the rate of exchange is allowed to change entirely in response to private market forces. The term "flexible" is generally preferred here as it has less of a normative content than either "free" or "floating" (with its connotation of a peaceful country pond) and does not, on the other hand, carry the impression that exchange rates necessarily "fluctuate" when there is no government intervention.

The analysis of the effects of exchange rate changes applies equally well to devaluation and revaluation (when the change in the currency's price arises from government decisions) as to depreciation and appreciation

Automatic
Monetary
Systems:
Flexible
Exchange
Rates

within a flexible rate regime. In the latter case, exchange rate changes are likely to be more frequent and less lumpy. Also, the cause of these changes may differ as compared to a system of managed exchange rates. But the effects of exchange rate changes on international competitiveness, absorption, and monetary aggregates are substantially the same, regardless of whether they arise from market forces or from policy decisions.

Like the gold standard, a flexible exchange rate system operates automatically and requires no government intervention. Also, the adjustment process under flexible rates relies on the same *types* of changes in relative prices, expenditure, and monetary behavior as the gold standard does. However, the apportionment of the burden of the adjustment among price, expenditure, and monetary changes is different.

Finally, there is no special international money asset in a flexible rate system. All payments and receipts are made in the national currencies of the countries involved. Any national currency is freely convertible into any other currency through the operation of the foreign exchange market, and its availability depends only on its price—the exchange rate. Thus, no reserves of international money are needed. Correspondingly, and as a first approximation to be examined at some length later, a flexible exchange rate system is alleged to allow nations maximum independence of economic policy.

The Adjustment Process Under Flexible Exchange Rates

Exchange Rate Changes and the Balance of Payments

Recall from Chapter 9 that one of the three major concepts of the balance of payments is the market balance.[1] The BOP is considered in equilibrium, according to this concept, when the quantity supplied and demanded of a country's currency are equal at a given price of that currency. Disequilibrium on the foreign exchange market consists of either excess supply or excess demand for the country's currency. In a regime of flexible exchange rates the outcome of disequilibrium is a change in the price of the currency. The exchange rate change restores BOP equilibrium in a similar fashion as a change in the price of, say, shoes, would clear the market for shoes.

The state of the market for the country's currency can be identified with the state of its balance of payments because demand and supply in the

---

[1] The other two concepts are the accounting balance and the program balance (see Chapter 9 for a discussion of all three concepts).

The
Adjustment
Process
Under
Flexible
Exchange
Rates

foreign exchange market are intimately related to the underlying demand for and supply of goods, services, and assets traded internationally.[2] Thus, the foreign demand for American computers, automobiles, hotel rooms, securities, productive assets, and so on, directly translates itself into a foreign demand for the dollars needed to purchase the goods and assets. The *demand for dollars* thus measures the sum total of autonomous credits in the U.S. balance of payments. Similarly, the U.S. demand for foreign goods, services, securities, and assets translates itself into a demand for the needed foreign currencies and is a measure of the sum of autonomous debits in the U.S. BOP. But, since the foreign currencies are obtained in exchange for dollars, the American demand for foreign moneys corresponds to a *supply of dollars* in the foreign exchange market.[3]

Autonomous credits are measured by the quantity of dollars foreigners need to get the American products they wish to buy. Autonomous debits are measured by the quantity of dollars Americans wish to exchange for the foreign currencies needed to get the foreign products they want. Since BOP equilibrium is best defined as an equality of autonomous credits (receipts) and autonomous debits (payments), it is also identified with equality between dollars demanded and supplied in the foreign exchange market, at a given exchange rate.

It easily follows that: (1) if the autonomous transactions are in disequilibrium, the market for the country's currency is also in disequilibrium (2) with the market for the currency in disequilibrium, the price of it (the exchange rate) changes; (3) the exchange rate change sets in motion certain effects that are expected to restore BOP equilibrium and hence equilibrium in the foreign exchange market.

All monetary systems work through a combination of price and expenditure effects. There are expenditure effects in a flexible rate monetary standard as there are in the gold standard. However, these may undercut or reinforce the effectiveness of the price changes rather than always reinforcing it as in the case of a fixed rate regime. They are discussed separately later in this chapter as important conditions of flexible rate effectiveness in bringing about payments equilibrium. This section examines only the price mechanisms of adjustment.

The working of the price mechanism of adjustment when exchange rates are free to move up or down is simple. Just keep in mind the often stated point that the price in an international transaction depends on both the price of the commodity in terms of one currency and on the exchange rate

---

[2] The identification of the foreign exchange market and autonomous BOP items is not a precise one, however, as some transactions, such as transfers of goods and services between branches of the same multinational corporation, do not call for purchases of foreign currencies.

[3] The Appendix shows the graphic derivation of the supply curve of dollars from the demand for imports.

Automatic
Monetary
Systems:
Flexible
Exchange
Rates

of that currency. Assume, for a start, that domestic prices do not change as a result of exchange rate appreciation or depreciation.

What happens if the U.S. BOP is in deficit at a given dollar exchange rate? The "real" deficit in the BOP translates itself into an excess supply of dollars on the foreign exchange market. Autonomous credits (receipts) being smaller than autonomous debits (expenditures), the quantity of dollars foreigners want in order to buy American products is smaller than the quantity of dollars Americans are supplying to the market to obtain the foreign moneys they want. In a flexible exchange rate regime, this state of excess supply of dollars leads to a decline in the dollar exchange rate, i.e., to depreciation of the dollar.

The cheaper dollar causes two interrelated phenomena. First, with U.S. domestic prices unchanged, depreciation of the dollar means lower foreign currency prices of U.S. goods, services, and assets. If the international demand for these depends in some measure on their price (which it normally does), the quantity of U.S. exports rises and the quantity of dollars demanded goes up along with it. The other side of the coin is that depreciation of the dollar by definition means appreciation of foreign currencies with respect to the dollar. With foreign prices unchanged, this means an increase in the dollar price of U.S. imports, and, under most circumstances, leads to a decline in the quantity of imports and in the American demand for foreign currencies. This may, or may not, cause the supply of dollars to decline (depending on the elasticities, discussed at length later). In the normal case, however, the combined net effect on the foreign exchange market of the increase in exports and decline in imports is to reduce the excess supply of dollars and lessen the BOP disequilibrium along with it. If the exchange rate is entirely free to vary, it continues to depreciate until the excess supply of dollars is wiped out and the BOP returns to equilibrium. (This conclusion is only a first approximation; it is subject to very important qualifications to be discussed later.[4]) The chain of price effects set in motion by external

---

[4] Nothing has been said about the capital account. In all probability, lending and portfolio investment are not affected much by the depreciation if interest rates do not rise as one of the consequences of depreciation. True, depreciation means that foreigners can buy the same bonds or stock shares for lower prices in terms of their own currency, but the interest or dividends earned are also denominated in the currency of the depreciating country and can be expected to be correspondingly lower. There may be a slight positive effect of depreciation on the inflow of direct investment funds, since the price of productive assets and the cost of acquiring control of a corporation probably fall as do prices of exports in general. But direct foreign investment is influenced by a great variety of motivations and concerns. The exchange rate mechanism can, however, operate to restore external balance even if depreciation has no effect beyond the trade balance. If, for example, a capital account deficit of a given magnitude is assumed, the currency continues to depreciate until an equivalent trade surplus is achieved, thus producing equilibrium in the BOP as a whole. Note, in any case, that goods and

The
Adjustment
Process
Under
Flexible
Exchange
Rates

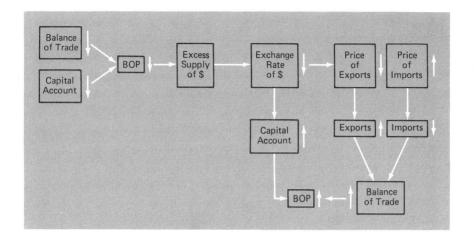

FIGURE 12.1

disequilibrium can roughly be summarized as shown in Figure 12.1 (a complete scheme is shown in Figure 12.3).

Depreciation: A Simple Diagrammatic Analysis

This section gives a simple diagrammatic example of how depreciation of the dollar works to influence U.S. exports and imports of specific commodities and, consequently, the quantity of dollars demanded and supplied. Appendix 1 contains a more complete diagrammatic analysis of equilibrium in the foreign exchange market.

Let's look at trade between the United States and West Germany. Suppose that the United States exports tractors to Germany and imports cameras, that the dollar price of a tractor and the German price of a camera remain unchanged at $10,000 and 1,800 DM, respectively, and that as the consequence of excess supply of dollars (U.S. BOP deficit) the U.S. dollar depreciates in half, from a rate of 6 DM to a rate of 3 DM per dollar. Assume also, for simplicity's sake, that all supply curves are perfectly elastic, i.e., that U.S. producers stand ready to sell at $10,000 apiece as few or as many tractors as anyone wishes to buy and that German producers are willing to sell any number of cameras as long as they get 1,800 DM for each.

The Export Side Before depreciation, an American tractor cost German buyers 60,000 DM ($1,000 times the exchange rate of $1 = 6 DM). At that

---

services account in most countries for the dominant share of international payments and receipts. Limiting to the trade account the influence of exchange rate changes does not constitute a serious drawback of the flexible rate adjustment process.

Automatic
Monetary
Systems:
Flexible
Exchange
Rates

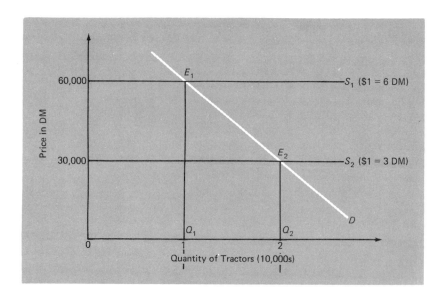

FIGURE 12.2a   U.S. Exports of Tractors to Germany: German Viewpoint

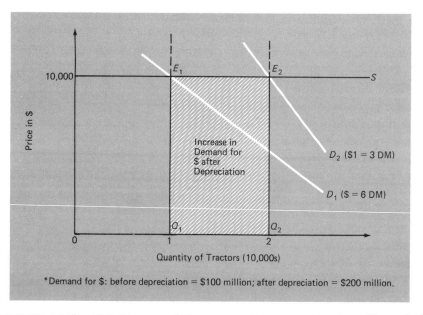

*Demand for $: before depreciation = $100 million; after depreciation = $200 million.

FIGURE 12.2b   U.S. Exports of Tractors to Germany: American Viewpoint°

price in terms of marks, Germans were willing to buy 10,000 American tractors, for which they needed to buy $100 million on the foreign ex-
change market. In Figure 12.2a equilibrium in the German market for imported American tractors was at E_1, the intersection of demand curve D with
supply curve S_1. As the result of dollar depreciation to $1 = 3$ DM, the

274

The
Adjustment
Process
Under
Flexible
Exchange
Rates

German price of an American tractor falls to 30,000 DM. From the viewpoint of the Germans, whose conditions of demand have not changed, this development is equivalent to an increase in the total supply of American tractors from S_1 to S_2. Equilibrium after depreciation is thus at E_2, implying German purchases of 20,000 tractors. As it happens, the total expenditure of German marks remains the same, with twice the amount being bought at half the unit price. But the German demand for dollars goes up. In Figure 12.2b, from the viewpoint of the American producer, whose cost conditions have not changed, depreciation is seen as an increase in total German demand for tractors from D_1 to D_2. Since the dollar price stays put at $10,000, the doubling of the quantity sold means a doubling of the quantity of dollars demanded, from $100 million to $200 million. The increase in the quantity of dollars demanded reduces the excess supply of dollars on the foreign exchange market and contributes to eliminating the BOP deficit.

The Import Side Figure 12.2c shows the American market for imported German cameras. (Only one graph is needed here, as the price of cameras is already in terms of dollars.) Before depreciation, a German camera cost in the United States $300 (1,800 DM times the exchange rate of 1 DM = $\frac{1}{6}$. At that price, demand conditions led to equilibrium at E_1, with Americans willing to buy 450,000 cameras and to spend a total of $135 million (450,000 × $300). Depreciation of the dollar results in doubling the price of a German camera to $600. This is seen from the American viewpoint as a decrease in the total supply from S_1 to S_2. Equilibrium shifts to E_2, with Americans reducing their imports of German cameras to 250,000. The American demand for German marks clearly declines, as fewer cameras are imported while their price in marks remains the same. But we are interested in the international market for dollars, hence in what happens to the supply of dollars as a result of depreciation. Total expenditure on German cameras after depreciation is $150 million (250,000 × $600), and this, of course, is also the new amount of dollars supplied in the foreign exchange market.

In this example, depreciation has a "perverse" effect on the import side, causing a $15 million increase in dollars supplied instead of the decrease needed to restore BOP equilibrium. This is because in this particular instance the demand for imports between E_2 and E_1 is relatively inelastic, with the percentage decline in quantity smaller than the percentage increase in price. The influence of elasticities on the effects of depreciation is examined at length in the next section. Suffice it to note here that, on both the export and the import side, the equilibrating effects of exchange rate changes are directly related to the foreign elasticity of demand for exports and to the domestic elasticity of demand for imports. The more elastic the demand for exports (the flatter is D in Figure 12.2a), the greater the increase in quantity demanded and, at an unchanged price in terms of dollars,

Automatic
Monetary
Systems:
Flexible
Exchange
Rates

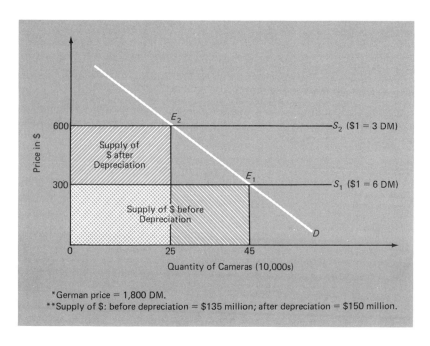

FIGURE 12.2c   U.S. Imports of Cameras from Germany°: American Viewpoint°°

the greater the increase in demand for dollars. The more elastic the demand for imports (the flatter is D in Figure 12.2c), the greater the decline in the quantity of imports and the greater the chance that this decline will translate itself into a decrease in supply of dollars. It is highly likely that the corrective effect on the export side is greater than any possible perverse effect of depreciation on the import side, so that, on balance, the depreciation does correct the initial disequilibrium in the foreign exchange market and in the BOP. In our hypothetical example, excess supply of dollars is reduced by $85 million: a $100 million increase in dollars demanded accompanied by a $15 million increase in dollars supplied.

Conditions of Flexible Rate Effectiveness

Depreciation improves the BOP by reducing the excess supply of the country's currency in the foreign exchange market, which is the monetary manifestation of a deficit in the autonomous transactions. It does so by increasing the foreign demand for the country's currency and, possibly, by reducing the supply of that currency. The increase in demand for the currency depends, in turn, on the increase in the quantity of exports demanded by foreigners; the reduction in supply of the currency is related to the decrease in the quantity of imports demanded. Whether depreciation improves the trade balance, and to what extent it does so, depends therefore to a major degree on the characteristics of world demand for the country's exports and of the country's demand for imported goods and services.

As you know, the quantity demanded of a specific commodity depends on:

1. the price of the commodity

2. the prices of other products complementary to the good in question or substitutes for it

3. money income of the buyers

4. "tastes," by which is meant all other influences on the quantity demanded, including tastes in the proper sense, but also expectations and random factors.

The functional relationship between the quantity demanded and the variables listed here is the **demand function.**

For the trade account as a whole, the quantity demanded of exports and imports thus depends on *relative* prices, on the level of national income and its distribution, and on tastes. Let us first assume that national income, income distribution, and tastes do not change as a consequence of currency depreciation and analyze how much of an effect the *relative price change* caused by depreciation has on the trade balance.

The Role of Price Elasticities

Price changes lead back to BOP equilibrium, of course, because they affect the country's exports and imports. Hence, other things being equal, these changes are all the more effective in restoring equilibrium when they greatly affect the quantities of exports and imports, i.e., the more responsive these quantities are to changes in price. Price elasticity is the familiar term denoting such responsiveness. Sticking for a while longer with the assumption of infinite elasticities of supply, it is clear that the elasticity of demand for internationally traded goods and services determines how much the balance of trade is affected by currency depreciation. *On the export side,* a relatively elastic foreign demand implies an increase in the volume of exports proportionately greater than the price change. The more elastic is the foreigners' demand for exports, the greater is the improvement in the balance of trade on this score. The volume of exports and the demand for the country's currency increase in all but the limiting case of zero

277

Automatic
Monetary
Systems:
Flexible
Exchange
Rates

elasticity of demand, when by definition the quantity demanded does not change at all in response to a change in price.

On the import side, the same relationship applies. The volume of imports decreases in all but the extreme case of zero elasticity of demand. But, as was seen earlier, it is quite possible for the decline in the volume of imports to be accompanied by an increase in total expenditure on imports, i.e., an increase in the quantity of dollars supplied. The supply of dollars falls, and the BOP disequilibrium is corrected, only if the elasticity of demand is greater than one. Unitary elasticity means by definition that the percentage fall in quantity is exactly equal to the percentage increase in price: total expenditure thus does not change. Demand elasticity lower than one means that the percentage price increase is greater than the percentage reduction in quantity. A smaller volume of imports comes in, but the more than proportional increase in price causes an increase in the supply of the currency to the foreign exchange market, thus undercutting the BOP improvement on the export side. If instead demand elasticity is greater than one, the effect of currency depreciation on the import side reinforces the BOP improvement coming from the increase in exports.

The role of demand elasticities in determining the effectiveness of exchange rate changes is formalized in a simple expression. This is commonly known as the **Marshall-Lerner condition** (it is sometimes also referred to as the *stability condition* or the *elasticities condition*).[5] *Depreciation improves the trade balance (and appreciation worsens it) if the sum of the elasticity of demand for imports and the foreign elasticity of demand for the country's exports is greater than one.* It instead worsens the trade balance, in a "perverse" way, if the sum of the two elasticities is less than one. This condition can be quickly and simply explained. Suppose that the elasticity of demand for exports is zero. No increase in exports, and no increase in demand for dollars, can on this score be expected from currency depreciation. In order for the sum of the two elasticities to equal one, the demand for imports must of course have an elasticity of one. If so, imports fall in the same proportion as their dollar price increases and the quantity of dollars supplied also remains the same. There is therefore no change in the market for dollars and in the BOP. If the elasticity of import demand (and thus the sum of the two elasticities) is less than one, the quantity of imports falls by a smaller percentage than the price increase and depreciation has the perverse effect of worsening the trade balance. If the elasticity of import demand is instead greater than one, the quantity of dollars supplied declines. With an unchanging quantity of dollars demanded, disequilibrium in the foreign exchange

[5] The elasticity condition applies to the effectiveness of the gold standard as well, since it is immaterial to buyers whether the price has changed because of currency depreciation with constant domestic prices or because of domestic price changes with a fixed exchange rate.

market is lessened and the flexible rate mechanism works as it is supposed to.[6]

Attention must then turn to the determinants of the elasticity of demand with respect to price. One of these is the availability of substitutes for the product in question. The fewer good substitutes available, the less responsive is the quantity demanded to a change in price. The demand for a product for which few good substitutes exist (salt, for instance) is inelastic: A change in price has little effect on the quantity that people wish to buy. But note that the demand for a particular brand of salt is much more elastic than the demand for salt in general since the other brands of the same commodity are perfectly good substitutes. Therefore, whatever the overall elasticity of demand for a commodity on the world market, the elasticity of foreign demand for exports of that commodity by one particular country, and of its demand for imports, is almost invariably higher. Foreign buyers have the option of obtaining the commodity from somewhere else, and importers can turn to domestically produced substitutes.

It is very improbable that a country will both have an inelastic demand for imports and face an inelastic world demand for its exports. The more important a country is as world supplier of a product, the less elastic is the foreign demand for its exports. But such a country is likely to be large and well-diversified and to produce domestically good substitutes for its imports. Consequently, the elasticity of its demand for imports is probably high. Similarly, a small country heavily dependent on imports might have an inelastic demand for imports (since domestic substitutes are not readily available), but its exports are likely to account for only a small proportion of world supplies and foreign demand is correspondingly elastic.[7]

---

[6] The Marshall-Lerner condition is actually a simplification of a more complex expression that takes into account all relevant price elasticities. A detailed analysis and demonstration is contained in Chapter 8 and the Appendix to Chapter 8 of L. B. Yeager, *International Monetary Relations* (New York: Harper & Row, 1976). See also Appendix G in C. P. Kindleberger, *International Economics*, 5th ed. (Homewood, Ill.: Irwin, 1973). It may be noted here that the Marshall-Lerner condition is sufficient for a properly working exchange rate mechanism, but not necessary. The condition obtains under the assumption of infinite supply elasticities and of an initial state of equilibrium in the trade balance. If instead supply elasticities are less than infinite, and/or the trade balance is initially in deficit, depreciation may improve the balance of trade even if the sum of demand elasticities is less than one. Appendix 1 to this chapter shows diagrammatically the stability and instability zones of the foreign exchange market, corresponding respectively to sufficient and insufficient price elasticities.

[7] An exception would be a small country that is a major world supplier of an important material for which few substitutes exist. For instance, the members of the Organization of Petroleum Exporting Countries (OPEC), taken as a group, may well face perverse effects of depreciation or appreciation of their currency. Their exports, heavily concentrated on petroleum, a commodity for which few good substitutes exist, constitute by far the dominant source of world supply of oil. The elasticity of demand for their overall exports is quite low. At the same time, they do not (as yet) have the capacity to produce domestically the foodstuffs, machinery, and arms that they import, and the elasticity of import demand is probably on the low side as well.

Automatic
Monetary
Systems:
Flexible
Exchange
Rates

A second major determinant of the elasticity of demand is the time needed by buyers to adjust their purchases to a change in price.[8] In the very short run, demand is inelastic. If when you get to the store you find that the price of hamburger has gone up, you are very unlikely to buy much less than you had intended. In the longer run, however, as you have time to adjust, you may well buy less hamburger and purchase more fish instead. One cannot therefore expect depreciation to have an immediate effect on the trade balance. Plans have been made, contracts signed, and so forth. Indeed, the evidence shows that it takes some weeks before the effects of exchange rate changes begin to be felt and one or two years for the balance of trade to improve significantly, even if the elasticities are basically right. The time element is in practice quite important. It is true that, given enough time, elasticities are always high. Thus, for example, given enough time to develop on a massive scale alternative sources of cheap energy, the demand for oil could become quite elastic. But this, of course, sidesteps a major issue. While things are fixing themselves up at their leisurely pace, hardships and economic difficulties can be widespread, governments can fall, riots and revolutions can happen. For the flexible rate mechanism to be judged effective in realistic terms, the relevant elasticities must be high enough within a reasonably short period.[9]

This introductory text should resist the temptation to conduct the reader through the involved arguments and empirical findings bearing on the issue of elasticity pessimism or optimism. It is sufficient for our purposes here to simply state the general (although by no means universal) consensus of the theoretical and empirical literature: Price elasticities in international trade are almost certainly high enough, within a reasonably short period of time, for the proper functioning of the flexible rate mechanism.

This conclusion is, however, a partial one, as the analysis has so far assumed that other things are equal. It is legitimate to assume that the repercussions on the economy as a whole of changes in the market for a specific commodity are insignificant (although they do exist) and can be disregarded. But it is hardly possible to assume that other things are equal

[8] The third determinant of demand elasticity is the percentage of income spent on the commodity. The demand for very expensive things, such as cars or houses, is generally more sensitive to price than the demand for inexpensive items. The reason is that an increase in the price of the former, with money income unchanged, causes a significant reduction in the buyers' purchasing power. Buyers thus purchase less of everything, including the commodity in question. This is known as the **income effect.** The switching of purchases from a commodity whose price has increased to a substitute product is known as the **substitution effect.**

[9] This point is really more relevant to the analysis of devaluation (an occasional large cut of the exchange rate) than to depreciation proper. Depreciation is the quick response of the market as a foreign exchange disequilibrium arises. The exchange rate in a flexible rate regime depreciates and appreciates much more often and by smaller amounts. Still, the effects on the trade balance would not be instantaneous even in a perfectly flexible exchange rate system.

when dealing with changes in the entire international trade sector of a country. In particular, Chapter 10 showed that changes in the trade balance are directly related to changes in national income and expenditure. The analysis of depreciation thus cannot stop with the price effects; it must also consider the income and expenditure effects.

Flexible Exchange Rates and National Expenditure: The Absorption Approach

Two intertwined issues are of special interest here. The first is the effect of currency depreciation on national spending and the repercussions of these changes in spending on the balance of trade. The second concerns the possible influence of depreciation on the country's terms of trade. This second issue, however, is not central to the functioning of the adjustment mechanism, and is discussed in Appendix 2.

Consideration of the role of price is sometimes called the *elasticities approach* to the analysis of depreciation, and consideration of the expenditure and income effects is termed the *absorption approach* (associated principally with the name of Sidney Alexander). These are actually misleading terms. What is at stake is examination of the various consequences of exchange rate changes, *all* of which can in principle be expected to occur in some degree. We are not dealing with different and mutually exclusive approaches to the analysis of the same phenomenon. Indeed, recalling the several determinants of demand and supply, the absorption approach amounts to little more than taking into explicit consideration the effects of changes in income (which had previously been assumed away) on the quantity of imports and exports. As explained shortly, doing so leads to an expansion and qualification of the conclusions of the previous section, not to a rejection of them.

With the theoretical building blocks already presented in earlier chapters, to take into account the income and expenditure effects is a relatively simple matter. A quick recapitulation from Chapter 10 might help. Aggregate supply (the value of national production) tends to equal aggregate demand (total national expenditure). Expenditure, in turn, consists of consumption, domestic investment, government spending, and foreign spending on the country's exports. From this, imports, which do not constitute spending on domestically produced goods and services, must be subtracted. In symbols

$$Y = C + I + G + X - M$$

Chapter 9 discussed the concept of **absorption.** Using the symbols above, absorption consists of $(C + I + G)$. And $(X - M)$, of course, is the trade balance. If we abbreviate $(C + I + G)$ as A, for absorption, and

Automatic
Monetary
Systems:
Flexible
Exchange
Rates

$(X - M)$ as B, for trade balance, we may write: $Y = A + B$. Hence, if the trade balance B is negative, domestic absorption A is greater than national production Y and, as previewed earlier, the country is "living beyond its income." Such a trade deficit is possible only if there is an equivalent surplus in the capital account (or foreign aid). What is of interest here is that if national production does not increase, the balance of trade can improve *only* if domestic absorption is somehow reduced. (One obtains, of course, the same result by starting from the equilibrium condition for an open economy: $S - I = X - M$; see Chapter 10.)

Currency depreciation would, if the elasticities are not too low, increase exports and reduce imports. But if the economy is at full employment, where are the resources needed to produce the greater volume of exports and of import-substitutes going to come from? An improvement in the balance of trade is impossible, regardless of how much relative prices change, unless domestic spending is somehow cut, thus releasing the resources needed to produce the extra exports and the additional domestic substitutes for imports.[10] Hence, some sacrifices have to be made by someone or some group in the nation if depreciation is to restore external equilibrium.

The puritanical nature of balance-of-payments adjustment raises its ugly head again. National savings must be increased, either voluntarily or in a forced manner through deliberate government policies. Policy-induced increases in national savings can arise through a more restrictive fiscal policy (increasing taxes or cutting government spending) or through inflation (discussed later in some detail). A voluntary increase in savings may result either from a real-cash-balances effect (also to be discussed later) or from a redistribution of national income in favor of the richer groups in society, which tend to have a higher marginal propensity to save. In an economy where commodities of mass consumption dominate the import picture and where exports are controlled by a few large corporations, the latter is a real possibility. The increase in the price of imports and the expansion of exports effectively redistribute income away from the population at large and toward the richer producers of export-type goods, who consume proportionately less. Obviously, the social implications would be considerable.

No sacrifices need be made if the economy is at less than full employment. Depreciation can in this case help to tighten up the slack by providing

---

[10] L. Yeager has pointed out that this is not necessarily true if exchange rate depreciation replaces quasi-adjustment policies, such as tariffs, which had been used to maintain BOP equilibrium with too high an exchange rate (an overvalued currency). As is known from Chapter 5, trade restrictions carry a cost for the economy as a whole. If they are eliminated at the same time as the exchange rate falls, the balance can improve even without a reduction in absorption. Resources are fully employed, true, but after removal of restrictions on trade they can be *reallocated* more in keeping with the country's structure of comparative efficiency. National production thus can increase in real terms and the balance of trade can improve along with it, provided that resources are internally mobile and that absorption is not allowed to rise.

sufficient price incentives to the producers of export-type goods and of import-substitutes to employ additional resources. National production can rise and the balance of trade improve along with it (provided only that the marginal propensity to spend is less than one) without any need for a cut in domestic spending. The country had been living beyond its current income, but only because it had not been producing as much as it was capable of.

To illustrate all this, let's go back to the farm family example used in Chapter 9. If the family purchases a greater value of goods and services than it sells, it has a balance-of-trade deficit. To correct it, it must either produce and sell more, or buy less, or some measure of both. If the land, labor, and equipment it owns are not fully utilized, it may succeed, by making a greater economic effort, to produce and "export" more without reducing its standard of living. If instead the trade deficit coexists with full employment of all resources, this avenue of balance-of-trade improvement is closed. To expand sales, the family must reallocate some of its resources out of the production of goods and services for its own use. For example, it may have to give up some turkey dinners to be able to sell more birds at Thanksgiving time, or it may have to reassign a family member away from the growing of vegetables for the family's own use to renting his services to outsiders for pay. To repeat, the family is living beyond its means. It has no way to correct the deficit other than increasing its "means" or reducing its "living." If the means (income) cannot be increased because the family is already exerting maximum economic effort, its standard of living (absorption) must be reduced.

Even if unemployment does exist before depreciation, taking into account the income and expenditure effects leads to an important qualification of the Marshall-Lerner elasticities condition. A *reversal factor* is at work here. To the extent that depreciation leads to a first-round improvement in the balance of trade, it also leads to an increase in national income, via the foreign trade multiplier explained in Chapter 10. And an increase in income induces imports to go up, in direct relation to the marginal propensity to import. In terms of the demand function, the quantity of imports demanded falls owing to the increase in their price, but it goes back up owing to the increase in income. (In diagrammatic terms, the import demand curve shifts to the right. See Figure 12.2c.) Imports will almost certainly not go back all the way to their previous level, since normally only a portion of the income increase is spent on additional imports. Still, this cuts down on the effectiveness of the price mechanism of adjustment.[11] Thus, unlike in the gold

[11] More rigorously, as pointed out among others by P. T. Ellsworth and J. C. Leith (*The International Economy*, p. 354), the existence of this reversal factor merely means that it takes a larger decrease in the exchange rate to restore BOP equilibrium since the exchange rate must continue to depreciate as long as a deficit persists. But, as will be

Automatic
Monetary
Systems:
Flexible
Exchange
Rates

standard, where expenditure effects proceed in the same direction as the price effects, in a flexible rate regime the two effects work to some extent at cross purposes. And this is readily understandable if you consider that under the gold standard a BOP deficit leads to a decline in national income and expenditure, whereas exchange depreciation tends to stimulate national production and employment.

The Role of Monetary Factors

Not a word has been said so far about the quantity of money circulating in the domestic economy. Yet, whether it is assumed that the domestic supply of money changes or remains constant as the exchange rate falls, monetary considerations have a bearing on the process of BOP adjustment. In general: (1) if the money supply is allowed to increase, domestic inflation is a probable result, and the rise in domestic prices can be an important factor of reversal of the BOP improvement from exchange depreciation; (2) if the money supply is instead kept at a constant level, the induced expenditure effects can reinforce the price mechanism of adjustment. Monetary phenomena can thus have significant price and expenditure effects of their own. Let's look at these two possibilities separately.

Depreciation and Inflation   It is practically assured that depreciation increases the price of imports in terms of domestic currency. And it has been assumed until now that the foreign currency price of a country's exports on the world market would fall as a result of exchange depreciation, as indeed it must if the quantity of exports demanded is to rise. It is clear that this can happen only if, and to the extent that, exporters don't raise their price. Except in the extreme case of perfect elasticity of export supply, however, some increase in the domestic price of exports is a certainty. If a significant monopoly element in the export industries exists, and/or if exports consist of differentiated products, the increase in exporters' price can be considerable. Such an increase in the domestic price of exports cuts down the competitive advantage achieved through exchange depreciation, and hence the expansion of exports. Still, the quantity demanded of the country's currency on the foreign exchange market does go up, whether from export expansion with an unchanged domestic price or from an increase in domestic price with an unchanged volume of exports.

---

seen in the later sections of this chapter, there are probable costs associated with depreciation, and they are greater the greater the extent of depreciation. Thus, the income-induced increase in imports does indeed reduce the effectiveness of the exchange rate mechanism of adjustment. The same is true of another important reversal factor, namely, the rise in domestic prices as a consequence of depreciation, which is discussed at length under the role of monetary factors in the next section.

Thus, depreciation almost certainly raises prices of internationally traded goods. But the more important issue is whether *overall* inflation occurs. Inflation is an increase in the general level of prices. To the extent that the increase in the prices of goods and services traded internationally is offset by an equivalent decline in other domestic prices depreciation need not have inflationary consequences. The question thus revolves around the possible existence of links between prices in the foreign trade sector and the general domestic price level.

Two important inflationary transmission mechanisms may be at work. The first is technological, the second institutional in nature. Both operate to spread inflation of the **cost-push** variety from the trade sector to the remainder of the economy.[12] *First*, if a large proportion of internationally traded goods (particularly imports) is made up of raw materials and intermediate goods, the increase in their price means an increase in production costs—and hence prices—for all domestic industries that use those materials and intermediates. *Second*, cost-of-living clauses can be a widespread feature of collective bargaining contracts. If workers' consumption depends heavily on imports, depreciation raises the cost of living for them and, through the operation of the "escalator" clauses, pushes up wages, production costs, and prices throughout the economy. In addition, when imports are heavily concentrated on intermediates and on mass-consumption goods, their demand is likely to be inelastic. As shown in Appendix 2, this means that the price of imports increases significantly. Thus, not only are there important transmission mechanisms but the original inflationary stimulus is likely to be stronger in the first place.[13] Finally, the probability of inflationary depreciation is increased even more by the well-known downward rigidity of prices in contemporary economies. Thus, even if the price rise does not spread from the trade sector to the remainder of the economy, it is highly improbable that a decline in the prices of nontraded goods can offset the increase in export and import prices.[14]

---

[12] The other main variety is **demand-pull inflation**, occurring when aggregate demand is greater than full-employment aggregate supply; colloquially, when too much spending is chasing too few goods. As national production cannot increase in real terms when all resources are fully employed, an attempt to get from the system more than it can produce bids up the general price level.

[13] The incidence of robberies in Italy is highest for jewelry stores, which is hardly surprising. But, reportedly, retail butchers rank second! With the marked fall in the exchange rate of the lira, the Italian dependence on imported meat, and the low elasticity of demand, the price of meat has gone so high that it has become almost as profitable to rob a butcher store as a jeweler. Even if apocryphal, this report illustrates just what can happen to the price of consumers goods as a result of currency depreciation.

[14] Once again, this need not happen if depreciation is accompanied by trade liberalization. Tariffs raise the domestic price of imports and can have an inflationary effect of their own. As L. B. Yeager (*International Monetary Relations*, p. 226) notes, replacing controls with a lower exchange rate may even diminish inflation, as it increases real income through a more efficient allocation of resources.

285

Automatic
Monetary
Systems:
Flexible
Exchange
Rates

But another viewpoint exists. As L. B. Yeager argues, a general increase in the level of prices is possible only if the quantity of money circulating in the economy is allowed to rise. Let's return to the quantity equation of exchange that is at the heart of the gold-specie-flow mechanism and of the gold-standard mode of BOP adjustment. As you know, the quantity of money times its turnover rate (the velocity of circulation) must be equal to the price level times physical production: $MV = PY$. If physical production and the velocity of money, Y and V, do not change, the inflationary consequences of depreciation can only occur if the quantity of money is allowed to rise. If it is instead held constant, some prices must decline somewhere in the economic system and offset the increase in the prices of internationally traded goods. (Even so, of course, one would simply be trading off this kind of income redistribution for the income redistribution effects characteristic of inflation.)

It is possible that V also increases as an indirect result of depreciation, and thus that the price level may go up even in the absence of monetary expansion. But it is implausible to presume that the velocity of circulation of money can keep increasing further and further to the point where people get rid of money as fast as they get it. Therefore, while it is a possible source of inflationary depreciation for some period of time, an increase in the rate of money turnover cannot be looked at as a continuing factor permitting systematic inflation.[15] Thus, the argument concludes, depreciation is inflationary only when domestic policy allows it to be by not holding down the quantity of money.

The argument is persuasive as far as it goes. But it does not seem to go far enough. *First*, the need for a restrictive monetary policy does serious damage to the claim that flexible exchange rates allow a country to pursue its own independent economic policy without fear of throwing the balance of payments out of whack. This point is dealt with further in the last section of this chapter.[16] *Second*, and even more serious, is the possibility that if prices are generally rigid downward, the price level may be allowed to rise, even with a constant money supply, by a fall in real national income. In symbols, Y could go down as P is increasing, although both M and V are constant. One would then face the nightmare that currency depreciation may cause both inflation and recession—a condition that has become a reality in many countries in recent years (although not necessarily as a result of flexible rates). The specific mechanism through which national in-

---

[15] However, as will be discussed in Chapter 14, self-feeding increases in the velocity of money were an important contributor to the hyperinflation in Germany in the early 1920s.

[16] In addition, the existence of a large international capital market, the Eurodollar market, lessens considerably the capacity of small countries to conduct monetary policy; see the Appendix to Chapter 14.

come may fall, ironically, is the same real-cash-balances effect to which "monetarist" advocates of flexible exchange rates attach a lot of importance.

Real Cash Balances and Interest Rates   In a fixed exchange rate system, a deficit causes a fall in the quantity of money. With domestic prices initially constant, the decline in the quantity of money in circulation leads to a reduction in the value of real cash balances held by individuals and institutions. In a flexible exchange rate system, the same relative shortage of money can result from a BOP deficit and the ensuing depreciation, but as a mirror image of the fixed rate effect.

With the quantity of money constant, the increase in prices caused by depreciation leads to reducing real cash balances. The size of the reduction probably differs under flexible rates more than it does under fixed exchange rates, but the effect is qualitatively the same. In their attempt to build up real cash balances back to the desired level, individuals, corporations, and institutions cut back their spending on imports and domestically produced goods and services alike. The subsequent decline in income reinforces the price mechanism of adjustment by lowering income induced imports.

A second monetary corrective has been emphasized by S. C. Tsiang. The trade balance improvement from depreciation initially leads to an increase in national income in money terms and to a reversal of the effect of depreciation through the rise in induced imports. But, with a constant supply of money, the increase in demand for money pushes up the rate of interest. This, in addition to improving the capital account, discourages investment and offsets, partly or totally, the income reversal effect. As noted earlier, if prices and wages are generally rigid downward, the combination of the real balances effect and the consequences of the rise in interest rates might conceivably allow both recession and inflation to result from depreciation even though the money supply is held down.

A Recapitulation

Consideration of the general policy question raised by flexible exchange rates will be left to the final section. Let us summarize here the more specific question of the functioning of flexible rates as a mechanism for restoration of BOP equilibrium. When only the price effects of exchange rate changes are considered, there are grounds for optimism that the adjustment mechanism works as it is supposed to, i.e., that depreciation improves the BOP and appreciation worsens it. But the analysis based only on elasticities pays no attention to the expenditure effects. These are taken into account by the absorption approach, which shows the need for complementary domestic policies to cut domestic spending. Skepticism that these policies will, or can, be undertaken, plus consideration of the reversal effect of income-induced increases in imports, leads to a less favorable prognosis on the effectiveness

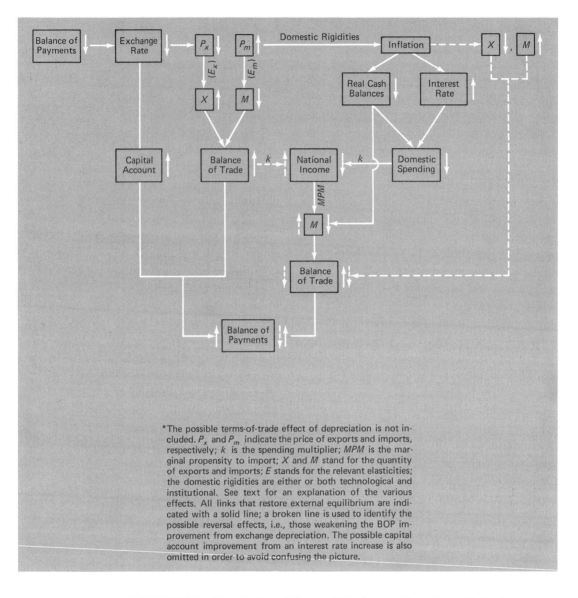

*The possible terms-of-trade effect of depreciation is not included. P_x and P_m indicate the price of exports and imports, respectively; k is the spending multiplier; MPM is the marginal propensity to import; X and M stand for the quantity of exports and imports; E stands for the relevant elasticities; the domestic rigidities are either or both technological and institutional. See text for an explanation of the various effects. All links that restore external equilibrium are indicated with a solid line; a broken line is used to identify the possible reversal effects, i.e., those weakening the BOP improvement from exchange depreciation. The possible capital account improvement from an interest rate increase is also omitted in order to avoid confusing the picture.

FIGURE 12.3   The Various Effects of Exchange Rate Depreciation°

of the exchange rate mechanism of adjustment. Taking into account the expenditure effects of *monetary* changes leads back to qualified optimism on the functioning of the flexible rate mode of adjustment. Emphasis on the second major reversal factor, instead, i.e., the inflationary consequences of depreciation, raises anew serious qualms about the effectiveness of flexible rates in correcting a BOP deficit (although it does not necessarily affect the performance of the system in correcting a surplus). Figure 12.3 summarizes the various effects of depreciation.

Insulation
of
the
Domestic
Economy?
Some
Policy
Considerations

Insulation of the Domestic Economy?
Some Policy Considerations

Recall the analogy in Chapter 11 that compared the operation of a fixed exchange rate system to unscrewing a burned out light bulb by holding it steady and walking around it, and that compared the operation of a flexible exchange rate system to standing still and turning your hand. It was stated as a first approximation that fixed exchange rates maximize economic *inter-dependence* among countries while flexible rates maximize economic *independence*. It is time to examine that preliminary statement, in light of the material of the previous pages.

Advocates of flexible exchange rates claim that the system insulates the domestic economy from the effects of foreign economic disturbances, and thus allows each country to pursue whatever economic policy it sees fit for the achievement of its goals. National economies are linked to one another via the foreign trade sector. Under fixed rates, economic disturbances spread to other countries through the trade-income linkage. Thus, a depression abroad adversely affects a country's exports and, if exchange rates are fixed, its national income as well. If, instead, rates are flexible, the balance-of-trade deficit caused by foreign depression is corrected *as it occurs* through the effects of the ensuing depreciation of the country's currency. Similarly, a country need not "import" foreign inflation, as the initial BOP surplus is corrected by appreciation of the currency. With the trade balance maintained in constant equilibrium by the ups and downs of the country's currency, the simple mechanism of transmission of foreign disturbances is jammed.

This picture of "splendid isolation" may be appealing, but not altogether warranted by the facts. Let us begin with the simple, but fundamental, proposition that insulation is advantageous or not depending on the nature of the foreign disturbance. Even if the insulation argument is granted, it is clear that a fluctuating rate of exchange insulates the country from favorable foreign events just as much as from unfavorable ones. Thus, if there arises a recession abroad when the country suffers from strong inflationary pressures, the net impact of the foreign disturbance would probably be considered desirable. Conversely, a country with unemployment problems can benefit from the effects of foreign inflation. Insulation from foreign economic events is good or bad depending on how well the country is doing on its own and on what it is being insulated from.

To be sure, it can be argued that it is the business of domestic economic policy to ensure internal balance (full employment with price stability) and that a foreign disturbance can have beneficial economic effect only if the country has pursued some incorrect policies in the past. Internal balance was assumed in the presentation of trade theory and commercial policy. It seems only fair to do so again in the discussion of financial policy. There

Automatic
Monetary
Systems:
Flexible
Exchange
Rates

is, however, a real question whether in fact flexible exchange rates do insulate the domestic economy from foreign disturbances.

To examine the possible policy conflict, recall that depreciation generally does improve the BOP but generates some domestic inflation, especially when unemployment is low, and that appreciation corrects a BOP surplus but adversely affects national income. Table 12.1 summarizes the ensuing policy problem. Note that the conflict-no conflict situation is the mirror image of that prevailing under fixed exchange rates (see Table 11.1), which is not surprising as the two systems are at opposite extremes.

The inflationary consequences of depreciation are reinforced when there is a link between the prices of goods traded internationally and the general price level. The link, in turn, exists only when certain domestic rigidities are present, either in the structure of production or through the prevailing institutional arrangements. It is therefore possible to argue that inflation does not result from depreciation per se, but from those government policies current and past that allowed those rigidities to emerge. This is correct, but it begs the issue. To say that depreciation would cause no inflation if policies over the past three or four generations had been different is no help at all to a government that must work with what it has. As the wag says: "If my parents had gone to the movies instead, I would not be here today." Circumstances in many countries are such that depreciation does exert significant inflationary pressures.

It is true that even with serious institutional rigidities, inflation is a much less likely consequence of currency depreciation if the government takes care of holding the money supply constant. But consider what this does to the insulation argument. Flexible exchange rates are supposed to allow a government maximum latitude in pursuing its own internal policy. However, in order for depreciation to be effective and inflation to be avoided, the government must refrain from exercising its autonomy in monetary policy! Also, remember the gist of the absorption approach: Depreciation cannot improve the trade balance unless appropriate policy measures are under-

TABLE 12.1   The General Policy Problem under Flexible Exchange Rates

Internal Situation	External Situation	
	BOP Deficit	*BOP Surplus*
Unemployment	**No Conflict:** Depreciation improves both external and internal balance.	**Conflict:** Appreciation corrects surplus but worsens unemployment.
Inflation	**Conflict:** Depreciation improves the BOP but worsens inflation.	**No Conflict:** Appreciation improves both external and internal balance.

taken to reduce domestic absorption or prevent it from rising. Flexible exchange rates do not allow a country complete economic policy autonomy.

Insulation
of
the
Domestic
Economy?
Some
Policy
Considerations

This scheme of the general policy problem under flexible exchange rates is, of course, incomplete. Exchange rate variation is not the only variable at work. Domestic economic policy instruments can also be used. Thus, *while it is not tenable to claim that flexible exchange rates totally insulate the domestic economy, it is possible to present the more modest conclusion that they allow a government greater policy flexibility than it possesses under a fixed exchange rate system.* Exchange rate *ap*preciation is a policy instrument additional to domestic monetary and fiscal policy. *De*preciation is not an additional instrument, but rather a more effective replacement for the use of domestic monetary policy to affect the BOP. Whatever the complexities of the economic situation facing a country, therefore, allowing the price of its currency to vary makes it less difficult to arrive at a coherent policy package for the achievement of conflicting objectives.

You should have at this point a reasonably good idea of the advantage of flexible rates. What of the disadvantages? Is it too much to hope that abandoning fixed exchange rates carries no costs? Yes. There are possible costs in terms of the volume of international trade, of resource reallocation, of integration of the world economy. These may, or may not, be seen as outweighing the contribution that flexible exchange rates can make to formulation of appropriate policies. There are fierce differences among economists on this. Even the most ardent proponents of flexible rates, however, stop short of arguing that flexible exchange rates are an all-purpose remedy comparable to the snake oil of the legendary West, and they freely admit that disadvantages exist.

First, the possibility of exchange rate changes introduces an element of uncertainty in international trade and discourages marginal transactions. Uncertainty can be removed through operating in the forward foreign exchange market, as was described in Chapter 9. But "there is no such thing as a free lunch": The costs of administering the forward market are ultimately borne by the traders. If expectations are neutral, the costs are in all probability minimal. When speculation is massive, however, the cost of forward cover can be considerable. Uncertainty on future exchange rates is sometimes airily dismissed with a wave of the hand toward the forward market, but it is a very real hindrance to international trade in certain sectors. Just imagine, for example, what havoc it causes for international travel and the pricing practices of international airlines, with flights scheduled to make stops in several countries and a single ticket issued for travel on different national airlines. When compared to the much greater uncertainties besetting international trade from other sources, however, this is probably not a determining, nor even a very important, disadvantage of flexible exchange rates.

Automatic
Monetary
Systems:
Flexible
Exchange
Rates

More serious is the possibility that a temporary and reversible change in the price of a currency causes *permanent* losses from the reallocation of economic resources back and forth. Suppose that excess supply of dollars on the foreign exchange market arises from a one-time outflow of capital from the United States. The dollar depreciates, exports become more competitive, imports more expensive. Resources are channeled to the export and import-competing industries, and away from other activities. As the one-time capital outflow comes to an end, the BOP finds itself in surplus at the lower dollar exchange rate. The ensuing appreciation of the dollar induces a reverse flow of resources back to their previous employments. It sounds easy on paper. But in the meantime, the factories that closed down can be reopened only at considerable cost, those that opened up must be closed, customers must be regained, people have been fired and others hired away from their previous jobs. In real life people, equipment, and materials are not reassigned with a stroke of the pen. There are very real costs to the reallocation of resources, which are worth paying only if the reallocation is warranted by a lasting, as opposed to transitory, change.

Finally, *interdependence* is in many ways a synonym for *integration*. In a general sense, the greater economic independence of countries under flexible exchange rates, to the extent that it does exist, is paid for by a loss in world economic integration. Clearly, the significance of this point extends far beyond considerations of economic efficiency and involves fundamental political goals of nations and groups of nations. For example, even if it were shown that the adjustment to payments disequilibria of states within the United States would be more efficient if each state possessed its own fluctuating currency, few would seriously argue that this advantage is worth the far-reaching political costs of economic disintegration of the union. Preventing damage to economic integration arrangements was the reason for the 1972 decision of the then-members of the European Economic Community (West Germany, France, Italy, Belgium, Holland, and Luxembourg) not to allow price fluctuations among their currencies beyond a narrow margin. (From the looks of the graph of exchange rates, this arrangement came to be known as the European "snake.") This is not to say that flexible exchange rates make international cooperation and integration impossible. They do, however, make it more difficult, just as they make it less difficult for individual countries to evolve policy packages suitable for their own internal objectives.[17]

---

[17] The attempt to define conditions under which fixed exchange rates (or a unified currency) are desirable has given rise to the concept of **optimum currency areas.** Very generally, the appropriateness of a unified currency for an entire area is directly related to the degree of mobility of productive resources among the regions of the area and to their economic dependence on one another. Thus, permanently fixed rates or a unified currency would be preferable to monetary independence if trade within the area is very large relative to trade with "outside" countries, if there is a good amount of central

Insulation
of
the
Domestic
Economy?
Some
Policy
Considerations

Throughout the discussion in the previous sections, it was clear that the size of the various effects of exchange rate changes depends to a great extent on the characteristics of the country in question. Thus, the price elasticities may, or may not, be sufficiently high for proper functioning of the exchange rate mechanism depending on the composition of the country's exports and imports, its share of the world market, and the geographic concentration of its foreign trade. The size of the income reversal effect is a function of the country's marginal propensity to import, and that, in turn, is related to a host of structural characteristics and policy variables. The terms of trade may improve or worsen through exchange rate changes. The strength of the monetary reversal effect through inflationary depreciation is related to the composition of imports, to the strength of the links beween export and import prices and the general price level, and to the monetary policy followed by the government. And the reinforcements of the adjustment mechanism through the real-cash-balances effect and the consequences of interest rate changes also depend on the characteristics of the country in question.

This recapitulation is meant to show that the effectiveness of flexible exchange rates as a BOP adjustment mechanism may be great for some countries and very limited for others and that the political and economic costs may be acceptable or not, depending on the country. It was possible in Chapter 11 to arrive at a generally unfavorable verdict on the feasibility of the gold standard in today's international economy. It is *not* possible to make a similarly general statement with respect to freely fluctuating exchange rates. Flexible rates can be effective or ineffective, desirable or undesirable, or anything else in between, depending on the country's situation, its capabilities, its goals, and its limitations.

What can easily be predicted, however, is that if the costs of exchange rate flexibility are deemed unacceptable, the country will take measures to abate them and/or limit exchange rate flexibility, provided that it has the political and economic autonomy to do so. The problem is that these measures usually include controls on foreign trade and investment, which carry their own costs in terms of economic efficiency for the country as well as for the world economy as a whole. To take an illustration from recent events (discussed further in Chapter 15), "...even after exchange rates came unglued, following the August 15, 1971 decision by the U.S. to make the dollar inconvertible into gold, controls proliferated rather than abated as countries acted to limit the extent of their exchange-rate flexibility."[18]

---

policy coordination for the entire area, and if the mobility of factors of production is great. We can't go into this in detail. But it should be intuitively clear that coordination of economic policy can help prevent serious payments imbalances from arising, and, when they do occur, the needed adjustment can be eased by an inflow of mobile capital into the region with a payments' deficit.

[18] R. M. Stern, "Tariffs and Other Measures of Trade Control: A Survey of Recent Developments," *Journal of Economic Literature*, September 1973, p. 865.

Automatic
Monetary
Systems:
Flexible
Exchange
Rates

By way of conclusion, it is well to remember that if the BOP is in fundamental disequilibrium that will not stop or reverse itself of its own accord, some adjustment must eventually occur in some form, and it will usually involve both price and income changes. What if the disequilibrium is not a fundamental one? Is there any way to get the best of both worlds, through some intermediate monetary system partaking to some extent of the characteristics of both fixed and flexible exchange rates? This general question leads to the next chapter.

Appendix 1: Equilibrium in the Foreign Exchange Market--A Diagrammatic Analysis

The text contains a very simple graphic analysis of the effects of depreciation on exports and imports of specific commodities. This Appendix goes further, to a diagrammatic analysis of the foreign exchange market as a whole. It still is, however, partial equilibrium analysis, as it assumes no shifts in the underlying conditions of demand and supply for the goods, services, and assets traded internationally. As was seen, exchange rate changes do have an effect on income and expenditure, and this, in turn, calls for some shift in demand and supply curves at the same time as the change in the currency price causes movements *along* the curves.

Assuming domestic prices to be unaffected by exchange rate changes, however, foreign demand for exports of all kinds can be translated into foreign demand for local currency, and domestic demand for imports can be translated into a supply of local currency, as explained herein. Let's take the market for dollars.

The amount of dollars foreigners demand is directly related to their demand for U.S. exports. The quantity of exports demanded is inversely related to the price of those exports. With U.S. prices constant, the price of exports is directly related to the dollar exchange rate. A 20 percent depreciation of the dollar, for example, means a 20 percent decrease in the world price of U.S. exports. Thus, there is an inverse relationship between the dollar exchange rate and the quantity of dollars demanded in the foreign exchange market. The demand for dollars has the same negative slope as the underlying demand for U.S. exports. More dollars are demanded at a lower exchange rate, fewer at a higher rate.

Not so for the supply of dollars. At a given price in terms of foreign currency, each point on the supply curve of dollars represents an *expenditure:* the quantity of imports demanded times the unit price in terms of dollars. For example, if a pair of Italian shoes costs 10,000 lire, and $1 exchanges for 1,000 lire, the price of the shoes in terms of dollars is $10. If at that price 1 million pairs of shoes are imported, the total dollar expenditure is $10 million. The $10 million is the quantity of dollars supplied at an exchange rate of $1 = 1,000 lire. If the dollar exchange rate falls to 500 lire per $1, the import price of the shoes goes up to $20 a pair. The quantity of shoes imported falls. Hence, there is a direct relationship between the exchange rate and the quantity demanded of imports. But the total expenditure, and thus the quantity of dollars supplied, may go up as well as down, depending on the elasticity of demand. If import demand is inelastic, so that for example the doubling of the price lowers the quantity demanded by only 10 percent, 900,000 pairs of shoes are imported after depreciation at a unit price of $20, and the quantity of dollars supplied rises to $18 million. If, instead, the demand is elastic, so that imports of shoes fall by more than the percentage of price change, the quantity of dollars supplied declines. The supply of dollars to the foreign exchange market thus has a positive slope when it corresponds to the elastic portions of the underlying demand curve for imports, but it changes direction and slopes upward and to the left in the portion corresponding to inelastic import demand.

Automatic
Monetary
Systems:
Flexible
Exchange
Rates

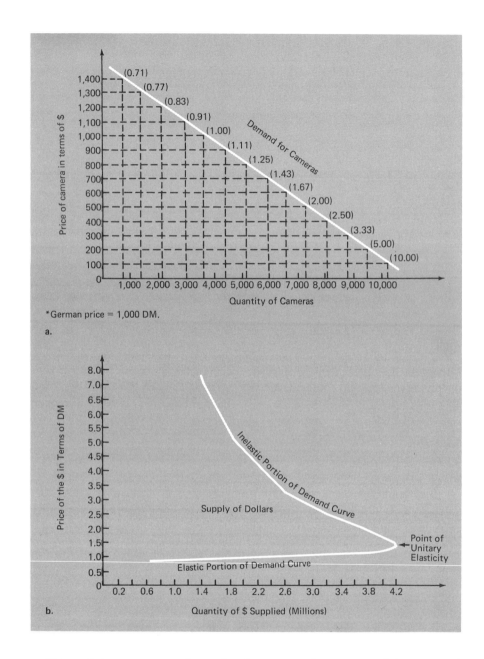

*German price = 1,000 DM.

a.

b.

FIGURE 12.4   Derivation of Supply of Currency from Demand for Imports*

Figure 12.4 shows the derivation of the supply of dollars from the demand for imports. Figure 12.4a shows the American demand for German cameras as a function of the dollar price of the camera. Naturally, it has the familiar negative slope, indicating an increase in the quantity demanded as the price declines. As a constant 1,000 DM price of the camera is assumed, the only way the price to the American importer can decline is through an *increase* in the dollar ex-

Appendix 1:
Equilibrium
in
the
Foreign
Exchange
Market—
A
Diagrammatic
Analysis

change rate. The dollar exchange rates corresponding to each price are shown in parentheses on top of the demand curve.

Each point on the supply curve of dollars shown in Figure 12.4b corresponds to an *area* in Figure 12.4a, as it is a product of a quantity and a price. For example, at an exchange rate of $1 = 5.00 DM, the dollar price of the camera is $200. From Figure 12.4a it is seen that at that price about 9,400 cameras are imported, for a total expenditure of about $1.8 million (9,400 times $200). This is the quantity of dollars supplied at an exchange rate of $1 = 5.00 DM, one point on the supply curve of dollars. (It is also the quantity of dollars supplied at an exchange rate of $1 = 0.8 DM.) The other points are derived in the same way from the demand for imports. Up to a point (corresponding in Figure 12.4 to an exchange rate of approximately $1 = 1.35 DM), the quantity of dollars supplied (total dollar expenditure on imports) increases as the exchange rate increases, but decreases thereafter. The inflection point on the supply curve of dollars corresponds to the point of unitary elasticity on the demand for imports. The portion of the supply curve of dollars below that point corresponds to the elastic portion of the import demand curve; the portion above that point corresponds to the inelastic portion of the import demand curve.

As has been mentioned, there is hardly any mystery about this. Elastic demand means by definition that the quantity demanded changes by a greater percentage than the price: If the price of imports increases, then total dollar expenditure goes down because the quantity bought falls more than in proportion. And the price of imports of course increases when the exchange rate goes down. Where, instead, the demand for imports is relatively inelastic, the import price increases caused by depreciation are accompanied by less-than-proportional decreases in the quantity of imports, and the total dollar expenditure (quantity of dollars supplied) rises.

Let's now put the two sides together. Figure 12.5 shows the market for dollars in terms of German marks. Since the dollar supply courve bends backward, there is a strong probability that the demand for dollars intersects it *twice*, once from above at E_u and once from below at E_s. *Two* equilibrium exchange rates, which equalize the quantity of dollars supplied and demanded, are thus possible. The market for dollars is cleared, hence the autonomous balance of payments is at equilibrium *either* when the dollar exchange rate is about 2.2 DM *or* when it is about 4.7 DM. But the higher equilibrium is unstable. Depreciation has in that case the perverse effect of causing excess supply of dollars, hence further depreciation and greater disequilibrium. Appreciation leads to excess demand and thus to the exchange rate moving up further and further away from E_u. E_s is instead stable equilibrium: A disturbance sets in motion forces that tend to restore the market to its previous position rather than leading it further away from it. A decline in the exchange rate from E_s generates excess demand for dollars and leads to appreciation back to E_s. And similarly for a temporary BOP deficit, which causes the exchange rate to fall back toward E_s. Thus, if the elasticities are sufficiently high, the exchange rate change is the instrument of restoration of BOP equilibrium.

Figure 12.5 can also be used to illuminate the workings of the gold standard. It clearly shows the difference between the two systems. Since in the gold standard the rate of exchange is fixed, a BOP disequilibrium leads to a realignment of domestic prices. The domestic price changes and expenditure effects of the payments imbalance cause the demand and supply curves to shift about until they again intersect at the fixed exchange rate, thus restoring external equilibrium.

Automatic
Monetary
Systems:
Flexible
Exchange
Rates

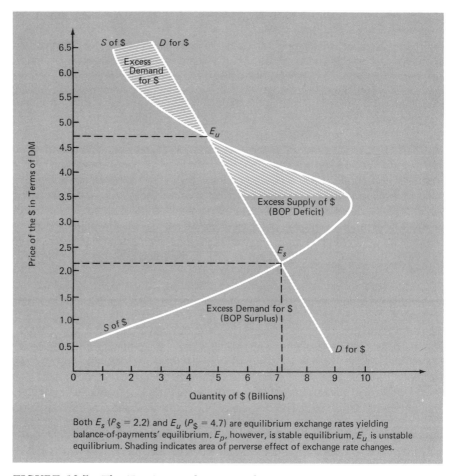

Both E_s ($P_\$ = 2.2$) and E_u ($P_\$ = 4.7$) are equilibrium exchange rates yielding balance-of-payments' equilibrium. E_p, however, is stable equilibrium, E_u is unstable equilibrium. Shading indicates area of perverse effect of exchange rate changes.

FIGURE 12.5   The Foreign Exchange Market

Appendix 2: Depreciation and the Terms of Trade

The effect of depreciation on a country's terms of trade may either reinforce or weaken the price mechanism of adjustment to external disequilibrium. The terms of trade in question are the same commodity or net barter terms of trade used throughout this book: the price of exports relative to the price of imports, (P_X/P_M). (As the entire trade sector is involved here, some suitable unit price index is relevant.) One of the oldest controversies in international economics centers around the issue of the impact of currency depreciation on a country's terms of trade. The issue is important because, as was seen in Chapter 5, an increase in the relative price of exports (an improvement in the terms of trade) is under most circumstances beneficial, and a worsening of the terms of trade harmful, to the economic welfare of a country.

It might seem that depreciation always must worsen the terms of trade. The price of exports goes down in terms of foreign currency and the price of imports increases in terms of domestic currency. The ratio between the two falls on both accounts. But this is the proverbial comparison of apples and oranges. Both export and import prices must be measured by reference to the same currency. It makes no conceptual difference whether domestic or foreign currency is used. Let's start with prices in terms of foreign currency.

At one extreme is the view that the terms of trade are entirely unaffected by changes in the exchange rate. This view is based on the assumption that the volume of a country's international sales and purchases has no effect on international prices. This is the usual assumption made about competitive markets. It is equivalent to saying that the world elasticity of demand for a country's exports is infinite and so is the elasticity of supply of its imports. A country can sell any amount at the given foreign price and buy all the imports it wants without in any way affecting their world price. World prices of exports and imports are then quite independent of any changes in a country's balance of trade.

This is the probable situation of a very small country, which accounts for an insignificant share of the world market and must either trade at the given world prices or not at all. Most countries, however, can exert some influence on prices through their international sales and purchases. It is at this point more convenient to switch to defining both export and import prices in terms of domestic currency. The earlier assumption of infinite elasticities of supply of exports and of imports must be abandoned also.

In all likelihood, under the usual conditions of increasing marginal cost, the increase in production of exports induced by depreciation does have the effect of raising to some extent the domestic price of commodities exported. But the price of imports in terms of domestic currency also goes up as a consequence of depreciation. With both the numerator and the denominator of the terms-of-trade ratio increasing, depreciation can in principle improve, worsen, or leave unaffected the ratio itself. If the domestic price of exports rises by the same percentage as the import price, depreciation does not affect the terms of trade. if the export price rises more than in proportion to the import price, depreciation improves a country's terms of trade, and vice versa.

Automatic
Monetary
Systems:
Flexible
Exchange
Rates

We find ourselves squarely in elasticities' territory again. It can be shown that high export and import *demand* elasticities are conducive to a terms-of-trade improvement, whereas high export and import *supply* elasticities militate against it. On balance, depreciation improves the terms of trade when the ratio of export demand elasticity to export supply elasticity is greater than the ratio of import supply elasticity to import demand elasticity, and worsens them in the contrary case.

Let's see how. On the export side, the increase in export price is first of all directly related to the increase in the quantity of exports demanded. And that, as is known, is a function of the elasticity of foreign demand. For a given increase in the quantity of exports, however, the rise in their price is also related to the elasticity of their supply, but in an inverse fashion: The less elastic the supply, the greater the price that has to be paid to exporters to induce them to expand production and sales. (This is because inelastic supply indicates that marginal cost rises quickly as production expands.) The increase in the price of exports is thus directly associated with the relationship between the elasticity of foreign demand and that of domestic supply. The higher the ratio between the two, the greater is the increase in export prices.

A similar reasoning applies to the import side. The more elastic the demand for imports, the greater the fall in the quantity of imports caused by depreciation. For a given decline in imports, the less elastic their supply, the more such decline causes the world price of imports to fall. The increase in the domestic price of imports is consequently smaller. Hence, the increase in the price of imports is directly associated with the relationship between the elasticity of supply of imports and that of their demand.

This is essentially the same argument encountered in Chapter 5, when discussing the terms-of-trade effect of a tariff, and in Chapter 6, when examining the optimum tariff case for import restriction. Depreciation is equivalent to raising the domestic price of all imports by a uniform tariff and to giving a uniform rate of subsidy to all products exported. An import tariff, as was seen earlier, either improves the terms of trade or leaves them unaffected. Depreciation, however, also implies an expansion in exports and, in principle, may worsen the terms of trade as well as improve them.

Putting the two sides together, a high ratio of export demand to export supply elasticity improves the terms of trade by raising the price of exports in domestic currency; a high ratio of import supply to import demand elasticity worsens them by raising the price of imports in domestic currency. Hence, depreciation improves the terms of trade when the ratio of export demand to export supply elasticity is greater than the ratio of import supply to import demand elasticity, and worsens them in the contrary case.

(For a detailed demonstration of this relationship and a fuller discussion of the possible influence of depreciation of the terms of trade see L. B. Yeager, *International Monetary Relations,* chap. 10 and Appendix.)

With these four variables interacting (and the limitations of partial equilibrium analysis), it is clear that there is no flat answer to the question of the effect of depreciation on the terms of trade. Depreciation probably does worsen the terms of trade if a country has the following general characteristics: (1) exports are highly concentrated on commodities with few international substitutes and are produced domestically under conditions of slowly rising marginal cost; (2) imports consist primarily of necessities, and the world *supply* of imports to the country is elastic. For example, a less developed country, which happens to be

a major international exporter of an important raw material, would have good reason to be concerned about the negative terms-of-trade effects of currency depreciation. Conversely, a large country with well-diversified exports and low unemployment might well add a likely terms-of-trade improvement to the advantages of depreciation in restoring equilibrium in its balance of payments.[19]

Other things being equal, a terms-of-trade improvement is equivalent to an increase in the country's real income. One can expect therefore a small reversal factor from the rise in imports induced by the income increase. If depreciation instead is accompanied by a worsening of the terms of trade, this particular expenditure effect works to reinforce the price mechanism of BOP adjustment by lowering imports a bit further.[20] Either way, however, it is unlikely that a possible terms-of-trade effect of depreciation plays a large role in the functioning of the adjustment mechanism.

Points for Review

1. Review your understanding of the relationship between autonomous BOP credits and the world's demand for a country's currency and between autonomous BOP debits and a country's supply of its own currency.

2. Other things being equal, what are the consequences of appreciation of the dollar on
a. The quantity of U.S. exports?
b. The quantity of U.S. imports?
c. The quantity of dollars demanded?
d. The quantity of dollars supplied?

3. Under the assumption of infinite supply elasticities, with other things being equal, use the hypothetical data here to calculate the effect of appreciation of the dollar in terms of English pounds on exports of U.S. cars and imports of English suits. Assume that both import demand and export demand are unitary elastic within the relevant range.
Before $1 = £0.5
           Price of U.S. car in dollars: $5,000
           Price of English suit in pounds: £50

[19] This issue should not be confused with the far more important problem of the long-term deterioration of the terms of trade of less developed countries.

[20] Again (see footnote 10), if depreciation is accompanied by a removal of restrictions on trade, its impact on the terms of trade is highly ambiguous. As was seen in Chapter 5, import tariffs may have improved the country's terms of trade by forcing down the world price of imports. Their removal would then reduce the price of the country's exports relative to that of its imports. The impact on the terms of trade of depreciation combined with liberalization is in this case even harder to predict in advance.

Automatic
Monetary
Systems:
Flexible
Exchange
Rates

Number of U.S. cars exported to England: 20,000
Number of English suits imported by U.S.: 500,000
Quantity of dollars demanded: $100 million
Quantity of dollars supplied: $50 million
Excess demand for dollars: $50 million

After $1 = £1
Price of U.S. car in dollars:
Price of English suit in pounds:
Number of U.S. cars exported to England:
Number of English suits imported by U.S.:
Quantity of dollars demanded:
Quantity of dollars supplied:
Excess demand for, or supply of, dollars:

4. In exercise 3, what would be the consequences of dollar appreciation if the elasticity of export demand were unitary but that of import demand were zero? What if the elasticity of import demand were zero and that of export demand were less than one, say, 0.5? In light of your results, review your understanding of the Marshall-Lerner stability condition.

5. In Figure 12.2, what difference, if any, would it make if the supply of imports were less than perfectly elastic (i.e., if it were upward sloping instead of horizontal)?

6. By reference to the determinants of demand (the demand function) review your understanding of the sense in which the elasticities and absorption approaches to the analysis of exchange rate changes are complementary rather than alternative views.

7. Why does domestic absorption need to be reduced for depreciation to improve the trade balance under full-employment conditions? What does such a reduction entail in actual practice?

8. With or without full employment, the absorption approach introduces an important reversal factor. What is it, and how does it work to partly counteract the effect of the relative price change?

9. Review your *general* understanding of the connection between trade elasticities and the terms-of-trade effects of exchange rate changes.

10. Depreciation raises the domestic price of both imports and exports. Can one therefore say that depreciation is necessarily inflationary?

11. Review your understanding of the possible inflationary transmission links between the prices of internationally traded goods and the general price level. Is such inflation of the cost-push or demand-pull type?

12. In terms of the simple equation of exchange: $MV = PY$, review your understanding of why inflation cannot occur unless either M or V go up, or Y goes down, or some combination thereof.

13. How does the real-cash-balances effect operate in a regime of flexible exchange rates?

14. How can a rise in interest rates counteract the income reversal factor?

15. Review your understanding of *each* of the links in the adjustment chains shown in Figure 12.3.

Questions for Discussion

1. The chapter began by listing automaticity among the general features of a flexible exchange rate system, and it concluded by doubting whether flexible rates do insulate the domestic economy from foreign disturbances. Is there an inconsistency between these two positions? Are they in fact at all related?

2. Is it *possible* for the exchange rate to appreciate or depreciate even though there is no disequilibrium in the autonomous BOP transactions?

3. Is it *likely* for the foreign exchange market to be in disequilibrium even though the basic balance of payments is not? In such a case, *should* the exchange rate be permitted to vary? (Refer to Chapter 9 for a definition of the basic balance and market balance concepts of the BOP.)

4. Explain the Marshall-Lerner condition by reversing the assumption made in the text, i.e., show that with zero elasticity of import demand it takes more than unitary elasticity of export demand in order for depreciation to improve, and appreciation to worsen, the trade balance.

5. What characteristics of a country's foreign trade sector would lead you to doubt the effectiveness of the price mechanism of BOP adjustment for that country?

6. It might be argued that the current characteristics of a country's foreign trade sector are immaterial in assessing the effectiveness of flexible rates, since in the long run all elasticities are high. Hence, the Marshall-Lerner condition is always more than satisfied, and the adjustment must eventually be complete. Is this a correct statement? Is it a useful statement?

7. If there is full employment, depreciation cannot improve the trade balance without a cut in domestic absorption. Is it also true that absorption must rise if appreciation is to reduce a trade surplus? What happens if domestic absorption does not rise?

8. Is the type of country for which perverse functioning of flexible exchange rates is a possibility (see discussion question 5) the same as the type of country whose terms of trade are likely to be worsened by depreciation? (Hint: As usual, go back to the relevant elasticities.)

9. The view that depreciation or appreciation cannot affect a country's terms of trade is sometimes called the "ultraclassical" view. Can you guess why?

10. The inflationary stimulus of depreciation is mainly of the cost-push variety. Can this stimulus not be counteracted by a reduction in demand-pull inflationary forces? What does this entail for domestic fiscal and monetary policy? What does it entail for the insulation of the domestic economy allegedly provided by flexible exchange rates?

11. Consider the following statement: "If past government policy had encouraged domestic competition and flexibility, and had prevented the institutionalization of escalator clauses in collective bargaining contracts, depreciation would not have inflationary consequences. Hence, any such consequences are to be laid at the door of past government policy and not of the flexible exchange rate mechanism." Is this a correct statement? Is it a useful one?

12. If depreciation can have inflationary consequences, do we need to be equally concerned about appreciation causing a general price decline?

Automatic
Monetary
Systems:
Flexible
Exchange
Rates

13. What does the possibility of interest rate changes do to the concept and calculation of the spending (Keynesian) multiplier?

14. As more and more factors were taken into account, the analysis in the chapter progressed from optimism on the effectiveness of the flexible exchange rate mechanism to pessimism, and back to either qualified optimism or qualified pessimism depending on which of the monetary effects is emphasized. What is at this point your own assessment of the effectiveness of flexible exchange rates as a *general* international monetary mechanism?

"Medio tutissimus ibis" (You will be most safe in the middle)

Ovid, *The Metamorphoses*

Discretionary Monetary Systems

13

What to Expect

This chapter rounds out the explanation of the essentials of the process of BOP adjustment and the discussion of the alternative monetary systems within which the process may operate. Chapters 14 and 15 illustrate the material presented earlier through a review of international financial history and of recent developments. This chapter discusses some of the possible monetary arrangements intermediate between the extremes of permanently fixed and completely flexible exchange rates. The first part describes an intermediate system fairly close to the fixed rate extreme. This is the Bretton Woods monetary arrangement that operated from the end of World War II until 1973. First, the background and rationale of the system are presented and the major institutions involved in its operation are described. Next examined, in parallel with the order of discussion in the previous two chapters, is the effectiveness of the Bretton Woods system. The three major issues discussed are the asymmetry of the adjustment mechanism, the problem of confidence and of destabilizing speculation, and the question of international liquidity. The second part of the chapter describes some monetary arrangements closer to the flexible rate end of the spectrum: the "wide band," the "crawling peg," "managed floating," and "dirty floating." The last part expands on the earlier hints concerning the financial means to suppress (rather than finance or adjust to) BOP disequilibrium, namely, exchange control.

In the previous two chapters it was seen that adjustment under both of the extreme international monetary systems carries significant costs for individual countries as well as for the world economy. Fixed exchange rates in a sense place the domestic economy at the mercy of the vagaries of foreign trade and investment. Flexible rates generate uncertainty and are an element of disintegration of the world economy. Intermediate monetary arrangements, partaking to some extent of the features of both fixed and flexible exchange rates, can generally be seen as attempts to get the best of both worlds. (It has also been argued, however, that they manage instead to get the worst of both.)

Any monetary system that is intermediate in the sense used here aims at modifying the result that would obtain from the operation of the private market and at preventing or managing changes in both the exchange rate and the domestic economy. An intermediate system therefore cannot be automatic, but it necessarily calls for some discretionary intervention by the public authorities to limit full exchange rate flexibility as well as unfettered adjustment of the domestic economy. But governments cannot intervene without the means to do so. Since the foreign exchange market is being discussed here, such intervention consists of governmental purchases and

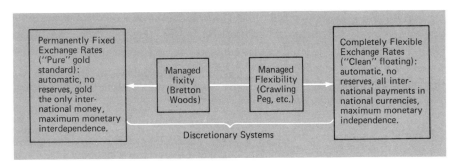

FIGURE 13.1   A Scheme of Alternative International Monetary Systems

sales of its currency in exchange for foreign currencies. It follows that in a discretionary monetary system governmental reserves of foreign currencies (and gold, if used as an international means of payment) are needed.

If reserves are not available, a BOP deficit cannot be financed by governmental operations on the foreign exchange market. In this case, direct controls to suppress BOP imbalances are the only option open to a government that wishes to prevent changes in the exchange rate and/or domestic economic realignment. Commercial policy restrictions to improve the BOP were discussed in Part II. The last section of this chapter examines the financial policy to suppress BOP disequilibrium, i.e., exchange control.

Discretionary, in-between international monetary arrangements can be closer to the gold standard or to the flexible exchange rate end of the spectrum. A convenient general classification is between those that maintain the exchange rate fixed over a fairly long period of time, while allowing occasional changes in it, and those that allow the exchange rate to fluctuate significantly but with intervention to prevent it from going beyond certain limits. The former may be referred to as **managed fixity** of exchange rates; the latter as **managed flexibility**. Please note, however, that the spectrum from full flexibility to completely fixed rates is a continuum. This classification (summarized in Figure 13.1) is used here only as a convenient memory aid.[1]

"Managed Fixity": The Bretton Woods System

The international monetary system that was in operation from the end of World War II until 1973 is known as the Bretton Woods system, from the name of the New Hampshire resort where the international negotiations

[1] Yet another intermediate solution consists of fixed exchange rates within *groups* of countries, with the currencies of one group floating jointly against the currencies of another bloc of countries. This is related to the optimum currency area notion mentioned in Chapter 12.

leading to its establishment took place in 1944. It is also called the **adjustable peg** system, as its principal characteristic is the "pegging" (fixing) of exchange rates with occasional adjustments of the peg being permitted. It also sometimes goes under the name of gold-dollar standard, from the fact that both gold and the U.S. dollar are the main international money assets.

The main features of the Bretton Woods system are as follows:

1. The exchange rate of each country's currency is fixed, but it may occasionally be changed by official government action in response to a "fundamental" BOP disequilibrium.

2. If external disturbances are not "fundamental," governments are committed to intervene in the foreign exchange market to prevent changes in the announced price of their currency.

3. An international institution, the International Monetary Fund, serves to facilitate the application of the rules of the system and to help national governments with the financing of temporary BOP disturbances.

In terms of the "two-out-of-three" rule discussed earlier (see Chapter 11), therefore, the Bretton Woods system attempts to preserve fixed exchange rates and monetary independence by sacrificing *short-term* BOP equilibrium. In the longer term, the presumption of the system is that it is the fixed exchange rate that will give way.

Rationale of the Bretton Woods System

The 1930s were marked by a lack of international policy coordination and by national economic policies of individual countries designed to export unemployment abroad or to defend themselves from the propagation of the Depression. Severe uncertainty was the resulting climate. Uncertainty concerning tariffs and quotas, uncertainty concerning the possible imposition of currency controls, and also uncertainty of other countries' capacity or willingness to maintain their exchange rate stable.

That period, among other things, saw a rash of currency devaluations. Only some of those devaluations were *competitive* in nature, i.e., designed to produce a trade surplus to stimulate the domestic economy at the expense of other countries, rather than to correct a payments' deficit. Others were *defensive*, designed to combat competitive devaluations by other countries, or they were forced by the depletion of reserves with which to maintain a stable rate of exchange.[2] Either way, the resulting exchange un-

---

[2] There is a major difference between beggar-my-neighbor commercial policy and competitive devaluation. As was seen in Chapter 4, tariffs and other trade restrictions are an obstacle between the world market and the domestic market, and they create a price difference between world and import prices over and above that caused by transport and other transfer costs. Devaluation, however, while increasing the price of

"Managed
Fixity":
The
Bretton
Woods
System

certainty and general economic instability of those years were considerable. And, in many instances devaluations were avoided only by imposing new commercial and currency restrictions on international trade and investment.

After World War II, the dominant preoccupation was therefore to construct an international monetary system that would minimize the chance of a recurrence of he 1930s uncertainty, instability, and widespread use of restraints of foreign trade. Thus, on the one hand, the certainty of fixed exchange rates and their advantages for policy-makers and private traders and investors alike had a strong appeal. On the other hand, it was also recognized that political and economic conditions in most countries were a far cry from those that would permit or tolerate the automatic operation of a gold-standard type of system with permanently fixed exchange rates. Consequently, while the principle was accepted that adjustment to external disequilibrium should take place via a change in the exchange rate, revaluations or devaluations were to be allowed only in response to a "fundamental" disequilibrium. Competitive devaluations were to be discouraged, and temporary or reversible BOP surpluses and deficits would not be permitted to induce frequent exchange rate changes and thereby impinge on the certainty and stable growth of world trade and investment.

Chapter 9 discussed at some length the notion of BOP equilibrium. The Bretton Woods rationale emphasizes that equilibrium has a *time dimension*. At one extreme, it would make as little sense to aim at balancing national payments and receipts on a day-to-day basis as it would for a person to try and spend in a given day exactly as much as he actually receives during that particular day. At the other extreme, to identify BOP equilibrium by reference to a very long period of time—for example that a country's BOP is in balance if a continuing deficit for 20 years is followed by a continuing surplus of the same magnitude for the next 20 years—would not make any sense either. How could a country manage to ride out a deficit for that long a time? A general principle (although a difficult one to translate into prac-

---

imports in terms of domestic currency, does not separate the world market from the domestic market. Thus, if all countries devalued competively and by the same percentage, in order to obtain a trade advantage over their rivals, at the end of the process *relative* prices would be the same and the volume of international trade need not be affected on this score. A complete round of beggar-my-neighbor tariffs and retaliatory tariffs, instead, would increase barriers between countries and reduce trade. What does happen through competitive devaluations is the needless shifting of resources back and forth. For example, if France devalues first to acquire a competitive advantage in relation to Britain, and later on Britain follows suit to defend itself, relative prices have not changed between the two countries. But in the meantime, productive resources in Britain have been first taken out of the import-competing and export sectors and channeled to other sectors in the economy, only to be reassigned to their original employments when the British defensive devaluation occurs. This is not a costless process. And the international hostility generated by exchange-rate warfare is no less intense than the ill will caused by beggar-my-neighbor commercial policies.

tice) can be to aim at BOP equilibrium over the country's *trade cycle* (say, 3 to 5 years), much as a person would consider his finances in balance if he spent his exact salary by the time the next paycheck is due, with a "surplus" in the early part of the week or month and a "deficit" later on.

However relatively long or short the cycle may be, the important implication is that no adjustment should be permitted in response to BOP disturbances within the cycle. The presumption being that the disturbance is temporary, the Bretton Woods policy is to *finance* the deficit or surplus and not allow it to disturb either the domestic economy or the exchange rate. Any form of adjustment carries certain costs, and these have to be borne if the adjustment is in fact needed. They instead can and should be avoided if the adjustment is unnecessary because the BOP disturbance will take care of itself in due course. To complete the light-bulb analogy used earlier, the Bretton Woods rationale is that the light bulb should not be changed at all unless one is reasonably sure that it has in fact burned out. If the lack of electric light is instead due to a temporary blackout, the better policy is to light candles until the power comes back.

The "candles" in the system are the country's monetary **reserves**. Reserves function as a buffer, a flywheel of the international financial mechanism. As already discussed, a BOP surplus translates into private excess demand for a country's currency on the foreign exchange market, at the current exchange rate. By the Bretton Woods rules, the government is expected to soak up that excess demand by selling its currency in exchange for foreign currencies. By doing so, it eliminates the upward pressure on the exchange rate and adds to its holdings of international monetary reserves. (In order that this not be allowed to expand the domesic money supply, and thus cause unwarranted changes in the domestic economy, the increase in foreign currency holdings must be "sterilized"; see footnote 23.)

A BOP deficit translates into private excess supply of the country's currency on the foreign exchange market. In this case, the government uses its reserve holdings of foreign currencies to absorb the excess supply and prevent the rate of exchange from falling. Like an accordion, therefore, monetary reserves expand and contract and serve to ride out temporary BOP deficits and surpluses.[3] If surpluses and deficits offset one another, so that over the cycle as a whole the BOP is in equilibrium, there occurs no net change in the country's reserves. The correspondence between this formulation of equilibrium and the official settlements definition of the BOP ex-

---

[3] Reserves are needed also in the gold standard (except in the case of a 100 percent gold standard). Their economic function is, however, diametrically opposite. In the gold standard, a country needs reserves in order that the process of adjustment to external disturbances may take place. In the Bretton Woods system, a country needs reserves in order to prevent adjustment from taking place in response to a "nonfundamental" disturbance.

"Managed
Fixity":
The
Bretton
Woods
System

plained in Chapter 9 should be apparent. The important difference, of course, is that we are now referring to payments' balance over some medium-term period presumably longer than 1 year.

By the logic of the Bretton Woods system, the preceding process of financing external imbalances must give way to a change in exchange rate when the imbalance is not temporary. If the BOP is "fundamentally" in disequilibrium, no longer will a surplus be followed by a deficit, and vice versa. A "fundamental" disequilibrium calls for adjustment, not financing. The country is then expected, usually after consultation with other governments, officially to revalue or devalue its currency. Revaluation and devaluation are nothing more than an official announcement that henceforth the government will support a different, but equally well-specified, rate of exchange. Since the government is the residual buyer and seller of its currency, the exchange rate ipso facto goes up or down to the new official support level.

The adjustment then takes place through price and expenditure effects in the same manner as would be the case under flexible exchange rates. The adjustment process described in Chapter 12 applies in almost every particular to revaluation and devaluation in the "adjustable peg" system, except of course that the parity change in the adjustable peg takes place all at one time by government decision and is consequently larger than the short-run appreciation and depreciation that arise from a flexible exchange rate system.

How Large a Devaluation? The Purchasing-power-parity Principle

Ideally, the announced change in parity is of the exact magnitude required to restore BOP equilibrium after a reasonable period of time. A change in the exchange rate smaller than required will necessitate further changes later on. A change larger than necessary will produce a BOP disturbance in the opposite direction. But how does one know in advance what new level of the exchange rate is just right? Given that, for example, a "fundamental" BOP deficit has been identified, and consequently that devaluation is called for, by how much is the peg to be adjusted?

In theory, we have all the elements necessary for such a determination. We know from the earlier analysis of depreciation that its corrective influence depends on the demand and supply elasticities of internationally traded goods and services, on the country's marginal propensity to spend, on the interest rate sensitivity of international capital flows and of domestic investment, on the strength of the real-cash-balances effect, and so forth. But the estimation in practice of any one of these factors is an econometric

311

problem of great difficulty.[4] The estimation of the *combined* influence of all of these factors on the magnitude of the effect of devaluation on the BOP is extraordinarily complex, especially when you consider that each factor exerts its influence over a different span of time.

A much simpler general guideline to the setting of equilibrium exchange rates is the so-called **purchasing-power-parity principle.** This principle, associated with the name of Gustav Cassel, was evolved in response to the question of the appropriate level of exchange rates to be established after World War I. It was generally understood at the time that the fixed-rate system of the prewar gold standard should be restored. But the wide-ranging dislocations caused by the war made it unthinkable simply to go back to the 1913 structure of exchange rates. Among other things, some prewar countries (the Austro-Hungarian empire, for example) no longer even existed! [5]

The purchasing-power-parity principle rests on the consideration that the exchange rate must bear a reasonable correspondence to the economic situation of the country in relation to the world economy. Recall from Chapter 2 the "law" of reciprocal demand, according to which international *relative* prices tend to settle at the level that balances trade. If this principle is turned around, foreign trade has a reasonable chance to be balanced only if exchange rates reflect international relative prices. A country's exchange rate, therefore, should be established (or adjusted, in the Bretton Woods context) at a level that reflects the relationship between the country's price level and world prices, i.e., the purchasing power of the country's currency.

In the relative version of the purchasing-power-parity principle, some past year when the BOP was in equilibrium is selected as the base year. The increase in the country's price level since the base year, relative to the increase in foreign countries' prices since then, determines the extent to which the currency should be revalued or devalued. For instance, if 1950 was a year when the U.S. BOP was in equilibrium, the U.S. price level had doubled and the worldwide general price level had tripled since 1950, the purchasing power of the U.S. dollar can be said to have gone up by 50 percent, and the dollar exchange rate should correspondingly be revalued upward by that same percentage.

The purchasing-power-parity principle is beset by statistical ambiguities, qualitatively different but perhaps just as great as the difficulties involved in the direct econometric estimation of the impact of exchange rate

---

[4] **Econometrics** is the branch of economics concerned with the theory and methodology of measuring economic phenomena and estimating the relationships among them.

[5] It is true that reestablishment of the automatic gold standard would eventually produce payments' equilibrium even if exchange rates were initially set at an unrealistic level. But people willing to accept the pain of necessary surgery might yet be very displeased if the operation could have been avoided with a little foresight and planning.

changes on the BOP. Nevertheless, the idea behind the principle is sound and the simplicity of calculation attractive enough to consider purchasing-power-parity a useful indicator of the order of magnitude of the needed change in exchange rates.[6]

The Bretton Woods Institutions

The postwar international order was conceived of as an integrated package, including institutions to coordinate national commercial policies, to foster economic reconstruction and development, and to assure international monetary stability. The International Trade Organization (ITO), which was to supervise the use of tariffs, quotas, and other commercial policy measures, never came into being. In its stead, the General Agreement on Tariffs and Trade (GATT) has served as a partial but helpful substitute (see Chapter 8). The other two organizations were created and are in existence today.

The International Bank for Reconstruction and Development (IBRD), commonly known as the World Bank, was established to provide financial support to economic development programs. Headquartered in Washington, D.C., the World Bank has been making loans to less developed countries for a generation. The loans carry a rate of interest lower than would be charged by private banks. In addition, the World Bank has a "soft loan" subsidiary, the International Development Association (IDA), which provides financial support at a minimal lending charge. A discussion of the operations of the World Bank and its affiliates belongs in an economic development text.[7] It

---

[6] In the absolute version of the principle, there is an attempt at comparing directly the absolute price levels of the countries involved. If, for example, the average price of a representative sample of goods and services were 10,000 lire in Italy and 100 francs in France, the purchasing-power-parity exchange rate would be 100 lire per franc. The difficulties of such a comparison are evident. Among other things, the French and Italian patterns of consumption would have to be identical and the qualities of the goods and services included in the representative basket the same, if the comparison is to be meaningful. The relative version of the theory suffers from its own statistical difficulties. The base year may not have been one of true BOP equilibrium. Or, things other than the domestic price level may have changed since the base year, and not only the prices themselves. However, the statistical problems inherent in purchasing-power-parity calculations should not lead one to dismiss the doctrine out of hand. It is true that the impact of devaluation can be directly estimated econometrically. But, as in the definition of BOP equilibrium, there is nothing to prevent one from using as many guidelines as are available. Provided that the theoretical underpinnings of different methods are valid, similar results via different routes strengthen one's confidence in the estimate.

[7] The World Bank has another subsidiary, the International Finance Corporation (IFC), established to provide financial assistance for private enterprise development. International aid institutions have emerged since 1960 on a regional basis as well, first with the establishment of the Inter-American Development Bank (IDB) and then with the creation of the Asian and African Development Banks. The United Nations has its own aid organ, the U.N. Development Programme (UNDP), with modest resources

should be noted here, however, that the institution is indirectly relevant also to international monetary stability. The availability of long-term loans for economic development purposes lessens the less developed countries' temptation to use their monetary reserves for those purposes, and, to that limited extent, it makes them better able to cushion short-term payments' disturbances.

The international institutional bulwark of the Bretton Woods system was the International Monetary Fund (IMF). The Bretton Woods arrangements expired in 1973, after a two-year coma. The IMF continues in existence, however, although its rules have been somewhat modified and its role is in a state of flux. Also headquartered in Washington, the IMF had 126 member nations in 1976. The so-called Group of Ten comprised the most influential member countries of the IMF.

The general goals of the IMF were in keeping with the concerns of the architects of the postwar international economic order. The IMF task was twofold. First, as already noted, it was intended to assure reasonably stable exchange rates. It also was expected to foster the financial counterpart of tariff and quota liberalization, i.e., the elimination of exchange controls and the restoration of convertibility of national currencies into one another. (On the latter point, see the last section of this chapter.)

In pursuance of these goals, the IMF has provided a forum for negotiations and a mechanism for systematic consultation on international financial issues similar to the role performed by GATT with respect to commercial policy (see Chapter 8). In addition, the IMF was given an important role in assuring that member governments would abide by their obligation to maintain stable exchange rates except in "fundamental" disequilibrium situations and to help them finance temporary BOP disturbances.

The Rules of the Game Under the Bretton Woods system, the U.S. dollar was pegged to gold, and most other currencies were pegged to the dollar. The U.S. government thus had the responsibility of assuring convertibility of the dollar into gold, by its commitment to buy and sell gold at the fixed price of $35 per ounce, and other participating governments had the obligation to intervene in the foreign exchange market to the extent necessary to keep their exchange rates approximately stable in terms of dollars. There was a narrow 2 percent band within which the exchange rate was permitted to fluctuate (approximately corresponding to the range between the gold

---

dedicated primarily to the provision of technical assistance. The European Community provides some financial support for the less developed countries associated with it. And, of course, individual industrialized nations have bilateral aid programs of their own. While the financial resources transferred to less developed countries by this array of institutions have been sizable, international aid has been far from adequate to support effectively the economic progress of two-thirds of the world's population. It has averaged in the last 20 or so years much less than $10 billion per year, amounting to less than one-half of one percent of the industrial nations' national income, or to about $3 *a year* per inhabitant of the less developed world.

"Managed
Fixity":
The
Bretton
Woods
System

points in the gold standard; see Chapter 11). A government did not have to intervene if the market exchange rate deviated from the announced parity by less than 1 percent in either direction.[8] It had to sell its currency when the exchange rate went to the upper limit of the band, and buy it up when the exchange rate fell to 1 percent below the parity.

Should a country come to the conclusion that the upward or downward pressure on the market exchange rate was due to a "fundamental" disturbance, and that an adjustment was needed, a change in the official parity became in order. The country could announce a change in the official parity on its own up to a maximum of 5 percent, without prior consultation or approval from any quarter. If it intended to revalue or devalue by more than 5 percent, the IMF entered into the picture. The IMF had to receive prior notification (on a highly confidential basis, of course) for a change of up to 10 percent, and it had the power to approve or disapprove an intended parity change greater than 10 percent.[9]

The Lending Function of the IMF   The IMF was not, and is not, an international central bank along the lines, say, of the U.S. Federal Reserve, as it cannot create its own international monetary assets.[10] The IMF, was, however, given the important role of "lender of last resort" in the world monetary system, to supplement governmental reserve holdings in helping to maintain exchange stability. Its operations in this respect resemble the workings of a checking account with built-in (but not automatic) overdraft privileges. The IMF lending works in the following way.

Each member country is assigned an IMF quota through a formula that takes into account the country's wealth, the importance of foreign trade, and the reserves it already holds.[11] Of the country's quota, 25 percent must be deposited with the IMF in gold and the remainder in the country's own currency. In exchange for this deposit, the country obtains a line of credits (called "drawing rights") of up to a maximum of 125 percent of its quota.[12] To finance BOP imbalances the country may borrow from the IMF the

[8] In an attempt to restore the tottering Bretton Woods system, the 1971 Smithsonian Agreement (discussed in the next chapter) widened the permissible band of fluctuation to 4.5 percent.

[9] Rumors almost inevitably filtered out and aggravated the destabilizing effect of speculation discussed later in this chapter.

[10] The Keynes Plan, presented, but not accepted, at the Bretton Woods conference in 1944 did call for a central-bank type international institution. Similar proposals have been advanced since then and are still very much alive. It is conceivable that future international agreements might yet expand the functions of the IMF in this direction.

[11] A member country's voting power is proportional to the size of its quota. The weighted voting, and the requirement of a qualified majority vote, assures both the United States and the European Community that no important decision can be taken without their concurrence.

[12] The limit has been extended, since the establishment of the IMF, for countries suffering from special problems. Thus, a compensatory financing facility has been

foreign currencies it needs by depositing an equivalent amount of its own currency. As the purpose of IMF lending is to assist in riding out temporary BOP difficulties, and not to provide long-term finance, it is expected that the country will repay the loan (repurchase its currency) within 3 to 5 years. Interest is also charged. The loan must be repaid in gold or fully convertible currencies in order that the IMF's own solvency as a lender of internationally accepted money not be endangered.

Credit for the first 25 percent of the country's quota (called the **gold tranche** as it had been deposited in gold) is for all practical purposes automatic. In fact, a country's gold tranche is counted as part of its official reserves. Although held by the IMF, it is virtually on call whenever the country so requires. The other four 25 percent "slices" of credit are called **credit tranches.** Drawing from the IMF becomes less and less easy as a member's outstanding indebtedness mounts. Loans within the second 25 percent (the first credit tranche) are no longer automatic. And, when the amount of the country's currency held by the IMF (the outstanding loans of foreign currency) gets close to the maximum allowable, approval of further loans by the IMF Board of Directors requires a satisfactory commitment by the member country concerning the policies it intends to follow to put its financial house in order. Recalling that the IMF also had the authority to approve or disapprove of exchange rate changes greater than 10 percent, you can see that the IMF had considerable potential influence (some called it interference) on member countries' policies.

The Role of the Dollar   In the Bretton Woods system, the U.S. dollar was, along with gold, the main international money. The international importance of the dollar somewhat diminished in the 1970s from its unchallenged prominence of the 1950s. It remains quite considerable, in parallel with the continuing economic and political weight of the United States in the world economy. During the early Bretton Woods years, however, the role of the dollar was dominant.

Mention has already been made of the major distinguishing characteristic of the dollar. The value of the dollar was fixed in terms of gold, whereas the value of most other currencies of participating countries was fixed in terms of dollars. This meant that it was not possible for the United States to revalue or devalue the dollar in terms of foreign currencies. If the value of $1 was fixed at 1/35 of an ounce of gold (as it was until 1971), dollar devaluation to, say, 1/42 of an ounce of gold was, of course, tantamount to an increase in gold price. But since other currencies were tied to the dollar

---

created to help countries faced with unexpected declines in their export earnings. Recently, an "oil facility" has been established to assist with the financial problems caused by increases in the price of imported oil.

itself and not to gold, their relationship to the dollar would not change on this score. The peg was therefore adjustable for all countries participating in the system *except* the United States, and its exchange rate was permanently fixed in the absence of a special international agreement to the contrary.

The exchange rate mechanism of adjustment was thus not available to the United States. Did this mean that a BOP disturbance affected the U.S. economy in the manner characteristic of permanently fixed exchange rates, as if the United States were on a straight gold standard? Clearly not. Unlike gold, the dollar, as the national currency, could in principle be printed in any desired amount by the U.S. government, and a BOP disturbance need not affect the domestic money supply. With both the exchange rate mechanism and the gold-standard type mechanism inoperable, it might be concluded that a BOP deficit could not give rise to any adjustment, and hence would continue unabated for as long as foreign countries were willing to accept dollars in settlement of the financial imbalance. As will be seen in the next chapter (and as the BOP statistics presented in Chapter 9 showed), this is precisely what happened in the 1960s.

The willingness to accept a monetary instrument as payment for real goods, services, and assets is, of course, at the heart of the definition of money. The dollar was the principal international monetary instrument because it was readily acceptable throughout the world as a medium of exchange, store of value, and unit of account. It was as good as gold. In fact, it was better than gold. Gold could only be put in a safe in some central bank basement and left there. Dollars could be deposited in American banks, or used to purchase U.S. securities, and earn interest.[13] It is not surprising, therefore, that foreign countries readily accepted dollars (until the 1960s, at least) both as monetary reserves and as transaction currency.

It remains to be asked why such near universal acceptability of the dollar existed. The two main reasons were that: (1) Many countries, especially in Europe, needed American products and hence the dollars with which to buy them; and (2) there was complete confidence that the overall system was on a sound basis and that the value of the dollar would not fall. As will be seen in the next chapter, the relative decline in the role of the dollar from its erstwhile paramount position proceeded in parallel with the weakening of the two reasons just mentioned. In more general terms, the international role of a national currency is linked to the economic and political weight of the country. The influence of the United States was paramount in the Western world after World War II; the unique role of the dollar was the financial corollary of U.S. economic and political dominance.

---

[13] This was easy to do owing to the efficiency and vast size of the securities market in New York City, which after the war replaced London as the financial capital of the Western world.

Effectiveness of the Bretton Woods System

There is nothing wrong with the internal logic of the Bretton Woods system, any more than there is with the internal coherence of both flexible exchange rates and the gold standard. To be sure, in hindsight it is apparent that the system was undermined by severe problems. These arose from countries' economic behavior and changes in the international economy, which the architects of the system had either not foreseen or had not sufficiently weighed.[14] At any rate, the problems eventually became severe enough to lead to the collapse of the system. The problems have been grouped under the headings of imperfections of the adjustment mechanism, speculation and lack of confidence, and insufficient international liquidity. These are intimately interrelated, but it is convenient to discuss them separately.

Imperfections of the Adjustment Mechanism Two of the assumptions implicit in the Bretton Woods rationale turned out to be highly dubious in practice. The first is that it is possible to tell whether an *on-going* BOP disturbance is temporary or "fundamental" in nature. (It is easy enough to tell after the fact.) The term "fundamental" has been placed within quotes throughout this chapter because it was not adequately spelled out by the authors of the system, nor has it become any clearer through the operation of the system. The presumption is that a BOP deficit within the "trade cycle" (another dubious concept) should be financed, while a net deficit over the cycle as a whole is a fundamental one that calls for devaluation. But how do you know in advance? How do you determine, for example, that a decline in exports is a mere "fluctuation" that will soon be offset by an equivalent upturn rather than the start of a less favorable long-term trend? There may be evidentiary hints and qualitative indications of various sorts, but there can be no certainty of what the future will bring. Lacking reasonable assurance that a given BOP disturbance was "fundamental," governments have shown a natural tendency to delay revaluation or devaluation until "all the evidence was in." In some cases, of course, the BOP disturbance did turn out to be temporary. In others, however, the delay in adjusting the exchange rate rendered the adjustment all the more painful when it was finally made and prolonged the situation of external instability, not only for the country in question but for its trade partners as well.

The second faulty assumption of the Bretton Woods system is that a move toward BOP equilibrium is viewed as desirable by both surplus and

---

[14] Ragnar Nurkse, perhaps the principal intellectual architect of the Bretton Woods system, did identify quite correctly one of the main prerequisites for the stable and effective operation of the system. He made it clear that the system could not be maintained for very long if participating countries allowed major deviations from *internal* balance. As we shall see, the United States and other countries instead permitted major inflationary pressures to build up, resulting in the U.S. case from the failure to dampen excessive spending related to the Vietnam war and the social programs of the late 1960s.

deficit countries. As has been seen, there is indeed a theoretical presumption that external equilibrium is preferable to either a deficit or a surplus. (Recall, in particular, that a trade surplus is tantamount to enjoying a standard of living lower than the country's production level permits.) But it has also been seen that adjustment does carry significant costs and that it harms important domestic constituencies. It is no wonder, then, that governments are generally reluctant to revalue or devalue until the adjustment becomes inevitable.[15]

But a revaluation is not inevitable. A devaluation eventually is. Revaluation is called for when a BOP surplus is "fundamental" in nature. The government can prevent the exchange rate from going up by selling domestic currency in exchange for foreign currencies or gold. And a government's printing presses, of course, are an inexhaustible source of domestic currency. Thus, as long as the government is willing to continue accumulating foreign currencies, revaluation can in general be avoided and the BOP surplus can be maintained.[16]

Not so in a deficit situation. Support of the current exchange rate must take the form of buying up the excess private supply of domestic currency in exchange for convertible foreign currencies or gold. No matter how large the country's reserves might initially be, or how much help it may get from the IMF, if the BOP deficit continues, the government must eventually run out of reserves. At that point, excess private supply becomes quite simply excess supply, and the exchange rate must fall as a result. (In actuality, of course, devaluation would be declared long before the reserves were altogether gone.)

The upshot of these considerations is that: (1) The exchange rate adjustment under the adjustable peg system is less frequent and less timely than economic circumstances call for; and (2) The adjustment mechanism is asymmetric, with devaluations taking place far more frequently than revaluations. The system has a **devaluation bias,** caused by the capacity of surplus countries to avoid revaluation without a matching capacity of deficit countries to avoid devaluation.[17]

The asymmetry of the adjustment mechanism is partly responsible for

[15] A government has a further reason to be reluctant to revalue its currency. A revaluation is equivalent to a devaluation of foreign currencies. If reserves are held in foreign currencies, a revaluation causes a loss in their value.

[16] There is in the IMF charter a provision authorizing member countries to discriminate against a nation with a persistent BOP surplus that refuses to revalue its currency. This provision, known as the "scarce currency" clause, was never applied, however.

[17] The devaluation bias is aggravated by the following consideration. For one reason or another, devaluation is viewed by governments as an admission of failure and by public opinion as a national shame. National shame it is not. It could well be a symptom of government failure and of garbled economic policies. Be that as it may, as long as a government does lose political capital by being forced to devalue, it might as well be on the safe side and devalue by *more* than it considers necessary.

an inflationary bias as well. In the previous chapter it was seen how depreciation engenders domestic inflation in the depreciating country. Devaluation, of course, has the same general effect. Thus, to the extent that a devaluation bias exists, there is a net worldwide inflationary pressure. In addition, if some devaluations are forced by speculative activity without being warranted by a "fundamental" BOP deficit (an issue discussed in the next section), the devaluation bias and the corresponding inflationary pressure are stronger than it was just implied.

There is more. Surplus countries' intervention to prevent a rise in the exchange rate may itself contribute to inflation. The government holds down the exchange rate by placing in circulation enough additional domestic currency to absorb the excess demand for it. If no other steps are taken, this represents an increase in the total supply of domestic money and is a source of inflationary pressure. It is possible to tighten credit and take money out of circulation elsewhere, thus keeping the total quantity of money constant. But, at the very least, resistance to revaluation adds to the complexities of policy-making in the surplus country.[18]

Confidence and Speculation In Chapter 11 the stabilizing effect of speculation under permanently fixed exchange rates was mentioned. If the price of a currency, for example, gets close to the lower of the gold points, people know that it has no place to go but up. Their purchases of the currency drive the exchange rate back up toward its mint parity, and the price of the currency consequently fluctuates even less than the narrow gold-point spread would allow. The devaluation bias of the Bretton Woods system, instead, makes destabilizing speculation the norm. Let's explain the phenomenon of speculation in the adjustable peg monetary system.

As a government intervenes on the foreign exchange market to keep the exchange rate from falling below the official peg by more than the allowable 1 percent, people know that reserves are being depleted, and that eventually the exchange rate has no place to go but *down*. Further, if a devaluation does occur, the exchange rate can be expected to decline by a significant amount. If a devaluation does not happen, the exchange rate might at most go up to 1 percent above the official parity. The asymmetry of the adjustment mechanism is thus reflected in an asymmetry between expected gains and losses from speculation. If speculators bet against a currency (usually by selling it forward), they stand to make a considerable profit if they are right and devaluation occurs before they have to make good on their forward contracts. They stand to suffer only a minor loss if they are wrong and devaluation does not take place. In these circumstances, it is hardly surprising that most

---

[18] It is the resistance to revaluation that is responsible for inflationary pressure, not the system per se. Also, a regime of floating rates can conceivably be just as inflationary (as discussed in Chapter 12).

speculative activity is **bearish** (betting on a price decline) rather than **bullish** (betting that the price will increase).

Insofar as the devaluation would occur anyway, speculation merely hastens it. Although the devaluation then in essence transfers income from the government (which had been buying up its own currency at the higher support price) to the speculators—a less than ideal redistribution of income from the government's viewpoint—international speculation would not be cause for great concern. If, instead, the speculative expectations are self-fulfilling, in the sense that speculation *itself* causes an otherwise avoidable devaluation, the entire rationale of the adjustable peg system goes out the window, with devaluations occurring whether or not there is a "fundamental" BOP deficit.

The likelihood that speculative activity causes devaluation is directly related to the massiveness of the speculative attack relative to the strength of the government's financial defenses. During the early Bretton Woods years, national and international reserves were, by and large, adequate to resist bearish speculation (the next section discusses their inadequate growth to finance the postwar expansion of world commerce). Since then, however, reserves grew at a relatively slow pace. By contrast, private holdings of foreign currencies increased enormously (partly on account of the remarkable growth of multinational corporations), currently amounting to hundreds of billions of dollars in value. When even a small fraction of this spectacular mass of money moves in unison against a currency (which can happen when most of the people who control it have similar exchange expectations), the financial currency defenses of any individual government are like a sand castle pitted against a tidal wave.

In the adjustable peg system, then, speculation grew to introduce a serious element of instability, an ironic epitaph for a monetary arrangement that had been designed to maximize exchange stability and certainty in international commerce. By contrast, speculation within the pure gold standard tends to have a mild stabilizing effect. What about speculation under flexible exchange rates?

Go back for a minute to the essential rationale of the Bretton Woods system: Exchange rates arising out of temporary BOP disturbances should not be permitted, to avoid the resulting uncertainty and the losses caused by shifting resources needlessly back and forth. For instance, it makes little sense to allow the currency to depreciate at Christmas time because of a strictly temporary BOP deficit due to seasonal imports of toys. But why suppose that private individuals would not know as well as the government does that the deficit is temporary and act accordingly? If there exists a body of foreign exchange speculators interested in making a profit, with sufficient funds and a good understanding of underlying economic conditions (or at least no worse than the government's own understanding), it is perfectly reasonable to suppose that they themselves prevent unwarranted exchange rate changes. They buy up the currency as soon as it begins to decline, in the correct expectation that after Christmas the price will go back up. By doing so, they make money and the exchange rate does not fluctuate significantly except when justified by a persistent BOP deficit. In that case, of course, devaluation is called for by the Bretton Woods logic itself. Thus, if it is assumed that speculation is stabilizing under most circumstances, the foundations of the Bretton Woods edifice are shattered.

Under what circumstances, it must then be asked, can speculation be destabilizing? Indeed, just what *is* destabilizing speculation? By the most common definition, speculation is destabilizing when speculators buy the currency when its price rises—thus driving it up even more—and sell it when the price falls—thus pushing it down further. Exchange rate fluctuations are then wider than they would be in the absence of speculative activity. But to buy at a high price and sell at a low price means losing money. Since people hardly do so on purpose, destabilizing speculation under flexible rates presupposes a lack of knowledge and foresight on the part of the speculators. Further, if speculation were a losing proposition, it would quickly wither away of its own accord. But foreign exchange speculation is a persistent feature of the international monetary landscape under any monetary system. Hence, speculators must be making money and speculation may accordingly be presumed to be stabilizing. So goes the basic a priori argument that speculation is stabilizing in the absence of government intervention.[19]

There is, as always, another side. C. P. Kindleberger has pointed out that it is perfectly possible for professional speculators to make money while the losses suffered by the much greater number of amateurs causes speculators as a group to lose. Speculation can thus be both persistent and destabilizing, with an unchanging money-making core of professionals and a fresh supply of new "losers" coming in all the time. (After all, this is how the stock market works much of the time.) This rebuttal, of course, only shows that speculation *could* be destabilizing, but it does not prove that it is. A degree of consensus has emerged (primarily on the evidence of the favorable Canadian experience with flexible exchange rates in the 1950s) that under flexible rates currency speculation is an element of stability in the foreign exchange market, except under unusual circumstances. However, the issue is still very much open. Since the demise of the Bretton Woods system, several major currencies have been allowed to float more or less freely. As this was written, these experiences were much too recent for a clear-cut conclusion one way or the other, except perhaps to answer that "it depends" on the country in question.[20] At any rate, soon there will be far more evidence on the role of

[19] Indeed, some writers come close to making the untenable argument that instability is not an important economic problem in its own right, along with the other major questions of efficiency, growth, and income distribution.

[20] Especially for currencies with a very "thin" market, such as those of smaller countries, it is perfectly possible for a few individuals to manipulate the market. But

"Managed
Fixity":
The
Bretton
Woods
System

speculation under flexible exchange rates than is provided by the overworked Canadian case.

International Liquidity   The issue of the level of reserves needed for the proper functioning of the Bretton Woods system is intimately related to the previous two problems: asymmetry of adjustment and destabilizing speculation. If there were no devaluation bias—i.e., if devaluations took place as often as revaluations—surplus countries would not accumulate reserves at the expense of deficit countries attempting to support their exchange rate. And, if bearish speculation were absent or quantitatively insignificant, unwarranted devaluations could be staved off with a much lower level of reserves.

In general one may presume that the quantity of international money, reserves, must bear some relationship to the volume of international transactions. If reserves are not unnecessarily high to begin with, an increase in international transactions calls for some increase in reserves (although not necessarily a proportional increase). If reserves do not grow in adequate amounts, the emerging shortage of international money may introduce a serious constraint to the further expansion of world trade and investment and, consequently, to the economic well-being of the participating countries.

In the Bretton Woods system, international money consisted of both gold and dollars. The production of newly mined gold turned out to be insufficient to finance trade expansion, partly because of the growing demand for nonmonetary gold in new industries such as electronics. If the amount of dollars circulating internationally also failed to increase, inadequate international liquidity would then limit the growth of commerce. This was the general situation during the early 1950s, when an international "dollar shortage" caused liquidity difficulties. On the other hand, the "dollar glut" arising from the substantial U.S. BOP deficits of the 1960s, while alleviating world liquidity problems, progressively whittled down international confidence that the value of the dollar would not change.[21] This was the peculiar dilemma of

---

even in more developed currency exchanges some apparent instances of destabilizing speculation have emerged in the recent years of floating rates. The situation during the few recent years of exchange flexibility has been summarized by Paul Volcker as follows: *. . . we have avoided the atmosphere of crisis and the sharp discontinuities in exchange rates that characterized the later years of the Bretton Woods system. However, with floating rates, actual exchange rate swings among some leading currencies have been very sizeable. The typical daily fluctuation is much larger than before and, more important, changes have cumulated to as much as 15 to 20 percent over a relatively short period of time only to be largely or entirely reversed in the ensuing months. (Federal Resrve Bank of New York, Monthly Review, January 1976, p. 7. Roman inserted.)*

[21] In 1960, the U.S. gold reserve was three times as large as its liquid foreign liabilities. Ten short years later, the situation was entirely reversed, with the amount of outstanding dollars (the dollar "overhang") several times greater than the U.S. gold stock.

the gold-dollar standard. Given inadequate supplies of new monetary gold, a dollar shortage would reinforce confidence in the dollar as international money, but international reserves would not grow sufficiently. Persistent U.S. BOP deficits could serve to finance world trade expansion, but would also eventually undermine the dollar's acceptability as a reserve asset and hence, by definition, the very "moneyness" of the dollar.[22]

Managed Flexibility

Monetary arrangements under this heading allow a greater degree of exchange rate flexibility than permitted by the Bretton Woods rules, but they still aim at preventing excessive swings in a currency's price, generally by trying to make destabilizing speculation unprofitable. Of the various ways to increase flexibility (short of completely flexible exchange rates) the following have been used in some form or other by different countries.

The "Wide Band"

Closest in spirit to the Bretton Woods arrangements, the "wide band" allows greater flexibility *at any given point in time* by simply permitting exchange rates to vary from their official parity by some percentage greater than the 1 percent allowed under the Bretton Woods rules. It is still essentially an adjustable peg system, with governments required to intervene to prevent rates from moving beyond the assigned limits, albeit less narrow limits.

A wider band can go some length toward alleviating the adjustable-peg problems discussed earlier. It may reduce the devaluation bias by allowing significant increases in the exchange rate without the need for formal revaluation. Correspondingly, the discrepancy between the expected benefits and costs of speculation is also lessened: Speculators face the possibility that the exchange rate may increase by a respectable margin, and the financial penalties for unjustifiably bearish speculation could well be significant. Finally, a wider band may reduce the maldistribution of monetary reserves

[22] The dilemma could have been avoided if the U.S. balance of trade had remained strong and if foreign investment had been greater in the years of the dollar shortage. U.S. foreign investment in the 1950s, while substantial, was inadequate as a source of increased international liquidity. It increased markedly in the 1960s, but precisely at a time when the U.S. balance of trade had begun to weaken and eventually to turn negative, thus producing mounting BOP deficits at a time when unquestioning confidence in the dollar was a thing of the past. It is interesting, though idle, to speculate on what might have happened to the international monetary system if the expansion of U.S. foreign investment had taken place a dozen years earlier, thus preventing the dollar shortage of the early 1950s while increasing the investment income component of the balance of goods and services during the following years.

by lessening the accumulation of foreign currencies by surplus countries resulting from their intervention to keep the exchange rate virtually identical to the official parity.

A wider band would do these things, of course, in direct relation to its width. Thus, the widening of the Bretton Woods band in December 1971 from the original 2 percent to 4.5 percent was a significant, but not a drastic, step. Instead, a permissible range of fluctuation of, say, 40 percent (plus or minus 20 percent of parity) would just about eliminate the problems of the adjustable peg system. It would also, of course, practically eliminate the system itself, and for most countries it would in fact correspond to a flexible rate regime, with the attendant drawbacks discussed in Chapter 12.

The "Crawling Peg"

This proposal (a variant of which was adopted in 1975 by Israel) permits greater exchange rate flexibility *over a period of time* by allowing the peg itself to "crawl" by some maximum stipulated amount within any one period of time. The "parity path" (the direction, magnitude, and timing of the change) would be established, and announced, in advance. The idea is to break up delayed, large, occasional parity changes into timelier, small, frequent, and predictable changes. Potential speculative profits would consequently be reduced, it is hoped to the point at which destabilizing speculation is no longer worth the bother, the commission charges, and the interest loss (if the country raises interest rates as part of the "crawling devaluation" process). At the same time, the predictability, although not the stability, of exchange rates would be preserved. By removing the need for infrequent and large parity changes, the crawling peg could also to some extent take revaluation and devaluation decisions out of politics.

The hitch is whether governments can predict the future well enough (and whether speculators believe that they can) to establish an appropriate parity path. If a crawling devaluation, for example, fails to keep pace with BOP detoriation or with speculators' expectations, we are back where we started. However, if adopted widely and subject to systematic international scrutiny, a crawling peg mechanism would at least have the probable advantage of lessening the Bretton Woods devaluation bias: More international pressure could be put on surplus countries to revalue their currency gradually; also those governments would face internal political costs lower than for a large one-time revaluation.

Figure 13.2 compares graphically the Bretton Woods band (diagram *a*), a hypothetical 15 percent wide band (diagram *b*), and a hypothetical downward parity path under a crawling peg system (diagram *c*). Diagrams *a* and *b* show demand and supply curves for a country's currency. These curves become horizontal (perfectly elastic) at the upper and lower limits of

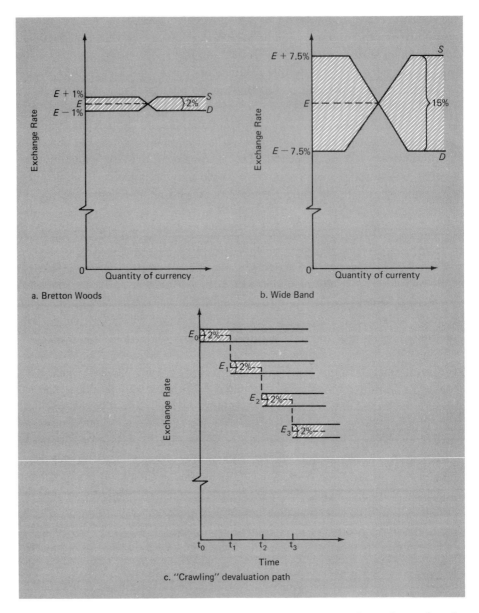

**FIGURE 13.2   Diagrammatic Representation of Bretton Woods, Wide Band, and
Crawling Peg.**

permissible fluctuations, since at those limits any amount of the currency
can be bought from, or sold to, the government. The official parity is designated as E.

There is no a priori reason why greater flexibility at one point in time
could not be combined with greater flexibility over time; a "crawling wide
band" has also been advocated.

Wide bands and crawling pegs are in the realm of proposals to allow greater flexibility within a generally specified structure of exchange rates, which governments are committed to maintain over the medium term. Closer to completely flexible exchange rates are arrangements to smooth out fluctuations in exchange rates without any prior specification of their "official" parities. Let's conclude this section with a brief look at these arrangements.

In the assumption that the public authorities are better able than private speculators to identify a trend in external payments and, consequently, the trend in equilibrium exchange rates, **official stabilization** may serve to smooth out fluctuations around that trend. The government buys the currency when the exchange rate declines and sells it when the price rises, *but* not in sufficient amounts to prevent a change from taking place altogether. Foreign currencies are expended from the stabilization fund to moderate a downward fluctuation from the trend and are bought back when the exchange rate rises above its trend value. Stabilization money thus has a quite different function from that of reserves in an adjustable peg system.

This is apparently an ideal situation. Exchange rate uncertainty is lessened, the costs of needless reallocation of resources back and forth are avoided, destabilizing speculation is prevented, and the exchange rate mechanism of BOP adjustment is allowed to operate smoothly. The difficulty is implicit in the assumption. The basic trend of equilibrium exchange rates may well be incorrectly identified by the government. If, for example, intervention is predicated on the assumption of a steady trend, while the true tendency is for the exchange rate to depreciate, intervention delays the needed adjustment and the stabilization fund is increasingly depleted. As it becomes more and more apparent that the means of financial intervention are shrinking, speculation surfaces again.[23] Stabilization of the type described may, however, have a useful place in international finance, particularly in volatile crisis times when panic replaces profit-and-loss calculations as the mainspring of speculative activity.

Official stabilization has been called by Gottfried Haberler "managed floating." Unlike managed floating, "dirty floating" has little to recommend it. Managed floating either takes place on the basis of some international agreement or at least calls for aboveboard stabilization activities of a kind and degree that are publicly and generally known. Dirty floating carries instead the connotation of cheating on agreed international rules of financial

---

[23] Another, but less serious, problem is the possible impact on the domestic money supply of the stabilization operations, with monetary expansion during exchange rate upswings and shrinkage when the currency is bought back by the government in times of a declining exchange rate. There are measures that can be taken to offset these inflationary or deflationary stimuli. Foreign funds can be "sterilized" and not allowed to influence the domestic money supply, as the British did, for example, through their Exchange Equalization Account of the 1930s.

behavior, or at least of surreptitious, underhanded activity. It may therefore become a dangerous source of international ill will. Dirty floating also tends to denote intervention to prevent exchange-rate changes or to make them smaller than is generally agreed that they ought to be on the basis of the underlying BOP situation. Dirty floating is thus the anarchic analogue of the adjustable peg, by which the faults of the Bretton Woods system are compounded by widespread uncertainty over the government's short-run intentions. In Haberler's definition, dirty floating is further characterized by direct controls over the foreign exchange market. This leads to the last topic of this chapter.

Suppressing External Disequilibrium: Exchange Control

The general heading of governmental restrictions on international transactions subsumes commercial policy, which affects the availability of the goods and services traded internationally, and exchange control, which affects the availability of the foreign currencies needed to do business with foreign residents. Commercial policy was examined at length in Part II. Exchange control as one important man-made obstacle to international commerce and investment was touched on in Chapter 4. In that context, however, the emphasis was primarily on the protective effects of financial restrictions. It is time to discuss briefly exchange control as a measure to suppress BOP disequilibrium.

A general distinction suggests itself, between *autonomous* interference in the foreign exchange market to pursue some specific objective of national policy and restrictions of foreign currency availability *forced* upon a government by a malfunctioning BOP adjustment mechanism. To the extent that the existing international monetary system is badly ineffective in preventing or correcting a BOP deficit, a participating country has only three alternatives: (1) suffer passively for some sort of adjustment to be forced upon it, with less-than-predictable and inevitably painful consequences (read again the statement quoted in Chapter 9, p. 217); (2) opt out of the system altogether (if it has the political and economic degrees of freedom to do so); *or* (3) suppress the disequilibrium by restricting payments abroad. Whatever valid or possibly valid arguments may be advanced in support of trade or investment controls (see Chapter 6), they generally do not apply (except by lucky accident) when exchange control is forced on a country by a malfunctioning international monetary system.

The mechanics of exchange control are simple in principle. Residents are required to surrender all their foreign exchange earnings to commercial banks. The banks are still the foreign exchange intermediaries, as in a free market. Here, however, they are intermediaries between private citizens and the public authorities, and they must act in accordance with government regulations concerning the disposition of foreign currency receipts. The system in practice requires, of course, the establishment of official penalties for failure to turn foreign currency receipts over to the government, the creation of an administrative organ, and a security apparatus to catch violators. Almost regardless of the severity of the penalties, a black market for foreign currencies usually emerges in some form.[24]

The general effect of exchange control is to diminish or destroy the convertibility of the domestic currency. A currency is convertible when it is generally accepted as a medium of international payments, and this is the case when it can be freely exchanged for any other currency in any desired amount. It follows that governmental restrictions on the availability of foreign currency render the country's own currency partially or totally inconvertible, depending on the scope and severity of the restrictions. In turn, less-than-complete convertibility of a currency prevents the country from taking full advantage of international specialization. For example, if country A's currency were not convertible into country B's currency, other countries importing from B would not readily accept A's currency in payment for their goods, since they could not turn around and use it to pay for B's goods. Country A may therefore be prevented from taking advantage of those countries' relative efficiency in certain sectors and may be obliged to resort to more expensive sources of imports.[25]

The more specific effects of exchange control are similar to those of quotas, discussed in Chapter 5. You can surely see the kinship between currency and quantitative restrictions. It makes little difference, for example, whether you are permitted to import a maximum of 1,000 Toyotas (which cost 1.5 million yen apiece) or to obtain a maximum of 1.5 billion yen (which pays for 1,000 Toyotas). Either way, imports are restricted.[26] In particular,

---

[24] This writer can still hear the singsong heard at all hours of the day in the street "markets" of Palermo, Italy, shortly after World War II: "I sell salt, perfume, Lucky Strikes, dollars, sterling, salt, perfume, Lucky Strikes, dollars . . ."

[25] The end result of nonconvertibility is **bilateral clearing**, by which a country accepts a foreign currency strictly to the extent that it intends to use it in the issuing country, and vice versa. The currency thus becomes incidental to what is essentially a barter process. Under **multilateral clearing**, participating countries accept one another's currencies, which are thus convertible within the group, while restrictions are imposed on the availability and use of currencies of nonmember countries. Clearly, the wider the scope of a multilateral agreement, the greater the degree of exchange convertibility in the world economy. At the limit, when all countries are members, restrictions on any foreign currency by definition cease and full convertibility of all currencies exists.

[26] A relative of exchange control is the **advance deposit requirement**, most recently imposed by Italy in 1976. By that requirement, importers must deposit a certain percentage of the value of imports in advance. The money is eventually returned to the importer, but, as no interest is paid, the requirement is a disguised tariff on all imports, equivalent to the opportunity cost of the deposit for the importer, and has the same restrictive effect on imports as any tariff would. The advance requirement also serves to prevent evasion of foreign exchange restrictions through the "over-invoicing" of imports, i.e., the "private" arrangement between importer and foreign seller to show an official price higher than that which is actually to be paid.

exchange control raises the same administrative difficulties as a quota does. Since the market is not allowed to function as the rationing device for scarce foreign exchange, some other rationing criterion must be applied. Whether the allocation of foreign exchange is on a first-come-first-served basis, or on an essential imports basis, or whatever, the giving out of licenses to buy the needed foreign currencies contains the same potential for favoritism, chicanery, and corruption as the administration of quotas.

Therefore, a general presumption is that exchange restrictions (like commercial policy restrictions) are not conducive to economic efficiency. But something should be said about the possible beneficial effects of exchange control that may offset this unfavorable preliminary verdict. General exchange control *may* be valuable either as the financial corollary of economic development programs or as an emergency device in transitional periods or in times of financial crisis and panics. In the first case, exchange control might be used to protect the infant manufacturing sector of a less developed country (not only an individual activity, as in the case of the infant industry tariff; see Chapter 6). In the second case, exchange restrictions may be needed in the aftermath of major disturbances (as for example in the years after World War II) and are often the only means to prevent "hot money" flight in times of severe uncertainty. One could hardly argue, for example, that a government should passively tolerate deliberate financial sabotage or the major destabilizing effects of panicky capital outflows. Clamping down *for a time* on the citizens' economic freedom to sell and buy foreign currency may be the only option.[27]

Exchange control, of course, need not be wholesale. Restrictions on the availability of foreign currencies for certain types of transactions may coexist with the absence of controls in other areas. Thus, restrictions on the use of foreign currencies for the purchase of "nonessential" imports are common throughout the less developed world. Selective exchange control is a form of disguised partial devaluation: In effect, a lower exchange rate (implying a higher price) applies to imports of nonessentials and a higher rate applies to other transactions. There may also be more than one official rate. Although a detailed discussion of dual and multiple exchange rates would take us to far afield, it should be mentioned that, when a meaningful distinction between categories of transactions can be made, a system of more than one exchange rate is conceivable and not necessarily inefficient. Thus, a less developed country that wishes to diversify out of its traditional exports may find it easiest and most effective to do so by applying a higher exchange rate (implying a higher price to foreign buyers) to those exports and a lower

---

[27] Indeed, the IMF charter explicitly authorizes the use of exchange control for this purpose.

exchange rate to other transactions.[28] Also, multiple exchange rates can conceivably be used to improve the country's terms of trade, by a reasoning similar to that encountered in the optimum tariff argument (see Chapter 6).

Points for Review

1. What is the difference between the Bretton Woods system, the adjustable peg, and the gold-dollar standard?

2. What are the principal features of the Bretton Woods system?

3. What is the Bretton Woods policy in regard to an imbalance in the BOP within the trade cycle?

4. What is the function of international reserves in the Bretton Woods system?

5. If a "fundamental" deficit points to the need for devaluation, how does one determine how much of a devaluation is needed?

6. What is the relationship between the law of reciprocal demand and the purchasing-power-parity principle?

7. Suppose that in 1960 the Italian BOP was in equilibrium and that Italian prices are today 400 percent of their 1960 level while prices in the rest of the world are 200 percent of the 1960 level. By the purchasing-power-parity principle, should the Italian lira be devalued or revalued, and by how much?

8. What are the functions of the International Monetary Fund (IMF)? Is the IMF an international central bank similar to the U.S. Federal Reserve system?

9. Were exchange rates in the Bretton Woods system *completely* fixed?

10. How are countries' borrowing privileges from the IMF related to the "quota"? Are these borrowing privileges automatic?

11. Could the dollar be devalued within the Bretton Woods arrangements?

12. Why was the dollar "better than gold" during the 1950s?

13. Review your understanding of the devaluation bias of Bretton Woods.

14. What is the connection between the devaluation bias and the inflationary bias of Bretton Woods?

15. Was speculation destabilizing in the Bretton Woods system because speculators lost money through making mistakes?

16. Review your understanding of the general controversy on whether or not speculation under *flexible* rates can be destabilizing.

[28] A subsidy on "new" exports or a tax on the traditional exports would accomplish the same purpose. The fiscal apparatus of the country may not, however, be developed enough to permit subsidization or taxation on the scale required.

17. What is a "crawling peg"? How and by whom is it decided by how much and when the peg should "crawl"?

18. How do you define "dirty" and "managed" floating?

19. What is the general effect of exchange control?

20. Review your understanding of the broad equivalence between exchange and quota restrictions.

Questions for Discussion

1. Discuss the Bretton Woods rationale in light of the lessons from the Great Depression of the 1930s.

2. On the one hand, BOP equilibrium on a minute-by-minute basis is absurd. On the other, it is very difficult to identify a "trade cycle." Do you have any observations on this apparent dilemma?

3. Why were the IMF and the World Bank established as *separate* institutions?

4. Do you agree with the statement made in the text that the role of a country's currency in international finance is linked to the country's economic and political status in the international economy?

5. How would you go about differentiating a temporary from a fundamental disequilibrium in your own personal financial position?

6. It is stated in the text that destabilizing speculation means that speculators, as a group, lose. Elsewhere, destabilizing speculation is viewed as part and parcel of the Bretton Woods arrangements. Just who lost from destabilizing speculation in the Bretton Woods days?

7. Why the frequent assertion in this chapter that in the Bretton Woods system adjustment, speculation, and liquidity problems were interrelated? If this is true, did it make sense to advocate, as many people did, "reforms" of one without touching the other two problems?

8. Given insufficient production of new gold, a U.S. BOP surplus within the gold-dollar standard results in a dollar shortage and thus in a shortage of international liquidity. A U.S. BOP deficit would increase international reserves but eventually undermine confidence in the dollar. Was this dilemma inevitable? Should it not have been foreseen by the architects of the Bretton Woods system?

9. Does a "wide band" differ in kind from the adjustable peg mechanism or only in degree?

10. Might the phenomenon of self-fulfilling expectations operate under a wide band, or crawling peg, as it did under the adjustable peg system?

11. Under what circumstances, and how, can multiple exchange rates improve a country's terms of trade?

*"There is always something to upset the most careful
of human calculations."*

Ihara Saikaku, *The Japanese Family Storehouse*

From Pax Britannica to Petrodollars:
International Finance in the
Twentieth Century

From
Pax
Britannica
to
Petrodollars:
International
Finance
in
the
Twentieth
Century

What to Expect

This chapter illustrates, through a review of international financial history to 1971, the considerations presented in the previous five chapters. The first section summarizes the main developments in international finance from the turn of the century to World War II. The second section examines the workings of the Bretton Woods system in practice. The structure of the second section parallels that of the presentation in Chapter 13 of the general problems of an adjustable peg system. It thus surveys the operation of the asymmetrical adjustment mechanism, the growing role of speculation, and the measures taken to expand international liquidity, concluding with an account of the events immediately preceding the system's collapse. The Appendix explains the sources and the role of the Euro-dollar market.

From Golden Age to Jungle: 1890–1939

The International Gold Standard before World War I

Advocates of a return to the gold-standard monetary system sometimes give the impression that the gold standard has been the norm in international financial dealings from time immemorial. On the contrary, although of course gold had been used as money for thousands of years, an international monetary system based on fixed exchange rates and adjustment of the BOP through maintenance of a linkage between gold stocks and domestic money ruled for only about as long as the 25 years of operation of the Bretton Woods system after World War II.

It is difficult to date with precision the birth of the international gold standard. What is known is that at the turn of the century practically all major industrial countries had followed Britain's early lead in maintaining a fixed exchange rate in terms of gold. Eighteen hundred ninety is probably as good a birth date as any; 1914 is unquestionably the last year of that period. While it lasted, the international gold standard worked quite well in maintaining or restoring equilibrium in the BOP of participating countries, much along the theoretical lines explained in Chapter 11. British policies provided a bench-mark to which other countries adjusted their own policies. In turn, British policies were generally in keeping with the gold-standard rules. The Bank of England would respond to a BOP surplus by lowering its **bank rate** (the interest rate charged on its loans to private financial intermediaries). This step would push down the entire structure of interest rates in the country, and the considerable international mobility of capital of those days would result in an outflow of capital to deficit countries. Although the price and expenditure effects of changes in interest rates were unknown or only imperfectly understood at the time, they existed nevertheless and contributed to keeping British external payments in approximate balance.[1]

The effectiveness of the gold standard depended, however, on a set of circumstances that, by and large, ceased to obtain after World War I and do not exist today. The most influential of these circumstances were:

1. The great international mobility of British capital, combined with Britain's strong balance-of-trade position. Britain's foreign investment could be counted on as a systematic counterweight of its trade surpluses. Owing to the responsiveness of capital flows to the Bank of England's lowering of the interest rate in times of surplus, the large British trade surpluses did not translate themselves into large overall BOP imbalances. It has been estimated that in the heyday of the system, from 1905 to 1913, Britain's foreign investment amounted to approximately 7 percent of her national income. (A corresponding proportion for the United States today would imply foreign investment upward of $100 billion every year!)[2]

In a very general sense, therefore, British foreign investment was *accommodating* rather than *autonomous* (although it was of course autonomous from the viewpoint of the private investors themselves). To see the importance of this for the working of the gold standard, consider the following

---

[1] Whether or not the Bank of England's policies followed the gold-standard "rules" strictly is a matter for continuing controversy. It has been argued that the Bank of England"s interest rate policy was not strict enough to cause the domestic money supply actually to contract in response to a gold outflow, as the gold-standard system calls for. And occasional instances of "sterilization" of gold flows—also against the rules—have been found by economic historians to have occurred in some countries. A strong case can be made therefore that the policy-makers' absolute self-discipline and obeisance to the system in the gold-standard years is largely mythical. Nevertheless, the adjustment process did work. Even if some deficit countries did not permit full contraction of the money supply, the surplus countries did allow it to expand. *Relative* prices still changed, and the gold standard worked, albeit less quickly than it would have if the rules had been scrupulously followed. And approximate equilibrium in the British BOP as well as the supplies of new gold helped to prevent serious imbalances from arising and to finance them when they did arise.

[2] The international mobility of capital and the central role of sterling as nearly universal transactions currency were facilitated by the well-developed and extremely efficient capital market in London, which was at the time the unquestioned center of gravity of world finance. Most British foreign investment consisted of lending (rather than equity investment) and generally went to infrastructural projects in lands of recent settlement (the United States, Australia, etc.), accompanying the great migratory waves of those years. By contrast, foreign investment after World War II, when the Western world's "frontier" lands had long been settled and international migration had been curtailed, has consisted increasingly of direct investments in manufacturing facilities. Thus, as R. Nurkse has pointed out, while British investment and labor movements before World War I were complementary to one another, foreign investment in recent years has occurred as a substitute to labor migration. The upshot is that foreign lending and investment by surplus countries can no longer be expected to be large enough to even approach the stabilizing influence of British investment in the gold-standard years.

From
Pax
Britannica
to
Petrodollars:
International
Finance
in
the
Twentieth
Century

obvious proposition: Other things being equal, the adjustment mechanism works better when disturbances are smaller. At the extreme, if all countries' payments are in balance, *any* international monetary system works well because no adjustment is necessary at all. Equilibrium in the BOP of Britain, the dominant actor on the economic scene of those years, was also a powerful contributor to balance in the external payments of other countries, and thus it made for considerable overall international economic stability. In addition, no major political or military disturbances occurred after the Franco-Prussian war of 1870–71. Skirmishes and colonial adventures were of course quite common, but not sufficient to generate serious international economic disturbances.

2. The political tolerance in most countries of the domestic economic consequences of BOP adjustment, combined with a significant degree of downward flexibility of wages and prices. As was seen in Chapter 11, the gold-standard adjustment to a BOP deficit need not cause production losses and unemployment if prices and wages are flexible in a downward direction. Undoubtedly, domestic prices and wages were far more pliant in the gold-standard age than in the later years of monopoly and trade-union power. To be sure, adjustment caused income to be redistributed away from wage earners in certain sectors and from other groups, but the fatalistic willingness to let the process of adjustment take its course (as well as the workers' lack of political power) permitted deficit countries to follow internal policies reasonably compatible with the functioning of the gold-standard mechanism.

3. Lastly, the discoveries of vast gold deposits in the 1890s and the ensuing large production of gold throughout the gold-standard years contributed significantly to exchange rate stability. Sales of new gold, counted as exports by the producing country but as additional monetary reserves by the recipient, allowed surpluses to be greater than deficits in the international economy as a whole, and they allowed deficit countries to finance their payments' imbalances for a longer time. Increases in world gold reserves thus served both to accommodate the worldwide net preference for BOP surpluses (see Chapter 13), and to allow deficit countries to remain on the gold standard without having to permit domestic deflation to the full extent required for adjustment.

Let's summarize. Britain's interest-rate policy and huge foreign lending prevented significant surpluses in her BOP and accordingly contributed to other countries' external balance. The payments' disturbances requiring adjustment were therefore relatively small throughout much of the system. When BOP disturbances did emerge, domestic wage-price flexibility made for a reasonably effective gold-standard type of adjustment. Finally, the growth in gold reserves allowed some countries to finance their deficits without abandoning fixed exchange rates, resulting in smaller disturbances, a more favorable adjustment climate, and a large monetary cushion. In hindsight, it is far from surprising that the international gold standard worked fairly well. (In fact, under those favorable conditions, it is probable that any other monetary system would have worked just as well—from flexible rates down through the intermediate arrangements discussed in the previous chapter.) Those favorable conditions were, however, to be radically altered by World War I and its aftermath. Perhaps the major underlying change was the shift in the balance of economic and political power away from Britain, whose sheer weight and external stability had firmly anchored the world economy prior to 1914.

A strong warning is in order here. The upshot of this section is that the international financial system was *stable*, that is all. That "stability" is not necessarily "happiness" is a point already made several times in this book. The gold-standard years were hardly a Garden of Eden for the great numbers of European factory workers subsisting in sweatshop conditions, nor was the colonial partition of most of the world among European powers particularly enjoyable for the millions of people on the receiving end of the colonial officer's swagger stick.

Self-deception in the 1920s

Along with the Romanovs, Hohenzollerns, and Hapsburgs, the newer gold-standard "dynasty" was also swept away by the world war. But for several years many of its loyal "subjects" refused to acknowledge its passing and continued to keep up the façade of the system. Britain's leading position, the political and economic mainstay of international stability, had been severely undermined—permanently, as it turned out. The United States, potentially the new center of gravity of the international economy, was not willing to behave as such. According to this "Kindleberger thesis," already noted in Chapter 10, the interwar period was marked by a power vacuum: Britain could no longer exercise international economic leadership; the United States would not yet do so.

After the war, there was a measure of consensus that a return to the gold standard was desirable. However, the difficult question of the new structure of exchange rates appropriate to the changed international pecking order had to be settled first. Chapter 13 discussed two routes to the determination of equilibrium exchange rates (the purchasing-power-parity principle and the direct econometric estimation of the impact of an exchange rate change). A third route was followed in the years after World War I: "Let the market tell you" what new exchange rate is appropriate by allowing the price of the currency to fluctuate freely. It should be emphasized that the currency floats during 1918–24 were intended purely as a transitional device to find the appropriate levels at which exchange rates should again be

From
Pax
Britannica
to
Petrodollars:
International
Finance
in
the
Twentieth
Century

fixed in order to restore the prewar international gold standard and not as an alternative monetary system in their own right.[3]

These were also the years of hyperinflation in the German Weimar Republic. The extraordinary German inflation of the early 1920s deserves a few separate words. Not only is it a fascinating phenomenon in its own right, but it was a national economic trauma that has conditioned inflation-shy German economic policies to the present day. A few incredible figures: one English pound exchanged for 75 DM in 1919, and for 1,250,000 DM in 1923; interest rates in Germany in 1923 averaged about 20 percent *per day* (even before the peak of inflation), and, even so, prices were rising faster and the real interest rate was negative; the German average price level at the peak of the inflationary spiral in the fall of 1923 was 100 billion times that of 1920, with a pack of cigarettes selling for 500 *billion* marks. Translating it into our own everyday terms, if on the day when you are reading this a quart of milk sells for 50 cents, an inflation rate comparable to that of the last months of the Weimar inflation would bring the price of milk to $300 a quart tomorrow.

Different lessons are drawn from this experience by different people. Advocates of fixed exchange rates use it to illustrate the dangers of unrestricted floating, as in their view much of the inflationary stimulus came from unwarranted depreciation of the mark on the foreign exchange market. Flexible rate proponents instead attribute the Weimar inflation to the extraordinary expansion of the money supply permitted by the German government. There is truth in both views. It is quite true that the government's printing presses were rolling overtime and producing ever-increasing amounts of ever more worthless paper money. But exchange rate depreciation contributed its share, too, as it often preceded domestic price increases. Chapter 12 presented the argument that inflationary depreciation can occur only if the domestic money supply is allowed to rise. The Weimar inflation contradicts that thesis to some degree, since the increase in domestic money, phenomenal as it was, did not keep pace with the rate of price increases. As national income was not undergoing major changes in those years, the inflationary consequences of depreciation were fueled also by increases in the velocity of money ($MV = PY$). And these, in turn, were partly the result of currency depreciation.

After the period of transitional floating, one country after another again pegged its exchange rate. Then, however, only some currencies were pegged directly to gold, while others were pegged to a major currency whose value was fixed in terms of gold. National monetary reserves thus came to include large amounts of foreign currencies, giving rise to the term **gold-exchange standard** to describe the monetary arrangement of those years.

[3] Other instances of this use of floating exchange rates have occurred in recent years, as for example the 3-week float of the German mark allowed by the West Germans in the fall of 1969 as an aid to deciding by how much the mark should be revalued.

Both the United States (right after the war) and Britain (in 1925) went back to approximately the prewar gold parity, implying a rate of exchange of $5 = £1. But the economic relationship between these two major powers was no longer the same. Prices had increased in Britain by more than they had in the United States. In addition, war-related disruption of foreign trade, far more damaging for Britain, had tilted the competitive balance even further toward the American side. And Britain's comfortable "rentier" position as recipient of considerable incomes from past foreign investments had sapped its earlier economic dynamism. As a result, the exchange rate was too high for the pound and too low for the dollar.[4]

As you know, the likely outcome would be British BOP deficits and American surpluses. Had the old gold standard rules been scrupulously followed, deflation in Britain and economic expansion in the United States would have intervened to eventually correct the imbalance and the international system might have survived. But the adjustment process was short-circuited by more and more countries, as circumstances were no longer the same as before the war. There was much less tolerance for deflationary adjustment, and U.S. financial isolationism kept American capital from flowing into the system to perform the equilibrating role of prewar British foreign investment. The situation was further aggravated by the return of the U.S. to high protective tariffs (see the discussion of the Fordney-McCumber Tariff in Chapter 8), worsening the trade balance of other countries, including Britain.[5] It is conceivable—just barely—that, given enough time, the monetary façade of the 1920s could have been reinforced and adapted to the changed background conditions. But the Great Depression intervened to destroy all but a few remnants of the international gold standard.

World Depression and Monetary Disintegration

Chapter 10 reviewed the spread of the Great Depression from the United States to the rest of the industrial world. By 1933 foreign payments by the United States (imports and capital outflow) had shrunk to less than one-

[4] The British decision to return to the prewar exchange rate was bitingly criticized by J. M. Keynes in his pamphlet *The Economic Consequences of Mr. Churchill* (who was at the time in charge of British economic policy). It is interesting that Winston Churchill's imperial conservatism reappeared 20 years later in his well-known remark that he had not been appointed Prime Minister "in order to preside over the liquidation of the British empire." It would have been quite in character had he said in 1925 that he had not been appointed in order to preside over the demise of British international monetary dominance.

[5] We have said often that a badly functioning international monetary system tends to lead to the adoption of quasi-adjustment measures to suppress BOP imbalances. The reverse is also true: Widespread additional restrictions, whether commercial or financial, place an extra burden on the BOP adjustment mechanism, which accordingly functions less well. The possibility of a vicious circle: monetary instability–restrictions–instability, etc., is a real one. However, the circularity of this, as of all other, economic processes,

From
Pax
Britannica
to
Petrodollars:
International
Finance
in
the
Twentieth
Century

third of their pre-1930 level. What happened to the world economy as a result is analogous to what would happen to the economy of Michigan if production of automobiles fell from 10 to 3 million cars per year.

A quick rundown of the 1930s monetary experiences includes the following major events. Even before the Depression, several small countries had already been forced to let go of fixed exchange rates, as must sooner or later happen when prevention of internal adjustment is accompanied by insufficient reserves to finance the BOP deficit. In 1931, the overvalued pound forced Britain itself off the gold standard.[6] With the pound floating, countries trading heavily with Britain had no viable option but to abandon the gold standard themselves and peg their currencies directly to the pound, thus creating a **sterling area.**[7] Germany, depreciation-shy from the inflationary experience with the 1920s floating mark, instead chose exchange control to suppress payments' imbalances, and so, eventually, did Italy. France took the import quota route. The U.S. BOP remained relatively strong, owing in part to the import-restricting effects of the 1930 Hawley-Smoot Tariff (see Chapter 8). But, as the foreign repercussions came home to roost in the form of reduced U.S. exports, and as one foreign currency after another was allowed to depreciate, the dollar became progressively less and less undervalued; the United States also let the dollar float in 1933–34.

An attempt was made in July 1933 at the World Economic Conference in London to put a stop to uncoordinated national actions that demonstrably redounded to the disadvantage of all. The Conference may well have failed of its own accord, but an "America First" message from President Roosevelt, essentially disavowing any intention to cooperate in international monetary stabilization if it appeared to conflict with internal American economic goals, ensured that little could come out of the London meetings. From the wreckage of the Conference emerged the **gold bloc,** an agreement by France, Italy, Switzerland, Holland, Belgium, and Poland to maintain their exchange rates fixed in terms of gold.

Somewhat paradoxically, it was the eventual inability of the gold bloc countries, particularly France, to maintain fixed exchange rates that led to the first step back toward international monetary sanity. Severe episodes of destabilizing speculation during the transitional floats of the 1920s had driven down the exchange rate of the franc even though the French BOP

---

can work for you as well as against you. Thus, given the requisite international cooperation, an improvement in international monetary arrangements can permit some trade and exchange liberalization, which renders the international monetary system more efficient, in turn fostering further liberalization, and so forth.

[6] At first, the pound was allowed to float freely; its exchange rate fell rapidly in the beginning and recovered somewhat thereafter. In 1932 the Exchange Equalization Account was established to function as a stabilization device (see Chapter 13).

[7] Before World War I, of course, nearly the whole industrial world was a sterling area, since sterling and gold were considered for all practical purposes synonymous.

The
Bretton
Woods
System
in
Action:
1945–71

was basically in surplus. This allowed France to fix its exchange rate at a relatively low level when it went back on the gold standard in 1926. The undervaluation of the franc lasted until about 1933, when it become France's turn to be the "beggared neighbor." At first, the French resorted to import quotas, but by 1936 massive speculation against the franc led the government to consider devaluation. Fearful, and with reason, that unilateral action in this respect would bring retaliation by other countries, France sought *advance* agreement for devaluation by Britain and the United States. The approval was given and embodied in the Tripartite Monetary Agreement of 1936.

The Tripartite Agreement was in a way the monetary counterpart of the Reciprocal Trade Agreements Program authorized by the U.S. Congress in 1934 (see Chapter 8). The Reciprocal Trade Agreement program had embodied the first operational recognition, in the arena of commercial policy, that isolated national actions in an interdependent world invite disaster for all. The Tripartite Monetary Agreement was the first, halting step toward the renewal of international cooperation in the arena of monetary policy.[8] World War II, of course, was to upset the apple cart again only 3 years thence.

The Bretton Woods System in Action: 1945–71

The adjustable peg system was discussed in general terms in Chapter 13. This section examines the operation of the system in actual practice and the steps that were taken to alleviate some of its problems. As has been noted, these can be classified under the headings of asymmetry of the adjustment mechanism, problems of speculation, and inadequate international liquidity. They did not, however, begin to cause serious difficulties until the 1960s. Let us start, therefore, with a brief look at the first postwar decade and at the restoration of currency convertibility.

European Recovery and the Restoration of Convertibility

European economic recovery from the ravages of war was the clear prerequisite for progress on any front. For the first 2 years after the war emergency aid, administered by the United Nations Relief and Recovery Administration

---

[8] It is significant that, unlike the Tripartite Monetary Agreement, its counterpart in more recent times (the Smithsonian Agreement of December 1971, discussed later in this chapter) took place *before* a round of serious competitive devaluations could start. It might be that, having learned the lesson of history, the world is not condemned to repeat it. The question for the future remains, how long does it take for a lesson to be forgotten?

From
Pax
Britannica
to
Petrodollars:
International
Finance
in
the
Twentieth
Century

(UNRRA), was provided European countries to prevent massive hardships and further collapse. In 1948, UNRRA was replaced by the Marshall Plan, a comprehensive aid program that in a 3-year period made grants totaling about $10 billion. There has been controversy among historians over the motivations and political success of the Marshall Plan. But there is little doubt that the aid substantially helped economic reconstruction in Europe. By 1951, economic recovery was practically complete, with production levels back to their prewar levels in most countries. The following decade was to witness a European "economic miracle" and remarkable rates of economic growth, particularly in West Germany, Italy, and France. On the other side of the planet, Japan was having its own economic miracle.

The years 1945–50 were those of the intense "dollar shortage." In fact, while the dollar was the most scarce, other foreign currencies were also in short supply in European countries, convertibility was almost nonexistent, and trade was carried on practically on a barter basis through a network of makeshift bilateral agreements. Instant convertibility was out of the question. It was feasible and clearly desirable, however, to gradually lessen exchange restrictions and increase convertibility in parallel with the pace of economic progress. As explained in Chapter 13, restrictions on the acquisition of foreign exchange are equivalent to import quotas in their effects on trade. The institution charged with coordinating efforts to remove quotas was the Organization for European Economic Cooperation (OEEC), which, in its first years of existence, also served to administer Marshall Plan aid.[9] The progressive removal of exchange controls was equally necessary for the expansion of international trade.

Intra-European currency convertibility was attempted first, with full convertibility the eventual goal. This was facilitated by a multilateral clearing mechanism established in 1950, the European Payments' Union (EPU), comprising the same membership as the OEEC.[10] The EPU was a clear improvement over bilateral agreements, allowing European countries at least to take advantage of each other's comparative efficiency. At the same

[9] At the end of the 1950s, when the liberalization of quantitative trade restrictions was accomplished, the OEEC was expanded to include the United States, Japan, Australia, and Canada, its name was changed to Organization for Economic Cooperation and Development (OECD), and its role diminished to that of a consultative and research organization (although a highly prestigious one).

[10] With multilateral clearing each member country concerns itself only with its overall financial position within the group and need not suffer the inefficiencies of trying to balance payments and receipts with each individual country it does business with. Country X deposits with the clearing organization its surplus in relation to country Y; country Y deposits its surplus in relation to country Z; and country Z deposits its surplus in relation to country X. The clearing organization nets it all out, and at the end of an agreed period of time only the net deficit or surplus needs to be settled. Member-country currencies are thus convertible into one another. A multilateral clearing organization of the EPU type also functions as a mini-IMF, lending to countries that have a net deficit within the group the currencies of surplus countries on the basis of agreed contributions and credit quotas.

The
Bretton
Woods
System
in
Action:
1945–71

time, by definition, it was a discriminatory arrangement against nonmember countries and, as such, gave European industries protection against competition from America and elsewhere. As would be the case for any protective arrangement, the EPU's end was resisted by protectionist interests in Europe, and it is probable that full convertibility could have been achieved a little sooner than it was. At any rate, at the end of 1958 the EPU was dissolved, exchange restrictions were eliminated in most industrial countries, and European currencies became convertible into dollars.

How Adjustable Was the Peg?

The previous chapter advanced the generalization that exchange rate adjustments in an adjustable peg system are likely to be biased toward devaluation. The historical record of the Bretton Woods years clearly confirms the point.

A first round of devaluations occurred in 1949, when practically all major countries, with the exception of Switzerland, Japan, and, of course, the United States, devalued in the wake of British devaluation of the pound from about $4.00 to $2.80. It may be argued that the devaluations of 1949 partook more of the nature of an *initial* establishment of a realistic structure of exchange rates to get the Bretton Woods system under way than of the nature of subsequent exchange rate adjustments. (After all, the dollar would not become overvalued for a good many years to come.) Even aside from the 1949 devaluations, however, adjustments of exchange rates in the Bretton Woods years were dominated by devaluations. The major exchange rate changes between 1950 and 1971 were the devaluations of the French franc in 1958 and again in 1969, the revaluations of the German mark in 1961 and in 1969, and the devaluation of the pound in 1967.[11]

Invariably, the devaluations were larger: France devalued by 15 percent in 1958 and 11 percent in 1969 and Britain by 14 percent in 1967, while West Germany revalued by only 5 percent in 1961 and by 9 percent in 1969. More importantly, unlike revaluations, devaluations of major currencies set off subsequent devaluations by client countries. (Thus, for example, Finland devalued by 25 percent following the 1967 devaluation of the pound.) Many major currencies, particularly the Japanese yen and the Swiss franc, were held at unquestionably undervalued parities, illustrating the asymmetry of adjustment explained in Chapter 13. In the later years of Bretton Woods, the cumulative effort of the devaluation bias had begun to lead

---

[11] Other events of some note were the floating of the Canadian dollar in 1950–62 and a 5 percent revaluation of the Dutch guilder accompanying the 1961 revaluation of the mark. Also, the mark was allowed to float for two brief periods in 1969 and in 1971—not as an experiment in a new monetary arrangement—but as a device to either get an idea of how much to revalue (in 1969) or to combat speculation (in 1971). The dollar devaluations of 1971 and 1973 are discussed later, as they did not fit the normal Bretton Woods arrangements.

From
Pax
Britannica
to
Petrodollars:
International
Finance
in
the
Twentieth
Century

back to the use of quasi-adjustment measures by deficit countries (after all the efforts to get rid of quotas in the 1950s!) and the growing mass of speculative funds was making it more and more difficult to prevent downward parity changes, even when they were unwarranted by the BOP situation.[12]

Speculation and the Multinational Firm

Parity adjustments in the Bretton Woods years were generally implemented in an atmosphere of crisis and were preceded by massive speculation. Particularly from 1967 on, there was an almost unbroken succession of speculative crises. First the pound, then the French franc, and finally King Dollar itself came under heavy speculative pressure.

The previous chapter stated that the likelihood that speculation itself causes exchange rate changes is directly related to the massiveness of the speculative attack relative to the strength of the government's financial defenses (its reserves). As speculative funds grew faster than monetary reserves, the capacity of the Bretton Woods system to preserve its own rationale for existence (maintaining the exchange rate fixed except in case of fundamental disequilibrium) became progressively weaker. The institutional development facilitating currency speculation has been the growth of the Eurodollar market, the sources and functions of which are discussed in the Appendix to this chapter. One major source of the increase in speculative funds has been the multinational corporation.

International capital flows before World War I consisted primarily of lending. After World War II, instead, a much greater proportion of capital flows has consisted of direct investment in manufacturing, mainly by U.S. firms in European countries. The book value of foreign manufacturing assets owned by U.S. corporations grew tenfold in the 20 years from 1950 to 1970. The growth of multinational enterprise is a complex phenomenon of importance for trade theory, policy, and finance. Here only the general implica-

[12] The dollar had become progressively overvalued in correspondence with the devaluations of other currencies. In the mid-1960s, restrictive measures were taken to alleviate the growing payments deficit, including the "tying" of foreign aid to the purchase of American products, restrictions on American investment abroad, and the **interest-equalization tax.** The latter aimed at offsetting the higher interest rates prevailing in foreign countries, particularly in Europe. While this may appear as the financial counterpart of the nonsense argument for scientific tariffs, there was a government limit on the interest U.S. banks could pay on savings accounts (the so-called Regulation Q). To the extent that this limit was responsible for the relatively lower U.S. interest rates, the interest equalization tax could be viewed as the economically legitimate corrective of an internal distortion, although only second-best to eliminating the distortion itself (see Chapter 6). In any case, both the capital controls and the interest equalization tax were eliminated in 1974, and aid was progressively "untied," although its volume was also considerably reduced.

The
Bretton
Woods
System
in
Action:
1945–71

tion of it for the stability of foreign exchange markets can be pointed out.[13]

International corporations hold substantial liquid funds denominated in a variety of foreign currencies in order to do business in the various countries where they have interests. The rapid growth of multinational enterprise has meant a parallel growth of these funds. In 1970, the value of liquid assets in the hands of U.S. corporations and international banks was over $30 billion, equivalent to about three times the value of the U.S. gold reserves in that year. Imagine the pressures on the pegged exchange rate of a currency when a couple of billions of dollars worth of it is sold on the foreign exchange market in a matter of weeks.

Why would a multinational firm engage in foreign exchange operations? The basic consideration is that the foreign currency composition of a multinational company's liquid holdings is determined by its head office in pursuance of the company's interests, not necessarily in keeping with the monetary policies of the countries where the company's subsidiaries are located. The two main reasons for changing the makeup of a company's foreign currency portfolio are to profit from interest rate differentials in different countries and to avoid losses from exchange rate changes. Sales and purchases of foreign currencies to profit from interest rate changes respond to the monetary policy of governments. An increase in interest rates can improve the capital account by attracting short-term capital from multinational corporations. And, since governments presumably raise or lower interest rates partly to stabilize the market for their currency, such foreign exchange activities of corporations in all probability contributed to the stability of the adjustable peg system. But probably far more important was the second motivation, i.e., not to suffer a capital loss should one of the currencies held be devalued. As P. B. Kenen has pointed out, a corporation treasurer wouldn't get fired if he missed out on taking advantage of a small interest differential, but he had better start looking for another job if he got caught holding a few dozen million dollars worth of a currency when it was devalued by 10 or 20 percent. Doubts on the willingness or the ability of a government to maintain the current exchange rate were thus likely to lead to massive unloading of the currency, on the "better safe than sorry" principle. In view of the huge amounts involved, there was a very good chance

---

[13] There exists an extensive body of literature on multinational enterprises. The more important contributions are listed in the Bibliography at the end of this book. The best-known treatment is R. Vernon, *Sovereignty at Bay: The Multinational Spread of U.S. Enterprise* (New York: Basic Books, 1971). In that book, among other things, Vernon makes the important point that the trade implications of the multinational corporation are quantitatively more important than the capital flows involved. In 1968, sales by US.-owned firms in advanced countries amounted to $44 billion, profit remittances to the parent corporation in the United States to only about $1 billion. "Because of the orders of magnitude involved, even a modest impact [on trade] can readily swamp those balance-of-payment effects that are recorded by way of profit remissions" (Vernon, p. 163).

From
Pax
Britannica
to
Petrodollars:
International
Finance
in
the
Twentieth
Century

that the government's own reserves and its IMF credit would be exhausted long before the excess private supply was mopped up and therefore that devaluation was forced whether or not the state of the BOP warranted it. Whereupon, of course, the company treasurers would be duly congratulated on their "foresight," and their destabilizing, albeit essentially defensive, behavior pattern would, like B. F. Skinner's pigeons, be reinforced. (To place this in better perspective, review the discussion in Chapter 13 of the possibility that speculation may be destabilizing also under flexible exchange rates.)

Measures to Expand International Liquidity

The third major problem of the Bretton Woods system, discussed in general terms in Chapter 13, was the inadequacy of international liquidity—or, to put it more rigorously, the reliance on U.S. BOP deficits for the provision of additional liquidity, which was bound to lead eventually to a crisis of confidence in the dollar and in the international monetary system that depended on it. Some observers viewed the inadequacy of reserves as the main problem of the Bretton Woods system. Others claimed that the difficulty lay in the asymmetry of the adjustment mechanism. The controversy was akin to arguing whether a chair totters because one of its legs is too short or because the others are too long. Existing reserves were inadequate exactly because the adjustment mechanism was faulty and the devaluation bias of the adjustable peg was aggravated by inadequacy of reserves.

Gold production had never, from the very beginning of the Bretton Woods system, kept up with the expansion of world trade and the growth of speculative funds with the ensuing need for greater reserves. The system thus did not enjoy the important advantage the international gold standard had in this respect before World War I. The world's gold stock, which had been 63 percent of global monetary reserves in 1951 accounted for only 37 percent of them in 1970. In particular, between 1951 and 1970 the U.S. gold holdings (the backing for the convertible dollar) had fallen from 43 percent to 13 percent of world reserves at the same time as dollar reserve holdings of foreign countries had climbed from less than one-third to almost one-half of global monetary reserves. The potential problem was recognized early on, but it was not until serious difficulties had emerged at the beginning of the 1960s that steps were taken to alleviate it. These included at first only a number of palliatives. Only later, too much later, was a major monetary innovation introduced in the form of the Special Drawing Rights (discussed below).

Stopgap Measures As we have seen, drawings from the IMF in excess of a country's gold tranche were not automatic. An improvement in IMF lending practice was the introduction of **standby agreements,** by which a country

The
Bretton
Woods
System
in
Action:
1945–71

would get advance IMF approval of a line of credit up to a certain maximum, which it could then use in whole or in part within a specified period of time if and when it decided to. Standby agreements improved the timing of IMF financial assistance, but they did not expand the amount of credit available to member countries.

A measure that did increase the capacity of governments to intervene on the foreign exchange market was the 1962 General Agreements to Borrow. Ten major countries agreed to lend the IMF up to a total for the group of $6 billion worth of their currencies. In addition several countries entered into **swap agreements,** by which they would exchange specified amounts of each other's currencies for a maximum period of 1 year. Since the currencies involved were convertible, each country could use the other's currency as an addition to its reserves. (The United States entered into about $12 billion worth of swap agreements with a dozen foreign countries.) Finally, **ad hoc cooperation** among central bankers of various countries in times of speculative crises affecting a country's currency often succeeded in staving off bearish speculation.

The IMF lending function itself was expanded through increasing countries' regular quotas and also through a **compensatory financing** facility established in 1963 and enlarged in 1966. Compensatory financing is available to countries, above and beyond their regular IMF credit line, that are affected by sudden and sharp declines in their export earnings. The facility proved to be very useful for many less developed countries, whose high commodity concentration of exports rendered them vulnerable to fluctuations in foreign exchange earnings. Total IMF lending in the Bretton Woods years is shown in Table 14.1.

The Special Drawing Rights While useful, the measures described above barely scratched the surface of the central problem: In the gold-dollar standard, increases in the availability of one international money (gold) were

TABLE 14.1   IMF Lending: 1947–71
(Millions of Dollars)

Years	Gross Lending	Repayments	Net Lending
Total: 1947–71	23,900	17,050	6,850
Annual Average: 1947–71	956	682	274
Annual averages in:			
1947–51	162	23	139
1952–56	220	195	25
1957–61	851	498	353
1962–66	1,350	800	550
1967–71	2,199	1,895	304

Source: IMF, *International Financial Statistics,* various issues.

From
Pax
Britannica
to
Petrodollars:
International
Finance
in
the
Twentieth
Century

minimal, and increases in the availability of the other (the dollar) undermined confidence in the system. A third international money was agreed upon in 1968 and first issued in 1970 under the undramatic technical name of **Special Drawing Rights** (SRD's) and the colloquial label of "paper gold."

As we noted earlier, the IMF credit facilities were expanded during the 1960s. The SDR's were instead an increase in each country's gold tranche, part of the country's owned reserves and on call whenever the country saw fit. It might seem peculiar that a bookkeeping change constituted the creation of a new form of money. But consider that the only requirement for a metal (such as gold), a piece of paper (such as the dollar), or a bookkeeping entry (such as the SDR's) to be money is that people accept it as such. The agreement of IMF member countries to accept each other's SDR's in exchange for national currencies ipso facto made SDR's a new form of international money. (Since 1974 the value of SDR's is calculated in terms of a weighted average of the prices of 16 major currencies.)

SDR's are, however, subject to some restrictions and are thus not quite "as good as gold" or as dollars used to be in the dollar shortage years. *First*, a country is not supposed to spend more than 70 percent of the SDR's allocated to it over a certain period, in order to avoid the risk that the international acceptability of "paper gold" be endangered by excessive circulation of it. *Second*, and more important, SDR's may be exchanged only among official governmental institutions and cannot be sold to private individuals. This means that they cannot be used for intervention on the foreign exchange market to sop up excess private supply of the country's currency.

What is the use of SDR's, then? Why, they increase world reserves. Take the following example. Italy has a $100 million BOP deficit, which it wishes to finance without internal adjustment or devaluation. Before the SDR's, it could do so by borrowing the $100 million from the IMF, which would then, naturally, no longer have them available for lending to some other country in financial trouble. With SDR's, instead, the IMF, functioning as intermediary, would "transfer" $100 million worth of SDR's from the Italian to the U.S. account and get *from the United States* the dollars Italy wants. As long as the United States is willing to accept SDR's in exchange for its dollars, as it is committed to do within the system's rules, global reserves are greater than in the absence of SDR's.

Allocation of SDR's among countries is made proportional to their IMF quota, which, as noted earlier, depends on national income, foreign trade, and reserves already owned. The first allocation of $3.5 billion was made in 1970, with further allocations of similar amounts thereafter. In comparison with gold and reserve currencies, however, these were relatively small sums. In 1976, total SDR's accounted for less than 5 percent of world monetary reserves. By that year, however, the complexion of the liquidity problem had been drastically changed by the previous collapse of the Bretton Woods system.

The
Bretton
Woods
System
in
Action:
1945–71

SDR's remain of great potential significance for international finance. They may yet, depending on future negotiations, become the monetary standard of which J. M. Keynes and others have dreamed, replacing both gold and reserve currencies with an international money, the creation and allocation of which is made to depend on the needs of the world economy and not on the vagaries of gold mining or on payments deficits of individual countries. For the purpose of rescuing the Bretton Woods system, however, creation of SDR's was the classic case of too little, too late.

Why, when liquidity problems had been recognized for years, did the international community not agree much earlier to SDR's creation in sufficient amounts? One answer is that the creation and allocation of money did and does require a difficult reconciliation of conflicting interests of different nations. Thus, deficit countries view an increase in international liquidity as needed to prevent an "undeserved" devaluation and the ensuing deflationary effects (see the discussion of the absorption approach in Chapter 12). But surplus countries, which tend to believe that the imbalance is caused by the profligacy of others, are likely instead to see liquidity as allowing a deficit country to continue to "live above its means" at their expense. And, even if an increase in total reserves is internationally agreed upon in principle, there remain to be determined the magnitude and timing of the increase, as well as the question of how the new money is to be equitably allocated among the various nations.

"Before the Fall"

Beginning in the mid-1960s, the moderate deficits of the U.S. BOP increased to sizable and eventually to alarming amounts. The U.S. share of world exports declined from 22 percent in 1951 to less than 15 percent in 1971, while the West German share doubled to 12 percent and that of Japan quadrupled to 8 percent over the same period. Most indicative of the American loss of international competitiveness was the emergence in 1971 of a U.S. balance of *trade* deficit, the first such deficit in over a generation.

To attempt a full explanation of a long-term trend of this importance would take us much too far afield. Two developments may, however, be singled out as contributing to the worsening foreign payments situation. The first was *external*. As was seen in Chapter 13, the dollar was the one Bretton Woods currency that could not be devalued in terms of other currencies. The devaluation bias of the adjustment mechanism thus necessarily implied progressive overvaluation of the dollar and a loss of international competitiveness on that account. The second development was *internal* to the United States. President Johnson insisted that the United States could have *both* "guns and butter," i.e., carry out an expensive foreign war in Indochina and wide-ranging domestic social programs at the same time.

349

From
Pax
Britannica
to
Petrodollars:
International
Finance
in
the
Twentieth
Century

His consequent refusal to propose a tax increase (as urged by his economic advisers in 1966) resulted in significant inflationary pressure on the U.S. economy. While it is true that even the accelerated rate of U.S. inflation in the late 1960s was lower than the rate prevalent in most other industrial countries, only U.S. price stability had until then made up for the loss of competitiveness from the overvalued dollar.[14]

By 1971 the U.S. gold stock was at an all-time low, massive bearish speculation had caught up with the dollar itself, and the 1971 BOP was in deficit at an annual rate of over $10 billion on the basic balance definition (it was twice as large on the liquidity criterion and almost $30 billion on the official settlements definition). The momentous first step in the official breakdown of the Bretton Woods system was the American suspension of dollar convertibility into gold on August 15, 1971.

"I have directed Secretary Connally to suspend temporarily the convertibility of dollars into gold or other reserve asset, except in amounts and conditions determined to be in the interest of monetary stability and in the best interests of the United States." This was President Nixon's announcement to the nation and to the world on August 15, 1971. The previous statements urging the defense of the Bretton Woods system had become "inoperative."

The official cessation of dollar convertibility into gold meant that the value of the dollar would henceforth be determined by the intervention of other countries on the foreign exchange market, placing them in a difficult bind. A government could continue to support the exchange rate of its currency only by absorbing ever greater amounts of depreciating dollars—a losing proposition. If it did not intervene, the currency would appreciate and the country's international competitiveness would be eroded. As could be expected, most countries adopted an intermediate course; "dirty floating" became the newest entry in the international vocabulary.[15]

---

[14] The policy problem under fixed rates (see Chapter 11) was dramatically illustrated by the 1971 events. The U.S. BOP deficit coexisted with a domestic recession. The policy course chosen was expansionary fiscal and monetary policy that, while ameliorating domestic economic problems, worsened the BOP deficit through the income-reduced increase in imports and the capital outflow from the reduction in interest rates. Since the dilemma was well understood, it may be argued that the August decision to suspend dollar convertibility had really been taken many months earlier. In August, there was no choice. But it is possible that the U.S. government deliberately put itself in that position to justify in front of the world a unilateral decision that it wanted to take anyway. (See the discussion in Chapter 15 of the U.S. position on international financial issues in the early 1970s.)

[15] France, Belgium, and, later, Italy, adopted in essence a dual exchange rate system, intervening to maintain stable the exchange rate for *trade* but allowing the exchange rate applicable to capital transactions to fluctuate. The idea was to discourage speculative capital flows without compromising the stability of exchange rates important for international traders. However, there are so many connections between the capital and the trade accounts, licit and illicit, visible and hidden, that the experiment was less than a total success. (On dual exchange rates, see Chapter 13.)

Appendix: The Eurodollar Market

This topic has implications both for the stability of the monetary system and for the basic question of financial interdependence among nations. *Eurodollars are deposits, denominated in dollars, in banks located outside of the United States.* The term has become a little misleading, as foreign bank deposits denominated in currencies other than the dollar have emerged and dollar deposits have come to be held also in non-European banks. Eurodollars encompass in fact all deposits denominated in currencies other than the currency of the country where the commercial bank is located. The bulk is still denominated in dollars, however, and held in European banks.

The Eurodollar market is a highly organized, although decentralized, network of commercial banks (Eurobanks) that accept checking account and savings deposits in dollars and make loans—also in dollars—on the basis of those deposits. Eurobanks are not special institutions. They are regular commercial banks that, in addition to their domestic financial intermediation role, accept deposits and make loans denominated in a foreign currency, thereby also acting as financial intermediaries between national capital markets. (Although a U.S. bank, by definition, cannot be a Eurodollar bank, the overseas branches of American banks may be; indeed, they are an important component of the Eurodollar market.)[16]

Eurodollars first emerged in the 1950s, when the Soviet Union deposited its dollar earnings in special accounts in European banks out of concern that they might some day be frozen by the U.S. government if deposited in America. After the restoration of currency convertibility in 1958, however, the growth of Eurodollars was motivated by more orthodox economic considerations. The previous chapter explained the special role of the dollar as international transactions currency and as intervention currency used by governments to maintain their exchange rate stable. This meant large dollar balances held by private individuals to finance their foreign transactions and by countries' central banks as part of their monetary reserves.

These dollars could, of course, be deposited in American banks. However, American banks were prohibited by government regulations from paying interest on checking accounts and could not pay more than a certain interest rate on savings accounts. (This was the so-called Regulation Q, which at the time of writing appeared to be on the verge of being repealed.) It was thus more profitable to put the dollars in short-term time deposits (averaging about 3 months) in a Eurobank, get a higher rate of interest, and still have them available whenever needed. Eurodollar deposits by both private individuals and foreign central banks thus grew continually as the expansion of world trade called for greater and greater holdings of dollar balances to use as transactions and intervention

---

[16] Eurobonds have also emerged. These are bond issues denominated in a given currency and sold simultaneously in various countries by a multinational syndicate. The interest and principal are payable in the designated currency. Between $5 and $10 billion worth of Eurobonds are floated each year, with the majority denominated in dollars and the remainder in German marks and other currencies.

From
Pax
Britannica
to
Petrodollars:
International
Finance
in
the
Twentieth
Century

currency.[17] Since 1962, when foreign official accounts became exempt from Regulation Q, central banks diminished in importance as a source of original Eurodollar deposits from over two-thirds of all deposits to less than one-third by the end of the decade. Two other important sources of Eurodollars, however, emerged to assure the continuing growth of the market. The first was the expansion of multinational enterprise. The second, since 1973, was the enormous deposits made by the monetary authorities of oil-exporting countries (see Chapter 15).

New Eurodollars may be created when banks use the dollars deposited with them in the same way as any commercial bank uses deposits, i.e., when they lend them out. The main end-use borrowers of Eurodollars comprise international traders and American multinational corporations. Although there are difficulties in estimating the size of the Eurodollar market, the broad orders of magnitude are impressive, and the growth of the market has been remarkable by any criterion. Including Eurocurrencies other than the dollar (mainly German marks and Swiss francs) the size of the market was about $1 billion in 1960, $7 billion in 1963, $25 billion in 1968, $90 billion in 1972, and way over $100 billion in 1976. L. B. Yeager placed the market in perspective by noting that its size is equivalent to over one-third of the total U.S. "narrow" money supply (M_1: currency and checking accounts).[18]

Eurodollars have great significance for international finance. The market is de facto an international capital market. As the financial expression of economic interdependence, Eurodollars have favorable as well as unfavorable implications. They facilitate the financing of international trade and investment, but they also interfere with the exercise of national monetary policies, particularly in the smaller countries. To see why, consider how easily a bank can evade tight money conditions in its own country by borrowing from a Eurobank in another country and how it can frustrate the intent of domestic interest rates declines by lending out its Eurodollar deposits to foreign Eurobanks at their higher rate of interest. Indeed, the bulk of Eurocurrency is owed by the Eurobanks themselves to one another. A government's influence over the domestic money supply and the rate of interest is significantly lessened by its lack of control over this large mass of liquid funds, even a small fraction of which can suffice to offset policy induced changes in money supply. Note that this is true regardless of the international mechanism of monetary adjustment, whether based on fixed rates, on flexible rates, or somewhere in between. Recall the argument presented in Chapter 12, according to which depreciation need not have inflationary consequences if the government prevents the total money supply from increasing. The existence of the Eurodollar market all but removes any lingering doubts that depreciation does in fact exert inflationary pressure.

Aside from how one chooses to judge the desirability of the basic role of Eurodollars as a link between national capital markets, two more specific fears have been expressed concerning the functioning of the Eurodollar market.[19]

---

[17] Eurodollar deposits also provide a hedge against the risk of possible imposition of foreign exchange restrictions. If one is concerned about the possibility of foreign exchange control, depositing one's foreign currency holdings in a foreign Eurobank prevents the government from getting at them.

[18] These figures may also be put in perspective by noting that, if $1 million in tightly packed $100 bills makes a stack about 1 foot high, $100 billion in $100 bills is a stack 100 times taller than the Empire State Building.

[19] A relatively minor question is the effect of the Eurocurrency market on BOP statistics, especially, of course, those of the United States. The market has little, if any,

First, existence of the market increases the amounts available for currency speculation and makes speculation easier. *If* circumstances are such that speculation is destabilizing, the Eurodollar market harms world monetary stability. Related to this point is the second concern: The Eurodollar market is not subject to financial safety regulations of the kind that apply to domestic credit creation in most countries, as there is no international monetary organization with regulatory authority over Eurobanks lending and Eurocurrency credit creation. It is therefore conceivable, if Eurobanks do not voluntarily operate on safe enough reserve margins, that the whole credit pyramid might collapse as a result of a panic in a segment of the market, with disastrous consequences for the international economy. It does not appear, however, that this is as yet a serious concern.

Points for Review

1. What major circumstances made for the effectiveness of the international gold standard before World War I?

2. Why is the monetary system of the 1920s sometimes called the gold-exchange standard?

3. Was the British pound repegged at too high a rate in 1925?

4. When, and why, did the sterling area arise?

5. To which approximate year can European economic recovery to pre-World War II levels be dated?

6. Why was the EPU established? How did it work? Was it successful?

7. Review your understanding of the functioning of a multilateral clearing mechanism.

8. Does the evidence of the Bretton Woods years confirm the generalization of Chapter 13 that an adjustable peg system has a devaluation bias?

9. Review the various stopgap measures taken during the 1960s to relieve world liquidity shortages.

---

effect on the basic balance, since practically all Eurodollar loans and deposits are short-term and, as you know, the basic balance only includes long-term capital. Eurodollars may have an effect on the apparent size of the official settlements balance. If a foreign central bank deposits some of its dollar reserves in a Eurobank, to earn a little more interest, recorded foreign official liabilities of the United States decline and private short-term liabilities to foreigners increase, with the consequence that the official settlements balance appears more favorable than it really is. Existence of the Eurodollar market is thus an additional reason to doubt the general validity of any single definition of the balance of payments, a point discussed in Chapter 9 and its Appendix 2.

From
Pax
Britannica
to
Petrodollars:
International
Finance
in
the
Twentieth
Century

10. Review your understanding of why SDR's are a new international monetary asset and why their issuance is a net increase in world reserves.

11. What are Eurodollars? Eurobanks?

12. Where do Eurodollars mostly come from? Where do they go to?

Questions for Discussion

1. Do you see any possibility that future years will see a resumption of foreign investment of the magnitude of the 1900–13 period?

2. Why was the Tripartite Agreement successfully negotiated in 1936 when the London Economic Conference of only 3 years earlier had failed?

3. Why was it considered necessary to establish both the EPU and the OEEC?

"We should be careful to get out of an experience only the wisdom that is in it, and stop there; lest we be like the cat that sits down on a hot stove lid. She will never sit down on a hot stove lid again—and that is well; but also she will never sit down on a cold one any more."

Mark Twain, *Following the Equator*

The Political Economy of International Financial Developments in the 1970s

The
Political
Economy
of
International
Financial
Developments
in
the
1970s

What to Expect

This chapter returns explicitly to the theme first stated in the introduction and running throughout the book; namely, that the hallmark of international economics is that a sovereign national government makes policy to further its national goals. First examined are the two major international financial developments of recent years in which the political and the economic aspects are especially closely intertwined: the progressive deemphasis of gold as international money and the emergence of the Organization of Petroleum Exporting Countries (OPEC) as a major actor on the international financial scene. The third section of the chapter reviews the progress of negotiations on the international monetary system in the 1970s. The broad outlines of the negotiating position and interests of the major industrial countries are sketched first. The section then proceeds to describing the outcomes of the principal international meetings on financial issues since the 1971 suspension of dollar-gold convertibility. This final chapter concludes with a capsule assessment of the state of the international monetary system at the beginning of 1977.

The introduction to this book argued that a sovereign national government quite naturally makes policy to further its own national goals. To the extent that these differ among countries, conflicts are to be expected between the interests of the international economy as a whole and those of individual nations. The probability and the manner of resolution of those conflicts necessarily involve major political questions, not only "technical" economic issues. It is for this general reason that the discussion in the previous chapters centered on the theoretical functioning of a particular monetary mechanism first and then went on to show how in practice the mechanism functioned, or is likely to function, in a political and economic international context dominated by the interplay of different national interests.

Of the recent financial developments, two in which the economic and the political aspects are especially closely intertwined are examined here: the demise of the role of gold in international finance and the financial and political implications of the emergence of OPEC and of petroleum as a major international issue. Both of these developments had a significant effect on the progress of international financial negotiations since the collapse of the Bretton Woods system. The negotiations, however, were also influenced by basic differences in the views of the major industrial countries.

Gold: The End of a 4,000-year-old Mystique?

In December 1974 the price of gold reached a peak of $198 per ounce; some people were predicting that it would soon go up to thousands of dollars. In August 1976 the price of gold had instead fallen back to a low of only $103 per ounce. Table 15.1 shows average yearly gold prices from the Bretton Woods days to 1976.

The principal events affecting the "moneyness" of gold and its price can be listed as follows. So long as no doubts existed on the soundness of the other international money—the dollar—there was no incentive to cash in dollars for gold and consequently no upward pressure on the dollar price of gold. The official price was $35 per ounce, and that was that. But, starting in the early 1960s, as the U.S. gold reserves fell more and more relative to the amount of outstanding dollars in circulation, the "moneyness" of the dollar declined; some central banks began to cash in some of their dollars for gold. This, naturally, meant a reduction in the absolute level of U.S. gold reserves and thus a further weakening of confidence in the dollar.

The DeGaulle government in France, in particular, was interested in forcing an increase in the dollar price of gold, in pursuance of its objective of an eventual return to the gold standard and an end to the dollar's special place among the world's currencies. That position was in keeping with De Gaulle's overall goal of reasserting France's status as a major world power. A second economic aspect of that overall goal was the curbing of American direct investment in European—and especially French—manufacturing. On the diplomatic side, French assertiveness manifested itself in the expulsion of NATO headquarters from their location in Paris; on the military side, in the establishment of an independent nuclear *force de frappe*. The forced devaluation of the dollar (*in terms of gold*) and the ensuing substantive and symbolic downgrading of American international financial dominance were thus an integral part of the general design.

TABLE 15.1   Gold Prices
(Dollars per Ounce, London, Yearly Averages: 1967–76)

Year	Price	Year	Price
1967 [a]	35	1972	60
1968	40	1973	105
1969	40	1974	165
1970	38	1975	150
1971	41	1976	120

[a] $35 per ounce was, of course, the official gold price, which, in the absence of a separate private gold market, was *the* price of gold for the entire Bretton Woods period up to the 1968 establishment of the two-tier system discussed later.

Source: IMF, *International Financial Statistics*, various issues.

The
Political
Economy
of
International
Financial
Developments
in
the
1970s

The mounting U.S. BOP deficits, quite aside from any intentional attempt to weaken the dollar, were in any case sufficient for the dollar to become "bad" international money. Gresham's Law ("bad money drives out the good") asserted itself, and speculative pressure pushing up the price of gold became serious. This pressure was staved off for a while by the formation of the **Gold Pool,** a cooperative arrangement whereby Britain, the United States, and the countries of the European Economic Community (except France, of course) agreed to joint intervention in the gold market to keep the price of gold from rising. But the sums involved became unmanageably large and, in 1968, the Gold Pool was replaced by an official agreement to formally separate the private market for gold from the official market. By this **"two-tier"** arrangement, the price of gold in the private market was allowed to fluctuate in response to supply and demand, while central banks remained committed to buy and sell gold to one another at the official $35 price.

The importance of the 1968 step was great. The speculative pressure could have been dealt with (as the French wished) by an increase in the official price of gold, thus strengthening its role as international money. On the contrary, the two-tier arrangement emerging from the 1968 crisis meant the effective downgrading of gold as international monetary standard. (Dollar-gold convertibility was at the same time unofficially restricted, however.)

It is more than a little ironic that DeGaulle's efforts to shake up the gold-dollar standard in the direction of strengthening the role of gold and eliminating the dollar as international money contributed, in the final analysis, to the opposite outcome: the demonetization of gold and the establishment(at least for the time being) of a de facto dollar standard. It is also an interesting historical coincidence that the beginning of the demise of gold was followed in short order by the political downfall of DeGaulle, gold's staunchest international advocate.

The next steps in the progressive "demonetization" of gold were the first issuance in 1970 of a new international monetary asset, the SDR's (see Chapter 14), and, of course, the official end of dollar-gold convertibility in August 1971. In November 1973 the two-tier system ended, not with a return of gold to dominant official reserve status, but, on the contrary, with a further weakening of its role. Central banks were henceforth permitted to sell gold to private individuals at the current market price. As the private price had climbed in the meantime to more than double the official price (despite two dollar devaluations in 1971 and 1973, which had raised the official price to $42), this step gave governments an incentive to unload their gold at a profit on the private market, thereby by definition ceasing to regard the metal as part of their official monetary reserves.

At the urging of the United States, an international agreement to drive another nail in gold's coffin was reached at the January 1976 IMF conference in Jamaica (discussed further later in this chapter). That conference declared the formal abolition of the official gold price, to be followed by IMF sales of one-sixth of the gold in its possession (the gold tranches of countries' quotas).[1] The IMF accordingly held a first auction of 780,000 ounces of gold in June 1976, followed by two more in July and September, in a program to unload the 25 million ounces over 4 years. These sales, reinforced by the impact of large Soviet gold sales to finance import requirements, and earlier profit-taking sales by the smarter among the "gold bugs" speculators, resulted in driving down the gold price to a 5-year low of slightly over $100 per ounce.

In the meantime, the international liquidity shortage of the Bretton Woods years had all but disappeared. You should not marvel at this apparently mysterious solution of a stubborn problem, if you remember the meaning of reserves and the functioning of the flexible exchange rate adjustment mechanism. In a flexible rate system, monetary reserves are by definition unnecessary, no international money exists, and all payments and receipts are made in the national currencies of the parties concerned. While the present state of affairs in international finance hardly corresponds to the automatic workings of pure flexible rates, it nevertheless incorporates a far greater degree of exchange flexibility than the Bretton Woods system did, and "adequate" reserves can be accordingly much lower. (Lest this development be viewed as an unqualified boon, however, also recall that many of the advantages of stable exchange rates have by the same token also ceased to exist.)

It is, of course, conceivable that at some future time gold may again be enthroned as an international monetary standard. As of the beginning of 1977, however, gold was a pleasant-looking yellow metal important in electronics, jewelry, and dentistry, but with a negligible role in the making of international payments. All available indications thus pointed to the yellow metal going the way of sheep, wampum, fish hooks, and all other moneys, that in due course were superseded by better monetary assets.

Whether this outcome is considered desirable depends largely on one's views regarding the capacity of governments to carry out sensible policies and/or to cooperate with one another in the management of international financial affairs. For, dependence of the international monetary system on the vagaries of gold discoveries, on technological progress in production of gold, and on political developments in the producing countries, is not defensible unless the alternative of a deliberately created international money managed by public authorities is deemed unacceptable. As someone has put it, con-

---

[1] The profits of the IMF sales over and above the former official gold price are earmarked for a trust fund to provide financial assistance to the poorest among less developed countries. Another sixth of the IMF gold (25 million ounces) is to be returned to member countries in proportion to their quotas. It should be pointed out that the Jamaica agreement on abolishing the official gold price had not yet, at the beginning of 1977, been ratified by all member countries.

The
Political
Economy
of
International
Financial
Developments
in
the
1970s

sider the silliness of getting at great expense a yellow metal out of a deep hole in the ground, refining and fashioning it into bars at additional expense, shipping it thousands of miles under tight guard, and then . . . putting it in another expensive hole in the ground under Fort Knox.

OPEC, Petrodollars, and World Finance

Whatever chances there may have existed to reach a consensus on reform of the international monetary system following the collapse of Bretton Woods were shattered in late 1973 by the huge increase in oil prices. "Arab boycotts," "international cartels," "energy crisis," "petrodollars," all surfaced in the very first rank of international issues. Oil is of unique importance for economic activity. Since different countries depend on imported oil to varying extents, the price increases had a significant impact on the relative economic position of industrial countries and hence on their BOP and appropriate structure of exchange rates.

A quick review of the essential facts. In 1960 the Organization of Petroleum Exporting Countries (OPEC) was established to "insure the stabilization of [oil] prices" and "the unification of petroleum policies for the member countries and the determination of the best means for safeguarding [their] interests." [2] OPEC accounts for about half of the world's production of crude oil and two-thirds of proven world oil reserves (including those of Communist countries). Its influence is potentially very great. However, OPEC was relatively ineffectual throughout the 1960s. In May 1970, a new Libyan government sent shock waves throughout the oil world by ordering production cutbacks to obtain higher prices for Libyan oil. Other OPEC countries followed suit and, in the Teheran Agreement of 1971, the fundamental precedent was established that producing countries' governments would have a say in establishing "posted" petroleum prices (oil pricing had been until then the exclusive preserve of the international oil companies). [3]

[2] The members of OPEC are Algeria, Ecuador, Gabon, Indonesia, Iran, Iraq, Kuwait, Libya, Nigeria, Qatar, Saudi Arabia, the United Arab Emirates, and Venezuela. The group of Arab countries, known as OPEAC, is most influential within OPEC not only because it accounts for the bulk of OPEC production, but also because those countries have a common culture and share some foreign policy interests.

[3] The posted price is the official price of oil used as the basis of computation of taxes and royalties to be paid by the oil companies. There is a general relationship between posted prices and actual prices, analogous to the relationship between the prime interest rate and other rates, in the sense that the posted level provides a general benchmark for the entire structure of oil prices. Actual prices depend, however, on a host of specific considerations, often incorporated in bilateral agreements between oil-producing and oil-importing countries. Needless to say, political considerations weigh heavily in the formulation of such agreements, as they do in the general setting of posted prices.

After the Yom Kippur War broke out in the Middle East in October 1973, the Teheran precedent served for an initial increase in the posted price of a barrel of crude oil from $1.20 to $2.00. This was only the beginning. Three months later, OPEC increased posted prices by 500 percent to $10.00 a barrel. A further increase was made in September 1975 to $11.50 a barrel. Thus, in less than 2 years oil prices had jumped tenfold.[4] The effects were felt everywhere, from the Pakistani farmer whose harvest slumped below subsistence levels owing to scarcity of petroleum-based fertilizer, to the Chicago tenant whose rent increased because of higher heating fuel costs, to the Italian car driver whose gasoline cost him $3 a gallon in 1976, and so forth throughout the entire world.[5]

A very important development occurred at the OPEC meeting of December 1976 in Qatar. At Saudi Arabia's insistence, no agreement was reached on a common OPEC price. Instead, Saudi oil (as well as that of the United Arab Emirates) would increase by only 5 percent, while the other 11 countries decided to increase their price by 15 percent. In addition, Saudi Arabia announced that it would remove its production ceiling, thus making it very difficult for the other OPEC members to implement their price increase in the face of the leading oil producer's intention to increase its supply. It would be very foolish to predict the imminent breakup of the oil cartel and the price rift will in all probability be patched up. Nevertheless, the Qatar events did not augur well for the cohesion of OPEC. The considerable tensions generated at that meeting were real.

These events have implications for virtually every facet of international economic *and* political relations. In a general political sense, OPEC (and, more specifically, the Arab countries within it) has come to constitute a new center of power in the world. This has meant some redistribution of world power and influence away from the established "poles" of East and West.[6]

---

[4] In his book *The Control of Oil* (New York: Pantheon Books, 1977), John M. Blair argued convincingly that the bilateral oligopoly characteristic of the international oil industry has engendered a commonality of interests between the OPEC countries and the major international oil corporations. Thus, the OPEC price increases were not only not resisted, but actually abetted by the oil companies themselves, which increased their own prices to an even greater extent through their vertical control of the refineries, tankers, and distribution facilities. Indeed, the OPEC price hikes were an opportunity for even greater profits for the companies. And, in fact, oil companies' profits did experience a remarkable increase in precisely the worst of the "oil shortage" days.

[5] The price increases were made possible, among other things, by the reduction in world oil supplies ensuing from the Arab countries' boycott of the United States and other industrial nations.

[6] A word of caution is in order here. The success of OPEC has lead many to assume that the same jackpot is there for the taking by countries producing other raw materials. While there are possibilities for the formation of other primary producer organizations, the extraordinary success of the oil cartel is due, quite simply, to the extraordinary importance of oil, and it cannot be duplicated. In economic terms, the capacity of a cartel to reap monopoly profits requires an inelastic demand for their product so that an increase in price does not self-defeatingly cause a significant decline

The
Political
Economy
of
International
Financial
Developments
in
the
1970s

Much too much has been made of this in the popular writings. Nevertheless, events since the 1971 Teheran meetings have shaken further the already tottering paradigm of a bipolar world. The OPEC members at first used their newfound influence only to maximize export earnings and push their more direct foreign policy interests, particularly in the Middle East. More recently, they have also attempted to stake a claim to leadership of, and spokesmanship for, the 3 billion people living in poverty in the less developed nations.

Less generally, the oil price increases have implications for the terms of trade and for the external financial position of countries. Oil prices have increased much faster than prices of manufactured goods, which the OPEC countries import. The terms of trade have unequivocally turned in favor of the oil exporters as a group. A large transfer of real income, therefore, has been and is taking place in favor of OPEC. The financial implications of this transfer vary according to the assumptions made. Some rather dramatic forecasts were fashionable in 1974: The Western world would be strangulated; petrodollars would wreck world finance; the sheiks would take up residence in Buckingham Palace and the White House. These apocalyptic predictions, like those in the "how-to-profit-from-monetary-crises-by-burying-gold-in-your-nuclear-shelter" books, have not materialized.[7]

The actual financial implications are striking enough. The increase in prices, combined with higher rates of taxes and royalties, yielded spectacular oil earnings for OPEC countries. For 1975, these were estimated at about $100 billion, an amount greater than the national product of any but the largest among industrial countries. In 1976, Saudi Arabia alone, the leading producer, received about $30 billion in earnings from oil exports. The OPEC

---

in purchases. In turn, this requires that the overall demand for the product be inelastic *and* that the cartel account for a large proportion of world supplies. OPEC, accounting for over half of world production of oil, an essential commodity with few substitutes, enjoys these advantages. Other international cartels would not, or at least certainly not to the same degree.

[7] As the writer who goes under the pseudonym of "Adam Smith" puts it: "Predict future events: that's easy, the hard part is making the event match the prediction." ("Adam Smith," *Powers of Mind*, New York: Ballantine Books, 1975, p. 356). Quoted on the same page is a passage from Shakespeare's *Henry IV:*

> GLENDOWER: I can call spirits from the vastly deep.
> HOTSPUR: Why, so can I, or so can any man;
> But will they come when you do call for them?

The apocalyptic predictions have come, however, close to economic reality for many less developed countries. The financial difficulties suffered by industrial countries from high oil prices pale into insignificance in comparison with the tragic consequences for the poorer among the less developed nations. For the 1 billion people involved, already living at a bare subsistence level, the scenario of mass starvation has been made all too real by the growing cost of imports of oil and of petroleum products. Some international efforts have been made to alleviate their plight, but so far these have not even come close to matching the seriousness of the problem.

countries had in 1976 over $50 billion in combined reserves. If these stupendous sums were thrown irresponsibly about the world capital markets, extremely serious financial instability would result. Instead, it appears that the oil recipients have so far been placing their money rather carefully and have by and large eschewed disruptive actions.

Where has all the money gone? Table 15.2 shows the estimated allocation for 1975.

Compared to 1974, principal developments included a decline in the OPEC countries' investable surplus, due primarily to a large rise in imports, only some of which reflected increased import prices; a deemphasis of investments in the Eurocurrency market (see the Appendix to Chapter 14) to less than one-third of total surplus, down from the 40 percent of 1974; and some increase in financial assistance to other countries. In addition, portfolio purchases of shares of foreign corporations have been on the rise. The most recent at the time of writing was the November 1976 purchase by Libya of 10 percent of the shares of FIAT—the Italian automobile company—for a reported bargain basement price of $415 million.

For the future, it is improbable that the oil countries will continue to practically double the value of their imports every year, as was the case from 1973 to 1974 and from 1974 to 1975. Therefore, although future oil price increases will not be in the same league with those of 1973–74, chances are that the investable surplus of the OPEC countries will be greater than the $32 billion of 1975. One may well expect further increases both in OPEC equity investments in industrial countries and in their financial assistance to the less developed world, particularly to the poorer countries hardest hit by oil shortages. The recycling of petrodollars will thus continue to be a crucial

TABLE 15.2   Allocation of OPEC Countries' Earnings: 1975

Item	Billions of Dollars	Percentage
Imports	60	—
Investable surplus	32	100
1. Eurocurrency placements	10	31
2. Investments in the United States	6	19
3. Investments in other countries	3	9
4. Financial assistance to other countries [a]	9	28
5. Deposits in international institutions [b]	4	13

[a] Primarily grants and soft loans to less developed countries. Includes $2.6 billion contribution to the IMF "oil facility."
[b] Excluding contributions to the IMF oil facility.

Source: Adapted from data in R. E. Debs, "Petrodollars, LDC's, and International Banks," *Monthly Review of the Federal Reserve Bank of New York*, January 1976.

The
Political
Economy
of
International
Financial
Developments
in
the
1970s

financial question. But it appears that it can take place in a reasonably orderly manner.

International Financial Negotiations in the 1970s

The General Economic and Political Setting

Recall the "two-out-of-three" principle explained at the end of Chapter 11: Of the three objectives of (1) BOP equilibrium, (2) fixed exchange rates, and (3) national economic policy autonomy, you can have only two. It is legitimate to advocate one particular type of international monetary system on the argument that the objective it sacrifices is less important than the remaining two it achieves. It is, however, not possible to accept the claim of economic ideologues of any stripe that *their* preferred international financial arrangement is costless.

With fixed exchange rates and total national policy autonomy, the BOP can be kept in "equilibrium" only by measures interfering with the flow of foreign trade and investment. Chapters 2 and 5 have demonstrated at length the costs of restricting international transactions.

BOP equilibrium and economic policy autonomy are compatible, at least in principle, provided that fixed exchange rates are abandoned. The concluding section of Chapter 12 discussed some of the likely costs of doing so: discouragement of foreign trade owing to exchange rate uncertainty, possible losses from unnecessary reallocation of resources back and forth, the hampering of world economic integration.

Finally, there is in principle the option of conserving both fixed exchange rates and BOP equilibrium, provided that economic policy is internationalized. Attractive as this may be as a long-run goal for internationally minded individuals, it is abundantly clear that at the present time countries have not the least intention of giving up their national economic sovereignty altogether.

Let's set out the two extreme cases. If there were *no* overlap at all between the national and the international interest (or if none were perceived—see the discussion of mercantilism in Chapter 2), the fact of national sovereignty would guarantee that no international agreement could ever be reached. If, at the other extreme, the interests of all countries coincided (or were thought to coincide) completely with one another, and hence with those of the international economy as a whole, the issue of negotiating international agreements would become moot. Reality, of course, is somewhere in between. Economic interdependence does exist, and it operates as a crucial restraint to the isolated exercise of national actions. But it is far from complete; the interests of countries differ in any number of fundamental respects.

This divergence of interests can, in turn, be attributed to two sets of factors. The first encompasses a country's specific economic circumstances; the second relates to its political aims and ideological preferences. In the evaluation of both the gold standard and the flexible rate system it was seen that the economic and political costs of the system depend to a great extent on the country's economic circumstances. Thus, for example, it is not coincidental that attachment to fixed exchange rates is generally strongest in small, open economies and weakest in the very large industrial countries whose dependence on foreign trade is relatively slight. For in the latter countries, such as the United States, fixed rates in the presence of institutional rigidities imply that it may take an intolerable increase in unemployment to eliminate a BOP deficit (without additional restrictions on imports or capital outflow). Conversely, the uncertainties of floating exchange rates are much more damaging in small countries with a relatively large foreign sector.

But different economic circumstances are not the entire story here (if they ever are). As Michael J. Brenner has pointed out in a very interesting recent study,[8] a country's foreign policy goals, its ideological preferences, and its historical past also contribute to the formation of its views on international financial issues. The negotiating posture of major industrial countries will be looked at in the next section. It should be quite clear at this point, however, that there are any number of solid reasons to expect countries to differ on issues of international finance, just as they are naturally expected to differ on issues of foreign policy and on the management of domestic affairs.

It follows that the search for international financial agreement, while inspired by the properties of the "pure" monetary systems, must be confined to arrangements that allow for the exercise of a measure of discretionary authority by the participating countries. The world does not allow financial purity any more than it encompasses perfection. Real national interests and preferences are at stake, and discretion *will* be exercised whenever governments deem it convenient from their national viewpoint. It is therefore far better that national discretionary authority be exercised within internationally agreed rules of financial behavior than it is to assume away the existence of differences in national interests, with unpredictable and almost inevitably unwanted consequences. Indeed, as will be seen in the concluding section, it was only when the two main opponents in the Western financial arena—France and the United States—came down in 1975 from doctrinaire advocacy of, respectively, fixed and completely flexible rates, that the door was open to eventual agreement on international monetary reform.

[8] M. J. Brenner, *The Politics of International Monetary Reform—The Exchange Crisis* (Cambridge, Mass.: Ballinger, 1976).

The
Political
Economy
of
International
Financial
Developments
in
the
1970s

The Negotiating Position of the Major Industrial Countries

The following is of necessity only a very general summary. It draws heavily from the study by Michael J. Brenner mentioned earlier, to which the interested reader is referred for a thorough understanding of the issues involved.

Probably the outstanding background characteristic of the 1970s transition was the lessening of American financial dominance, combined, however, with ample remaining power to give the United States a veto on any proposal of which it disapproved. The decrease in U.S. financial dominance of the West meant, almost by definition, greater autonomy of the other Western developed countries and hence an increased reluctance on their part to agree to new international rules that would inevitably lessen that newfound autonomy.

The United States At the root of the American position on monetary issues was the conflict between domestic economic goals and the international role of the dollar. The 1960s had seen attempts at resolving this conflict by restrictions on the outflow of American capital. The failure of that approach (aside from the real economic costs involved) had become apparent as BOP deficits increased more and more. In the American view, the blame was to be laid at the door of countries with a BOP surplus and was attributed to their unreasonable resistance to revaluation. There was implicit in that view a temptation to *force* the other countries to deal with the international financial imbalance. If the dollar was so important to the Western world as transaction and intervention currency, let the other countries shoulder the costs of maintaining its value, *or,* if they choose, let them accept a floating—and depreciating—dollar and the ensuing relative appreciation of their own currencies.

The temptation implicit in the policies of the 1960s surfaced in the Nixon administration's attitude of "benign neglect" on international monetary issues (not unlike the policy of the same name advocated by the Moynihan memorandum with respect to internal race relations). That is: Do nothing to stem speculation against the dollar or to cut down on the amount of outstanding dollars in circulation (the "dollar overhang"); let the other countries worry about it, unless and until they become willing to cooperate actively in removing their commercial barriers to U.S. exports (especially nontariff barriers), and in revaluing their own currencies.

As was noted earlier (Chapter 14, footnote 14), this was one of the effects of the 1971 suspension of dollar-gold convertibility. It would seem, after the fact, that the policy had the intended effect, with the eventual substantive revaluations and appreciations of surplus countries' currencies (see the last section of this chapter). What might have been the outcome, without the commendable restraint shown by most countries in 1973–75, will fortunately never be known. There was certainly more than a trace of brinkmanship in the "let's take care of Number One" attitude on the part of the foremost financial power in the developed Western world.[9]

West Germany   The national trauma conditioning much of the German views on economic issues, including those of international finance, was the Weimar inflation of the 1920s (see Chapter 14), which, most observers believe, was a major contributing factor to the eventual rise of the Nazis to power. Postwar German economic policies have tended, therefore, to place a high premium on price stability. If these policies result in large trade surpluses in relation to less "disciplined" countries, why should Germans be required to bear the costs of the adjustment? In their view, the main culprit for international monetary instability was the United States and its 1960s policies of monetary expansion without corresponding fiscal retrenchment. Also to blame was the Bretton Woods network of cooperative international financial arrangements, which went much too quickly to the rescue of "undisciplined" countries.

In addition, owing to the low inflation rate and the high trade surplus, the German mark was an excellent haven for the bullish side of speculation against the lira, the pound, the dollar, or whatever. The resulting inflow of funds (averaging $200 million *per day* in January–March 1973) created serious inflationary pressures—just what German economic policies had been designed to avoid in the first place. The West German attitude was thus not unlike that of the neat homeowner who has to put up with vermin from next door because of his neighbors' unsanitary habits. More specifically, the West German government was led to conclude that, in view of the enormous mass of speculative funds, exchange rate intervention was useless. Instead, the economy could be best insulated against imported inflation by a floating mark, which would also obviate the need for controls on capital flows.

France   As we noted earlier in this chapter, France had been most critical of the special role of the dollar and had been trying since the early 1960s to reduce it. As the French saw it, the international use of the dollar as reserve currency allowed the United States to finance "imperial" pursuits of which

[9] Brinkmanship was evident at least in the attitude shown by Treasury Secretary John Connally during the secret discussions at Camp David preceding the August 15 announcement. William Safire (*Before the Fall: An Inside View of the Pre-Watergate White House* [New York: Belmont Tower Books, 1975], p. 514) reports the following exchange between Connally, Treasury Undersecretary Paul Volcker, and Federal Reserve Chairman Arthur F. Burns, on the suspension of dollar-gold convertibility:

CONNALLY:"So the other countries don't like it. So what?"

VOLCKER: "But don't let's close the [gold] window and sit—let's get other governments to negotiate new rates."

CONNALLY: "Why do we have to be reasonable? Canada wasn't."

BURNS: "They can retaliate."

CONNALLY: "Let 'em. What can they do?"

367

The
Political
Economy
of
International
Financial
Developments
in
the
1970s

they disapproved, both economically (investments in European industries) and politically (the Vietnam war). On the other hand, the French (traditionally as worried about unemployment as the Germans are about inflation) were also concerned about the adverse effects of dollar devaluation or depreciation (*in terms of the French franc*) on their trade balance and hence on domestic employment. The twin goals of reducing American financial dominance while maintaining French competitiveness in foreign trade led France to advocacy of a dual exchange rate system: essentially fixed exchange rates for trade transactions and, for capital transactions, either floating rates or the imposition of controls combined with international action to reduce speculative activity.

Britain Britain had been suffering through the late 1950s and the 1960s from an almost textbook case of the policy conflict under fixed exchange rates (see the last section of Chapter 11). Economic contractionary policies ("stop") would improve the BOP at the expense of domestic employment. The subsequent expansion ("go") would bring back the external deficit. The "stop-go" cycle could be, in principle, stopped by devaluing the pound. Devaluation would, however, have an adverse effect on the remnants of Britain's imperial responsibilities.

In a sense, therefore, the 1967 devaluation of the pound can be seen as the financial expression of the official end of the British empire, paralleling the continuing liquidation of the remaining colonial political links. Having swallowed that pill, it was only a matter of time before British official attitudes swung to supporting flexible exchange rates. The intellectual changeover can probably be dated to 1969, when the influential *Economist* headlined "It's Better To Float." This became translated into policy in June 1972, when the pound was allowed to find its own value in the foreign exchange market. By and large, their favorable experience with the Equalization Account of the 1930s (see Chapter 14, footnote 6) led the British to favor some form of managed floating in accordance with agreed international rules, while their "ideological" preference led them to oppose controls on capital flows.

Japan Japan, Brenner argues, maintained a fairly passive attitude throughout this period. This nonassertive low profile was consistent with the "dirty floating" practices the Japanese monetary authorities adopted almost immediately after the August 1971 statement and have continued as this was being written.

It is not surprising, therefore, that to the extent that Japan has had a firm position on reform of the international monetary system, it has also been generally favorable to managed floating. Unlike Britain, however, Japan has advocated coupling managed flexibility with controls on capital flows, in keeping with the wide acceptance of governmental controls of various sorts within the Japanese economy itself.

Major International Negotiating Developments: 1971–76

The 1971 suspension of dollar-gold convertibility was intended to be, at least in principle, temporary. The step was accompanied by the imposition of a 10 percent import surcharge (mentioned in Chapter 6 as an example of a bargaining tariff). The understanding was that the surcharge would be removed (and it was) following satisfactory settlement of the monetary question and some progress on the liberalization of foreign nontariff barriers to U.S. exports.

The unilateral nature of the American action of August 15, 1971, generated considerable resentment in both Europe and Japan (which had just been stunned only one month before by the U.S. opening to China with no consultation or even prior notification). Aggravated by the negotiating heavy-handedness of Secretary Connally, this resentment might well have been vented in economic reprisals against U.S. exports and capital, with the possibility of setting off a retaliatory spiral of the kind that had all but destroyed world trade 40 years earlier. Luckily, instead, the lesson of the 1930s had not been forgotten, and a comprehensive international agreement was reached on December 18, after meetings at Washington's Smithsonian Institution.

The Smithsonian Agreement was more significant for the *fact* of agreement than for the contents of it, which were to last only about a year. The agreement, in addition to removing the U.S. import surcharge, established a new relationship among major currencies and modified the adjustment mechanism itself. On the subject of exchange rate realignment, the dispute had centered on whether the crisis was to be resolved by devaluation of the dollar or by revaluation of surplus countries' currencies. This was not a purely semantic quarrel (of the type of the "shape-of-the-table" argument at the 1968 Paris negotiations on Vietnam).

There was also an economically substantive issue at stake. Dollar devaluation would be tantamount to revaluation of all foreign currencies, even those of countries in shaky financial circumstances. Revaluation could instead apply selectively to "chronic" surplus countries, particularly Japan and West Germany. The dispute did, however, carry important political symbolism. From the viewpoint of the surplus countries, dollar devaluation would be public acknowledgment that U.S. policies were responsible for the monetary crisis. From the American viewpoint, revaluation of some foreign currencies would indicate that the U.S. BOP deficit had been caused by the surplus countries' resistance to carrying *their* fair share of the adjustment burden.

As in most issues of political importance, the agreement involved a compromise between the two opposing positions. The Smithsonian Agreement

The
Political
Economy
of
International
Financial
Developments
in
the
1970s

called both for devaluation of the dollar and for revaluation of the yen and mark in terms of gold. The dollar was devalued by 8.5 percent, to $38 per ounce of gold. The mark price of gold was lowered by 5 percent and that of the yen by 8.5 percent; in relation to the dollar, therefore, the mark was revalued by 13.5 percent and the yen by 17 percent. The value of the other major currencies remained constant in terms of gold, implying, of course, their 8.5 percent revaluation in terms of the dollar.[10] Dollar convertibility into gold, however, was not restored. Officially, it was intended to be restored after the U.S. BOP showed a substantial improvement. But by the time the improvement had taken place, 2 years later, the collapse of the Bretton Woods system had made dollar-gold convertibility virtually moot.

Another important component of the Smithsonian package was the agreement to modify the adjustment mechanism itself by widening the band of permissible fluctuations of a currency's price from the Bretton Woods 2 percent relative to the dollar to 4.5 percent, which, as explained in Chapter 13, meant a 9 percent maximum fluctuation between currencies other than the dollar. As was discussed in Chapter 13, a wider band lessened the certainty of exchange rates in order to weaken bearish speculation and hence the devaluation bias of the adjustable peg. Three months later, however, the countries of the European Economic Community decided, from concern with their economic integration, to allow a narrower 4.5 percent maximum fluctuation of their currencies in relation to one another, and hence only 2.25 percent relative to the dollar, just about the same as the old Bretton Woods band. This smaller European band moved as a unit within the wider Smithsonian band. From the looks of the exchange rate graph, it came to be called the European "snake" in the Smithsonian "tunnel."

The Smithsonian Agreement would not last very long. First, in 1972, bearish speculation against the pound led to a British decision to let the pound float, while the bullish side of that speculative coin led the Japanese to establish controls on the resulting capital inflows, rather than allowing the yen to appreciate. Then, in early 1973, massive sales of dollars in exchange for Swiss francs resulted, after further international consultations, in a second devaluation of the dollar, to $42 per ounce of gold. As we have seen, all attempts at reviving the Bretton Woods corpse were abandoned in March 1973 when the European currencies were allowed to float jointly against the dollar.

Since that time, international financial practices have included free floats, lightly managed and heavily managed floats, dirty floats, European

---

[10] Other parity changes in terms of gold included very small devaluations of the Italian and Swedish currencies, small revaluations of the Belgian and Dutch currencies, and sizable revaluations of the Austrian schilling and the Swiss franc. The average devaluation of the dollar in relation to all foreign currencies was in the neighborhood of 10 percent.

"snakes," and even remnants of Bretton Woods in the form of the pegging of the currencies of many smaller countries to the dollar or to the currency of a large trade partner. This mixture, running the gamut from nonintervention to rigid maintenance of exchange rate parity, was officially in violation of the IMF rules, which formally remained as originally written and modified by the Smithsonian Agreement of 1971. No general agreement on guidelines for governments' international monetary behavior was to replace the adjustable peg rules until the Jamaica Conference of January 1976.

Throughout this confusing and highly dangerous period systematic intergovernmental contacts were preserved, largely by the consultative mechanism provided by the IMF. Lines of communication were kept open, and governments by and large refrained from disruptive isolated actions of the 1930s type. Still, virtually no progress on monetary reform was made until the fall of 1975.[11] This was in large measure because the dust from the oil price increases of 1973–74 had not yet begun to settle. Another factor contributing to the negotiating standstill was the lack of American leadership, stemming from the "benign neglect" posture discussed earlier as well as the all-consuming preoccupation of the Nixon administration with the Watergate scandal.[12]

The contemporary analogue of the abortive 1933 World Economic Conference in London (see Chapter 14) was the November 1975 summit meeting of industrial countries' heads of state at the castle of Rambouillet near Paris. The Rambouillet meetings produced no concrete agreement (nor were they meant to), but they established an indispensable spirit of cooperation for the solutions of common problems and set the stage for real progress to follow. First, the United States and France, after negotiations conducted in complete secrecy, agreed to support monetary reform based on some sort of managed floating. (As we have seen, managed floating was already favored by the British, the Japanese, and—to some extent the West Germans.) The American side came down from its strong advocacy of freely flexible exchange rates and agreed to some stabilizing intervention. The French in return moderated their stand in favor of a speedy return to fixed rates and agreed in principle to exchange flexibility for the indefinite future.

The Franco-American agreement was the skeleton on which the cooperative "spirit of Rambouillet" was fleshed out 2 months later at the January 1976 meeting of the IMF in Jamaica. The resolve not to allow a repetition of the 1930s was strengthened at a second summit meeting in Puerto Rico in the summer of 1976. At the time of writing, the latest confer-

[11] The British magazine *Economist* aptly headlined its September 28, 1974, preview of the forthcoming IMF annual meeting: "A Centipede is not a Speedy Beast."

[12] "I don't give a [expletive deleted] about the lira!" was one of the more profound statements of Richard Nixon's on the international financial situation (as recorded in the White House tapes).

The
Political
Economy
of
International
Financial
Developments
in
the
1970s

ence had been the May 1977 summit in London. That meeting produced no unpleasant surprises inconsistent with the earlier monetary agreements. The atmosphere was one of guarded confidence, stemming in part from the favorable developments regarding the economic recovery of industrial countries from the 1975–76 recession and the slowing down of their rate of inflation from the two-digit levels recorded in 1975.

The International Monetary System of the Beginning of 1977

Events following the Smithsonian Agreement of 1971, and particularly the differential impact of the oil price increases on the various countries, caused significant changes in the value of the world's currencies. As of the fall of 1976, among the major currencies the greatest appreciation against the dollar since 1971 had been shown by the Swiss franc, and the steepest depreciation by the British pound and the Italian lira, while the dollar depreciated only slightly from its Smithsonian average value in terms of other currencies.

Most exchange rates fluctuated considerably on the way to their 1976 levels. For example, the relatively small depreciation of the dollar was the combined result of sharp downturns in 1973 and 1974 followed by a strengthening of the dollar later on (partly owing to the lesser dependence of the United States on imported oil). Figure 15.1 shows the changes in the exchange rates of selected major currencies, from their Smithsonian parities in terms of the dollar to their market prices in the fall of 1976.

The IMF Conference of January 1976 in Jamaica produced agreement on the outline of a new international monetary system, although a very general one and subject to later ratification by IMF member countries. The three main points of the agreement are as follows: *First*, on the issue of the international monetary standard, the official gold price was abolished and the IMF was authorized to return one-sixth of its gold to member countries and sell another sixth on the private market (as discussed earlier in this chapter). *Second*, the IMF was given an aid function through the agreement to establish a gold trust fund to provide financial assistance to poor countries. *Third*, and most importantly, it was agreed that "optional managed floating" would henceforth be the official mechanism of international monetary adjustment. That is, countries would legally be allowed to let their currencies float, *if they chose to*, but would *also* be committed to stabilizing intervention on the foreign exchange market to prevent erratic or purely speculative movements in their exchange rate. The international economy again rests on agreed monetary guidelines, albeit far less prescriptive and detailed than the Bretton Woods arrangements.

Will the agreement stick and the system last? Like the writing of fugues,

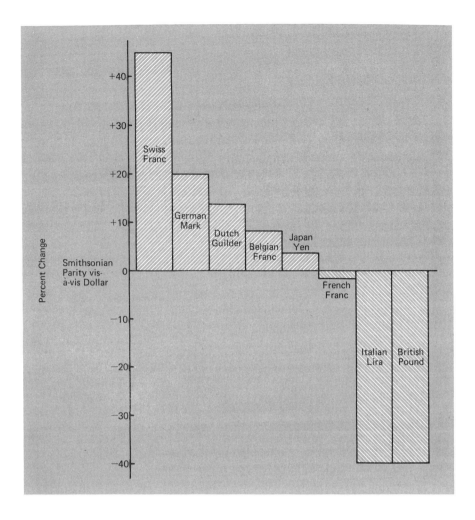

FIGURE 15.1 Approximate Percentage Changes in Major Currencies'
Exchange Rates: 1972–76

H. L. Mencken said, the prophesying business is fatal to all save the person
of absolute genius. It is true that, unlike the Bretton Woods system, optional
managed floating has emerged from actual monetary practices and not as an
a priori scheme (no matter how well thought-out), and thus it appears to
have an excellent chance of surviving in the foreseeable future. Still, in view
of the many sources of potential instability, from oil to the rising debt of
less developed countries, the most appropriate note on which to close this
chapter (and this book) is the following line from Mark Twain's *Life on
the Mississippi:* "I was gratified to be able to answer promptly, and I did.
I said I didn't know."

The
Political
Economy
of
International
Financial
Developments
in
the
1970s

Points for Review

1. Review the main steps leading to the deemphasis of the role of gold in the international monetary system.

2. Review the essential facts concerning the formation of the OPEC cartel and the increases in oil prices since the fall of 1973 (including the argument presented in footnote 4).

3. What was the position of the French government in the 1960s regarding the international role of gold as compared to that of the dollar? Was that position vindicated by the later events?

4. Review the international allocation of OPEC countries' earnings. Why does the text say that the "recycling" of petrodollars has been so far relatively orderly?

5. Are different economic circumstances the only source of differences of views among countries on international monetary issues?

6. Review the positions of the United States, West Germany, France, Britain, and Japan on reform of the international monetary system in the 1970s.

7. List the main ingredients of the Smithsonian package of December 1971.

8. List the main components of the Jamaica Conference agreement of January 1976.

Questions for Discussion

1. International inadequacy of a particular monetary asset can be remedied either by increasing the availability of it or by agreeing to get rid of that form of money altogether. Is this statement correct? Discuss it in light of the progressive demonetization of gold since 1968.

2. Do you see any similarity between the sterling area of the interwar period and the 1970s European "snake" arrangement on exchange rates?

3. Do you see any parallels between the French-American controversies on monetary issues in the 1930s and their contemporary positions until the Rambouillet summit of 1975?

4. There is, broadly speaking, a crucial difference between the Tripartite Agreement of 1936 (marking the beginning of the end of commercial and financial disorder) and the Jamaica accords of 1976: the Jamaica negotiations succeeded *before* the real damage could take place. To what would you attribute this fortunate difference, aside from the politicians' good memory?

5. There are several possible parallels between the international negotiating stage of the 1930s and that of the 1970s. Can you think of some?

6. Do you see a theme in contemporary international relations resembling the Kindleberger thesis that the underlying cause of international collapse in the 1930s was the American unwillingness to assume responsibilities consonant with the U.S. weight?

7. The positions of the major industrial countries, as summarized from the Brenner study, all appear to be justified and reasonable. Which sounds more convincing to you? Which country was "right"? Does it matter at all?

8. The Nixon administration exhibited a similar attitude toward both race relations in America and the international financial system. Do you agree? To what an extent could the "neglect" reasonably be called "benign"?

9. The Smithsonian Agreement of December 1971 was announced by President Nixon as "the greatest monetary agreement in the history of the world." Do you concur? Why is it argued in the text that the *fact* of agreement was more important than the contents of it? (Hint: Go back to your discussion of question 4.)

10. Why was the European "snake" arrangement considered important for European economic integration purposes? (Hint: Go back to the evaluation of flexible exchange rates at the end of Chapter 12.)

11. The text does not take a firm position on the staying power of optional managed floating, the international monetary reform agreed to at the Jamaica conference of 1976. What is your own assessment of the prospects for the international monetary system in the foreseeable future?

Bibliography

General References

Among textbooks, the following more advanced and comprehensive treatments may be mentioned:

CAVES, R. E. and R. W. JONES. *World Trade and Payments*, 2nd ed. Boston: Little, Brown, 1977. (Somewhat more difficult than this book.)

KINDLEBERGER, C. P. *International Economics*, 5th ed. Homewood, Ill.: Irwin, 1973. (Also somewhat more advanced than this book.)

TAKAYAMA, A. *International Trade.* New York: Holt, Rinehart and Winston, 1972. (Advanced, heavily mathematical treatment of international trade theory.)

YEAGER, L. B. *International Monetary Relations: Theory, History and Policy.* New York: Harper & Row, 1976. (Thorough treatise on international finance.)

Of textbooks more elementary than the present one, the following may profitably be used for reviewing some of the essential points:

KENEN, P. B. and R. LUBITZ. *International Economics*, 3rd ed. Englewood Cliffs, N.J.: Prentice-Hall, 1971.

Most other textbooks in international economics are at about the same level of difficulty as this book. They are, however, longer. As stated in the preface, this book is explicitly designed as a one-semester text. As such, it barely touches on some important issues that lie beyond the essentials of an introduction to theory and policy. Some leads are given in the last section of this bibliography. Students' first means of exposure to those issues, and of expanding their understanding of the material included in this book, should be perusal of a collection of readings in international economics. Of the several currently in circulation, BALDWIN, R. E. and J. D. RICHARDSON, eds. *International Trade and Finance* (Boston: Little, Brown, 1974) may be cited as a comprehensive collection of reasonably accessible material. A much more difficult set of articles is reprinted in a 1968 collection sponsored by the American Economic Association: CAVES, R. and H. JOHNSON, eds. *Readings in International Economics*, Homewood, Ill.: Irwin, 1968.

For students interested in researching novel topics, a look at BERGSTEN, C. F., ed., *The Future of the International Economic Order: An Agenda for Research* (Lexington, Mass.: Lexington Books, 1973), and KENEN, P. B., ed., *International Trade and Finance: Frontiers for Research* (Cambridge: Cambridge University Press, 1975), is advisable. Although new contributions to the field appear in most of the reputable economics journals, the *Journal of International Economics* and the *International Economics Review* are two among the specialized publications in this field. Finally, the well-prepared

377

students interested in advanced applied research would do well to consult H. GLEISER, ed., *Quantitative Studies of International Economic Relations* (Amsterdam: North-Holland, 1976).

This book is explicitly intended to present "mainstream" theory. For those interested in a radical perspective on international economic problems, a good general start is H. MAGDOFF, *The Age of Imperialism* (New York: Monthly Review Press, 1969), and ROSEN, S. J. and J. R. KURTH, *Testing Theories of Economic Imperialism* (Lexington, Mass.: Lexington Books, 1974). Also consult: Union for Radical Political Economics (URPE), *Radical Perspectives on the Economic Crisis of Monopoly Capitalism*, New York, 1969. For current articles from a radical perspective, see *Monthly Review* and the *URPE Review*.

Data Sources

There is a flood of data on international trade and finance. (In fact, data availability in this field has historically tended to be better than in other areas of economics.) The following should be sufficient for most undergraduate research projects. On international trade: United Nations, *Yearbook of International Trade Statistics* (expect a 2-year lag), and for current data the U.N. *Monthly Bulletin of Statistics*. On international finance: International Monetary Fund, *International Financial Statistics*. On U.S. developments, the single best source is the Commerce Department's *Survey of Current Business*. More detailed data on international economic relations among developed countries can be found in publications of the Organization for Economic Cooperation and Development (OECD). On statistical aggregates for industrial countries from 1950 to 1974 consult the OECD publication *National Accounts of OECD Countries* (Paris, April 1976). Trade of less developed countries is the special concern of the U.N. Conference on Trade and Development (UNCTAD). Naturally, for any research project that involves a particular country, national governments' publications should be consulted.

Selected Readings (In addition to references mentioned in the text)

On Interdependence and Political Aspects of International Economics (Chapter 1)

In the burgeoning literature on economic interdependence and on the relationships between international economics and foreign policy, the following are stimulating works:

BOYER DE LA GIRODAY, F. "Myths and Reality in the Development of International Affairs." *Essays in International Finance.* No. 105, Princeton University Press, 1974.

COOPER, R. N. *Economic Interdependence: Economic Policy in the Atlantic Community.* New York: McGraw-Hill, 1968.

HOFFMAN, S. *Gulliver's Troubles, Or, The Setting of American Foreign Policy.* New York: McGraw-Hill, 1968.

KENEN, P. B. *Giant Among Nations.* New York: Harcourt Brace Jovanovich, 1960.

KINDLEBERGER, C. P. *Power and Money.* New York: Basic Books, 1970.

SPERO, J. E. *The Politics of International Economic Relations.* New York: St. Martin's Press, 1977.

Of collections of articles on foreign economic policy issues the following may be mentioned:

BERGSTEN, C. F. and L. B. KRAUSE, eds. *World Politics and International Economics.* Washington, D.C.: The Brookings Institution, 1975.

COHEN, B., ed. *American Foreign Economic Policy.* New York: Harper & Row, 1968.

U.S. Commission on International Trade and Investment Policy. *U.S. International Economic Policy in an Interdependent World.* Washington, D.C.: Government Printing Office, 1971.

International Organization. "World Politics and International Economics," Special Issue, Winter 1975.

The journal *Foreign Affairs* often publishes articles of international economic relevance, within the broad context of foreign policy concerns.

On Trade Theory (Chapters 2–3)

BALASSA, B. "An Empirical Demonstration of Classical Comparative Cost Theory." *Review of Economics and Statistics.* August 1963.

BALDWIN, R. "Determinants of the Commodity Structure of U.S. Trade." *American Economic Review.* March 1971.

BHAGWATI, J. "The Pure Theory of International Trade: A Survey." *Economic Journal.* March 1964.

BLUMENTHAL, T. "Exports and Economic Growth: The Case of Japan." *Quarterly Journal of Economics.* November 1972.

Bibliography

CAVES, R. E. *Trade and Economic Structure.* Cambridge, Mass.: Harvard University Press, 1960.

CHENERY, H. B. "Comparative Advantage and Development Policy." *American Economic Review.* March 1961.

CHIPMAN, J. S. "Factor Price Equalization and the Stolper-Samuelson Theorem." *International Economic Review.* October 1969.

CORDEN, W. M. "Recent Developments in the Theory of International Trade." *Special Papers in International Economics*, No. 7. Princeton University Press, 1965.

FALVEY, R. E. "Transport Costs in the Pure Theory of International Trade." *Economic Journal.* September 1976.

GRUBEL, H. G., and P. J. LLOYD. *Intra-industry Trade: The Theory and Measurement of International Trade in Differentiated Products.* New York: Halsted Press, 1975.

HECKSCHER, E. "The Effects of Foreign Trade on the Distribution of Income." Reprinted in H. ELLIS and L. METZLER, eds. *Readings in the Theory of International Trade.* Homewood, Ill.: Irwin, 1949.

HELLER, P. S. "Factor Endowment Changes and Comparative Advantage: The Case of Japan, 1956–69." *Review of Economics and Statistics.* August 1976.

HOUTHAKKER, H. S. "An International Comparison of Household Expenditure Patterns." *Econometrica.* October 1957.

HUFBAUER, G. C. *Synthetic Materials and the Theory of International Trade.* Cambridge, Mass.: Harvard University Press, 1966.

JOHNSON, H. G. "Factor Endowments, International Trade, and Factor Prices." *Manchester School of Economic and Social Studies.* September 1957.

JONES, R. "Factor Proportions and the Heckscher-Ohlin Model." *Review of Economic Studies.* October 1956.

KEESING, D. B. "The Impact of Research and Development on U.S. Trade." *Journal of Political Economy.* February 1967.

KEMP, M. *The Pure Theory of International Trade and Investment.* Englewood Cliffs, N.J: Prentice-Hall, 1969.

KENEN, P. B. "Nature, Capital, and Trade." *Journal of Political Economy.* October 1965.

KINDLEBERGER, C. P. *Foreign Trade and the National Economy.* New Haven: Yale University Press, 1962.

LEONTIEF, W. "Factor Proportions and the Structure of American Foreign Trade." *Review of Economics and Statistics.* November 1956.

Linder, S. B. *An Essay on Trade and Transformation.* New York: John Wiley, 1961.

MacDougall, G. D. A. "British and American Exports: A Study Suggested by the Theory of Comparative Costs." *Economic Journal.* December 1951.

Meade, J. E. *A Geometry of International Trade.* London: Allen & Unwin, 1951.

Ohlin, B. *International and Interregional Trade.* Cambridge, Mass.: Harvard Economic Studies, 1933; revised edition, 1967.

Schweinberger, A. G. "The Heckscher-Ohlin Model and Traded Intermediate Products." *Review of Economic Studies.* April 1975.

Stern, R. "British and American Productivity and Comparative Costs in International Trade." *Oxford Economic Papers.* October 1962.

Stolper, W. F. and P. A. Samuelson. "Protection and Real Wages." *Review of Economic Studies.* November 1941.

Uekawa, Y. "Generalization of the Stolper-Samuelson Theorem." *Econometrica.* March 1971.

Vanek, J. *The Natural Resource Content of U.S. Foreign Trade 1870–1955.* Cambridge, Mass.: M.I.T. Press, 1963.

Vernon, R. "International Investment and International Trade in the Product Cycle." *Quarterly Journal of Economics.* May 1966.

———, ed. *The Technology Factor in International Trade.* New York: National Bureau of Economic Research, 1970.

On the Theory of Commercial Policy (Chapters 4–6)

Balassa, B. *The Theory of Economic Integration.* Homewood, Ill.: Irwin, 1961.

———. "Tariff Protection in Industrial Countries: An Evaluation." *Journal of Political Economy.* December 1965.

——— and D. M. Schydlowsky. "Domestic Resource Costs and Effective Protection Once Again." *Journal of Political Economy.* January-February 1972.

Baldwin, R. E. "The Effects of Tariffs on International and Domestic Prices." *Quarterly Journal of Economics.* February 1960.

———. "The Case Against Infant-Industry Tariff Protection." *Journal of Political Economy.* May-June 1969.

———. *Non-tariff Distortions of International Trade.* Washington, D.C.: The Brookings Institution, 1970.

Bibliography

BHAGWATI, J. "Protection, Real Wages, and Real Incomes." *Economic Journal*. December 1959.

———. *Trade, Tariffs, and Growth*. London: Weidenfeld and Nicolson, 1969.

——— and H. JOHNSON, "A Generalized Theory of the Effects of Tariffs on the Terms of Trade." *Oxford Economic Papers*. October 1961.

——— et al. *Trade, Balance of Payments, and Growth*. Amsterdam: North-Holland, 1971.

——— and B. HANSEN, "A Theoretical Analysis of Smuggling." *Quarterly Journal of Economics*. May 1973.

BLACK, J. "Arguments for Tariffs." *Oxford Economic Papers*. June 1959.

BOHM, P. "On the Theory of Second Best." *Review of Economic Studies*. July 1967.

CORDEN, W. M. "Protection and Foreign Investment." *Economic Record*. June 1967.

———. "The Structure of a Tariff System and the Effective Protective Rate." *Journal of Political Economy*. June 1966.

———. *The Theory of Protection*. Oxford: Clarendon Press, 1971.

———. *Trade Policy and Economic Welfare*. London: Oxford University Press, 1974.

DELL, S. *Trade Blocs and Common Markets*. New York: Knopf, 1963.

DENTON, G. R., ed. *Economic Integration in Europe*. London: Weidenfeld and Nicolson, 1969.

GRUBEL, H. G. and H. G. JOHNSON, eds. *Effective Tariff Protection*. Geneva: General Agreement on Tariffs and Trade, 1971.

HAGEN, E. "An Economic Justification of Protectionism." *Quarterly Journal of Economics*. November 1958.

HOLZMAN, F. D. "Comparison of Different Forms of Trade Barriers." *Review of Economics and Statistics*. May 1969.

JOHNSON, H. G. "Optimum Tariffs and Retaliation." *Review of Economic Studies*. 1953–54.

———. "The Gains from Freer Trade with Europe: An Estimate." *Manchester School of Economic and Social Studies*. September 1958.

———. "The Cost of Protection and the Scientific Tariff." *Journal of Political Economy*. August 1960.

———. "The Cost of Protection and Self-Sufficiency." *Quarterly Journal of Economics*. August 1965.

———. *Aspects of the Theory of Tariffs*. London: Allen & Unwin, 1971.

JONES, R. "International Capital Movements and the Theory of Tariffs and Trade." *Quarterly Journal of Economics*. February 1967.

KEMP, M. "The Mill-Bastable Infant Industry Dogma." *Journal of Political Economy*. February 1960.

KRAUSE, L. B. *European Economic Integration and the United States*. Washington, D.C.: Brookings Institution, 1968.

KREININ, M. "On the Dynamic Effects of a Customs Union." *Journal of Political Economy*. April 1964.

LEITH, J. C. "The Effect of Tariffs on Production, Consumption, and Trade: A Revised Analysis." *American Economic Review*. March 1971.

LIPSEY, R. G. and K. LANCASTER. "The General Theory of Second Best." *Review of Economic Studies*. 1956–57.

MAGEE, S. P. "Factor Market Distortions, Production, and Trade: A Survey." *Oxford Economic Papers*. March 1973.

McDOUGALL, I. A. and R. H. SNAPE, eds. *Studies in International Economics*. Amsterdam: North-Holland, 1970.

MEADE, J. E. *Trade and Welfare*. London: Oxford University Press, 1955.

METZLER, L. "Tariffs, the Terms of Trade and the Distribution of National Income." *Journal of Political Economy*. February 1949.

MONETA, C. "The Estimation of Transportation Costs in International Trade." *Journal of Political Economy*. February 1959.

PAXTON, J. *The Developing Common Market*. Boulder, Colo.: Westview Press, 1976.

SALANT, W. and B. VACCARA. *Import Liberalization and Employment*. Washington, D.C.: Brookings Institution, 1961.

SCHIAVO-CAMPO, S. *Import Structure and Import Substitution in the Central American Common Market*. SIECA Monograph Series, No. 1, Guatemala, 1972.

SCITOVSKY, T. *Economic Theory and Western European Integration*. Stanford: Stanford University Press, 1958.

STERN, R. "Tariffs and Other Measures of Trade Control: A Survey of Recent Developments." *Journal of Economic Literature*. March 1973.

SWANN, D. *The Economics of the Common Market*, 3rd ed. Harmondsworth, England: Penguin, 1975.

VERNON, R. "Foreign Trade and National Defense." *Foreign Affairs*. October 1955.

VINER, J. *The Customs Union Issue*. New York: Carnegie Endowment for International Peace, 1950.

Bibliography

On the Political Economy and History of Tariffs
(Chapters 7–8)

ALTING VON GESAU, F. A. M., ed. *The External Relations of the European Community.* Farnborough, England: Saxon House, 1974.

BERGSTEN, C. F. and W. G. TYLER, eds. *Leading Issues in International Economic Policy.* Lexington, Mass.: Lexington Books, 1973.

CASADIO, G. P. *Transatlantic Trade: U.S.A.–E.E.C. Confrontation in the GATT Negotiations.* Farnborough, England: Saxon House, 1973.

CHEH, J. H. "U.S. Concessions in the Kennedy Round and Short-run Labor Adjustment Costs." *Journal of International Economics.* November 1974.

CURZON, G. *Multilateral Commercial Diplomacy.* London: Michael Joseph, 1965.

CZEMPIEL, E. O. and D. A. RUSTOW, eds. *The Euro-American System.* Boulder, Colo.: Westview Press, 1976.

HAMILTON, A. *Report on Manufactures*, 1791. Reprinted in F. W. TAUSSIG, ed. *Selected Readings in International Trade and Tariff Problems.* Boston: Ginn, 1921.

IQBAL, Z. "The Generalized System of Preferences Examined." *Finance and Development.* September 1975.

KELLY, W. "The Expanded Trade Agreements Escape Clause, 1955–61." *Journal of Political Economy.* February 1961.

KINDLEBERGER, C. P. *The World in Depression, 1929–39.* Berkeley: University of California Press, 1973.

KOJIMA, K. *Japan and a New World Economic Order.* Boulder, Colo.: Westview Press, 1976.

MURRAY, T. and M. EDGMAND. "Full Employment, Trade Expansion, and Adjustment Assistance." *Southern Economic Journal.* April 1970.

Organization for Economic Cooperation and Development. *Policy Perspectives for International Trade and Economic Relations.* Paris, 1972.

PATTERSON, G. *Discrimination in International Trade: The Policy Issues, 1945–65.* Princeton, N.J.: Princeton University Press, 1966.

PINCUS, J. "Pressure Groups and the Patterns of Tariffs." *Journal of Political Economy.* August 1975.

SHONFIELD, A., ed. *International Economic Relations of the Western World, 1959–1971.* Royal Institute of International Affairs. London: Oxford University Press, 1976.

YEAGER, L. B. and D. TUERCK. *Foreign Trade and U.S. Policy: The Case for Free International Trade.* New York: Praeger, 1976. (This is a major revision of their 1966 book *Trade Policy and the Price System,* discussed in Chapter 7.)

On the Foreign Exchange Market and the BOP
(Chapter 9)

ALIBER, R. Z., ed. *The International Market for Foreign Exchange.* New York: Praeger, 1969.

COHEN, B. J. *Balance-of-Payments Policy.* Harmondsworth, England: Penguin, 1969.

EINZIG, P. *A Textbook of Foreign Exchange.* New York: St. Martin's Press, 1966.

GRUBEL, H. *Forward Exchange, Speculation, and International Capital Flows.* Stanford: Stanford University Press, 1966.

HENNING, C. *International Finance.* New York: Harper & Row, 1958.

HOLMES, A. R. and F. H. SCHOTT. *The New York Foreign Exchange Market.* New York: Federal Reserve Bank of New York, 1965.

International Monetary Fund. "Terms Used in Balance-of-Payments Analysis." *IMS Survey.* November 12, 23, and December 17, 1973.

MEADE, J. E. *The Balance of Payments.* London: Oxford University Press, 1951.

Report of the Review Committee for Balance-of-Payments Statistics. *The Balance of Payments Statistics of the United States: A Review and Appraisal.* Washington, D.C.: U.S. Government Printing Office, 1965.

"Report of the Advisory Committee on the Presentation of Balance-of-Payments Statistics." *Survey of Current Business.* June 1976.

TSIANG, S. C. "The Theory of Forward Exchange and Effects of Government Intervention on the Forward Exchange Market." *I.M.F. Staff Papers.* April 1959.

On the Theory of International Monetary Adjustment
(Chapters 10–13)

ALEXANDER, S. "The Effects of a Devaluation on the Trade Balance." *I.M.F. Staff Papers.* April 1952.

———. "Effects of a Devaluation: A Simplified Synthesis of Elasticities and Absorption Approaches." *American Economic Review.* March 1959.

BALASSA, B. "The Purchasing-Power-Parity Doctrine: A Reappraisal." *Journal of Political Economy.* December 1964.

Bibliography

BLACK, J. "A Geometrical Analysis of the Foreign Trade Multiplier." *Economic Journal*. June 1957.

BRANSON, W. H. "Monetarist and Keynesian Models of the Transmission of Inflation." *American Economic Review*. May 1975.

CASSELL, F. *International Adjustment and the Dollar*. Federal Reserve Bank of Minneapolis, June 1970 (revised April 1976).

CONNOLLY, M. and D. TAYLOR. "Adjustment to Devaluation with Money and Non-Traded Goods." *Journal of International Economics*. August 1976.

COOPER, R. N. "Macroeconomic Policy Adjustment in Interdependent Economies." *Quarterly Journal of Economics*. February 1969.

FRENKEL, J. and H. G. JOHNSON, eds. *The Monetary Approach to the Balance of Payments*. London: Allen & Unwin, 1975.

HALM, G. N. "The 'Band' Proposal: The Limit of Permissible Exchange Rate Variations." *Princeton Special Papers in International Economics*, No. 6. Princeton University Press, 1965.

HARBERGER, A. C. "Some Evidence on the International Price Mechanism." *Journal of Political Economy*. December 1957.

HELLIWELL, J. "Monetary and Fiscal Policies for an Open Economy." *Oxford Economic Papers*. March 1969.

HOUTHAKKER, H. and S. MAGEE. "Income and Price Elasticities in World Trade." *Review of Economics and Statistics*. May 1969.

INGRAM, J. "State and Regional Payments Mechanism." *Quarterly Journal of Economics*. November 1959.

ISHIYAMA, Y. "The Theory of Optimum Currency Areas." *I.M.F. Staff Papers*. July 1975.

JOHNSON, H. G. "Theoretical Problems of the International Monetary System." *Pakistan Development Review*, Vol. 7. Reprinted in R. N. COOPER, ed., *International Finance*. Harmondsworth, England: Penguin, 1969.

———. "The Case for Flexible Exchange Rates." In R. E. BALDWIN and J. D. RICHARDSON, eds. *Selected Topics in International Finance*. Boston: Little, Brown, 1973.

LEE, M. H. *Purchasing Power Parity*. New York: Dekker, 1976.

LINDBECK, A. "Approaches to Exchange Rate Analysis: An Introduction." *Scandinavian Journal of Economics*. No. 2, 1976.

———. "Stabilization Policies in Open Economies with Endogenous Politicians." *American Economic Review*. May 1976.

MACHLUP, F. "Relative Prices and Aggregate Spending in the Analysis of Devaluation." *American Economic Review*. June 1955.

———. "The Terms-of-Trade Effects of Devaluation upon Real Income and the Balance of Trade." *Kyklos*. IX, 1956.

McKINNON, R. "Optimum Currency Areas." *American Economic Review*. September 1963.

MICHAELI, M. *Balance of Payments Adjustment Policies*. New York: National Bureau of Economic Research, 1968.

MUNDELL, R. A. "A Theory of Optimum Currency Areas." *American Economic Review*. September 1961.

———. "The Appropriate Use of Monetary and Fiscal Policy for Internal and External Stability." *I.M.F. Staff Papers*. March 1962.

———. "Capital Mobility and Stabilization Policy under Fixed and Flexible Exchange Rates." *Canadian Journal of Economics and Political Science*. November 1963.

——— and A. K. SWOBODA, eds. *Monetary Problems of the International Economy*. Chicago: University of Chicago Press, 1969.

PARKIN, M. and G. ZIS, eds. *Inflation in the World Economy*. Toronto: University of Toronto Press, 1976.

SALANT, W. "International Reserves and Payments Adjustment." *Banca Nazionale del Lavoro Quarterly Review*. September 1969.

SCITOVSKY, T. *Money and the Balance of Payments*. Chicago: Rand McNally, 1969.

SOHMEN, E. *Flexible Exchange Rates*, rev. ed. Chicago: University of Chicago Press, 1969.

TEW, B. "The Use of Restrictions to Suppress External Deficits." *Manchester School of Social and Economic Studies*. September 1960.

WHITMAN, M. *Policies for Internal and External Balance*. Special Papers in International Economics, No. 9. Princeton University Press, 1970.

WILLIAMS, J. *Postwar Monetary Plans and Other Essays*. New York: Knopf, 1944.

WILLIAMSON, J. G. *American Growth and the Balance of Payments, 1820–1913: A Study of the Long Swing*. Chapel Hill, N.C.: University of North Carolina Press, 1963.

WILLIAMSON, J. H. "The Crawling Peg." *Essays in International Finance*. No. 50, Princeton University Press, 1965.

On International Financial Policy and History
(Chapters 14–15)

BELL, G. *The Eurodollar Market and the International Financial System*. New York: Halsted Press, 1973.

BEN-SHAHAR, H. *The Petromoney Question.* Lexington, Mass.: Lexington Books, 1976.

BERGSTEN, C. F. et al., eds. *The Bürgenstock Papers.* Princeton: Princeton University Press, 1970.

———. *The Dilemmas of the Dollar.* Council on Foreign Relations, New York University Press, 1976.

BERNSTEIN, E. et al. "Reflections on Jamaica." *Essays in International Finance.* No. 115, Princeton University Press, 1976.

BLOOMFIELD, A. *Monetary Policy under the International Gold Standard, 1880–1914.* Federal Reserve Bank of New York, 1959.

BROWN, W. A., JR. *The Gold Standard Re-Interpreted, 1914–1934.* New York: National Bureau of Economic Research, 1934.

CHOUCRI, N. with V. FERRARO. *International Politics of Energy Interdependence.* Lexington, Mass.: Lexington Books, 1976.

COOMBS, C. A. *The Arena of International Finance.* New York: John Wiley, 1976.

DE GRAUWE, P. *Monetary Interdependence and International Monetary Reform.* Farnborough, England: Saxon House, 1976.

DEPRES, E., ed. *International Economic Reform.* New York: Oxford University Press, 1973.

DUNN, R. M. "Exchange Rigidities, Investments Distortions, and the Failure of Bretton Woods." *Essays in International Finance.* No. 97, Princeton University Press, February 1973.

EINZIG, P. *Eurodollar System: Practice and Theory of International Interest Rates.* New York: St. Martin's Press, 1964.

EMMINGER, O. "The International Monetary Situation: A European View." *The Banker.* July 1975.

Federal Reserve Bank of Boston. *The International Adjustment Mechanism* (a Symposium). Chicago, 1972.

FLOYD, J. E. "The Overvaluation of the Dollar." *American Economic Review.* March 1965.

FOURNIER, H. and J. E. WADSWORTH, eds. *Floating Exchange Rates: The Lessons of Recent Experience.* Leyden, Holland: Sijthoff, 1976.

HEWSON, J. R. and E. SAKAIBARA. *The Eurocurrency Markets and Their Implications.* Lexington, Mass.: Lexington Books, 1975.

HORSEFIELD, J. K., ed. *The International Monetary Fund, 1945–65.* Washington, D.C.: International Monetary Fund, 1969.

International Monetary Fund. *Reform of the International Monetary System.* A Report by the Executive Directors to the Board of Governors. Washington, D.C., 1972.

Journal of International Economics, Special Issue: A Symposium on the International Monetary System, September 1972.

KINDLEBERGER, C. P. Lessons of Floating Exchange Rates." *Journal of Monetary Economics*, vol. 3, Supplementary Series, 1976. (See also, in the same issue, P. B. KENEN's "Assessing Experience with Floating Exchange Rates," and R. I. McKINNON's "Floating Foreign Exchange Rates 1973–74: 'The Emperor's New Clothes'.")

LITTLE, J. S. *Eurodollars: The Money Market Gypsies.* New York: Harper & Row, 1975.

MADELIN, H. *Oil and Politics.* Farnborough, England: Saxon House, 1975.

MAGNIFICO, G. *European Monetary Unification.* London: Macmillan, 1973.

MONROE, W. F. *International Monetary Reconstruction.* Lexington, Mass.: Lexington Books, 1974.

MYHRMAN, J. "Experiences of Flexible Exchange Rates in Earlier Periods: Theories, Evidence, and a New View." *Scandinavian Journal of Economics.* No. 2, 1976.

NURKSE, R. *International Currency Experience: Lessons of the Inter-War Period.* Geneva: League of Nations, 1944.

——. "International Investment Today in the Light of 19th Century Experience." *Economic Journal.* March 1954.

PARK, Y. S. *Oil Money and the World Economy.* Boulder, Colo.: Westview Press, 1976.

PARKIN, M. and G. ZIS, eds. *Inflation in Open Economies.* Toronto: University of Toronto Press, 1977.

SALANT, W. *International Reserves and Payments Adjustment,* Reprint No. 175. Washington, D.C.: Brookings Institution, 1970.

TRIFFIN, R. *Gold and the Dollar Crisis.* New Haven: Yale University Press, 1960.

VERNON, R., ed. *The Oil Crisis.* New York: Norton, 1976.

WILLIAMSON, J. "The Future Exchange Rate Regime." *Banca Nazionale del Lavoro Quarterly Review.* June 1975.

On Other Major International Policy Issues

As stated in the preface, and often repeated throughout the text, it was considered preferable to leave out entirely discussion of some very important current policy issues rather than to provide a cursory treatment that might easily be misleading. Of these, three are of undoubted importance: East-

Bibliography

West trade, the multinational corporation, and the trade problems of less developed countries. There is a rich literature in all these fields. The following references are a very limited, indicative selection.

1. East-West Trade

HOLZMAN, F. D. *International Trade under Communism—Politics and Economics.* New York: Basic Books, 1976.

MASNATA, A. *East-West Economic Cooperation: Problems and Solutions.* Farnborough, England: Saxon House, 1974.

McMILLAN, C., ed. *Changing Perspectives in East-West Commerce.* Lexington, Mass.: Lexington Books, 1975

PISAR, S. *Coexistence and Commerce: Guidelines for Transactions Between East and West.* New York: McGraw-Hill, 1970.

WILCZYNSKI, J. *The Economics and Politics of East-West Trade.* New York: Praeger, 1969.

WILES, P. J. D. *Communist International Economics.* New York: Praeger, 1969.

2. Multinational Enterprise

BROOKE, M. Z. and H. L. REMMERS. *The Strategy of the Multinational Enterprise.* London: Longmans, 1971. (Especially useful on the internal organization of multinational enterprise, on the relationship between parent company and subsidiary, and on financial practices.)

GILPIN, R. *U.S. Power and the Multinational Corporation.* New York: Basic Books, 1975. (Chapter 5 has an excellent summary of the literature on multinational enterprise to 1974, and is probably the best place for an interested person to start.)

SAUVANT, K. P. and F. G. LAVIPOUR, eds. *Controlling Multinational Enterprise.* Boulder, Colo.: Westview Press, 1976. (An interesting collection of papers.)

TUGENDHAT, C. *The Multinationals.* New York: Random House, 1972. (Primarily an account of the rise and practices of large multinational corporations, and of their internal operations.)

VERNON, R. *Sovereignty at Bay.* New York: Basic Books, 1971. (Undoubtedly the best-known treatment of the subject.)

3. Trade and Development

BALASSA, B., C. CLAGUE, and I. WALTER. "Commercial Policy and Less Developed Countries." *American Economic Review.* May 1971.

Declaration on the Establishment of a New International Economic Order. Resolutions adopted by the United Nations General Assembly in May 1974, and Programme of Action. (Obtainable from the Office of Public Information, United Nations, New York.)

Di Marco, L. I., ed. *International Economics and Development: Essays in Honor of Raoul Prebisch.* New York: Academic Press, 1972.

Erb, G. F. and S. Schiavo-Campo. "Export Instability, Level of Development and Economic Size of Less Developed Countries." *Oxford University Bulletin of Economics and Statistics.* November 1969.

Johnson, H. *Economic Policies Toward Less Developed Countries.* Washington, D.C.: Brookings Institution, 1966.

Linder, S. B. *Trade and Trade Policy for Development.* New York: Praeger, 1967.

Little, I., T. Scitovsky, and M. Scott. *Industry and Trade in Some Developing Countries.* London: Oxford University Press, 1970.

MacBean, A. *Export Instability and Economic Development.* Cambridge, Mass.: Harvard University Press, 1966.

Prebisch, R. *Towards a Trade Policy for Development.* New York: United Nations, 1964.

Schiavo-Campo, S. and H. W. Singer. *Perspectives of Economic Development.* Boston: Houghton-Mifflin, 1970 (especially Parts IV and V).

Index

Compromise Tariff, 172
Connally, J., 367n., 369
Consumers' surplus, 96
  diagrammatic analysis, 103–4
Constant cost, 37n., 56
Consumption effect of tariffs, 95
  diagrammatic analysis, 103
Convertibility. See Currency convertibility
Corden, W. M., 110
Corn Laws, repeal, 173
Cost
  comparative, 60–61
  constant, 37n., 56
  decreasing, 56, 63–65
  of fixed exchange rates, 260–62
  of flexible exchange rates, 289–91
  increasing, 37ff.
  opportunity, 25, 32, 218
Council of Mutual Economic Assistance (COMECON), 114
Countervailing duties, 144
  in 1974 Trade Act, 190
Cover, in foreign exchange market, 204
Crawling peg, 325–26
Credits, in BOP, 207
Credit tranches, in IMF lending, 316
Cultural-sociological argument for tariffs, 132
Currency
  appreciation and depreciation, 199, 269
  arbitrage, 201–2
  convertibility, 82–83, 329, 342
    1971 suspension, 350
  devaluation and revaluation, 199
  hard and soft, 82
Current account, 207, 209–10
Current account balance, 208
Customs duties. See Tariffs
Customs union, defined, 113

Dale, E. D., 136n., 180n.
Debits, in BOP, 207
Debs, R. E., 363n.
Decreasing returns. See Increasing cost
Deficit, in BOP. See Balance of payments, measures
DeGaulle, C., 357
Dell, S., 117
Demand function, 47
Demand reversals, 47n., 55
Demonstration effect, 47, 132
Dependence, 9–10. See also Interdependence
  and arguments for tariffs, 131–32
Depreciation
  and absorption, 281–84
  and inflation, 284–87
  price effects, 272–73
    diagrammatic analysis, 273–76
  and real cash balances, 287
Detente, 159, 190
Devaluation, 199, 269, 308
Devaluation bias, in Bretton Woods system, 318–19, 325

Devaluations
  in Bretton Woods system, 343–44
  in 1970s, 370, 372
Dingley Tariff, 173
Direct investment, 210
Dirty floating, 199, 327–28, 350
Discrimination, in commercial policy, 85, 89, 112. See also Economic integration
  and GATT rules, 177
Discriminatory tariffs. See Discrimination
Disraeli, B., 129
Distortions. See Market distortions
Distributional arguments for tariffs, 133–35
Division of labor
  and role of trade, 9
  and specialization, 242
Dollar, role in Bretton Woods system, 316–17
Dollar glut, 323
Dollar overhang, 221n., 323n., 366
Dollar shortage, 221n., 323, 342
Drawing rights. See International Monetary Fund, rules
Dual exchange rates, 330, 350n.
Dumping, 142–44
  in 1974 Trade Act, 190
Dynamic effects of trade, 56–59

East African Community, 114n.
East-West trade, provisions in 1974 Trade Act, 190
Eberle, W. D., 180n.
Economic growth
  effect of tariffs on, 109
  and international trade, 56ff.
Economic integration, 112–17
  defined, 113
  dynamic effects, 116
  static effects, 115–16
Economic liberalism. See Laissez faire
Economic policy rules, 160–61
Economic union, 114
Economic warfare, 80, 129
Economies of scale, 56, 63–65
Edgeworth-Bowley box diagram, 32–33
Effective protection, 87ff.
1816 Tariff, 171
Elasticity, income
  defined, 47n.
  and demand reversals, 47n.
  empirical evidence, 55
Elasticity, price
  defined, 95n.
  determinants, 101n., 279–80
  and dumping, 143
  role in size of tariff effects, 100–101
  and terms-of-trade effect of depreciation, 300–301
Elasticity condition. See Marshall-Lerner condition
Elasticity of substitution
  and factor reversals, 50n.
  and infant industry, 145n.

Ellsworth, P. T., 283n.
Emerson, R. W., 158
Enlightenment, 23
Equalization of factor prices, 51–52
Equilibrium, 79, 95n., 204–5
  in balance of payments, 211–14
  in foreign exchange market, 270–71
    diagrammatic analysis, 295–98
  "fundamental," in Bretton Woods system, 308ff.
  of national income, 231, 235–36
  partial and general, 79, 95n.
  stable and unstable, 297
"Errors and omissions," in BOP, 207
Escape clause, in commercial treaties, 178–79
Eurobank, 351
Eurobonds, 351n.
Eurodollars, 286n., 351–53
European Coal and Steel Community, 114
European Common Market. See European Community
European Community, 114–15, 159, 177n., 179, 184, 191
European Economic Community. See European Community
European Payments Union (EPU), 342–43
European "snake," 292, 370
Exchange control. See Foreign exchange control
Exchange Equalization Account, 327n., 340n.
Exchange rate
  defined, 4, 198
  dual, 330, 350n.
  multiple, 330
  and risk, 5, 204
  spot and forward, 203–4
Exchange risk, 5, 204
Expansion of the market, argument for tariffs, 64
Expectations, on exchange rates, 204
Export quotas, 81
Export tariffs, 85
External economies. See Externalities
Externalities, 57–58
  and infant industry, 146–47

Factor endowments, 48
Factor endowments theorem, 49ff.
  mathematical proof, 67–68
Factor intensity, 50
Factor mobility, 3–4
  and adjustments to import competition, 135
  effect of tariff, 109, 136
Factor-price equalization, 51–52
Factor prices, 48
Factor reversals, 50n., 56
FIAT, sales of shares to Libya, 363
Findlay, R., 67
Fiscal and monetary policy, for internal and external balance, 264–65, 290
Fixed exchange rates, 251. See also

Optimum tariff, 100, 137–38
Optional managed floating, 372
"Orderly market arrangement." *See*
Voluntary quotas
Organization for Economic Cooperation and Development (OECD), 342n.
Organization for European Economic Cooperation (OEEC), 342
Organization of Petroleum Exporting Arab Countries (OPEAC), 360n.
Organization of Petroleum Exporting Countries (OPEC), 191, 279n., 360–64
Overhang. *See* Dollar overhang

Paine, Tom, 171
"Paper gold." *See* Special Drawing Rights
Patterson, G., 113n.
Payne-Aldrich Tariff, 125n., 158, 174, 185
Peril-point provisions, 179
Perry, J. M., 182
Petrodollars. *See* Oil prices
Pigou, A. C., 258
Policy conflicts
under flexible exchange rates, 289–93
under gold standard, 262–63
Portfolio investment, 210
Posted price of oil, 360n.
Preferences, 112, 191. *See also* Discrimination
Price elasticity. *See* Elasticity, price
Price rigidities, and flexible-rate adjustment, 285
and gold-standard adjustment, 261–62
Producers' surplus, 96–97
diagrammatic analysis, 103–4
Production effect of tariffs, 95
diagrammatic analysis, 103
Production function, 26, 48, 50
Productivity of labor. *See* Labor productivity
Profit, 230
Program balance, in BOP, 213
Prohibition of usury, 18
Prohibitive tariff, 111n., 128
Propensity. *See* Marginal propensity
Puerto Rico summit conference of 1976, 371
Purchasing-power-parity principle, 311–13
Pure competition, assumption in trade theory, 54

Quantitative restrictions. *See* Quotas
Quantity equation of exchange, 260, 286
Quantity theory of money, 260–61
Quasi-adjustment policies, 252, 264
Quotas, 81–82
on agriculture in Europe, 184
differences from tariffs, 110–12

effects, 109–12
equivalence with tariffs, 110
on exports, 81
on imports, 81–82
influence on competition, 111

Rambouillet summit conference of 1975, 371
Rate of transformation, in production, consumption, exchange, 39–40
Ratner, S., 173n.
Real cash balances, role in BOP adjustment, 257, 287
Reciprocal demand, 28–29, 42, 53, 312
Reciprocal Trade Agreements, 175–76, 341
Redistribution effect of tariffs, 97
diagrammatic analysis, 104–5
Regulation Q, and growth of Eurodollars, 351
Renaissance, 19
Research and development, and international trade, 64–65
Reserves
function in Bretton Woods system, 310
shortage in Bretton Woods years, 323
Retaliation, in commercial policy, 159–60, 174–75. *See also* Mercantilist arguments for tariffs
Revaluation, 199, 269
Revenue effect of tariffs, 97
diagrammatic analysis, 104–5
Reversal factors, in flexible-rate system. *See also* Absorption, Inflation
from income changes, 283–84
from price changes, 284–87
Ricardo, D., 24, 46, 49, 60
Risk. *See also* Uncertainty
in arbitrage operations, 201n.
in foreign exchange, 5, 204
and international trade, 75
Robertson, J., 165n.
Robertson, R. M., 182

Safire, W., 367n.
Salvemini, G., 158
Samuelson, P., 49
Saving, 231
Say, J. B., 145
Scarce currency clause, 319n.
Schiavo-Campo, S., 89n., 131n.
Schlesinger, A., 175n.
"Scientific" tariff, 127–28, 158, 174
Second-best. *See* Theorem of second-best
Singer, H. W., 89n.
Size of market, and division of labor, 9
Skinner, B. F., 346
Smith, Adam, 8n., 23n., 24, 46n., 61, 125, 129

Smithsonian Agreement of 1971, 341n., 369–70
"Snake." *See* European "snake"
Special Drawing Rights (SDR's), 347–49
Specialization
and division of labor, 9, 242
partial, 41–42
Specific tariffs, 85
Speculation, 200, 202
bearish and bullish, 321
in Bretton Woods system, 320–23
defined, 200
under flexible exchange rates, 321–23
and forward foreign exchange rates, 219
and multinational corporations, 344–46
Stability condition, in foreign exchange market. *See* Marshall-Lerner condition
Stabilization, official, 327
Stagflation, 265
Staley, C. E., 130n., 131
Standby Agreements, 346–47. *See also* International Monetary Fund
Statistical discrepancy, in BOP, 207
Steel import quotas, 187n.
Sterling Area, 340
Stern, R. M., 132n., 159
Stocks and flows, 205, 211, 217
Stolper-Samuelson theorem, 35, 52, 127, 133
Stop-go policies, 368. *See also* Gold standard, policy conflicts
Structural tariff discrimination, 89–90
Subsidies, 133, 140n., 161–63
for infant industry, 147
Substitution effect, 41, 280n.
Surplus in BOP. *See* Balance of payments, measures
Swap Agreements, 347

Takayama, A., 53, 138n.
Tariff negotiations, unilateral vs. reciprocal, 157
Tariff Nullification Act of 1832, 172
Tariff of Abominations, 172, 185
Tariff-rate quote, 85n.
Tariffs
ad valorem vs. specific, 85
averaging problems, 86–87
for bargaining purposes, 139
compound, 85
defined, 85
discriminatory, 85
effective, 87–90
on exports and on imports, 85–86
historical cycle, 185–86
and income distribution, 133–35
macroeconomic effects, 107ff.
microeconomic effects, 95ff.
diagrammatic analysis, 101ff.
nominal, 87–90
prohibitive, 111n.
revenue vs. protective, 86